© 2009 Peter Reaburn
PhD BHMS(Ed) Grad Cert Flex Learn

ISBN 978-0-9805466-2-0

This publication is copyright.
No part of it may be reproduced or transmitted in
any form without written permission.

Book orders:

www.mastersathlete.com.au

Published by
  David Fenech

Info Publishing Pty Ltd
PO Box 1466, Mackay, Qld 4740
Phone (07) 4944 1982
Email david@infopublishing.com.au

Cover by

**Nellie Designgraphics**
0431 382 923
Janelle Cooke
Phone (07) 4928 0769

## Disclaimer

*The information, recommendations and guidelines provided in this book are not intended as medical advice or to replace advice given by trained medical or allied health professionals or qualified coaches. In the case of illness, disease, injury or other medical condition, a doctor or health professional should be consulted prior to commencing an exercise training or nutrition program. Masters athletes with known medical conditions or a family history of health problems should always check with their family doctor before undertaking exercise.
 Info Publishing, the author and their officers, employees and agents give no warranty and make no representation that the information, recommendations and guidelines contained in this book are suitable for any purpose or are free from error and they accept no responsibility for any person acting or relying upon the information, recommendations and guidelines contained in this book, and disclaim all liability for any loss, damage, cost or expense incurred by reason of any person using or relying on the information, recommendations and guidelines or by reason of any error, omission, defect, or misstatement contained in such information, recommendations and guidelines..*

# Contents

Acknowledgements .................................................................................... 4
Foreword ................................................................................................... 5

**Chapter 1**
    The Aging Process and Keys To Successful Aging ............................. 7

**Chapter 2**
    Age-Related Declines In Performance And Implications For Training ............. 26

**Chapter 3**
    Medical Screening and the Masters Athlete ...................................... 39

**Chapter 4**
    The Principles of Training the Masters Athlete ................................. 51

**Chapter 5**
    Coaching the Masters Athlete ............................................................ 62

**Chapter 6**
    Endurance Development for The Masters Athlete ............................. 71

**Chapter 7**
    Strength and Power Training for the Masters Athlete ....................... 98

**Chapter 8**
    Speed and Power Development in the Masters Athlete ................... 117

**Chapter 9**
    Developing Flexibility in Masters Athletes ....................................... 134

**Chapter 10**
    Periodisation and Peaking for the Masters Athlete ........................... 143

**Chapter 11**
    Exercising in the Heat and Cold ...................................................... 168

**Chapter 12**
    Injury Prevention and Management for the Masters Athlete ............ 177

**Chapter 13**
    Overtraining and the Masters Athlete .............................................. 196

**Chapter 14**
    Staying Healthy and Illness-Free ...................................................... 205

**Chapter 15**
    Recovery Strategies for the Masters Athlete ..................................... 218

**Chapter 16**
    Nutrition for the Masters Athlete ..................................................... 237

**Chapter 17**
    Weight Control and the Masters Athlete ......................................... 275

**Chapter 18**
    Performance-Enhancing Supplements and the Masters Athlete ........ 296

**Chapter 19**
    The Female Masters Athlete ............................................................ 310

# ACKNOWLEDGEMENTS

Like training for a goal in sport, writing a book such as this takes time, energy, sacrifice and commitment.

I wish to thank my parents Bob and Noela Reaburn for instilling a lifetime love of sport and learning into this old boy! Now as a parent of two beautiful girls, I can reflect on those early years of my development and can only marvel at how you both survived instilling these qualities into five active and lively children.

To my University lecturers who fuelled my passion for learning about sport, fitness and health through the years of undergraduate and postgraduate studies, a big thanks. In particular Professor Max Howell, raconteur and lover of life, who taught me that learning does indeed go on for life and that putting pen to paper in a book is the way to express that learning.

To all the many aging athletes I have talked to, competed against, still train and race with, and researched, I shall always value the wisdom of the years. In particular, I wish to acknowldege some aging athletes who have inspired me as a person and athlete. Triathlete, Greg Reddan who used to amaze me with his triathlon training feats, low heart rates in training, and love of the training journey. Distance runners Dr Andrew Semple and Ron Grant who both inspired me with their experiences as runners and ability to give back to sport and the community. Masters swimmers, Gordon Metcalfe and Max Gillespie who taught me that sport and its associated fitness is to be loved well into the advancing years and that "it's never too late".

Finally, to my wonderful family. My girls Rebecca and Megan who give meaning to my world and I hope realise one day that dad has done some good things in his life. To my big girl, Claire, who supports my passion for training and competing, sacrifices for me in so many ways, and puts up with those early starts and lowering bank statements, the biggest thanks of all. We are a great team!

# Foreword

This book is written for masters athletes and the growing number of coaches looking after this crazy bunch! Whether you are a self-coached aging athlete, train in a squad set-up for older athletes, work-out with the younger athletes or coach aging athletes, you will get something from this unique book. It is for those people who want to learn more about the aging process and its effect on sports performance. It is for those people who want to know the correct ways to maximize speed, endurance and strength and slow the inevitable age-related decline in performance. While I don't try to suggest that every aging athlete is the same and can improve their performances to the same extent by

*Peter Reaburn PhD*

reading this book, I do know that aging athletes are smart and well-educated. They have a thirst for the what, when, where and why's of training. This book aims to educate the aging athlete as to why we should be eating, recovering, and training in particular ways and how we should be doing that based on sound science.

This book is also a labor of love on a number of fronts. First, I am a lover of sports (cricket, horseracing and motorsport excepted!). I still enjoy competing at a high level after 45 years, I read the headlines on a newspaper starting from the back page, television-viewing starts at 7pm with SBS's World of Sports, Inside Sport is my favorite magazine (for the insightful journalism of course!), and weekend sport on TV is "Dad's time-out". Secondly, as a sports scientist, I am amazed at how little knowledge is out there relating to the aging athlete. In 1989 I commenced my PhD at The University of Queensland in the area of Exercise Physiology. I examined the strength, speed and endurance characteristics of a group of lifetime athletes over the age of 60 years who had been in training since they were kids. As a competitive aging athlete and sports scientist, I was shocked during those years at the lack of written scientific or layman's literature available addressing the aging athlete. After completion of my PhD, I edited a periodical called The Masters Athlete that attempted to focus on the aging athlete and how they might improve sports performance. My wife Claire was the business side of the publication and I was the writer. We had upwards of 1,000 dedicated readers who seemed to have a thirst for wanting to know more about the aging process, its effect on sports performance, and what can be done to slow the inevitable decline in speed, endurance and strength.

Together as we move closer to retiring from work, we are about to launch a website that will 'bridge the gap' between sport, exercise and health science and the aging athlete. Watch out for it at: www.mastersathlete.com.au

Finally, I have always been a believer that too much sport and exercise science sits in the heads of the researchers or in obscure journals in University libraries readable only to those with sport science degrees. While The Masters Athlete enabled me to satisfy that urge to "bridge the gap" between theory and practice, I also felt it was time to synthesize my 45 years competitive and training experiences and scientific knowledge of masters athletes into a book that an older athlete could easily pick up and read. I hope I have achieved this goal with this book.

The objective of the book is to enable the aging athletes who read it to both improve performance and better understand their body's responses to exercise as they age. From my observations, too many aging athletes just train without training smart. This book is based on science and tried and true systems of developing strength, speed and endurance. Every attempt has been made to relate current scientific thinking and research to the aging athlete. While little scientific research is available that specifically relates to the aging athlete, my challenge was to relate the vast scientific literature on aging non-athletes and relate it to what is known about sports performance and training practices of young athletes. I hope this book goes a long way to bridging the gap between sports science and the aging athlete.

Enjoy the contents and keep training - *age shall not weary us!*

Peter Reaburn PhD

# CHAPTER 1

# THE AGING PROCESS AND KEYS TO SUCCESSFUL AGING

*We do not stop playing because we are old;*
*We grow old because we stop playing.*

**George Bernard Shaw**

## Introduction

I love getting older for the wisdom it brings. I hate getting older for the slower times it brings! Like it or not, aging as an athlete means eventual declines in performance. There are just too many natural processes that we can't control that determine how fast or slow we age physically.

While we are all aging, we do not age at the same rate. While some people experience rapid declines in physiological and psychological functioning as they age, others age much more slowly. Our parents' genes play an important role that we can't control while other important factors such as nutrition, fitness, stress, smoking and lifestyle are factors we can control. As aging athletes, such a healthy lifestyle probably comes naturally to us. As you will see in this chapter, science has shown there are enormous benefits to aging healthy and aging fit. Before we look at these benefits, let's look at how scientists define aging and what theories exist as to why and at what rate we age.

## Definitions of Aging

Most of us agree that aging is simply the passage of time since our birth. But why is it that some of my 50 year-old buddies look 40 (and act 25!) and some look 60 (and act 70!). Gerontologists, those scientists that study aging, define aging in five ways:

1. *Chronological Age* is our age in years since birth. However, all of us have friends that can't do what we as aging athletes can do physically, despite being the same age in years. Indeed, some are incapacitated or in homes. Not the picture I have of myself in 20-30 years time!

2. *Functional Age* refers to how able an aged person is to function physically, psychologically or socially. Research has shown that a 12-week progressive fitness training program can increase strength and endurance by as much as 20%, the equivalent of up to 20 years reversal in these important capacities of functional aging. Given this, I ask the question, why aren't more people out there doing what we do?

3. *Biological Age* refers to our physical and physiological age. A person with numerous medical complications or disabilities is seen to have a relatively poor biological age.

In contrast, aging athletes may have a biological age 10-15 years younger than their chronological age.

4. *Psychological Age* refers to our ability to function psychologically and includes things such as self-esteem, problem solving ability, ability to learn and memory. Again, we all know older people that are as sharp as razors and others who have "lost it" as they age. Research has consistently shown that regular exercise helps maintain psychological function into older age.

5. *Social Age* refers to how, for our age, we behave within the community. For example, historically it may have been seen as inappropriate for older people to train or exercise to stay physically fit. Thank goodness this "take it easy old fella" philosophy is being broken down and we are seeing a dramatic increase in the number of older people getting back into sport and taking years off their chronological age by mixing it with youngsters!

6. *Training Age* While few books on aging will ever mention this term, it refers to how long a person has been training for, either within a particular sport or in sport in general. Research strongly suggests that the greater the training age of a person, the more quickly they adapt to and recover from training stimuli.

A recurring theme in the limited research on older athletes and physically active aging people is that they are functionally, biologically, psychologically and socially much younger that their chronological age. Let's keep it that way!

## Theories of Aging

The reasons for aging appear a combination of genetic factors, environmental factors (e.g. hot and cold weather, altitude, pollution, illness exposure or vulnerability, and psychological stress) and lifestyle factors (e.g. cigarette smoking, alcohol consumption, and diet and physical activity levels). The complexity of the aging process is reflected in the number of theories on how or why we age. Indeed, there does not seem to be any one theory that explains why we age.

Over the years, numerous theories have been proposed to explain the changes associated with aging. These include:

### *Genetic Theories*

Numerous studies have been done on identical and non-identical twins to show that mum and dad's genetic material determines how well we age just as it determines about 70-75% of whether we are going to be sprinters, endurance animals or just mongrels! There is also no doubt that regardless of how healthy a lifestyle we live, genetic programming is the major determinant of how well we age or how long we live for.

The majority of researchers believe that genes program aging from birth to death. These theories suggest that our body's' cells have a biological clock that influences a number of mechanisms that regulate the rate of loss of function in key cells within our body. With aging we see a progressive slowing of growth-stimulating processes, a gradual failure of repair processes, and a gradual build up of metabolic errors in the body's cells that slow our ability to deal with illnesses, toxic substances or damaged cells. There also appears no doubt that genetics appears to increase an individual's susceptibility to various causes of disability and premature death. For example, the genes affecting obesity will also affect the risk of diabetes, cardiovascular disease, and various forms of cancer and osteoporosis, all of which are linked to obesity. Furthermore, specific gene combinations have been identified that influence the immune response and thus our resistance to disease or cancers.

The likelihood of a gene expressing itself will also depend on the interaction of the gene with environmental factors. For example, a person with a genetic predisposition to lung disease is more likely to develop that disease if exposed for prolonged periods to cigarette smoke or other air pollutants.

In summary, there is no doubt that both genetic (pick your mum and dad well folks!) and environmental factors play a role in how quickly we age.

### *Cellular Theories*

This theory of aging suggests there are degenerative changes within each cell in the body. The most common belief is that of *free-radical oxidation*. A free radical is an unstable molecule of oxygen that wants to react with other molecules in any cell in the body. This process ultimately destroys cells. In healthy and fit people, there are chemicals called oxidases that keep these free radicals in equilibrium. However, as we age, there appears to be a reduction in the activity of these 'good' oxidases, and increased exposure to chemical carcinogens and radiation that increase the free radical activity. Together, this means increased free radical oxidation that leads to changes in our connective tissue (ligaments, tendons, covering of muscle) strength, a breakdown of our immune system, decreases in skin and joint elasticity leading to decreased flexibility, and the destruction of the genetic material DNA meaning our ability to remake good cells such as muscle cells is decreased.

Thankfully, regular exercise increases the amount of the good oxidases, meaning the ability of the free radicals to damage cells is significantly reduced in aging athletes.

### *Control Theories*

These theories of aging suggest that specific functions or systems on our body such as the immune or hormone systems change with age and influence many other body functions. For example, research has shown an age-related decrease in the quality of the aging immune system response to germs, bacteria or viruses. Furthermore, the genes controlling the immune system have also been shown to slow the production of those chemicals called oxidases that protect our aging cells from free-radical oxidation as discussed above. This will lead to a destruction of cells in our body including muscle and nerve cells. Again, the good news is that a high level of fitness into older age can help produce more of these oxidases that fight those free radicals.

The hormone system also exerts a strong influence over all bodily functions. For example, an age-related decline in testosterone production is commonly observed that negatively influences many other bodily systems such as the strength and regeneration ability of muscles, ligaments, tendons and cartilage.

*Wear and Tear Theory*

Proteins play a major role in the structure and function of all cells, tissues and organs in the body. This theory suggests that with aging there is a negative change in protein formation such that bodily functions are compromised. These changes may be caused by cell damage from internal (temperature, viruses, free radicals) or external (radiation, pollution, food, smoke) causes.

*Waste-Product Accumulation Theory*

This theory proposes that with aging there is a progressive accumulation of waste within the body's cells to the point that the function of that cell is compromised. One such compound is called lipofuscin that is a by-product of the free-radical damage referred to above. Research has shown that lipofuscin can account for up to 7% of a cell's volume by age 90 years.

*Cross-Linkage Theory*

This theory suggests that molecules within cells join together and form larger molecules that are resistant to the normal breakdown and repair processes the body undergoes. This theory is widely used to explain the tightening of ligaments, tendons and the covering of muscles, all of which contribute to an age-related decrease in flexibility and performance.

Thus, there appears no one theory on aging that explains all the changes that occur as we get older. Importantly, the quality of our life can greatly influence how we age biologically. Preventing disease, controlling many of the above environmental factors, eating well and a life of physical fitness are now seen to be a key to aging well. However, despite these theories, there are large individual differences in the rate and extent of aging in each individual.

## Individual Differences and Lifestyle Interventions

Numerous studies have shown that it is possible for individuals to deviate from the normal aging pattern and to delay or postpone the inevitable consequences of aging. There is no doubt that people who engage in healthy behaviours such as regular exercise, healthy nutrition, and smoking cessation can both reduce the rate of aging and live longer. For example, cardiovascular fitness capacity, as measured by $VO_2max$ (the maximum volume of oxygen that can be transported to, and consumed by, the working muscles), declines at the rate of 10% per decade in "normal" people. However, in people with a poor functional age it might decline at 15% per decade while in aging endurance athletes it might be 5% per decade (see Figure 1.1). Thus, a highly trained 60 year-old marathoner might have the same $VO_2max$ as a 25 year-old person with a poor functional age.

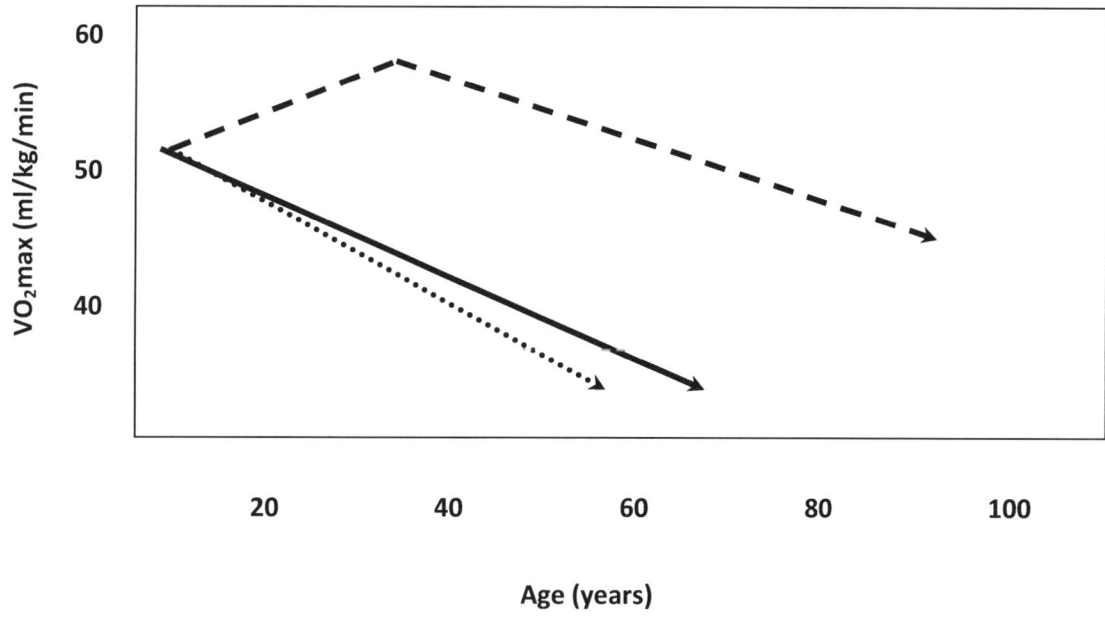

*Figure 1.1:* An example of different rates of aging among individuals.
────── Normal aging.   ....... Poor functional aging.   ─ ─ High functioning age.

Despite all the physiological declines that occur with aging, research consistently shows that an individual's attitude to aging is crucial in determining how well they cope with the inevitability of the aging process. Although changing slowly, society appears to have the attitude that aging is associated with retirement, sitting back and watching the younger generation, wrinkles, rocking chairs, mental slowness and getting fat and lazy. There pervades an attitude that nothing can be done to avoid these inevitable life changes. My personal experience and those of many aging athletes I have read about and know personally, is that a lifetime of physical training has enormous benefits that say goodbye to society's pervading attitude. Aging athletes I know look, think and act younger and are actively involved in activities supposedly reserved for the youngsters.

Let's now turn our attention to looking at the scientifically-proven benefits of high fitness levels that masters athletes exhibit and how this fitness relates to both a better quantity and quality of life.

## Aging, Fitness and Longevity

For years now we've known that healthier active people live longer than aging people who have disease states or have given in to a sedentary lifestyle and / or poor nutrition habits. Perhaps the most well-known study conducted by a United States scientist named Ralph Paffenberger who has followed 17,000 former Harvard University graduates over 40 years. He suggested that burning up more than 8.4 megajoules (2,100 Calories) per week in physical activity (walking burns up 0.08 Calories per minute per kilogram, running at 8km/hr about 0.2 Calories per minute per kilogram) lowered the death rate by 25-30% compared to those who did little exercise. The active group also lived just over two years longer and had a much greater quality of life. Most researchers also agree that the more "vigorous" the physical activity, the lower the death rate in older exercisers.

So what about highly fit people such as aging athletes compared to those older people who are just physically active by walking or gardening regularly. These days, low fitness levels are seen as an equal to or greater risk factor of heart disease than smoking, high blood cholesterol, high blood pressure, blood glucose, obesity or genetics. Stephen Blair, a world leader in this type of research, compared the death rates of 'most fit' versus 'least fit' (as measured by $VO_2$max tested on a treadmill) men and women and found that the 'least fit' men were 3.5 times and the 'least fit' women 4.5 times more likely to die compared to the 'most fit' groups. Even if the men or women had two or three other risk factors of heart disease, the rates of death were still lower in those who were more aerobically fit. Blair also studied a group of 'least fit' men as they improved their aerobic fitness to a high fit level over a five-year period. A 44% reduction in death rate was observed in these people with the greatest change in the 50-59 year age group who lowered their death rate by 70% after getting fit.

In summary, the existing research suggests that light to moderate physical activity (golfing, gardening, dancing, housekeeping, boating, bowling) confers little to no benefit to longevity, while vigorous activity such as jogging and swimming does. Sadly, while light to moderate physical activity might be more palatable to most people who have not seen the light or doctors or exercise specialists who see low levels of intensity as an easier way to get people to be a little bit active, all the evidence suggests that vigorous activity is the way to go for not only quantity of life but quality of life. Exercise is anti-aging medicine!

Why do women live longer than men? While genetics plays a part, it appears that many factors might explain the difference. Up until recently, women have not served in the armed forces with the associated high death rates. Again, until recently, women have had lower rates of death from lung cancer or heart attacks. This is probably due to the preventative action of the female hormone oestrogen against heart disease and the lower rates of cigarette smoking compared to men, although these rates appear to be changing. Prior to menopause, research has also shown that the risk of sudden death during vigorous physical activity is 10 times greater in men than women. However, while they might live longer than men, research suggests that women of the same age as men have lower aerobic fitness and muscular strength than men. Thus, apart from not being able to compete at the same level in sport as men, they are more likely to have a less active lifestyle into old age due to reduced strength and endurance. Indeed, United States research has shown that men have an average 10.8 years of disabled life years while women have 14.0 years of disability. These figures present a huge argument for muscle strengthening and aerobic fitness development in older people.

Apart from gender and physical activity, a number of other lifestyle and environmental factors have been shown to influence our genetic potential as to how long we live. These include:

- *Hot weather* causes an increased demand for blood flow to the skin so that the heat generated by muscles can be taken by the blood to the relatively cooler skin. This causes an increased load on the heart due to competing demands by muscles and skin for blood. An impaired ability to regulate skin blood flow and an accumulation of body fat in older people, particularly women, exacerbate this problem. In unhealthy older persons who may have high blood pressure or diabetes, the load on the heart becomes even greater. Older people with a low aerobic capacity also have a reduced ability to turn on the sweat mechanism together with a lower sweat rate. In older athletes who retain a relatively high aerobic capacity, these abilities appear to be maintained.
- *Cold weather* also poses a challenge to the elderly. In contrast to hot weather where skin blood vessels open up to cool the blood, in cold weather the skin blood vessels constrict. This does two things – increases blood pressure and reduces the amount of blood coming back to the heart for each beat. This means the heart has to increase its rate of beating to get the same amount of blood out to working muscles. Thus, the risk of death in a susceptible person increases. Once cold, we not only close down skin blood vessels but we shiver to generate heat. One of the inevitable age-related changes we have is a decrease in muscle mass. Less muscle mass means a reduced ability to generate heat from shivering. Thus, older people may be more susceptible to death in cold weather.
- *High altitude* means a reduced ability for the bloodstream to take up oxygen that in turn increases the risk that physical activity may precipitate a cardiac event in older persons.
- *Air pollution* causes DNA, the genetic material in each cell of our body, to age the lung tissue in people who exercise and use their lungs in polluted areas.
- *Exposure to disease* in some communities or countries, older people with a poor genetic ability to fight infection or disease are at increased risk of illness or death. Aging itself leads to a depressed immune system and a reduced ability to fight infection and disease. In contrast, moderate levels of exercise lead to long term improved ability to fight infection in older people.
- *Psychological stress* has been shown to be conclusively linked to longevity. Obviously the frequency and severity of adverse life events, level of external support, and individual coping skills will affect the stress response. Research has also shown us that a higher level of trust is associated with greater life satisfaction, better health and enhanced longevity. Furthermore the type B personality (less stressed than type A) is more prevalent in older people, especially females. Being involved with masters sport or physical activity has been shown to maintain social contacts, sustain mental functioning and enhance mental health, thus helping we masters athletes cope better with life stressors.
- *Smoking* has been shown to shorten life expectancy in males by eight years and females

by five years. Physical activity in smokers improves longevity but to a much smaller extent than non-smokers.
- *Alcohol consumption* to excess has a negative effect on the normal age-related deterioration in liver and heart functioning. A study of longevity in Russian workers after retiring from heavy industry showed that between 1986 and 1994, the life expectancy of this heavy drinking group dropped from 65 years to 59 years in men and 74.8 to 73.2 years in women.
- *Dietary factors* strongly affect longevity. An accumulation of body fat to obesity levels directly affects health and the risk of heart disease. In laboratory animals, life span has been increased by dietary restriction and death rates increased by increasing energy intake as a result of increased cell breakdown in the big eating rats. In humans, taller and thinner people tend to live longer than shorter muscular people. High fibre diets (fruit, vegetables, cereals) rich in omega-three unsaturated fats (fish) have also been linked to longevity.
- *Race* also influences longevity. High death rates and reduced longevity are commonly seen in economically disadvantaged countries or communities where inadequate physical activity, poor diet, high smoking rates and excessive alcohol consumption are seen. Indeed, recent evidence from the Australian Institute of Health and Welfare suggests that lower socio-economic groups are at least twice as likely to die of cardiovascular diseases as those least disadvantaged, with indigenous Australians suffering cardiovascular death rates seven to ten times those of average Australians.

## Aging, Fitness and Quality of Life

Aging athletes are the converted. We appreciate and understand the benefits of fitness, as opposed to just being physically active. For many of us who enjoy competing against ourselves, against our own age group or peers, or "keeping the youngsters honest", a high level of fitness brings both performance benefits and keeps us biologically, functionally, psychologically and socially young.

We know that physical activity and fitness positively affect the many chronic health conditions (e.g. heart disease, hypertension, diabetes) that have been linked to premature death or disability in older age. However, there are numerous other benefits from aging fit. These include physiological, health, psychological and social benefits.

### Physiological Benefits

a. *Increased maximal oxygen consumption ($VO_2max$)*. As noted earlier this endurance capacity declines at the rate of around 10% per decade in non-athletes but only 5% per decade in older endurance athletes. Endurance training, particularly if it is intense, can improve $VO_2max$ by 10-30% in previously untrained older people but as much as 10% over a season in trained endurance athletes, young or old.

b. *Increased muscle strength*. Primarily due to an age-related decrease in muscle mass, there is an age-related decrease in muscle strength, even in aging athletes. Historically, it was felt that weight training was of no benefit to older people but the studies that suggested this did not use weights intense enough to get a benefit. These days, weight training using high resistance (> 80% maximum) has conclusively been shown to improve muscle strength and power, even in 90-plus year olds who doubled their strength above initial levels. In non-athletes, weight training not only increases muscle strength but also bone density, resting metabolic rate, endurance capacity, glucose metabolism and overall physical functioning. For older athletes, weight training becomes absolutely essential due to the need to hold on to muscle mass to develop strength and power in older power athletes and to take up more oxygen in endurance athletes. More on this in a later chapter.

c. *Flexibility.* Aging is associated with a significant decrease in the elastic properties of muscle and the connective tissue around joints, ligaments and tendons. These inevitable age-related changes result in significant decreases in the range of motion around a joint. For older non-athletes, this will lead to a decreased ability to bend and twist, thus compromising many of the tasks of daily living. For aging athletes, a reduced range of motion will lead to increased risk of injury but more importantly smaller stride or stroke lengths in running or water sports, respectively. Thus, as will be emphasised in a later chapter in this book, stretching, like weight training, is absolutely essential for the older competitive athlete.

d. *Lung functioning.* The elasticity of the lungs declines with age resulting in decreased lung capacity and power. While physical training in young people appears not to increase lung capacity, in older people who commence training, there is a benefit to improving lung function.

e. *Blood pressure.* Around 30% of the adult population of Australia have borderline or high blood pressure (140/90) with over 20 million older Americans experiencing this serious medical problem. There is a dramatic age-related increase in both systolic (when the heart pumps) and diastolic (when the heart is filling) blood pressures to the point where by age 55 approximately 55% of the people over 55 years of age suffer hypertension. A number of studies have shown that low to moderate intensity aerobic training can significantly lower both blood pressures in borderline or higher hypertensive adults. In a study we did at the 1994 World Masters Games in Brisbane, Australia, just over 35% of competitors were using hypertension drugs. This finding suggests that hypertension is prevalent in masters athletes but at a lower rate than people of similar age.

f. *Blood lipids.* Aging is associated with increases in both total blood cholesterol, the bad low density lipoprotein (LDL) cholesterol and triglycerides, all of which are risk factors in coronary heart disease. These blood fat profiles are improved with both endurance training and weight training, probably secondary to reduced body fat stores that accompany such training. Aging endurance athletes have been shown to have low levels of LDL cholesterol (the bad guy) and high levels of HDL cholesterol (the good guy). However, research has shown that these changes are transient and that regular training or physical activity is required to maintain this favourable blood fat profile.

g.  *Blood glucose (sugar)*. Physical activity has been shown to positively benefit blood glucose levels by increasing our sensitivity to insulin and reducing the insulin response to an increase in blood glucose after eating or drinking carbohydrates.

h.  *Sleep quality*. Physical activity has been shown to enhance sleep quality and quantity in all age groups. For older athletes needing longer to recover, this benefit cannot be underestimated as we will discuss in the Recovery Chapter later in the book.

i.  *Other benefits*. These include improved balance and coordination and improved velocity of movement, factors that in non-active or athletic people decline with age, but for older athletes are absolutely essential.

**Health Benefits.**

The Australian Institute of Health and Welfare has shown that 80% of Australians adults have at least one cardiovascular disease risk factor. It also showed that over half of Australian adults were overweight or obese, 16% had high blood pressure (> 140/90), about half had higher than desirable cholesterol levels (5.5 mmol/L, 200 mg/dl), and 30% did insufficient physical activity to benefit health. In the United States, similar data has been developed as shown in Figure 1.2 below.

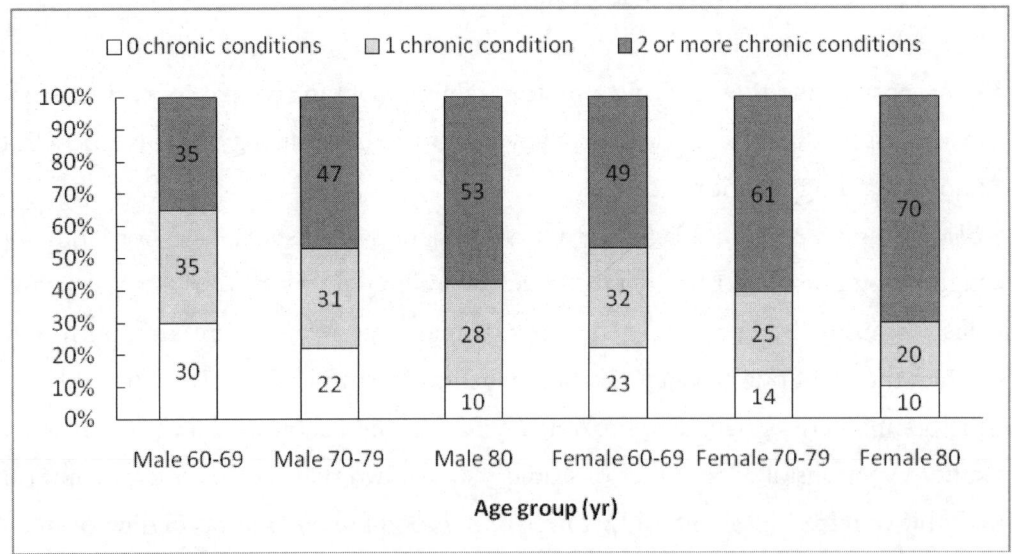

*Figure 1.2:* Approximate percent distribution of male and female USA population over 60 years of age with number of chronic conditions.

Physical activity and fitness have been shown to lower the incidence of illness, disability and death from the following health concerns:

- Coronary heart disease
- Type II diabetes
- Hypertension
- Osteoporosis
- Obesity
- Colon cancer
- Breast cancer
- Hip fracture

It appears that *current* activity levels are more protective than *past* activity. However, *cumulative* lifetime activity patterns may be a more influential factor for most of the above diseases, especially those with a long term developmental period such as cancer, osteoporosis and obesity. Scientists from Holland have suggested that high levels of physical fitness during adolescence and young adulthood is predictive of a healthy cardiovascular disease profile at a later age. In contrast, high physical activity, as opposed to high physical fitness during youth, does not seem to be predictive of reduced risk of cardiovascular disease in older age. Similarly, researchers from Finland have shown that older people who participated in endurance or team sports during their youth, had a lower risk of hypertension as adults. Having participated in power sports as youths did not convey any benefit.

### *Psychological Benefits.*

In the short term, regular exercise has been shown to enhance relaxation, reduce stress and anxiety, and enhance mood state. In the long term, benefits include:

a. *General well-being.* Psychologists have observed improved life satisfaction, enhanced self esteem, and reduced mood swings in people who undertake regular, long term training.

b. *Depression and anxiety.* The incidence of depression increases significantly with age with around 20-30% of adults experiencing these common lifetime disorders in a lifetime. However, in those older people who are physically active, this association is significantly reduced, particularly in older people with mild-to-moderate depression.

c. *Mental functioning.* Age-related decreases in the ability to problem solve, complete tasks that require fast and complex processing, react to stimuli, and control movement are common in non-active older people, but far less so in physically active older people. There is also scientific evidence to show that new skills can be learned and existing skills refined by all people, regardless of age. That is, old dogs *can* learn new tricks!

### *Social Benefits.*

Aging is associated with the need to adapt to changing roles. Marriage, children, careers, deaths of spouses or friends, retirement, financial hardship, ill-health and social isolation force many older people to search for a new identity. The short term benefits of being physically active into old age include empowering by reducing dependence and encouraging self-sufficiency through improved strength and endurance. Another short term benefit is social integration where physical activity programs conducted in small groups such as masters swim squads enhance social interaction. This is the very reason why AUSSI Masters Swimming have the motto *Fun, Fitness and Friendship*. Other social benefits include new friendships, a wider circle of social contacts, a more stimulating environment to maintain an active role in the community, and improved opportunities for mixing with younger and older generations.

In conclusion, numerous physiological, health, psychological and social benefits accrue from being physically active and fit. Taken together, these factors contribute to a much improved quality of life for the older athlete who remains fit and physically active.

## The Aging Athlete and Health Benefits

During the last three decades there has been an enormous increase in the number of older people engaging in regular exercise for the health benefits and sheer enjoyment of being involved in sport and exercise. Many of these older people are now becoming recreational or competitive athletes focussed on sports performance. For example, the inaugural World Masters Games held in Toronto, Canada in 1985 had 8,305 participants across 22 sports; the 2002 Melbourne, Australia World Masters Games 24,886 participants across 26 sports, and the upcoming 2009 World Masters Games being held in Sydney, Australia is anticipating the biggest mass participation (30,000), multi-sport (28 sports), multi-national, festival in the world. Furthermore, in the late 1980s, 44 Australian sporting organizations had introduced a masters (veterans, seniors, golden oldies) component. At the beginning of the new millennium, over 70 Australian sporting organizations now cater for the aging athlete with many conducting state and national championships and at least 30 hosting world championships and forming their own international federations.

In one of the few studies to examine the health benefits of masters athletes, Canadian researchers examined the long-term health value of regular endurance training in 551 men and 199 women aged 40-81 years over a seven-year period. The results showed:

- 1.4% suffered a non-fatal heart attack
- 90% were interested in good health
- 76% considered themselves less vulnerable to illness than their peers
- 68% considered their quality of life better than their non-exercising friends
- 37% of the smokers said training had helped them give up the addiction
- 59% had regular check-ups
- 88% said they slept well

An American researcher, Frank Kasch, and his colleagues, followed two groups (one group was endurance-trained, the other did no exercise) of 15 older men over a period of 23 years. At the end of the 23 year period:

- The athletes had lost 3.4 kg, the non-exercisers gained 3.2 kg
- The athletes had a 15.9% body fat, the non-exercisers 25.7%
- The athletes had a resting pulse 10 beats lower than the non-exercisers
- The athletes had lower blood pressures than non-exercisers with 9 of the non-exercisers being diagnosed as hypertensive
- The athlete's VO$_2$max had dropped 13%, the non-exercisers by 41%
- The exercisers had a maximum heart rate that was 20 beats/min higher than the non-exercisers

These results strongly suggest that a lifetime of physical training goes a long way to maintaining a young biological age.

### The Benefits of Endurance versus Weight Training?

As a sport physiologist with a passion for bridging the gap between sport and exercise science and athletes, I am often asked by people which is the best form of exercise to do as we get older. The answer is *both*. However, depending on what you want to achieve, endurance (aerobic) training or weight training have different health and performance outcomes as shown below in Table 1.1.

*Table 1.1:* A comparison of the effects of endurance training and strength training on health and fitness factors.

| Factor | Aerobic Training | Weight Training |
|---|---|---|
| VO₂max (aerobic capacity) | ↑↑↑ | ↑ |
| Resting heart rate | ↓↓ | ↓ |
| Stroke volume (ml blood/beat) | ↑↑ | ↑ |
| Blood pressure | | |
|     Systolic | ↓↓ | |
|     Diastolic | ↓↓ | ↓ |
| Body fat | ↓↓ | ↓ |
| Energy expenditure and body composition | | |
|     Resting metabolic rate | | |
|     Energy expenditure | ↑ | ↑↑ |
|     Fat mass | ↑↑ | ↑↑ |
|     Muscle mass | ↓↓ | ↓↓ |
|     Bone mineral density | ↑ | ↑↑↑ |
| | ↑ | ↑↑ |
| Strength | ↑↑ | ↑↑↑ |
| Blood Fats | | |
|     Total cholesterol | ↓↓ | ↓ |
|     HDL | ↑↑ | ↑ |
|     LDL | ↓↓ | ↓ |
|     Triglycerides | ↓↓ | ↓ |
| Glucose metabolism | | |
|     Insulin response to glucose | ↓↓ | ↓↓ |
|     Resting insulin levels | ↓ | ↓ |
|     Insulin sensitivity | ↑↑ | ↑↑ |
| Reduced injury risk | ↓ | ↓↓ |
| Low back pain | | ↑↑ |
| Psychological function | ↑ | ↑ |
| Physical function | ↑↑ | ↑↑↑ |

### Successful Aging

I cannot finish this chapter without mentioning the ten key factors that have been linked to successful aging by the American Academy of Anti-Aging Medicine (A4M) (http://www.worldhealth.net/). This group of medical professionals believe that successful aging is a four-

strategy approach involving
1. Diet,
2. Exercise,
3. Early detection of degenerative conditions, and
4. Pharmacologic interventions that influence metabolism such as growth hormone.

While the 8,500 strong doctor members' A4M organization has its critics who say the research evidence isn't out there to support some of their suggested anti-aging practices, they rightly say that death is a terminal illness and we cannot wait 30 years to see what the research data says about some anti-aging products.

The A4M suggests the following 10 factors are the key to successful aging:
1. Sleep 7 to 8 hours a night
2. Eat breakfast
3. Control body weight
4. Snack seldom
5. Exercise regularly
6. Become more educated
7. Limit alcohol intake
8. Stay socially connected
9. Don't smoke
10. Maintain optimism and happiness

For older athletes keen to maintain or prolong their vitality and competitiveness into older age, a more relevant list of 10 biomarkers was produced by two of the world's leading scientists in the area of aging, exercise and sports performance, Drs Bill Evans and Irwin Rosenberg. Based on years of their own and others research, the following 10 biomarkers they see as essential to monitor in order to maintain vitality into older age:

*Muscle mass.*

We lose about 3 kilograms of muscle mass per decade of life after adulthood with this loss accelerating after age 45 years. Apart from genetics, exercise and hormone (NB testosterone) levels determine our muscle mass. For older athletes, given the illegality of anabolic steroid use, doing hypertrophy (muscle building) weight training is strongly recommended to hold onto muscle mass, especially in masters speed, strength and power athletes. Muscles are made up of slow twitch fibres that contract relatively slowly but have good endurance, and fast twitch fibres that contract relatively quickly but fatigue quickly. Research has shown that the slow twitch fibres are used during low intensity activities and the fast twitch during hard or fast work. Sadly, it is the force-producing fast twitch fibres that, in both non-athletes and athletes, decrease in number and size with age. This means that our performance will decline in events requiring speed and power. Strength training and high intensity or speed work selectively develops the fast twitch fibre size. Thus weight training and speed work should become a must the older an athlete becomes.

An age-related decrease in muscle mass also affects a number of the biomarkers below:
- A decrease in resting metabolic rate
- An increase in body fat
- A decrease in aerobic capacity
- A reduced blood sugar tolerance, and
- A loss in bone density

*Strength.*

This biomarker is related to the decrease in muscle mass. Again, speed work and weight training, especially hypertrophy (muscle enlargement) weight training, will go a along way to maintaining or delaying the age-related changes in muscle strength.

*Resting metabolic rate (RMR).*

The RMR is the amount of energy (kilojoules or Calories) that you use at rest to just function (breathe, pump blood, and maintain body temperature). Apart from RMR, our daily energy expenditure also includes the energy cost of exercise and the increase in energy usage after eating are the three factors that affect our daily use of Calories or kilojoules. The RMR is by far the greatest contributor to our daily energy expenditure at about 60%. Crucially, RMR decreases with age (about 2% per decade) and is highly related to the major user of energy while at rest - muscle mass which decreases with age. An average 70 year-old needs about 500 Calories (about 2000 kilojoules) less per day than a 20 year old. However, few older people slow down their food energy intake. Too much energy intake, with too little exercise, a reduced muscle mass and a slower RMR, mean an increase in body fat. Again, weight training is crucial to maintain muscle mass, maintain RMR, and thus reduce an age-related increase in body fat.

*Percent body fat.*

As discussed above, body fat increases significantly with age. In women, the average body fat for a 25 year old is 25%, at 65 year it is 43%. In men, it increases from 18% to 38% from age 25 to 65 years. Importantly, it is not the weight on the scales that is important, it is the body fat versus the good lean body mass (muscle, organs, bones) that we should worry about. In general, when we start an exercise or training program as an older athlete, we may not change body weight at all. What is most likely is that we are gaining muscle mass but losing fat mass, thus not changing our body weight when we look at a set of scales. This is exactly what we want, losing weight by dieting may mean a loss of some fat mass, but it also may mean a loss of muscle mass that will work against us in that a loss of muscle mass lowers our RMR. This is why the best way to lose fat is to combine a diet with exercise - we lose fat and gain or maintain muscle mass that long term will help us lose more fat by increasing our RMR.

Interestingly, it is not only the *total* body fat that is important to overall health and vitality, but *where* that body fat is stored. Research has shown that men and women who store the majority of their body fat *above their hips* have a higher risk of developing heart disease, stroke and diabetes than those who store it *below their hips*. The safe combination of diet combined with exercise will see the body fat being removed from where it is stored the most, not from what part of the body you exercise – doing a lot of sit-ups will not necessarily see a drop in the size of the beer belly!

For aging athletes wanting to lose weight, the combination of diet and exercise, and in particular, weight training, is strongly recommended. We will discuss this area of weight control for aging athletes in detail in a later chapter.

### *Aerobic capacity.*

This is the maximum capacity of the body to transport and consume oxygen, sometimes called VO$_2$max. As a biomarker of vital aging, a relatively high VO$_2$max is essential. Why? It indicates healthy lungs (to get the oxygen into the blood), a powerful heart (to transport the oxygen in the blood), a good blood network (arteries/veins), and effectively working muscles (to take up the oxygen made available in the blood). Sadly, by age 65 years, the VO$_2$max decreases by 30-40% compared to that of a 25 year old. Three major reasons explain this drop in aerobic capacity:

- An age-related decrease in physical activity or decreased intensity of training
- An inevitable age-related decrease in the maximum heart rate meaning less blood, and thus oxygen, is pumped to the muscles
- An age-related decrease in muscle mass meaning less muscle to take up the available oxygen.

To help develop or maintain VO$_2$max into older age , it is therefore important that older endurance athletes should do high intensity training and/or muscle-building weight training. More on how to do this in a later chapter.

### *Blood sugar tolerance.*

Our body's ability to control blood sugar levels is called *glucose tolerance*. Sadly with aging, particularly aging non-athletes, comes a loss in the ability to take up and use the blood glucose. Too much blood glucose will lead to what we call *type II diabetes* or *adult-onset diabetes.* By age 70, about 20% of men and 30% of women have an abnormal glucose tolerance, increasing the risk of type II diabetes. Researchers have shown that this poor glucose tolerance is due to a number of factors that are also age-related:

- Decreased physical activity – this lowers both muscle mass and the sensitivity of tissues to insulin that helps lower blood glucose levels. The result is a creeping increase in blood glucose
- Increased body fat – this disturbs the body's ability to control fat and glucose in the blood
- Lower muscle mass – muscle is the major organ the insulin stimulates to take up the glucose and store or use for energy production. Less muscle means less ability to take up the blood glucose and again an age-related increase in blood sugar

Sadly, the creep in blood glucose upwards also directly contributes to heart disease, high blood pressure, and high blood cholesterol. However, regular physical training combined with a low fat, high fibre complex carbohydrate diet helps control diabetes. For older people, exercise, in particular weight training, helps use up the blood glucose as an energy source, helps maintain the muscle mass that uses the glucose made available in the blood, and maintains or increases the sensitivity of tissues to insulin that cause blood glucose levels to drop.

*Cholesterol/HDL ratio.*

Cholesterol is a fatty substance that is essential for the body's normal functioning. It plays an essential role in the making of all the body's cell membranes and the production of many of our sex hormones. It is transported in the blood by attaching to proteins, the combination of which is called lipoproteins – HDL (high density lipoprotein), or LDL (low density lipoprotein) cholesterol. The LDL-cholesterol contributes to the build up of plaque in blood vessels that contributes to artery blocking. In contrast, HDL- cholesterol takes the plaque away and back to the liver, thus helping keep the arteries clear.

We take cholesterol into our body via foods (kidney, liver, egg yolk, prawns) but the majority is made by the liver. That's why we don't need it in our diet in large quantities. However, a high saturated fat diet also contains cholesterol. That's also why a "low cholesterol" or "no cholesterol" food label that still has saturated fat, could increase cholesterol levels.

While total cholesterol levels are important, it is the ratio of total cholesterol to HDL-cholesterol that is more important. A high HDL-cholesterol (normally about 20-30% of total cholesterol) suggests a low LDL-cholesterol (normally about 60-70% of total cholesterol), with both these factors being important in heart disease prevention. Your cholesterol/HDL ratio should be 4.5 or lower. In normal aging it appears the total cholesterol appears to increase while the HDL-cholesterol remains constant, suggesting the LDL-cholesterol is increasing.

Apart from genetics, we need to control the factors that influence the blood lipoproteins – diet, exercise, obesity, oral contraceptives, alcohol and smoking. A low fat diet will lower LDL-cholesterol levels and help control obesity but have no influence on the good HDL-cholesterol. Only exercise and lower body fat can elevate the HDL-cholesterol levels. Stopping smoking, drinking alcohol in small amounts and going off birth control pills also help increase HDL-cholesterol levels. Thus, for the aging athlete, aerobic training helps lower total cholesterol and increase HDL-cholesterol, contributing to a prolonged quantity and quality of life.

*Blood pressure.*

Apart from obesity, this is one of the major health problems in the western world. The causes of high blood pressure include obesity, lack of exercise, a diet too high in fat, salt and alcohol intake, and smoking. Normal blood pressure is below 140/90 which means 140 mm mercury pressure when the heart contracts (systolic blood pressure) and 90 mm mercury pressure when the heart is filling (diastolic blood pressure). If blood pressure is continually high, it causes the artery walls to stiffen and thicken, making the heart work harder than it needs to. In unhealthy people with other risk factors, this predisposes a person to a heart attack.

While lowering salt content of food to 4 grams/day (avoid processed, salted – ham, bacon, sausages, takeaway foods) can assist about 10% of people with high blood pressure who respond to this, regular moderate exercise (brisk walking, swimming, cycling to increase heart rate and breathing (30 minutes a day total most days of the week) has been shown to consistently lower blood pressure in those with high blood pressure. Other lifestyle changes to reduce blood pressure include

- Giving up or reducing smoking
- Eating plant-based foods (fruit, vegetables)
- Eating moderate to low-fat dairy products
- Eating mono- and unsaturated fats
- Eating lean unprocessed meat, poultry and fish
- Drink one (women) to two (men) standard drinks a day and have two alcohol-free days a week
- Maintain a healthy weight target (94 cm waist for men, 80 cm for women and body mass index [weight in kgs / height in m$^2$] less than 25)

*Bone density.*

There is an age-related decrease in the mineral content of bones that to less dense and therefore weaker and more brittle bones. The causes of the age-related decrease in bone density are poor calcium intake, hormonal changes, deficient calcium absorption, and lack of physical activity. Contrary to popular opinion decreased bone density affects both men and women but is more common in postmenopausal women (or women with a hysterectomy or ovary resection) because of the associated hormonal changes. From the age of 25 years, we lose about 1% of our bone mass per year. However, for every gram of bone mineral lost by women, men lose about 0.66 gram. Before menopause, women only lose bone mass at around 0.3% per year but after menopause when the production of oestrogen drops dramatically, the rate accelerates to 2.5-3% per year.

Obviously, diet and exercise can help. Specifically, the dietary intervention requires older people to take in 800 mg/day or more of calcium before menopause and 1000-1200 mg/day during pregnancy or after menopause. Research has shown that most women take in only around 500 mg/day, despite knowing the importance of calcium. Combined with adequate intake of vitamin D and carbohydrate, both of which aid calcium absorption, eating calcium-rich foods such as low fat dairy products, will help reduce bone mineral loss. Exercise requires muscular movement that stresses bone that then adapts by increasing its density. Historically, weight-bearing exercise (e.g. walking, running) was seen as the best exercise prescription, but recent research has shown that weight training is equally or more effective in increasing bone mineral density.

*Ability to regulate body temperature.*

Our body likes to operate at around 37.5 degrees C. When our body gets hot such as during hot weather and/or during exercise, we sweat to produce fluids to evaporate which in turn cools us down. With age, our ability to regulate body temperature in the heat (and cold) drops due to:

- Decreased muscle mass that means less heat producing shivering
- Reduced ability to sense thirst
- Reduced number of sweat glands
- Reduced sweat production per unit area of skin.
- The sweat mechanism turns on at a higher body temperature than a younger person.
- Kidney function is impaired to the point where at age 70 years they can filter only at about half the rate they did at age 30 years. When dehydrated, a younger person's kidneys work to reduce urine output in order to conserve water. In older people this is therefore not as effective.

Importantly, many of these factors are related to the age-related decrease in $VO_2max$. For older athletes that maintain or develop their $VO_2max$, many of these declines can be avoided by regular endurance training.

## Conclusion

Aging is a multi-faceted process with the rate of aging being strongly determined by genetic factors but able to be influenced by both lifestyle and environmental factors. There is no doubt that maintenance of a physically active lifestyle into old age is associated with better health, greater quantity and quality of life, and less disability. There is also no doubt that vigorous versus light to moderate physical activity confers greater quantity and quality of life than light to moderate intensity exercise. For the aging athlete, these are side-benefits to remaining competitive while enjoying a life full of fun, fitness and friendship.

The American Academy of Anti-Aging Medicine and some of the world's leading researchers in exercise and aging have also strongly recommended a higher level of physical activity as we age. Importantly for both performance and health reasons, all the research points towards the aging athlete undertaking weight training, flexibility and some high intensity endurance training and focussing on a healthy diet to control body fat.

# CHAPTER 2

# AGE-RELATED DECLINES IN PERFORMANCE AND IMPLICATIONS FOR TRAINING

*I'm in better shape now than when I was 100.*

**103-year-old shot-put competitor in World Masters Games**

## Aging and Activity Levels

Scientists define *physical activity* as movement caused by muscle contractions that increase energy expenditure. In contrast, *exercise* is defined as repetitive bodily movement undertaken to improve or maintain physical fitness. Thus, walking, housecleaning, and gardening are considered physical activity while swimming, running and weight training are considered exercise.

Regardless of which definition is used, research has conclusively shown that older adults are less active than younger adults, and that older women are less active than older men. However, the following factors have been shown to negatively affect involvement in physical activity or exercise:

- Socioeconomics – the smaller the household income, the less likely to be active
- Race – indigenous persons less likely to be active
- Education level – less well-educated persons less likely to be active
- Health status – less healthy persons less likely to be active
- Smoking – smokers less likely to be active
- Stress – stressed persons less likely to be active
- Exercise knowledge – persons with little knowledge of benefits are less likely to be active

The most recent information available suggests that western society is becoming less active at a dramatic rate, with obvious health consequences. For example, a survey of 3,841 Australians recently found that although 88% of people believed their health could be improved by being more active, the proportion of people inactive increased from 13 to 15% over the previous two years. Importantly, the proportion of physically inactive Australians increased in people aged 30-44 years (12 to 17% over two years) and among those with tertiary qualifications (6 to 11%).

A recent Australian Bureau of Statistics survey found that 54.7% of the Australian population aged 18 years and over participated as players in one or more sports or physical activities (Table 2.1). Participation rates were highest for the 18-24 year age group (73.5%), and declined steadily with age with only 33.8% of the population aged 65 years and over having participated in a sport or recreational physical activity. Males had a higher participation rate than females in every age group. Overall, males had a participation rate of 58.5% compared with 50.9% for females.

*Table 2.1:* The decline in participation in sport and physical activity with increasing age.

| Age Group | Males (%) | Females (%) | Overall (%) |
|---|---|---|---|
| 18-24 | 79.7 | 67 | 73.5 |
| 25-34 | 68.9 | 64.2 | 66.6 |
| 35-44 | 58.5 | 57.7 | 58.1 |
| 45-54 | 51.9 | 45 | 48.5 |
| 55-64 | 48.8 | 37.6 | 43.2 |
| 65 and over | 39.4 | 29.2 | 33.8 |
| Total | 58.5 | 50.9 | 54.7 |

The existing research suggests that physical inactivity ranks second only to tobacco smoking in importance for the burden of disease and disability from all-causes in Australia. The role of physical inactivity as a health risk factor is at least as significant as high blood pressure or high cholesterol in contributing to cardiovascular disease. Furthermore, physical activity protects against several forms of cancer, reduces the risk of diabetes, improves mental health and may reduce the risks of falls and injury in the aged.

The *Physical Activity Patterns of Australian Adults* survey has recently shown that the percentage of Australians achieving sufficient levels of physical activity for a health benefit is declining. For example, over a two year period, this figure dropped from 62% to 57% with the drop greatest in women (61 to 54%) and 30-44 year-olds (64 to 54%).

While no actual breakdown into exercise intensities or types of exercise is available, this disturbing trend of decreased physical activity levels is occurring quickly. Table 2.2 shows the total participation changes in physical activity and sport by age group over the years 1998-99 and 1999-2000. The results clearly show an age-related decline in physical activity levels with age with people over the age of 65 years the least active.

*Table 2.2:* Total participation changes in physical activity and sport by age group over the years 1998-99 and 1999-2000.

| Age Group | 1998-99 (%) | 1999-2000 (%) | Change (%) |
|---|---|---|---|
| 18-24 | 80.4 | 73.5 | -6.9 |
| 25-34 | 70.1 | 66.6 | -3.5 |
| 35-44 | 61.1 | 58.1 | -3.0 |
| 45-54 | 56.4 | 48.5 | -7.9 |
| 55-64 | 47.8 | 43.2 | -4.6 |
| 65+ | 36.8 | 33.8 | -3.0 |

Further analysis of these figures shows that of this age group, 39.4% of males and only 29.2% of females are physically active.

These results are very similar to Canadian and United States figures. Studies from Canada have shown that, even though 89% of older adults know of the health benefits of physical activity into older age, about 69% of them are not participating in physical activity to gain those benefits.

## Early-Life Activity and its Relationship to Adult Activity

Exercising appears to be a relatively stable lifestyle characteristic from adolescence to adulthood and across various ages during adulthood. A number of studies have shown that perceived well-being and movement confidence were the best predictors of later life exercise. A recent Scandinavian study of 642 people aged 65 years and over showed that, for both men and women, participation in competitive sport from as early as 10-19 years of age was a significant predictor of maintaining physical activity into old age. The early positive experiences with sport (encouragement, skill development, social, self-confidence) were strong influences in later life involvement. The same study also highlighted that women's participation in recreational sports at age 40-64 years predicted physical activity involvement after 65 years of age. Once into older age groups, research has shown that people over 55 years of age with low levels of physical activity were four times more likely to be inactive after eight years than those who were most physically active at the baseline age of 55 years. Thus, it appears that people active in sports during childhood and youth are far more likely to remain active into older age. Moreover, once into adulthood, the earlier an inactive person becomes active, the more likely they are to remain active into older age.

## Performance Declines in Aging Athletes

Age-related decreases in performance in speed, power, strength and endurance events are commonly observed. For example, Olympic weightlifting performance (snatch, clean and jerk) in aging lifters has been shown to decrease about 1-1.5% annually beyond the age of 30 and then decrease at a faster rate after age 70 years.

Figures 2.1 and 2.2 show the age-related declines in swimming performances for aging men and women in both a speed and power event (50m freestyle) and endurance event (1500m freestyle).

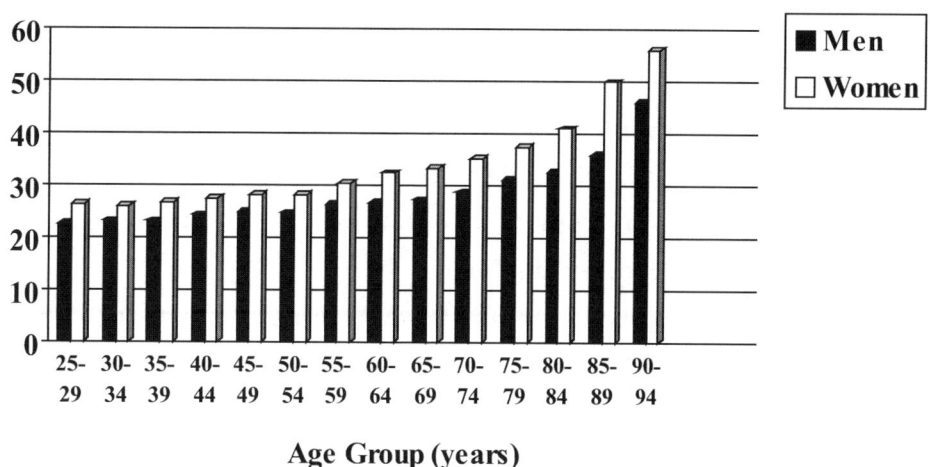

*Figure 2.1:* Male and female age-group records for 50m (sec) freestyle swimming.

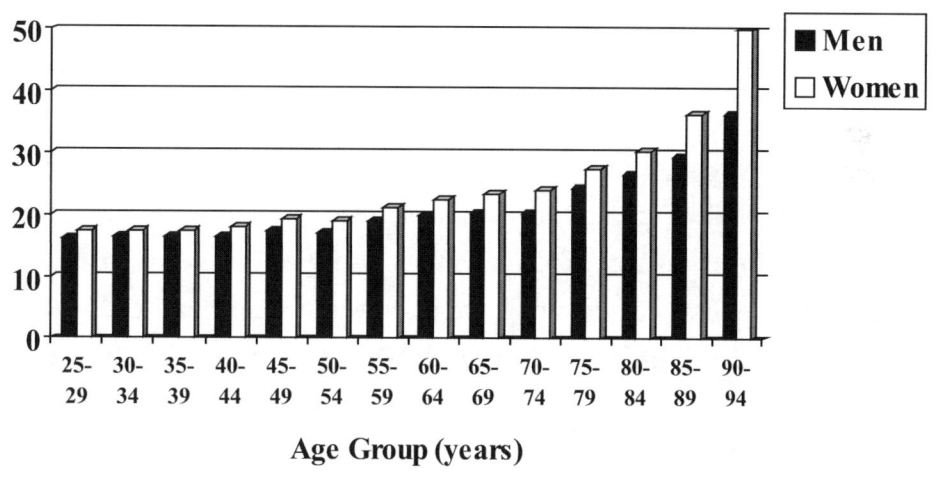

*Figure 2.2:* Male and female age-group records for 1500m (min) freestyle swimming.

A close analysis of these swimming world records suggests that performance levels peak at age-group 35-40 years, decrease linearly until age 70 years, and then the rate of decline accelerates. These performance declines reflect age-related declines in muscle mass and strength and strongly suggest the need for strength training in aging athletes. Moreover, age-related declines in aerobic capacity explain the decline in 1500m endurance capacity.

## Physiological Declines and Implications for the Aging Athlete

The aging process is accompanied by declines in the cardiovascular, musculoskeletal, nervous, immune and thermoregulation systems that affect the endurance, speed, power, flexibility and body composition of aging athletes. The purpose of this section is to explain exactly what changes do occur in aging athletes and more importantly, what we can do to slow these declines.

1. *Cardiovascular System* The capacity of heart and blood system is measured in a laboratory as maximal oxygen consumption or VO$_2$max. In non-athletes this value declines at the rate of 10% per decade. However, in older male and female endurance athletes, it declines at about half this rate, primarily due to a decrease in the maximum heart rate that reduces the ability of the heart to get enough blood and oxygen to the working muscles. Some research suggests that older endurance athletes who train intensely, can maintain VO$_2$max for a decade or more, before declining.

    The research has shown conclusively that previously inactive older people can improve their VO$_2$max by 20-30%, just as young people can. Thus, it is never too late to start. For the aging athlete, research has conclusively shown that high intensity exercise (> 85% of maximum heart rate) can improve or help maintain VO$_2$max into older age.

    The major reason for the age-related decline in VO$_2$max is an age-related decline in maximum heart rate (MHR)

    $$MHR = 220 - Age \pm 10 \text{ years (historical formula)}$$
    $$MHR = 205.8 - (0.685 \times age) \text{ (new formula)}$$

    For older athletes, the good news is that fitter older people tend to have a higher MHR than those the same age that are unfit.

    Another reason for the age-related decrease in VO$_2$max is an age-related decline in the amount of blood pumped per heartbeat, what scientists call the stroke volume. Older endurance athletes appear to maintain their stroke volume much better than non-athletes. Importantly, stroke volume can be increased with low intensity endurance training in aging non-athletes, and high intensity training (e.g. interval training) in older athletes. The lower MHR and stroke volume often observed in older endurance athletes means less blood and thus oxygen being made available to muscles. Interestingly, the muscle blood flow also drops in aging muscle meaning not only less oxygen delivery but also less removal of waste products such as carbon dioxide and lactic acid, the accumulation of which hinder muscle performance. Less blood flow also means a reduced ability to recover between intervals, between training sessions, and from an injury. The arteries and capillaries of aging muscles also appear to have a reduced ability to dilate (get larger) compared to younger people. This also means reduced muscle blood flow and thus reduced oxygen delivery to working muscles in aging muscles.

2. *Connective Tissue* These tissues provide support and structure to the body. The covering of muscles, tendons (join muscle to bone) and ligaments (connect bone to bone) are the major connective tissues. They get bigger and stronger with training, and weaker and smaller when not used. The strength of the connective tissue is dependent upon the number of cross-linkages between the small fibres that make up the connective tissue. Connective tissue also has elastic properties that help generate forces when stretched and cause decreased flexibility when tight. Aging causes the connective tissue to lose the number of cross-links it has and also its elasticity, thus reducing the strength and flexibility of the connective tissue. Aging also sees a decrease in the water content of these tissues.

This means a reduction in the shock absorbing capacity of the tissues as well as a loss of compliance of connective tissue to stretch and be elastic.

Thus, age-related changes in the connective tissue make an aging athlete more susceptible to injury and contribute to a loss in flexibility that not only affects the risk of injury, but reduces performance in sports or events requiring a range of motion about a joint.

3. *Skin* has a number of important functions that include:
   - An energy storage site
   - A barrier to infection
   - A barrier to ultraviolet light and rain
   - An important part of our thermoregulation system

   While age-related changes in this tissue can affect a number of exercise-related functions, athletes are also exposed to other factors (sunlight, heat, cold and wind) that age the skin faster than an inactive older person. Specifically, the skin becomes thinner that compromises the ability to insulate against the cold. Thinner skin reduces the ability to cushion against impacts making an older person more susceptible to bruising. An age-related decrease in the skin elasticity makes an older person's skin easier to tear when falling, hitting something, or tearing off a band-aid. A reduced skin blood flow means cuts, bruises or scratches heal more slowly and our ability to get rid of heat to the skin surface is reduced. Aged skin also loses about 2% of its pigment per year after age 30 years, making older people more susceptible to skin damage from ultraviolet radiation. Thus, an older person needs to be more sun-safe than younger people.

4. *Respiratory System Changes* The lungs and their associated airways are essential for life and a highly efficient system crucial for success in sport. While pollution, previous airway disease, smoking, lack of exercise, and genetics all lead to deterioration in this system, it appears that aging itself is also a major contributor. Thus, aging athletes experience breathlessness at a lighter intensity of exercise than younger athletes. The age-related changes in the respiratory system include lower lung and airway elasticity that means the respiratory muscles (diaphragm, rib muscles) must work harder to get air in and out of the lungs, thus taking up valuable oxygen that the muscles want to use. With aging, these respiratory muscles lose strength and the ligaments and connective tissue surrounding the muscles becomes stiffer. These changes reduce the ability of the lungs to fill which in turn reduces the ability of the respiratory system to deliver air and oxygen to the blood flowing through the lungs, the rate of which also decreases with age. Furthermore, the membranes of the tiny air sacs (alveoli) where the exchange of oxygen and carbon dioxide take place get thicker due to an age-related increase in the thickness of the connective tissue where the exchange of these gases takes place. This creates a barrier to the gas exchange so important in athletes.

   Thus, the lung capacity and power of the lungs decreases with age at about 25 ml/year after the age 20 in non-athletes. Together with a reduced ability to exchange oxygen and carbon dioxide, this decreased lung function means aging athletes have a reduced aerobic capacity compared to younger athletes. However, the age-related changes above occur at a slower rate in aging athletes compared to non-athletes due to the strengthening of the respiratory muscles that regular exercise provides.

5. *Neuromuscular System* The major age-related change in this system is a decreased muscle mass that drops 25-30% in non-exercising 60-70 year olds compared to young adults. The research suggests that muscle mass starts decreasing slowly after age 30 years but decreases 3 to 6% per decade after 60 years of age. By age 50 years there has been a 10% decrease in total muscle area. After 50 years of age, the rate of muscle loss is accelerated with an even faster rate of decline after 70 years of age.

The reduced muscle mass is caused partially by an age-related decrease in the production of muscle building hormones testosterone and growth hormone, but is primarily due to a loss of the total muscle fibre number and a reduction in the size of each muscle fibre. Crucially for the older athlete, these decreases in the number and size of muscle fibres appear to occur in the fast-twitch muscle fibres which are the speed and power producing fibres. Research has shown that the number of fast twitch muscle fibres in young men is 50-60% of the total fibres but at age 80 years is about 30%. Interestingly, the decrease of fast twitch fibre number is made up for by an increase in the number of slow twitch fibres, suggesting that the nerves, the thing that determines fibre contraction speed, detach from the fast twitch fibres and attach onto slow twitch fibres. Because strength and power are greatly dependent upon muscle size and in particular the number and size of fast twitch fibres, decreases in muscle fibre size and number with age, mean decreased strength and power. However, and research supports this, the endurance of aging muscle appears to be maintained into old age due to an increased slow twitch fibre number within a muscle.

For muscles to work effectively in generating strength and power, they also need nerve input. Sadly, as we age, a number of negative changes occur in the nervous system that will slow us down. These include:
- Reduced nerve connections to muscle fibres
- Reduced nerve conduction velocity
- Slower transmission of the electrical impulse from the nerve to the muscle
- Reduced muscle contraction velocity

Taken together, the changes that occur in the neuromuscular system result in a reduced ability to generate force, speed and power. These changes mean a decrease in performance with aging, particularly in speed and power events.

A number of studies have shown that older athletes have similar muscle strength, muscle power, muscle size, fast twitch fibre number and size as young non-athletes but that compared to young athletes, all these capacities decrease.

The implications for the aging athlete are that:
- Weight training, specifically hypertrophy weight training that builds muscle size,

has been shown to increase muscle size in older non-athletes and aging athletes. More importantly, resistance training has been shown to significantly increase muscle strength (double in fact in 90 year olds who've never done weights) and muscle size. Research undertaken by myself at The University of Queensland in the mid-1990s showed that veteran sprint runners who did hypertrophy (muscle size increasing) weight training consisting of 8 weeks of 80% plus of maximum lifts done 8-12 times per session, increased not only their muscle size, but their 100 and 300m run performance on the track. More in the strength training chapter later in this book.

- Speed and overspeed (higher rating than used in the sport – downhill running, treadmill sprints, towing) work that stimulates the nervous system and fast twitch muscle fibres becomes crucial for both aging endurance and speed and power athletes.

6. *Skeletal System.* Aging is associated with osteoporosis, the loss of bone mineral density that results in reduced bone strength in both men and women. This decrease in bone strength increases the risk of bone fractures in older people. Sadly, the death rate following the most common bone fracture in older people, a hip fracture, is approximately 50% within two years of the event. Both men and women lose bone mass at around 0.3% per year after 50 years of age. However, women at menopause lose the ability to produce the hormone oestrogen that is so important for maintaining or increasing bone density. After menopause women lose bone mass at a much greater rate up to 2.5% per year. While the loss of bone mass is not fully understood as yet, it is associated with reduced skeletal blood flow, physical inactivity, insufficient calcium intake, decreased calcium absorption by the gut, a reduced hormone function, and genetics. Both weight-bearing exercise (walking or jogging) and weight training have been shown to directly increase bone mineral density by increasing the forces transmitted to muscles, tendons, ligaments and bone, causing the bones to remodel and get stronger.

   In a recent study, Canadian researchers observed that bone mineral density in the lower limbs of 40-55 year old male endurance runners was significantly higher than a group of age-matched men who exercised two to four times a week, suggesting that such exercise confers a decreased risk of osteoporosis. However, the implications an age-related loss of bone mass and strength means older athletes, especially menopausal or post-menopausal women, who display a fracture following minor trauma or high intensity training, should be suspected of having low bone density. The same group(s) should also commence an exercise or training program slowly and progressively to allow the skeletal system to adapt. Indeed, the research suggests that aged bone can still gain strength and bone mass similar to that of younger people.

7. *Other Nervous System Changes* The nervous system is a complex system of several billion cells that function as the body's internal communication network. Aging causes decreases in the efficiency of this network. Well known are:

- age-related hearing loss that suggests coaches, team mates or conditioners need to speak louder or place themselves closer to the aged athlete
- age-related vision losses that suggest regular eye tests and/or correction (glasses, corrective surgery)
- age-related decrease in reaction time due to a reduced rate of muscle contraction, decreased rate of nerve conduction velocity, reduced rate of perceptual processing, and a slower processing of sensory stimulation

While the slower reaction time occurs in both aging non-athletes and athletes, it is pleasing to know that the reaction time of older athletes is better than young non-athletes but not as quick as younger athletes.

The ability of older athletes to focus attention under competition stress has also been studied. The results suggest that older athletes become over-aroused during competition compared to younger athletes and they cannot focus for as long on a task. Obviously, the more skilled the aging athlete, the easier it will be to focus, while inexperienced older athletes need to concentrate more just to do the basic skills of a task. This would suggest that coaches of older athletes should prepare older athletes by placing them in stressful situations in training.

The nervous system is also involved in determining sleep patterns. It appears that there is an age-related decrease in the sleep *quality*, rather than a decrease in sleep *quantity*. That is, more time needs to be spent in bed to attain the same benefits sleep offers such as recovering. Research has shown that older people have more difficulty remaining asleep than falling asleep, they wake more often, and once awake, stay awake for longer than younger people. For older athletes, these changes suggest the recovery process from training or competition may be compromised. The tips on better sleep quality are discussed at length in the recovery chapter in this book.

8. *Flexibility* is defined as the range of motion about a joint. Research has shown that flexibility decreases with age approximately 20-30% between the ages of 30 and 70 years. Reasons for this age-related decline appear to be decreased physical activity levels, decreased water content and thus elasticity of the connective tissue (tendons, ligaments, joint capsule) surrounding a joint, and increased cross-linking between the connective tissue fibres. My experience as an aging athlete would also suggest that sitting a lot, a fact of life in my desk- or meeting-bound job also helps shorten connective tissue. I also feel that many micro-tears of the connective tissue (from years of training) surrounding muscles and joints leads to scar tissue build-up which over many years may cause a tightening of the joints. While flexibility is important for older non-athletes to remain functionally independent into old age, for older athletes it assists in injury prevention and crucially a longer stride or stroke length that can greatly assist performance. Thus, along with weight training, I strongly believe that flexibility training, not just as part of warm-up or cool-down, is crucial for the competitive aging athlete.

9. *Body Composition* is related to the proportion of lean body mass (muscle, bone and

organs) and percentage of body fat. In general, aging is associated with a decline in lean body (muscle) mass and an increase in fat mass. Importantly, aging is associated with a preferential depositing of body fat around the abdomen with high levels of "central" fat being closely linked to many heart disease risk factors. These changes are determined by a combination of genetic factors, physical activity and energy intake. We also know that an age-related increased fat mass is associated with increased blood pressure, increased risk of diabetes, increased risk of heart disease, and reduced strength and flexibility. For older athletes, the importance of keeping body fat levels low is crucial for both health and performance reasons. A whole chapter of this book is focused on this topic.

10. *Thermoregulation.* This system is responsible for the regulation and maintenance of the body temperature. While the affect of age on this system is examined in depth later in the book, a number of factors such as reduced $VO_2max$, reduced skin blood flow, reduced sweat rate, and reduced total body water suggest that aging athletes have a reduced ability to thermoregulate.

11. *Immune System* The immune system is responsible for fighting infections within the body. Unfortunately, like most of the human body's systems, it also undergoes age-related changes that potentially lead to an increased risk of infection, greater rates of illness and an increased risk of death in older people. The immune system consists of a host of cells that are released into the body to fight and destroy the invading cell (virus, bacteria). The production and response of these cells slows with aging. A number of stress-related hormones (adrenalin, cortisol, endorphin) regulate the production and response of these cells during an invasion by a foreign body. During exercise, these hormones suppress the release of these cells. Aging sees a decrease in the adrenalin levels at rest but a similar increase with exercise as that seen in younger people. In older people, research suggests the stress hormone cortisol is increased both at rest and during exercise compared to younger people. Taken together, during exercise, the body appears more susceptible to infection because the immune system is suppressed. This response is particularly evident with high intensity exercise where the stress hormones remain high after exercise making a person more susceptible to infection at a time when they are mixing with others talking about the event in a group setting.

The limited research examining the immune system in trained older people would suggest that during exercise, the levels of these stress hormones are reduced compared to older non-exercisers. This means that the immune system is more able to fight the invading cells if they enter the body because the hormones haven't suppressed the release of the infection-fighting cells. Research has also conclusively shown that older endurance-trained people have a much more responsive immune system than older non-exercisers. This means that older athletes are far more resistant to infection and when infected can fight the infection at a faster rate, thus recovering more quickly to resume training and competing.

12. *Recovery from Muscle Damage.* A number of studies on both rats and humans have suggested that there are age-related differences in the susceptibility of skeletal muscle to

exercise-induced muscle damage and the ability for post-damage repair. It appears that for the same relative intensity (% of maximum) of exercise, older muscles are damaged more, at least in older non-athletes. A recent study, however, found that after eight weeks of strength training, younger (20-30 years) and older (65-75 years) men displayed similar muscle damage when examined under an electron microscope. This suggests that training may help prevent muscle damage in older people.

Most human and rat studies suggest that recovery from a training session that induces muscle damage is impaired in aging people. Certainly my own anecdotal evidence based on years of observing my own response to training and listening and observing other aging athletes from endurance sports, is that recovery takes longer from intense training sessions.

A number of reasons have been put forward for this increased muscle damage and longer recovery and include:

- The age-related decrease in muscle size and strength makes the muscle(s) more susceptible to damage. Strength training is thus an obvious solution to overcome this factor.
- The age-related decrease in flexibility or range of motion about a joint means that when an aging person exercises, damage is more likely to occur in the connective tissue that is less elastic, less lubricated, and less pliable.
- The age-related decrease in antioxidant and antioxidant agents (enzymes) within most tissues including muscle and connective tissue.
- The age-related decrease in the inflammatory response within muscle means that the appearance of cells to remove damaged cells is compromised, delaying the repair of muscle and connective tissue.
- The age-related decrease in muscle protein synthesis (building) rates may slow the rebuilding of muscle and connective tissue after training-induced damage.

For the aging athlete, the consequences of the normal aging process can be summarised in Table 2.3 opposite.

*Table 2.3:* Summary of age-related changes and consequences that occur in normal aging.

| Change with Age | Consequence | Solution |
|---|---|---|
| **Cardiovascular** | | |
| Maximum HR ↓ | Blood pumped ↓ | High intensity training |
| Stroke volume ↓ | Blood pumped ↓ | High intensity training |
| Muscle blood flow ↓ | Recovery ↓ | High intensity training |
| Capillaries/fibre ↓ | Oxygen uptake ↓ | Aerobic training |
| Blood volume ↓ | Oxygen uptake ↓ | Aerobic training |
| **Muscle size/strength ↓** | Speed/Strength/Power ↓  Aerobic capacity ↓ | Weight training |
| **Fast twitch fibres** | | Weight training |
| Number ↓ | Speed/Strength/Power ↓ | High intensity training |
| Size ↓ | Speed/Strength/Power ↓ | Speed training |
| Contraction velocity ↓ | Speed/Strength/Power ↓ | |
| **Elasticity ↓** | Flexibility ↓ | Stretching |
| **Nerve cell ↓** | Speed/Strength/Power/Coordination ↓ | Weights/Speed training |
| **Immune system ↓** | Increased susceptibility to illness ↑ | Aerobic training |

## Physiological Declines in Aging Athletes

Limited research has examined the age-related changes that occur in aging athletes. While a number of studies have examined elite older athletes and how their strength, body composition and aerobic capacity compares with similarly-trained younger elite athletes, few of these studies have tracked aging athletes over time and if they have, they've had small numbers of elite male endurance athletes to examine. A consistent finding has been a small change in body composition (decreased muscle mass and increased fat mass), a drop in fast twitch fibre size, a drop in strength and a drop of about 0.5%/year in aerobic capacity.

A classic study by sport scientists in Florida, USA, has been tracking a group of older track athletes body composition and maximum aerobic capacity over 20 years from age 50 to age 70 years. At age 70 years, the group of 21 athletes was divided into three groups – those who maintained high intensity training, those who maintained regular moderate to vigorous training, and those who had greatly reduced their training. The findings were:
- Each group dropped their VO₂max but the high intensity group dropped the least (8-15%) and the low trained group the most (18-34%).
- Maximum heart rate dropped by 5-7 beats/decade regardless of training intensity.
- Body weight remained stable for the high and moderate-trained groups but body fat increased 2-5%.
- Muscle mass dropped in each group but was best maintained in those that had commenced weight training.

Only recently has a 20-year long-term study commenced that is examining 146 male and

82 female normal masters athletes between the ages of 40 and 86 years. The first results included measures of body composition, heart health, maximum aerobic capacity, blood chemistry (glucose, trigycerides, cholesterol and HDL-cholesterol), bone mineral density, muscular strength, and training and competitive performance. The results to date suggest that aerobic capacity, strength and muscle mass are decreased with age while bone mineral density decreased in the women only.

However, the results also support other studies on aging athletes that all confirm that aging athletes train with significantly less time and with lower intensity than younger athletes. Indeed, aging athletes appear to train primarily for endurance, rather than strength. A 2002 study observed the same pattern of an endurance-training focus in aging swimmers that contrasts with younger swimmers who train for endurance, strength, speed and power. The researchers rightly suggest that the declines observed in performance and many of the physiological capacities such as aerobic capacity, strength and muscle mass may be due to this decreased intensity of training in aging athletes.

**Conclusion**

Limited research has examined the age-related changes that occur in the numerous body systems that affect sports performance of masters athletes. However, it appears that while performance in speed, power and endurance sports is reduced with age in masters athletes as a result of these age-related decreases in the major systems of the body, high intensity endurance and speed training, combined with hypertrophy and then power training in the gym, pool or track, combined with longer recovery and flexibility training, are the keys to maintaining performance or reducing the rate of decline in performance over the years.

# CHAPTER 3

# MEDICAL SCREENING AND THE MASTERS ATHLETE

*Health lies in labour, and there is no royal road to it but through toil.*
Wendell Phillips

## Introduction

As the number of older people taking up sport increases, it would be expected that there would also be an increase in death and disability in this group. Furthermore, it is also commonly accepted that factors such as poor training program design, incorrect technique, improper training surfaces, poor biomechanical alignment, muscle or flexibility imbalances, poor equipment and violence are factors leading to sporting injuries. The *pre-participation medical screening* (PPMS) has been well accepted as a screening tool and a significant factor in reducing sudden death and preventing injury prevention, and improving performance in athletes of all ages.

The purpose of this chapter is to review the available literature relating to medical screening in athletes, with particular emphasis being placed on guidelines from leading agencies such as the International Federation of Sports Medicine (FIMS), Sports Medicine Australia (SMA), the Australian Association for Exercise and Sports Sciences (AAESS), the American College of Sports Medicine (ACSM) and the American Heart Association (AHA) that relate to the medical screening of the aging athlete. However, no consensus has been reached by these leading agencies because of the varying philosophies of each of the medical specialties and agency. The aging athlete and medical practitioner are therefore challenged to individualise the PPMS for themselves based on the aging athlete's medical history, physical examination, fitness and cardiovascular profile as well as the unique demands of the athlete's chosen sport.

## The Purpose of Pre-participation Medical Screening

The Australian Association for Exercise and Sports Science (AAESS), together with Sports Medicine Australia (SMA), have published pre-exercise screening guidelines based on those already developed by the American College of Sports Medicine. These guidelines recommend that males over 45 years and females over 55 years who plan to undertake vigorous exercise (> 60% $VO_2max$ or 70-75% maximum heart rate) should undertake both a PPMS and a fitness test with exercise electrocardiogram (ECG) under the supervision of a medical practitioner. Depending on the specific demands of the sport, the fitness test should include a measure of $VO_2max$, and anaerobic threshold, both of which are available at most sports science departments within Universities.

Apart from examining an older individual's exercise capacity and tolerance, the aims of a

PPMS for the aging athlete are:
- Identify factors (e.g. poor flexibility, muscle imbalances) that may lead to injury
- detect any defects that may contraindicate participation in sport
- exclude medical problems that may lead to sudden death
- address any current medical problems
- identify medications that may inhibit or preclude involvement in masters sport
- identify further tests or referrals to other trained professionals
- institute treatment that may help the athlete achieve optimal performance
- enhanced enjoyment and performance in masters sport

## Components of the PPMS

The available scientific literature pertaining to PPMS suggests that a medical history and physical examination are essential components of a comprehensive PPMS.

### Medical History

It is widely accepted that the medical history is the most important part of the PPMS with a previous study suggesting that a medical history can identify up to 74% of all sport-related problems in younger athletes. The history should include the following areas:.

*a. Cardiovascular risks*

Two questions may be enough when screening athletes for cardiovascular risks:
   i. Has anyone in the athlete's family died suddenly before the age of 50 years?
   ii. Has the athlete ever passed out during exercise or stopped exercise because of dizziness?

However, more recently, AAESS and SMA have formulated cardiovascular risk factor guidelines (see Table 3.1 below) that have relied heavily on existing guidelines from both the American College of Sports Medicine and the Australian National Heart Foundation. It is suggested these guidelines are far more appropriate for the older and more "at risk" exerciser.

*Table 3.1:* Australian Association for Exercise and Sport Science / Sports Medicine Australia cardiovascular risk factor classification.

| | |
|---|---|
| 1. | Smoking |
| 2. | Diagnosed hypertension or resting blood pressure >140/90 mm Hg on at least two occasions, or on anti-hypertensive medication |
| 3. | Serum cholesterol > 5.5 mmol.L-1 |
| 4. | Serum triglyceride > 2.0 mmol.L-1 |
| 5. | Diabetes mellitus. Individuals with insulin dependent diabetes mellitus (IDDM) who are over 30 years of age, or have had IDDM for longer than 15 years, and persons with non-insulin dependent diabetes mellitus (NIDDM) who are over 35 years of age |
| 6. | Family history of coronary or other atherosclerotic disease in parents or siblings prior to age 55 |

In addition to the cardiovascular risk factors outlined in Table 3.1, the AAESS/

SMA guidelines suggest a screening for major symptoms and signs of cardiopulmonary or metabolic disease (see Table 3.2 below), as long as these factors are interpreted in a clinical context.

*Table 3.2:* Australian Association for Exercise and Sport Science / Sports Medicine Australia screening guidelines for major signs and symptoms of cardiopulmonary or metabolic disease.

| | |
|---|---|
| 1. | Pain or discomfort in the chest or surrounding areas that appears ischaemic in nature. |
| 2. | Unaccustomed shortness of breath or shortness of breath with mild exertion |
| 3. | Dizziness or syncope (fainting) |
| 4. | Orthopnea (difficulty breathing when lying flat) / paroxysmal dyspnea (breathlessness attacks during sleep) |
| 5. | Ankle oedema (swelling) |
| 6. | Palpitations or tachycardia (high heart rate) |
| 7. | Claudication (limping or pain in the le.g. or calf bought on by poor blood supply) |
| 8. | Known heart murmur |

A more detailed discussion on some of these major symptoms and signs as they pertain to the aging athlete will be addressed later in this chapter.

*b. Exercise-induced asthma*

As part of the medical history, a medical practitioner needs to question whether the athlete has a history of asthma, hay fever or coughing spells after exercise. The purpose of the question is not to disqualify the athlete from sports participation but to both initiate additional screening (peak flow measures pre- and post-exercise and lung function testing) and control of the condition via appropriate medication.

*c. Musculoskeletal injury*

If the older athlete has ever broken a bone, had to wear a cast, had an injury to a joint, or suffered from osteoarthritis, they may suffer more recurrent injuries, particularly if the previous injury was in the knee and ankle. Moreover, the risk of further injury is greater in joints that have persistent weakness or instability. Given that one of the most common physiological declines with age is muscular strength, the importance of resistance training in an injured older athletes training program cannot be underestimated in overcoming both muscle or joint weakness and joint instability.

It might be suggested that aging athletes who are less aerobically fit, have lower bone density, have some degenerative joint disease, or are less skilful than younger athletes, might suffer more injuries than younger athletes. However, research has shown that older athletes suffer sports injuries at rates similar to younger athletes. The most common sites of injury in both age groups appear to be the knee and ankle with the aging athletes appearing to suffer more from metatarsalgia (pain and inflammation in the ball of the foot), plantar fasciitis and cartilage injuries than younger athletes. Furthermore, previous research suggests that overuse injuries are more common in older versus younger athletes possibly as a result of older athletes (NB Runners) training with a higher mileage than younger athletes.

Acute injuries are common in aging athletes participating in sports that demand high levels of coordination, reaction time, balance and agility such as ball games and martial arts. Table 3.3 below shows the more common sports and the associated injuries observed in aging athletes.

*Table 3.3:* Common sports and injury sites observed in aging athletes. Nervous System Injury

| SPORT | COMMON INJURIES | | |
|---|---|---|---|
| Running | • Achilles tendonitis<br>• Plantar fascitis<br>• Chondromalacia patella<br>• Ankle sprains | | • Shin splints<br>• ITB Syndrome<br>• Heel pain<br>• Stress fracture |
| Swimming | **Shoulder**<br>• Impingement<br>• Rotator cuff rupture<br>• Biceps tendon tear<br>• Arthritis | **Spine**<br>• Arthritis<br>• Degenerative disc<br>• Osteoporosis | **Lower Limb**<br>• Arthritis of hip and knee<br>• Arthritis of patello-femoral joint |
| Cycling | **Accidents**<br>• Clavicle, forearm, wrist fracture<br>• A-C and shoulder dislocations<br>• Lacerations / abrasions<br>• Sprains - lower limb | | **Overuse**<br>• Compression syndromes<br>  ◦ Cubital tunnel<br>  ◦ Carpal tunnel<br>• Inflammatory syndromes<br>  ◦ lateral epicondylitis<br>  ◦ patellar tendonitis<br>  ◦ achilles tendonitis<br>  ◦ Retropatellar chondromalacia<br>• Muscular strains |
| Tennis | **Acute**<br>• Meniscal tears<br>• Achilles rupture<br>• Gastrocnemius tear<br>• Rotator cuff rupture | | **Chronic**<br>• Tennis elbow<br>• Rotator cuff tendonitis<br>• Back pain<br>• Degenerative knee changes |
| Rowing | Chondromalacia, ITB syndrome, patellar tendonitis, low back pain, rib stress fractures and extensor tenosynovitis | | |

A history of traumatic nervous system injury such as a concussion or loss of consciousness is of major importance in the contact and collision sports such as the football codes and martial arts. In younger athletes, it has been well documented that football players with a previous concussion have a fourfold greater risk of intracerebral haemorrhage. An aging player of the contact sports in this category, particularly with a history of recurrent concussions, may warrant a neurological examination by the medical practitioner or a referral to a specialist.

### d. Heat-related illness

Most summers, particularly in northern Australia, are characterised by hot and humid conditions. Research has shown that individuals who have previously had a heat illness are more susceptible to another bout of heat illness, probably due to residual or permanent damage to the hypothalamus, the heat-sensing and controlling part of the brain.

Older athletes may be more susceptible to heat illness as a result of a 25-40% lower skin blood flow and reduced sweat output compared to younger athletes of the same level of aerobic fitness. Previous research has also shown that a large number of older people suffer diabetes and hypertension, both of which can lower the ability to exercise in the heat. Furthermore, some prescription drugs (diuretics, vasodilators, adrenergic blockers, anticholinergics) are widely used by aging athletes and may affect the ability to tolerate heat. However, it appears that, regardless of age, the level of aerobic fitness (VO$_2$max), degree of acclimatisation and the hydration levels of the individual athlete are more important in determining safe sports participation in the heat than age itself.

*e. Medical Conditions*

A number of common medical conditions are observed in both young and older athletes. Apart from the cardiovascular disease risk factors outlined in Table 3.1 above, a number of symptoms are a concern if observed during exercise. These include chest pain; breathlessness suggestive of low fitness levels, airway obstruction, lung or cardiac disease; heart palpations, particularly when associated with chest pain, dizziness, or breathlessness; dizziness or fainting, or fatigue. Fatigue may be related to poor fitness, illness, overtraining or medication such as tranquillisers or beta-blockers.

As expected, osteoarthritis (OA) appears to be more common in the aging athlete, particularly in the knee joint of endurance athlete. Once OA has developed, running may have to be reduced or stopped. Exercises that maintain muscle strength and joint mobility are important, particularly in the knee, lower back and abdominal areas. Hydrotherapy (water running, aquarobics) in a heated pool is suggested as an alternative training methodology.

*f. Medications*

Many aging athletes take medications to control medical conditions. Doctors and pharmacists need to educate aging athletes about the possible complications or interactions that some of these medications may have when training or competing. It is also incumbent on the aging athlete to know the effects of their medications on sports performance and to be aware of the rules governing their use in their sport. Some common medications used by active older people are:

- Blood pressure medications (beta-blockers and calcium-channel blockers) that keep the heart rate low and may mask the symptoms of low blood glucose. Beta-blockers can impair the uptake of glucose by working muscles
- Diuretic agents that contribute to dehydration, electrolyte imbalances, cramping or fainting
- Anti-depressant medications and tranquilizers can cause fainting
- Psychotropic medications can contribute to heat injury and dehydration
- Insulin and sulfonylureas (anti diabetic drugs) increase the risk of low blood glucose
- Anticoagulants increase the risk of serious bleeding if an aging athlete is injured

A number of drugs are commonly used to treat cardiovascular disease. Use of *Digoxin* may slow the pulse rate, lead to loss of appetite, and make the athlete sluggish but has no effect on performance, nor is it an International Olympic Committee (IOC) banned drug. *Anginine* is used to treat angina and may lead to headaches, low blood pressure, and susceptibility to fainting. However, it may improve the tolerance to exercise in older people with angina. *Beta-blockers* are a group of drugs that help control high blood pressure by slowing down the heart rate. They also reduce hand and arm tremor and are therefore banned by the IOC because sports such as archery, shooting, diving, and modern pentathlon may benefit. However, beta-blockers reduce aerobic performance and may cause lethargy, insomnia, and possible aggravation of asthma.

Athletes wanting to lose weight quickly through increased fluid loss via the kidneys commonly use diuretics. They may lead to dehydration, low blood pressure, increased blood sugar, and muscle cramps. However, despite being an IOC-banned drug group, they may improve exercise tolerance in people with heart failure. *Anticoagulants* prevent blood clotting and therefore lead to increased susceptibility to bleeding in contact sport players and or anaemia in injured endurance or team game athletes.

Many of the commonly used *analgesics* (e.g. *codeine*) and *decongestants* (e.g. *ephidrine*) are banned substances due to their beneficial effects on exercise performance. Pre-exercise medication using a *beta-adrenergic agonist* (e.g. *salbutamol, terbutaline,* or *sodium chromoglycate - Ventolin, Bricanyl, Respolin*) is beneficial in preventing or reducing the severity of an asthma attack. While these substances are banned by the International Olympic Committee, the masters sports drug policy allows use of these drugs for medicinal purposes. The major drug treatment for arthritic conditions is *analgesics* such as *paracetamol, codeine* (an IOC banned drug), *aspirin* and *Non-Steroidal Anti-Inflammatory Drugs (NSAIDS)*. The majority of NSAIDS are metabolised in the liver and excreted in the kidneys so that lower doses should be used in masters athletes where kidney function may be impaired due to age.

It has recently been suggested that menopausal female masters athletes should be encouraged to take oestrogen to relieve menopausal problems while testosterone replacement may restore libido, improve energy levels, prevent bone loss, and deal with the breast soreness attributed to oestrogen. The ethical problem facing masters sports administrators is that testosterone is a banned IOC drug for younger athletes.

The growth and increasing competitiveness of masters sport has lead to the suggestion that drug testing may become an institution within the movement. The dilemma facing masters sports administrators is that many IOC-banned drugs are prescribed or regularly used by masters athletes for health maintenance or treatment of diseases. However, in most cases where a product contains a banned drug, there are alternative drugs to treat the problem. At present, the World Anti-Doping Association (WADA) do not have a policy for masters athletes. However, many national and international masters sporting events have developed drugs policies. For example, the 2009 12th Australian Masters Games (AMG) Drugs Policy states:

> *12AMG condemns the use of substances for the purposes of performance enhancement, which is contrary to the ethics of sport and incompatible with the philosophy of Masters sport. Participants may be required to undertake random drug testing.*

The drugs listed as banned substances by the IOC have been adopted by the World Masters Games. The International Masters Games Association supports the World Anti-

Doping Agency (WADA) and its opposition to the use of banned substances by athletes to enhance athletic performance. Indeed, during the Sydney 2009 World Masters Games all registered competitors are subject to the possibility that they may be required to make themselves available for a doping test, if requested by games organisers. However, due to the nature of the World Masters Games, the organisers recognise many of the competitors participating in the Sydney 2009 World Masters Games may be taking medications that appear on the WADA banned list for therapeutic purposes.

The following groups of drugs have been banned by the IOC:
- Stimulants (caffeine, cocaine, amphetamines, *Sudafed, Orthoxicol, Actifed,* and *Demazin*)
- Anabolic steroids (*Deca-Durabolin, Stanazol,* and *Primobolan*)
- Diuretics (*Lasix* and *Aldactone*)
- Narcotic analgesics (*Palfium, Di-Gesic, Codeine, Panadeine. Codral,* and *Dymadon*).
- Peptide hormones and analogues (human growth hormone, human chorionic gonadotrophin and corticotrophin)
- Blood doping (Hematocrit [% of blood made up of red and white blood cells] > 50)
- Beta-Blockers (*Betaloc, Inderal, Lopresor,* and *Tenormin*) in sports such as archery, shooting or diving.

It is strongly suggested that the family medical practitioner draw the aging athlete's attention to the above regulations during any medical screening.

## The Physical Examination

Following the taking of the medical history, a thorough physical examination of the aging athlete should be undertaken. It is widely accepted that there are three essential components that contribute to the greatest diagnostic utility and form the core of the physical examination:

i. *Blood pressure measurement.* Apart from being a significant CVD risk factor, early treatment modifies long-term risks and lessens organ damage.

ii. *Musculoskeletal examination.* It is strongly recommended that a sports physiotherapist or sports physician screen an aging athlete. Both of these specialists are trained in musculoskeletal examination techniques. An evaluation should evaluate signs of poor flexibility or hyper mobility, muscular weakness and / or muscle imbalances front to back or side to side.

An early study observed 11% of 2,670 young athletes examined had identifiable risk factors for sports participation with 66% of these problems being musculoskeletal. While no evidence is available on aging athletes, it might be suggested given age-related declines in muscular strength, flexibility and endurance, the aging athlete may present even higher rates of musculoskeletal problems. Given the high rates of knee and ankle injuries in both young and older athletes, these joints should become a priority in the physical examination. Specifically, tests of the knee joint for the twisting sports such as field or court games, hamstring / quadriceps strength ratio tests in sports with high rates of hamstring strains (e.g. track and field), ligament laxity tests in contact sports, rigid foot type tests in sports with high rates of stress fractures (e.g. distance running), and one-leg hyperextension tests in fast bowlers, divers or gymnasts. Moreover, identifying ankle laxity or proprioceptive (feeling) loss should be followed by thorough rehabilitation before sports participation.

Musculoskeletal examinations must be specific to the sport. For example, older swimmers and water polo players should be screened for rotator cuff and shoulder girdle function with muscle imbalances between internal (usually strong) and external (usually weaker) rotators often present in swimmers. Osteochondritis dissecans (poor blood supply to the end of bones) is often observed in throwers and may be detected by examination and / or supported by X-ray examination. Jumpers such as basketballers, volleyballers, or field athletes have increased risk of patellar (knee cap) tendinitis diagnosed on the presence of localised pain or tenderness of the patellar tendon (joins knee cap to lower leg) and rehabilitated with eccentric strengthening of the muscles around the knee joint.

Musculoskeletal alignment becomes an important consideration in activities such as long distance running, where older athletes, particularly females with increased Q (hip to knee) angles, may become more prone to patellofemoral tracking disorders. A patellar compression test and visual inspection of Q angles during the PPMS may lead to referral to a podiatrist or physiotherapist.

iii. *Cardiovascular Tests*

Sudden death in aging athletes appears caused by atherosclerotic coronary heart disease or cerebrovascular disease, rather than cardiovascular abnormalities that explain most sudden deaths in young competitive athletes. While the frequency of sudden death in older marathoners is approximately 1:50,000 or 1:900,000 exercise hours in 50-69 year old men, the risk is three-fold increased during strenuous exercise with over 90% of victims male. While the media fuels the interest in sudden deaths of aging athletes, there is a relatively low risk of sudden death in older persons exercising.

A number of leading agencies such as FIMS and AHA, together with practitioners have suggested the need for the cardiovascular examination to include:

- precordial auscultation (heart sounds) at the left sternal border beginning after the first heart sound in both the supine (lying) and standing positions to identify heart murmurs consistent with dynamic ventricular outflow obstruction. While murmurs are common in well-trained athletes, murmurs should be further investigated if other than systolic (heart filling), constant or high grade systolic, or systolic with suspicious clinical features
- assessment of the femoral artery (groin) pulses to exclude coarctation (narrowing) of the aorta
- Any doubt as to the nature of a murmur or other cardiovascular abnormality indicates

referral to a cardiologist for confirmation or further evaluation.

To prevent sudden death in older athletes, the American Heart Association thus recommend a complete medical and family history for males over 40 years (females over 50 years) similar to those recommended by the AAESS / SMA guidelines outlined in the earlier tables. In addition, the FIMS, AHA and AAESS / SMA guidelines each recommend that older individuals planning to undertake vigorous exercise greater than 70% of maximal heart rate (220-age), should undertake a maximal exercise test with ECG under the supervision of a medical practitioner with skills and experience in the area. Such tests determine functional capacity, possible arrhythmia (irregular pulses) or other ECG abnormalities.

While sports specific testing such as treadmill running for runners or cycle ergometry for cyclists is recommended, it is suggested that older people unaccustomed to vigorous exercise be evaluated on a treadmill due to the higher heart rates and $VO_2max$ values observed on treadmills and the dependence on quadriceps strength required in maximal cycling tests. Furthermore, in previously inactive older people seeking a medical clearance, initial test workloads should be low with workload advances in small increments. The older person should be familiarised with the equipment of choice, with the optimal duration of the maximal test being between 8 and 12 minutes. This allows time for changes in heart rate, blood pressure, and ECG changes to occur, while avoiding undue fatigue, musculoskeletal discomfort, or boredom.

   *iv.* *Other tests* Blood analysis may be suggested in an aging athlete with a history of anaemia or who complains of fatigue, particularly if an endurance athlete and / or female and menstruating, or who has never been screened for blood lipids. Blood tests should include ferritin, iron studies, haemoglobin, liver function tests (LFT), full blood examination (FBE) for anaemic or fatigued athletes and blood lipids (triglycerides, total cholesterol, HDL- and LDL-cholesterol) for the aging, previously unscreened person.

Vision and hearing tests may also be indicated in some older individuals depending on the sport or degree of impairment. Tests might include the Standard *Snellen Chart* at six (6) metres with and without correction (glasses / contact lenses) or a test of colour vision using the *Isiharra* test. Hearing might be examined through observation of any abnormality of auditory canals, Eustachian tubes or eardrums or observation that the patient can hear conversational voice at two metres. A dermatological (skin) examination may also be warranted with specific emphasis on signs of solar damage, particularly in those aging athletes involved with outdoor pursuits such as field and court games or endurance events.

Given the age of the athlete, an assessment or referral for assessment may also be suggested for the following:
- nutrition status and habits (sports dietician)
- physical work capacities such as strength, aerobic and anaerobic capacities (exercise physiologist within a University Sports Science Program).

## The Female Masters Athlete

Females are becoming increasingly involved in masters sport. Although most of the PPMS is similar for males and females, medical practitioners need to focus on particular factors to address female athletes' specific concerns, particularly for the aging female athlete. For example, in the premenopausal female athlete, gynaecologic questions pertaining to length and frequency of periods, menstrual flow rates, signs of secondary amenorrhea / dysmenorrhea / menstrual dysfunction, frequency of urinary tract infections may be appropriate.

Some musculoskeletal conditions have been observed to occur more often in women. For example, patellofemoral (knee cap) pain, ankle sprains and laxity of the shoulder joint warrant investigation depending on the women's sport of choice and medical history.

The risk of injury in the menopausal athlete is of primary concern. Therefore, appropriate activities for menopausal women beginning to exercise include low impact aerobics, walking, cycling, swimming, aquarobics, and circuit weight training under supervision. Osteoporosis primarily occurs in post-menopausal women and predisposes them to fractures of the hip, wrist and spine. Low levels of oestrogen (also observed in pre-menopausal women who lose their periods due to high levels of training), low levels of calcium intake, family history, smoking, certain medications and lack of weight bearing or weight training exercise are factors contributing to osteoporosis and should be screened for, particularly in the postmenopausal woman. A recent study examined bone mineral density (BMD) in 42-50 year old long term (>20 years) female athletes from high (netball/basketball), medium (running/hockey) and non-impact (swimming) sports and observed that the high impact athletes had significantly higher BMD than the non-impact athletes and a group of sedentary controls.

Hormone replacement therapy (HRT) involves the administration of an oestrogen / progesterone / testosterone combination, in addition to adequate calcium and Vitamin D intake and weight bearing exercise, to post-menopausal women. While no studies have been completed that have examined the effect of HRT on sports performance per se, a number of recent studies have observed increased strength, more favourable CVD risk factors, and reduced menopausal symptoms in HRT - treated menopausal women. However, studies have also shown increased risk of breast cancer in women undertaking HRT.

## A Self-Administered Screening Test

While I strongly recommend a visit to your family doctor or preferably a sports physician for men over 45 and women over 55 years starting to train, the reality is that most aging athletes feel they are healthy enough or "it can't happen to me". Furthermore, a study by exercise scientists from the University of South Australia suggested that, if the above AAESS/SMA guidelines were strictly enforced, between 43-73% of men and 44-61% of females would require medical clearance prior to commencing an exercise program. They costed this out to represent between $250 million and $1.2 Billion. The scientists suggested that rigorous application of the guidelines would not only be expensive but would hinder aging people getting involved with physical activity, physical fitness or masters sport. In light of this, Dr Maria Fiatarone, a highly respected exercise scientist specialising in exercise and aging, developed the following questionnaire for use in a large scale community exercise program for over 50s. She suggested that *people who answered yes to any one of the following questions should see their doctor before starting a training program.*

1. Do I get chest pain while at rest and/or during exertion?
2. If the answer to question 1 is "yes" is it true that I have not had a physician diagnose these pains yet?
3. Have I ever had a heart attack?
4. If the answer to question 3 is "yes" was my heart attack within the last year?
5. Do I have high blood pressure?
6. If you do not know the answer to question 5, answer this: Was my last blood pressure reading more than 150/100?
7. Am I short of breath after extremely mild exertion and sometimes even at rest or at night in bed?
8. Do I have any ulcerated wounds or cuts on my feet that do not seem to heal?
9. Have I lost 10 pounds (5 kg) or more in the last 6 months without trying and to my surprise?
10. Do I get pain in my buttocks or the back of my legs – my thighs and calves – when I walk?
11. While at rest, do I frequently experience fast irregular heartbeats or, at the other extreme, very slow beats? (Although a low HR can be a sign of an efficient and well-conditioned heart, a very low rate can also indicate a nearly complete heart block).
12. Am I currently being treated for any heart or circulatory condition, such as vascular disease, stroke, angina, hypertension, congestive heart failure, poor circulation in the legs, valvular heart disease, blood clots, or pulmonary disease?
13. As an adult, have I ever had a fracture of the hip, spine or wrist?
14. Did I fall more than twice in the past year (no matter what the reason)?
15. Do I have diabetes?

### Risk of Exercise

In general, apparently healthy adults can safely engage in exercise unless they are planning vigorous exercise over 60% of their maximum heart rate. Most aging athletes fall into this group. The *American College of Cardiology* and *American Heart Association* recommend exercise stress testing in men over 40 years of age and women over 50 years of age before they start vigorous exercise.

There now exist clear guidelines as to the need for pre-exercise screening, contraindications to exercising and guidelines as to when to halt an exercise or test session. However, the risks of a heart attack or death during exercise are very low. Each year, between 0.75 and 0.13 per 100,000 young athletes and 6 per 100,000 middle-aged men die during vigorous exercise. A Finnish study has shown that the incidence of death during vigorous exercise in men is 1 in 11 million hours at age 20-39 years, 1 in 1.3 million hours between ages 40 and 49 years, and 1 in 900,000 million exercise hours between 60 and 69 years of age.

A heart attack is 5-50 times (depends on how hard the activity is) more likely in a person who is exercising than when the same person is carrying out some non-exercise activity for an equivalent amount of time. However, these hazards are offset by a three-fold drop in heart attack risk between exercise sessions. Thus, irrespective of medical screening, a person is far better advised to engage in moderate activity than remaining inactive. Indeed, the majority of chronic conditions likely to be detected by medical screening (arthritis, diabetes, coronary heart disease, chronic obstructive lung disease, depression, gait or balance disorders, and susceptibility to falls) respond positively to exercise programs.

In some aging people "at risk" of a cardiac event or aggravating a pre-existing disease or condition (angina, arthritis, osteoporosis, hypertension), the risk of exercise may outweigh the potential benefits. However, the potential risks can be greatly reduced by conducting a medical history, undertaking a physical examination, determining exercise tolerances, close and qualified supervision and education.

## Conclusion

It has been well documented that even highly motivated older athletes can be complacent about the need for periodic medical examinations. However, medical practitioners should rarely be in a situation where a PPMS will prevent an older person becoming involved in masters sport. Referral may be warranted to cardiologists for cardiovascular clearances, sports physicians or sports physiotherapists for expert musculoskeletal profiling and rehabilitation, sports dieticians for dietary advice or exercise specialists for physical training programs. However, once screened using a PPMS, the older person should be encouraged to actively participate in masters sport, particularly given the preventative health benefits of exercise to quantity and quality of life into old age.

The aging athlete is strongly advised to undertake a regular medical check-up by a sports physician or qualified sports medicine specialist prior to commencing training for an event. This becomes more important the older the athlete becomes, the harder they intend to train or if the athlete is commencing training after years away from sport.

# CHAPTER 4

## THE PRINCIPLES OF TRAINING THE MASTERS ATHLETE

*Place the sidewalks where the people walk.*

**Anonymous**

*Those who are enamoured of practice without science are like a pilot who goes into a ship without a rudder or compass and never has any certainty of where they are going.*

**Leonardo da Vinci**

*The body will do what you tell it if you learn how to tell it.*

**Donald Ronan**

### Introduction

Now that we have an appreciation of the factors that may explain a decline in performance as we age, the important question is how can we prevent that slowing-down process. Regardless of whether we are 20 years old or going on 100, a lifetime aging athlete or novice, there are certain training principles that all athletes need to adhere to when planning their training program.

### Principles of Training

While there are numerous methods, strategies and techniques to improve endurance, speed, power, strength or flexibility, the principles below are based on research and experience. They need to be followed to remain injury free and develop whatever physical capacity you are focusing on. Your training plan needs to cause a *progressive overload* on your body that is *sports specific*, adheres to the principles of *FITT (frequency, intensity, time, type)* and allows you *adequate recovery*.

1. **Specificity**. We should analyse the needs of the chosen sport or event and specifically train for those demands. A sprinter should do sprint and resistance training, an endurance athlete should focus on endurance training. The exercises we use in flexibility or strength training should simulate the body positions and joint movements used in the event or sport. I see too many aging athletes train for speed events in competition by endurance training methods. While endurance training methods are great for health reasons (weight control and heart disease prevention) and as a base for speed work, the aging athlete

will find they will lose speed by continually training with long, slow distance work. It is critical that the competitive aging athlete prepare through training for the exact stresses competition will place on the body. While this might suggest that playing the sport is the best training, it's not. Why? Because it does not overload any one physical capacity (speed, strength, endurance, flexibility), it works them all in small ways.

2. **Progressive Overload**. Training needs to place demands on the body. The body will adapt if the training is regular and at a level *above* those normally done. Once the body has adapted, it is time to again overload. Endurance athletes might do the same time for a set distance or achieve a lower heart rate for a set speed; power and strength athletes might be able to easily do a set distance in a certain time at a set intensity or lift a certain weight more times. It's thus time to overload the body again. Progressive overload means gradually training harder, more often, or for longer in a session. If you specifically require endurance, you should progressively increase how long or how hard you train. If you are a sprinter, you can progressively increase how hard you do your speed work. Generally the harder we train, the longer the recoveries should be. Gradually training harder, more often, or for longer will allow your body to adapt slowly and prevent injuries or overtraining.

It has been well documented that aging athletes train with lower volumes and lower relative intensities than younger athletes, possibly due to lack of motivation or lack of time as a result of family or work commitments. However, it might be suggested much of the decrease in aging athletes' speed and endurance might be explained by decreased training intensity or volume relative to younger athletes. This may be due to the reasons outlined above or to the myth that the older person shouldn't train hard for cardiovascular or injury risk reasons. I am totally opposed to this attitude - an attitude I see all too often in both the general community and the medical profession. I see no reason the aging athlete cannot train as hard as the youngsters - on the assumption that the aging athlete is healthy and has been pre-screened by a sports physician and / or sports physiotherapist.

The more experienced aging athlete will have no problems with the principle of progressive overload. However, many aging athletes will be competing for the first time in many years. The more experienced and specifically fit we are, the more quickly we will adapt to our training because we have a longer training age. Those of us who are "making a comeback" or competing for the first time in years must realize that the principle of progressive overload is even more important - start easy, and gradually build the intensity, frequency, and volume of your training.

The general rule of thumb on percentage increase in training load is 10% per training block (e.g. per week). For the aging athlete, I suggest gradually build the time or distance, then the frequency, then the intensity and once that is done work on the hard-easy principle. That is, alternate hard days (long or hard) with easy days (short and easy or complete rest).

3. **FITT (Frequency, Intensity, Time, Type)**

Manipulating any of the FITT principles over time, will allow us to progressively overload the body.

- *Frequency (how often?)*

    Research has shown that to *develop* a fitness component (e.g. speed, strength, endurance) we need three sessions/week. To *maintain* fitness, we need two sessions as long as they are relatively intense. As a general rule, similar sessions should be limited to four times per week so as to maximize recovery, minimize injury risk or avoid burnout. These similar sessions should be frequent rather than spread out over time.

    Beginners should start at twice per week and progressively over time increase the number of training sessions per week.

- *Intensity (how hard?)*

    Endurance athletes use heart rates to determine how hard they work, sprinters a percent of maximum speed for that distance, strength athletes a % of their maximum lift for that exercise. Specific details on each of these will be discussed in the relevant chapters later in the book. However, there is another universally accepted scale that can be used across all types of training and across all people. It accounts for individual differences in fitness and pain tolerances and should be used extensively, particularly by novice aging athletes. It is called the Borg (he's the smart bugger who developed it!) Scale or sometimes called the RPE (Rating of Perceived Exertion) Scale. Table 4.1 below details the old 6-20 scale and the new 1-10 scale and later chapters will address these in detail.

*Table 4.1:* Rating of Perceived Exertion (RPE): A subjective method of monitoring intensity or pain levels.

| OLD 6-20 SCALE | | NEW 1-10 SCALE | |
|---|---|---|---|
| Rating | Description | Rating | Description |
| 6 | No exertion | 1 | Very, very light |
| 7 | Extremely light | 2 | Very light |
| 8 | | 3 | Fairly light |
| 9 | Very light | 4 | Light |
| 10 | | 5 | Somewhat hard |
| 11 | Light | 6 | Moderately hard |
| 12 | | 7 | Hard |
| 13 | Somewhat hard | 8 | Very hard |
| 14 | | 9 | Very, very hard |
| 15 | Hard | 10 | Extremely hard |
| 16 | | | |
| 17 | Very hard | | |
| 18 | | | |
| 19 | Extremely hard | | |
| 20 | Maximal exertion | | |

There is no doubt that intensity has been shown to be the key to improvement in performance yet it is also the factor that leads to overtraining and injury. There is no doubt that aging athletes have been shown to train with lower intensity, suggesting that if they want to improve performance, they need to lift that intensity or they will slow down. The key is to regularly monitor intensity and your responses to that intensity. As a general rule, beginning aging athletes need to start at a low intensity and progressively lift that intensity until competition intensities are reached.

- *Time (how long?)*

Time or training volume can be measured a number of ways. Time (e.g. 2 hr ride) or a distance (e.g. 3k swim) or number of repetitions or sets (e.g. 80 reps or 4 sets of 20) are typical ways of expressing time. Again, a progressive increase in time spent, distance covered, or repetitions completed over time will contribute to improved performance.

- *Type (what to do?)*

There are three common methods of doing exercises:

a. Continuous – completing the designated time or distance without a break or change in intensity

b. Continuous-interval - completing the designated time or distance with a change in intensity

c. Stop-start interval – breaking the session down into repetitions (each individual exercise or distance), sets (block of repetitions) and rest periods.

Table 4.2 below shows some examples of interval-based sessions that I suggest are the key to improved performance in aging athletes in that they allow relatively high intensity (speed) with adequate recovery while stimulating those fast-twitch muscle fibres that decrease in number and size as we age.

4. **Be Prepared to Adapt more Slowly than you did as a Kid**

For the aging athlete the rule of thumb should be "start low and build slowly". While little research has been completed on the adaptation of aging athletes to training, a number of studies on older non-athletes doing endurance or strength training have consistently shown that older people do adapt to the same degree that younger people do, *but they take significantly longer to adapt*. This is particularly important to the aging athlete who is *coming back* to sport after years away from it. That is, a person with a relatively young training age. These aging athletes tend to *think* of themselves as just as physically capable and fit as when they trained 20 years ago, but soon find out that *physically* they can't cope with the distance, frequency and intensity of training like they used to. As a general rule, the older and less fit the athlete, the lower they should start and the more slowly they should progress.

*Table 4.2:* Examples of interval-based training sessions.

| Training | Frequency | Intensity | Exercise | Reps | Sets | Rest between Reps | Rest between Sets |
|---|---|---|---|---|---|---|---|
| Strength | 2/week | 75% 1RM* | Leg Press | 10 | 3 | 0 | 2 min |
| Sprint | 1/week | 100% | 25 m | 6 | 4 | 30 sec | 3 min |
| Endurance | 2/week | Level 4 ** | 4 min | 3 | 2 | 4 min | 2 min |

\* 1 Repetition Maximum (see Chapter 7)   \*\* Intensity level (see Chapter 6)

5. **Train Intensely.** The bottom line is that training intensely is the key to success in sport, regardless of the age of the athlete. For we aging athletes where age-related declines in all our exercise capacities are slowing us down, keeping the heart, nerves, muscles, lungs and other body systems working to the highest level is even more important in maintaining performance or at least slowing the age-related declines in speed, endurance and strength. While building and maintaining base endurance and strength is important, a higher priority should be given to intense workouts that should include strength training in the gym or at home, power training at the gym or at home, and intense workouts when training. Intense workouts should include heart rate zones 5-6 (85-100% maximum heart rate) interval training for endurance athletes, and speed and strength and power workouts for aging strength, speed and endurance athletes that have good health and no cardiovascular complications.

6. **Use Intensity Sparingly.** No more than three intense workouts should be done by the experienced and competitive aging athlete per week. For recreational aging athletes two intense workouts are enough. These workouts should be preceded by easy workouts and you should be fresh to make the most of the intense work. Other days should be devoted to lower intensity work and technique development.

7. **Always Warm-Up and Cool-Down**

    To prevent injuries, reduce the risk of a cardiac event and maximize training or racing performance, warm-up is essential. Warm-up should be done in the following order:
    a. General – any aerobic work that works up a light sweat.
    b. Stretching – static stretches of the joints and muscles used in the sport/event. If the sport or event demands dynamic flexibility, then progress from slow dynamic stretches within range, to slow to end of range, then fast dynamic within range then fast dynamic to end of range.
    c. Low intensity sport-specific activity.
    d. Sport- or event-specific intensity work.
    e. Short cool down.
    f. Race or compete.

*Effective Warm-up Techniques*

The warm-up prepares the aging athlete for the demands of the workout and aids in injury prevention. There are basically three components to an effective warm-up and they should be

performed in this order:
1. *Cardiovascular.* The cardiovascular warm-up heats the body thus facilitating energy producing reactions to occur more quickly. The heart is also stimulated to deliver oxygen to the exercising muscles via the cardiovascular system, thus enabling the muscles to rely less on anaerobic (lack of oxygen) energy sources that produce lactic acid.
2. *Muscular.* The muscular warm-up slowly increases the length of muscles (ie. stretching muscles) for injury prevention and better force generation.
3. *Skills.* The skills warm-up depends on the sport and involves replicating the skills you will need to use in the game or event. A power event should thus have some sport- or event-specific power work in the warm-up to stimulate the nervous system while a ball-handling event should include specific ball handling drills as part of the warm-up.

### Guidelines For Warm-up

a. Include cardiovascular work followed by muscular stretching and then skills practice (depending on your sport).
b. Warm-up for at least 10 minutes; if you haven't got 10 minutes, 3 minutes is better than nothing.
c. Under cold environmental conditions warm-up longer; in hot conditions, shorter.
d. Keep warm with appropriate clothing after warm-up if you are not working out immediately.
e. Include some of the same activity as you will do in the main body of your workout in the warm-up. Do the same intensity but shorter duration and if it's a skill sport, do the skill work at game intensity.
f. If you can't actively warm-up then do so passively using warm clothing, warm showers, jog on the spot and stretch.
g. Practice the warm-up which you are going to use before competing.
h. Warm-up as close as possible to the start of your event. For endurance events this gets the heart rate up and the blood carrying oxygen to the working muscles so when the event starts, you are less reliant on anaerobic sources of energy. For power and speed events, it primes the nervous system for action.

8. **Include Flexibility Training**

Flexibility is the range of motion at a joint or series of joints. In some sports this is extremely important. In the aging athlete, research has shown that flexibility decreases, particularly in the hip joint. This finding has strong implications for the older sprint runner who needs hip flexibility to ensure stride length, a major contributor to speed. Apart from performance enhancement, the main reason for including flexibility training into your workouts is for prevention of injury and optimal skill development. While many aging athletes stretch before a workout, too few focus extended time on stretching routines outside of warm-ups. To prevent injury, increase range of movement and thus force application, help recover from workouts, and for helping prevent or treat some debilitating diseases, stretch in front of the TV 2-3 times per week. While a whole chapter of this book is devoted to flexibility training, below are some guidelines.

## Guidelines For Stretching

The following principles should be adhered to for a safe and effective static stretching program:

a. *Warm-up for 10 minutes to increase body temperature and increase blood flow to muscles and connective tissue that limit flexibility (ligaments, tendons).* Stretching itself will not warm-up these tissues while a warm-up (light calisthentics, jog, swim or cycle followed by joint rotations, twisting, bending) will enhance muscle and connective tissue extensibility. In cold weather, the warm-up might be more intense and more clothes worn to stay warm during the stretching routine. I do my stretching routines immediately after a shower at night and in front of the TV. The shower warms me up and doing it in front of the TV enables my wife and/or kids to sometimes join me to have a laugh at some of the positions I get into or show me up with how good they are at some of the stretches I do.

b. *Isolate the muscle group to be stretched.* Michael Alter's book, *Sports Stretch* (www.humankinetics.com) gives excellent examples for 41 sports.

c. *Use correct alignment and technique.* Again, Alter's book is excellent for this with great diagrams and dot-pointed explanations.

d. *Exhale going into the stretch* to facilitate relaxation during the stretch.

e. *Breathe normally during the stretch* but accentuate exhaling when going deeper into the stretch.

f. *Hold the stretch at the point of tension, not pain.*

g. *Hold the stretch for 10 to 30 seconds.* A 1994 study found holding a hamstring stretch for 60 seconds just as effective as a 30-second stretch.

h. *Come out of the stretch as carefully as you go into it.*

i. *Do 2-3 repetitions of a 10-second stretch or one of a 30-second stretch.* Given that the lack of flexibility is due to connective tissue tightness, research has shown that low force, long duration stretching is the most effective to get increased range of motion about a joint.

j. *Stretch 3-5 days per week.*

k. *If your sport demands dynamic flexibility, incorporate a progressive velocity flexibility strategy.* That is, stretch in the following order:

   i. Static

   ii. Slow, short of end of range stretching (below 75% of actual sport speed)

   iii. Slow, full range stretching (again below 75% of actual sport speed)

   i. Fast, short of end of range stretching

   ii. Fast, full range stretching

Consult a sports physiotherapist for advice on a flexibility program that will both enhance performance and prevent injury.

While the above guidelines recommend static or passive stretching, ballistic stretching may be recommended for athletes involved in ballistic activities at the end of the joints stretch range. Examples might be kickers, sprinters, or jumpers. However, ballistic stretching should always be preceded by a period of static stretching.

A whole chapter of this book is devoted to flexibility training to highlight just how important it is for the aging athlete. Please read the chapter carefully and make the effort to visit a sports physiotherapist for help in this area or at least check out the Michael Alter book called *Sports Stretch* (www.humankinetics.com).

9. **Strength Train Year Round.** The muscle mass and strength of aging athletes drops, regardless of high intensity training into old age. These decreases start to occur at age 50 but accelerate quickly past the age of 65 - 70 years. Thus, the older we become, the more important strength training should become. Because muscle mass is so important for sports performance, especially strength, speed and power sports, muscle enlargement and maintenance weight training should be done all year round and initially under the guidance of a strength specialist. While the increases in strength will be dramatic, increases in muscle mass, particularly in aging women, may not be that noticeable. Apart from the performance benefits, strength training will go a long way to preventing injury, particularly when doing intense training.

10. **Maintain Leg and Arm Speed.** Along with a decline in muscle mass comes a decline in the fast twitch fiber size and number, the force and speed producing muscle fibers. One possible reason for this loss of fast twitch fiber size and number is that they are not stimulated. Thus, speed work becomes crucial for the aging athlete. Short efforts 5-20 seconds in duration with long rests and 5-10 repetitions is all that is required once a week. This work should be done after development of a strong base of endurance and strength.

11. **Reversibility.** Sport fitness is so hard to get, yet so easy to lose. When consistent, fitness-producing training is interrupted by illness, injury, burnout, overtraining, family or work commitments, the body slips back to its pre-training levels. For the endurance athlete, losses in fitness are noticeable after two weeks. Table 4.3 shows some of the changes.

For the anaerobic athlete, the decline is slower but obvious after three-four weeks. Strength remains relatively constant after four weeks of no training but power (strength done fast) drops by about 15% over the same time period. Sadly, the more highly-conditioned the athlete, the faster the decline in fitness. If you need to take time off from regular training, one-two *intense* workouts a week appear to help prevent the slide in performance. If you must take a break be prepared to work twice as long as the break to get the fitness back.

*Table 4.3:* Losses in endurance fitness parameters after two weeks of no training.

| Measure of Fitness | Change (%) |
|---|---|
| $VO_2max$ | -8 |
| Stroke volume (blood pumped per beat) | -10 |
| Blood volume | -12 |
| Aerobic chemicals in muscle | -29 |
| Anaerobic threshold | -7 |
| Blood lactic acid levels | +88 |
| Use of fat as a fuel | -52 |
| Time to fatigue | -10 |

12. **Individuality.** While this book is based on the findings of science, every individual ages, gets fit, and gets unfit at their own rate. For example, one study showed that a group of older people improved their fitness an average of 14% after a period of endurance training. However, despite all doing the same training, one person improved only 4% while another improved 40%. Genetics has determined that some people are *slow responders* to training, some *fast responders* and the majority *average responders* to any type, frequency, intensity and duration of training. This is why every training program, no matter how scientifically based, based on someone else, or that of an elite athlete, may not work for you. It is the reason why this book is based on principles rather than prescription.

13. **Periodisation** This principle involves working hard at times and easy at times. We work hard at times to stress our body and we work easy at times to allow recovery from the stress. This concept of periodisation involves breaking up your training season into short blocks of time (e.g. one week), longer blocks of time (e.g. three-six weeks), and even longer blocks - the season. It is generally acknowledged that within a week we work hard at times and easy at times - the old hard / easy principle. Within a three-week block we might have a hard week, a medium week, and an easy week. During the season, we generally lift intensity from three-week block to three-week block.

The importance of gradually building intensity and allowing time to adapt to this increased training stress cannot be emphasised enough. For the older sprint or power athlete, two maximal speed or power workouts at the most are suggested in a hard week. Generally maximal speed work should be done when fully recovered, so take the long recoveries between hard workouts. The aging endurance athlete needs to work on the easy - medium - hard principle from week to week and the hard - easy principle during a week. If the emphasis is on building mileage during the May - June period (e.g. cycle road racer), then hard is long easy miles, medium is shorter easy miles, and easy shorter again. During the next three-week block a hard week might be one long ride, two strong rides, and one aerobic interval session with the medium week being two easy longer rides, one strong ride and one aerobic interval session. We can thus manipulate intensity and duration, depending on the demands of our event and what phase of training we are in, and whether we are in a hard, medium, or easy week.

14. **Recover Hard and Smart.** Research on older non-athletes and anecdotal personal experience and those of other older athletes suggest that aging athletes need more rest between quality training sessions and/or need to focus more aggressively on nutritional and physical recovery strategies. Train hard for 2-3 weeks then recover and rest. Not enough athletes young or old use recovery training. They see training hard in the pool, on the track, in the boat or on the road as what its all about. The smart aging athlete will focus just as much energy on recovery training and use the methods suggested in Chapter 15 of this book. We must allow our body to adapt to the training loads placed on it. This allows the body to adapt and develop. Too little recovery leads to injury, overtraining and decreased performance, or burnout. Recovery can include eating and drinking immediately after training or competing, spas, massages, light swims, or recovery jogs. A whole chapter of this book has been devoted to it to emphasise its importance.

15. **Variety.** Variety in training intensity, workout structure, venue, type of training etc. all provide that break from the routine we all need at times to prevent staleness. While I usually run and swim train separately, I occasionally enjoy throwing on my back or "bum" pack and running to the pool hard, have an easy swim, then run to feel on the way home.

16. **Injury Prevention** is also a critical principle of training, particularly for those athletes returning to competition after not having competed or trained for an extended period. A number of factors need to be considered in preventing injury. These include your previous injury history, common injury sites in your sport / event / position, your technique (good or bad), and whether you progressively overload your training. I strongly recommend that aging athletes, particularly those inexperienced, visit a sports physiotherapist who understands your sport. Ask them for a musculo-skeletal profile after telling them your history and what sports and/or events you are training for. For the power athletes I also strongly recommend strength training under a suitably qualified person (Australian Strength and Conditioning Association (ASCA) or appropriate degree). In addition, I also suggest that a coach be used to oversee technique, particularly for those involved in power or endurance events.

17. **Be Consistent.** Too many aging athletes get sick, injured, burnout or overtrain. When these occur, they are generally due to pushing too hard, too often without recovering smart. The downtime that results from these problems means lost fitness and the hard road back to that fitness level. Consistent training, not hard training, is the smart way to fitness. It means using the recovery methods discussed in this book when the body is tired, taking a day off when the throat starts to tickle, not doing that planned interval training session but going for a walk.

18. **Train More Time Efficiently.** Aging athletes generally have far less time to train and recover due to work and family commitments and pressures. They therefore need to train smarter. The more experienced the aging athlete, the more you will be able to determine which type of training, drill, training patterns or workouts work for you as an individual.

The purpose of the training chapters in this book is to educate aging athletes on exactly how to do just that.

19. **Listen To Your Body**. The most important training principle of all. As aging athletes we are experienced enough to know when it's time to ease back on how hard or often we train. If the body is "creaking", "niggling", or tired, ease back, use the recovery strategies suggested in Chapter 15, or rest completely. If the "bod" continues to complain, see a sports medicine-trained professional who understands your sport.

## Conclusion

In summary, the aging athlete must gradually lift intensity, frequency and / or duration of training depending on what event / sport / position we are training for. We must work hard at times to stress our body and train easy or rest at times to allow our bodies to adapt to the hard work. The longer we have been away from training the greater the need to follow the principles above. By specific training and listening to our bodies as we train progressively harder, we can hopefully achieve our own personal goals.

## CHAPTER 5

# COACHING THE MASTERS ATHLETE

*Regardless of age, every athlete should be treated by the coach as an individual. The enthusiasm, the desire, and the commitment to perform does not abate with age and the coach must assist those...who wish to perform and achieve at the highest level...help them in their quest for excellence...*

Dr John Daly, OAM.

*You're never a master, always a student.*

Murray Rose

### Introduction

The media has created an incorrect image of the aging athlete. Aging athletes are portrayed by the media as either "very old" or former greats – what I call the "Dawn Fraser Syndrome". The truth is that research has shown that the majority of aging athletes are 30-54 years of age, well educated, in full-time work, married or have a partner, have a disposable income and are normal people with a wide variety of interests and motivations. Together with these different motivations, aging athletes vary enormously in health status, fitness levels, physical abilities, life experiences, previous sports experience, source and degree of motivation, available time, needs and goals, interests and physiologies. This variation becomes greater the older the athlete becomes. An astute coach of the aging athlete should get to know each individual athlete under their care, particularly their motivations for being involved in aging sport.

### Where are the Coaches?

Very few sports in Australia, AUSSI Masters Swimming excluded, have a specific coach accreditation scheme. As evidenced by the rapid growth in the number of Masters Games over the last decade, aging sport is the largest growing sector within sport. However, few sports have taken up the challenge to harness the experience, energies and dollars this segment of the sport and recreation industry can offer them.

There is a market for coaches of aging athletes. However, until National Sporting Organizations appreciate the value of the aging athlete to their organization, as surf lifesaving appear to have done; few specialist coaches of aging athletes exist in Australia or overseas. The purpose of this chapter is to further educate coaches who might already be coaching aging athletes and to better prepare already accredited coaches into taking up the challenge of coaching the "vet".

## Reasons for Involvement

Research has shown that over 80% of aging athletes were active in their chosen sport as younger athletes with research suggesting that the majority of aging athletes "dropped out" for reasons of family or work commitments, the tediousness of regular training and competition, friends had dropped out, or because of injury or illness. As a result, most "vets" have had a past active interest in sport and are keen to become involved again in their chosen sport.

Aging athletes are, in general, involved in sport for "Fun, Fitness and Friendship". While competing against others is important for some, competing against self is more important for most aging athletes. However, as with younger athletes, the reasons for involvement vary enormously. They include:

- Keeping physically fit – the major factor
- Sharing the enjoyment of sport with a group
- Developing skills and abilities
- Weight loss
- Relaxation
- Meeting new people
- Socialising
- Develop self confidence and independence
- Travelling
- Competing

A study of New Zealand masters swimmers showed that there might be different motivations for aging men and women to be involved in their sport. While the factors above were common to both genders, men rated competing more important than women, while females rated losing weight more important than males.

The astute coach must be aware that every aging athlete is participating for different reasons. Knowledge of why an individual is involved in the sport will maximise adherence to training and thus attainment of each athlete's personal goal.

## Barriers to Exercise Involvement

While the above physical, mental and social benefits are major motivators for older people to get involved in sport, there are a number of perceived barriers that keep older people away from sport. These include:

1. *Health Status.* Arthritic or joint pain, fatigue, and a host of pathologies (hypertension, heart disease, diabetes, obesity). Sadly, physical activity and in particular physical fitness, impacts positively on all these pathologies. The table overleaf shows some Canadian data reflecting the physical conditions that may limit exercise involvement and gender differences.

*Table 5.1:* Health conditions responsible for limiting physical activity involvement in Canadians 65 years and over (1996-1997). Figures are %.

| Gender | Nervous System | Back Problem | Limb Problem | Respiratory Problem | Arthritis | Heart Problem |
|---|---|---|---|---|---|---|
| Male | 13 | 10 | 10 | 9 | 11 | 18 |
| Female | 11 | 7 | 10 | 6 | 27 | 13 |

2. *Fear of Injury*. Fear of falling in the very old, and fear of heart attack are often cited as barriers. Highlighting the benefits of strength training and aerobic fitness is required to overcome this fear.

3. *Urinary Incontinence*. The involuntary loss of urine is embarrassing and can be a reason older women in particular don't become involved in sport. Coughing, laughing, straining, jumping or running can cause the loss of small amounts of urine. One study of 326 regularly-exercising women (average age 38.5 years) found 47% had some degree of incontinence that became more severe with high-impact exercises.

4. *Lack of Time*. This is the most often cited barrier in career- and/or family-focussed aging people. However, the older the age group, the less a barrier this becomes unless caring for relatives, grandchildren, partners and/or maintaining a full or part-time job. Time management and prioritising exercise for health and wellness reasons need to be considered.

5. *Lack of Money*. A limited or fixed income may prohibit joining a community facility, buying appropriate clothing or shoes or travelling to a facility. Programs for aging athletes should be accessible and cost-effective.

6. *Lack of Support*. Particularly in aging women who have focussed for years on partners or family, the coach, administrator, and fellow athletes need to support the aging athlete coming back into sport or trying sport for the very first time.

7. *Body Image*. The emphasis on appearance and the knowledge that with advancing years the body changes shape creates a barrier to participation. This is particularly the case in women who are faced with media images of sportswomen. Coaches of sports requiring the wearing of swim costumes or shorts need to be aware of this.

8. *Fear of Failure*. Inexperience in sport, in older women in particular, may contribute to aging people not wanting to try a new sport for fear of failure. A supportive environment with emphasis on participation, fun, fitness and friendship will help.

9. *Lack of Confidence*. For many aging people wanting to get involved with sport, a lack of confidence comes from a lack of skill, particularly in women who for historical reasons have not been as active as boys in sport as children. A low-key, non-threatening sporting environment created by the coach is therefore essential.

10. *Lack of Awareness*. Sport in the media is portrayed as an activity for young people. Moreover, sport for aging athletes is portrayed as something for the ex-elite. Coaches and administrators of sport for the aged need to promote in the media the "fun, fitness and friendship" side of sport.

11. *Negative Attitudes to Physical Activity.* Research has consistently shown that a positive attitude to physical activity is associated with higher levels of physical activity.
12. *Knowledge.* In poor socio-economic or educational groups, lack of knowledge about the benefits of physical activity is a factor in preventing involvement in masters sport. Research has shown that older people in general lack knowledge as to the frequency, duration, and intensity of physical activity or exercise required to gain health benefits.

## Current Training Practices

Previous research suggests that the "average" aging athlete trains 2-3 times per week for around an hour a session. The concern is that the vast majority of "vets" develop training programs based on previous experience or simply practice the game by playing the game. The same research also suggested that advice from friends is rated more important than reading about programs written by expert coaches or sports scientists. This finding raises the issues of aging athletes thinking they are as capable as they were 20 years ago and overestimating abilities and fitness; not being in touch with current coaching methods and training practices; and, including training practices that might be detrimental to health.

At the 1994 World Masters Games in Brisbane, we conducted research suggesting that warm-up / cool-down strategies were seldom included with training, particularly in the older age groups. This finding has obvious performance and injury implications for the older age groups.

Another important observation from the 1994 research was the fact that aging athletes, in general, train with less intensity than when they were younger athletes. For many aging athletes training for "fun, fitness or friendship", training intensity can be low to moderate. However, for the healthy, non-at-risk performance-oriented "vet", quality work that includes higher intensity training is strongly recommended since intensity has conclusively been shown to be the key to improved performance in all age groups.

## Problems Encountered with Adults Exercising

A number of problems are often encountered when coaching the aging athlete, particularly in the initial stages of commencing a training program. Table 5.2 below highlights the major concerns for the coach.

## Physiological Changes with Aging

Unfortunately for those of us still competing in masters sport, many of the physiological changes that occur with aging are inevitable. However, many of these declines may be due to inactivity as a result of taking a break from sport or decreased training volumes and intensities rather than aging per se. These changes and their implications for coaching are listed in Table 5.3 overleaf:

*Table 5.2:* Problems often encountered when an aging athlete commences training after years away from exercise.

| Problem | Coaching Implication |
|---|---|
| 1. Overestimate ability | Stress need for progressive overload<br>Spend time with initial briefing |
| 2. Embarrassed at lack of ability | Encouragement<br>Link with other similar ability people |
| 3. Ashamed of physique | Link with similar body typed individuals<br>Encouragement |
| 4. Impatience at slow progress | Initial education that progress will be slow<br>Mentoring with other athletes |
| 5. Muscle weakness | Need for gym work in sport specific areas<br>Graduated program |
| 6. Joint problems and immobility | Professional referral and input<br>Possibly sacrifice biomechanical correct technique to suit athlete<br>Flexibility training |
| 7. Cardiac risk | Medical screening (see below)<br>Be aware of use of medications and side-effects |
| 8. Overweight | Encouragement<br>Education as to dietary and exercise control |
| 9. Increased risk of injury | Warm-up<br>Flexibility training<br>Technique training |
| 10. Sight or hearing loss | Coach positioning and voice projection |
| 11. Urinary incontinence | Reduce high impact activities<br>Wear pad during exercise<br>Pelvic floor exercises |
| 12. Medical conditions | Need for pre-screening by medical professional<br>Need for coach awareness of medication side-effects and exercise guidelines for chronic medical conditions |

## Training Adaptations

Initially, the aging athlete coming back after a long lay-off from training may show poor exercise tolerance. However, with a graduated and progressive training program, they can adapt well to physical training. The percentage improvement in strength, speed, power and endurance in the older person appear to be the same as the younger person commencing training. However, they will not, in general, attain the fitness levels they had as a younger athlete. Moreover, research also suggests that older persons take longer to adapt to both strength and endurance training programs.

Anecdotal evidence also suggests older athletes also take longer to recover from training. This would suggest that recovery strategies such as massage, nutrition (high carbohydrate intake, fluids), hydrotherapy (spas, hot/cold showers in those without cardiac risk), and active recovery (longer cool-downs, cross-training) be incorporated into training. Furthermore, longer breaks between quality workouts are recommended with lighter work between those quality workouts.

*Table 5.3:* Changes that occur with aging and their implications for coaching.

| Physiological Changes | Effect on Performance | Coach Implications |
|---|---|---|
| Decreased aerobic capacity | • Decreased endurance<br>• Slower to "get going"<br>• Decreased thermoregulatory ability | • Train competitive athletes with intensity<br>• Need longer between intervals<br>• Ensure warm-up includes intensity and is close to start of race<br>• Take longer to adapt<br>• Prevent heat injuries |
| Decreased anaerobic capacity | • Decreased speed | • Include resistance training<br>• Ensure quality speed work |
| Decreased flexibility | • Decreased joint range of motion<br>• Poor technique | • Need for flexibility training<br>• Increased susceptibility to injury |
| Decreased strength / power | • Decreased strength and power due to loss of muscle mass<br>• Poor technique | • Hypertrophy strength training<br>• Lower volume, not intensity, of intense work. |
| Decreased basal metabolic rate | • Tend over time to put on fat-weight unless dietary intake not tapered | • Include resistance training to maintain muscle mass<br>• Monitor skinfolds / body fat<br>• Monitor athlete's diet |
| Decreased nervous system activity | • Slower reactions and speed | • Maintain quality work that stimulates nervous system maximally |
| Decreased vision and hearing | • Decreased performance | • Coach positioning and communication |
| Decreased health | • Decreased tolerance to quality work in unhealthy individuals | • Need for pre-participation screening by sports physicians, physiotherapists, dietitians |
| Decreased muscle mass | • Decreased speed and basal metabolism | • Hypertrophy weight training to increase or maintain muscle mass |
| Decreased bone density | • Increased risk of stress fractures | • Include weight bearing activity<br>• Monitor calcium intake<br>• Consider hormone replacement therapy<br>• Prevent falls by strengthening muscles<br>• Prevent repetitive intense work |
| Menopause | • Decreased performance<br>• Increased recovery time<br>• Increased fatigue<br>• Increased irritability | • Encourage athlete to maintain a training diary<br>• Longer recovery within and between training sessions<br>• Reduce training intensity and volume<br>• Demonstrate patience and understanding |

## Training Recommendations

There is no doubt the older athlete's physical capacities decline with age. However, both research and anecdotal evidence would strongly suggest the following strategies to enhance or maintain performance with age:

1. Ensure all athletes are screened for health and cardiac risk factors prior to commencing training (see next section).
2. Include resistance training to maintain or develop muscle mass, particularly for persons over age 50 years.
3. Include flexibility training as an integral component of training.
4. For competitive "vets" include intensity in workouts.
5. Monitor recovery rates and include recovery training into the program.
6. Use the same principles of training as with younger athletes - specificity, progression, overload, recovery, variation and individuality.

Most importantly, the astute coach of aging athletes must be aware that older athletes have a wide variety of motivations and physiologies that impact strongly upon training program design. Individualization of training thus becomes far more important the older the athlete being coached.

## Safety Guidelines for Older Exercisers

The following precautions apply to all forms of exercise that an older athlete undertakes. These precautions become more important depending on an individual aging athlete's health status, fitness level and competitive drive.

- Obtain medical clearance from a sports-orientated doctor or the family doctor.
- Never hold the breath – this holds particularly during strength or flexibility training and particularly for those with blood pressure or heart conditions.
- Do not hyperextend the joints.
- Discourage a competitive atmosphere in those who are motivated to PB's rather than gold medals.
- Limit overhead arm work, particularly in those with blood pressure and/or heart problems.
- Teach a neutral spine position to avoid twisting and/or flexing of the spine.
- Avoid excessive vertical loading of the spine, particularly in those with or suspected of osteoporosis (e.g. post-menopausal women).
- Modify methods of training or exercises that are not well tolerated. If an exercise causes pain, modify or replace it.
- Implement slow and gradual progression by manipulating frequency, intensity and duration of training.
- Avoid high-risk activities such as straight-le.g. sit-ups, neck rotations, exercises that bend and twist at the same time, or sudden high intensity exercise without warm-up

and progressive increases in intensity.
- Always err on the side of safety.

## Pre-participation Screening

With increasing age comes an increased risk of heart disease and other health risk factors. The Australian Association for Exercise and Sports Science (AAESS) and Sports Medicine Australia (SMA) have developed a set of guidelines for persons commencing an exercise program.

Prior to commencing training after many years away from sport, the following guidelines are recommended:

- A male over 45 or female over 55 years age who undertakes **moderate** exercise (< 75% of 220-age heart rate) and is "apparently healthy" (no heart disease risk factors - blood pressure > 140/90; serum cholesterol > 5.5 mmol.$L^{-1}$; serum triglyceride > 2.0 mmol.$L^{-1}$; smoking; diabetes; family history) does **NOT** need a medical screening by a doctor - ideally a sports physician.
- A male over 45 or female over 55 years age who undertakes **vigorous** exercise (> 75% of 220-age heart rate) and is "apparently healthy" (see above) **MUST** have a medical screening and electrocardiogram by a doctor or sports physician prior to commencing training at any level.
- All persons who are at "higher risk" (have two or more of the heart disease risk factors above) or who are known to be "with disease" **MUST** have a medical screening and electrocardiogram prior to commencing training at any level.

In addition to the medical screenings suggested above, it is strongly recommended that the aging athlete undertake the following additional screenings:

- Sports Physiotherapist - for a musculokeletal profile where muscle imbalances and / or flexibility problems are identified that may lead to injury or technique problems.
- Sports Dietician - to examine current dietary intakes of macronutrients (carbohydrate, fat and protein) and micronutrients (vitamins and minerals) as well as advice on the additional intakes or precautions needed for athletes commencing an exercise program, particularly in some groups of aging athletes (e.g. menopausal women or endurance athletes).

Following the above screenings, the competitive aging athlete who decides to undertake a weight training program should also strongly consider making contact with a strength and conditioning specialist who is trained to give the best advice on strength training for enhancing performance.

## Coach Implications

Given the problems shown in Table 5.2 and the anatomical and the physiological changes that occur in aging individuals (Table 5.3), the coach of aging athletes needs to be aware of each person's:

- reasons for becoming involved
- current fitness level
- previous sporting experience and level attained
- injury or disability history
- self image
- current lifestyle
- time available to train
- goals and level of commitment

Moreover, the successful coach of aging athletes needs to include the following features into their program:

- skill development
- fitness development
- variety
- competition if desired by the athlete
- encouragement and praise
- individualised assessment
- fun and friendship

**Conclusion**

Aging athletes participate in aging sporting events for a variety of reasons apart from competition. These different motivations, together with the variability in physiologies and rates of decline in physical capacities, make the coaching of the aging athlete a challenge. In return, the coach of the older athlete gains enormous rewards in seeing their charges not only win medals but achieve much more in terms of achievement of personal goals that may be as simple as completing an event or beating a colleague in training.

# CHAPTER 6

# ENDURANCE DEVELOPMENT FOR THE MASTERS ATHLETE

*Permanence, perseverance, and persistence in spite of all obstacles, discouragements, and impossibilities: it is this that in all things distinguishes the strong soul from the weak.*

**Thomas Carlyle.**

*Genius is one percent inspiration and 99 percent perspiration. I never did anything worth doing by accident, nor did any of my inventions come by accident; they came by work.*

**Thomas Edison**

*The secret of success is constancy of purpose.*

**Benjamin Disraeli**

## Introduction

Endurance is the ability to last. Whether it is to survive a marathon run, a 40 kilometer time trial on the bike, a six-minute rowing race, or a 1500m swim, we must have the capacity to finish the event. Team players such as touch players, netballers or footballers must also have endurance, not only to last the duration game but to recover from both sprints in the game and from game to game if playing in a number of games in a day or on successive days.

The purpose of this chapter is to outline the factors that affect endurance capacity, the factors related to successful endurance performance, and then to give practical advice on how to maximize endurance development for masters athletes.

## Factors influencing endurance ability

Five factors determine our abilities to be good endurance athletes. These include:

1. *Genetics.* It has been estimated through studies on identical twins that 70-75% of endurance ability is genetic. That is, our parents have given us (or forgotten to give us!) the ability to be an endurance athlete. Our parents have given us a particular body type, an endurance physiology, a high or low percent of slow twitch endurance muscle fibers, the ability to recover from or adapt to training stress, or the mental constitution for endurance. If we don't have these factors in our favor, we are going to find it difficult to do well in endurance events.

2. *Gender.* Female athletes *generally* have a 10% lower aerobic capacity than male endurance athletes. This is due to the fact that females have smaller hearts (therefore pumping less blood and oxygen), a smaller concentration of hemoglobin (the substance in the blood that carries oxygen), and they carry greater amounts of body fat than men. While it might be argued that extra fat may lead to better flotation in female distance swimmers, it is generally agreed that the extra fat found in most females is a hindrance to endurance performance when compared to males.
3. *Body composition.* Low levels of body fat are very important to the endurance athlete. No endurance athlete wants to carry extra "bricks" around on a bike, running track, playing field or through the water.
4. *Age.* Age is a critical factor influencing aerobic capacity. Aerobic capacity declines in non-exercising older people at approximately 1% per year, and in we aging athletes at about 0.5% per year till approximately 70 years after which it escalates. The major factor explaining this decline is a reduction in maximum heart rate at the rate of approximately one beat per year.
5. *Training.* Endurance training improves both the ability of the heart to pump blood to muscles and the ability of those trained muscles to take up and use the oxygen made available by the heart and blood. Research suggests that training can increase our aerobic capacity by up to 25%.

While there is little we can do about genetics, gender, and age, we can diet and exercise safely to reduce body fat and dramatically improve endurance performance by using correct training methods. We will discuss these training methods shortly, but let us firstly examine the physiological factors that lead to successful endurance performance.

**Physiological factors related to successful endurance performance**

Sports science has conclusively shown that performance in endurance events or sports is due not only to the factors outlined above but to a number of specific physiological characteristics. These are discussed in detail below.

1. *Maximum oxygen uptake ($VO_2max$) or aerobic capacity.* $VO_2max$ is the greatest rate at which oxygen can be transported by the blood and consumed by an athlete's working tissues. The units of $VO_2max$ are ml/kg/min and values of some outstanding athletes are (were): Said Aouita (5000m runner) - 83.0; John Walker (miler) - 82.0; Sebastian Coe (miler) - 77.0; Greta Waitz (female marathon) - 73.5; Peter Snell (miler) - 72.3; Derek Clayton (marathon) - 69.7. Values in young, elite male runners might be 65-75 ml/kg/min but in 60-plus year-old male runners they are around 50-55 ml/kg/min with females about 10% lower. Swimmers and cyclists usually have a lower aerobic capacity due to the smaller muscle mass involved that can therefore take up less oxygen (see Table 6.1).

*Table 6.1:* Typical maximum oxygen uptake values in 20-30 year old high performance athletes. Age-related declines occur at approximately 5% per decade in masters athletes.

| Sport | VO$_2$max (ml/kg/min) Male | VO$_2$max (ml/kg/min) Female |
|---|---|---|
| **Endurance sports** | | |
| Long-distance running | 75-80 | 65-70 |
| Middle-distance running | 70-75 | 65-68 |
| Road cycling | 70-75 | 60-65 |
| Orienteering | 65-72 | 60-65 |
| Swimming | 65-70 | 55-60 |
| Rowing | 65-69 | 55-60 |
| Canoeing | 60-68 | 50-55 |
| Race walking | 60-65 | 55-60 |
| **Games** | | |
| Football (soccer) | 50-60 | 45-50 |
| Volleyball | 55-60 | 48-52 |
| Basketball | 50-55 | 40-45 |
| Tennis | 48-52 | 40-45 |
| Table tennis | 40-45 | 38-42 |
| **Combative sports** | | |
| Boxing | 60-65 | 50-55 |
| Wrestling | 60-65 | - |
| Judo | 55-60 | 48-52 |
| Fencing | 45-50 | 40-45 |
| **Power sports** | | |
| Track sprint runners | 48-52 | 43-47 |
| Field athletes | 40-50 | 35-40 |
| Decathlete / heptathlete | 60-65 | 50-55 |
| **Acrobatic sports** | | |
| Gymnastics / rhythmic gymnastics | 45-50 | 40-45 |
| Figure skating | 50-55 | 45-50 |

Historically, it was thought (and still is by many coaches and athletes!) that VO$_2$max was the most critical factor in endurance performance. Wrong! While it is an important factor, it is not the most critical factor when it comes to performance on the track, road, lake, river or pool. A far better predictor of endurance performance is what fraction or percentage of that VO$_2$max can be maintained for the duration of an event - a concept called the anaerobic threshold.

2. *Anaerobic threshold.* This is the percentage of the athlete's aerobic capacity that can be used at race pace – what I call the "hurt but hold" intensity. Top marathoners and road cyclists can maintain 80-90% of their $VO_2$max while less elite athletes can only sustain 70-75% of their $VO_2$max for the same distance. Above this pace the muscles start to produce lactic acid that upsets the muscle contraction process and slows the breakdown of carbohydrate so that energy production is compromised.

   To highlight the importance of the anaerobic threshold to endurance performance, let's look at one of the world's greatest former marathoners - Australian Derek Clayton. Derek held the world marathon record for over a decade in the 1960-70s. Lab tests showed that Derek's $VO_2$max was lower than most of his competitors. However, his anaerobic threshold was relatively higher than theirs, giving him an edge when it came to racing. History also tells us he was tough - he passed blood in urine and faeces for days after breaking the world record! Later we will discuss ways to measure the anaerobic threshold and ways to help raise it so that we can race harder and not accumulate lactic acid.

3. *Fatigue resistance.* This is the ability of an endurance athlete to maintain pace during prolonged endurance exercise. A major adaptation to long duration, low intensity endurance training is fatigue resistance. The long slow distance and "miles in the arms or legs" concept thus allows us to resist fatigue.

4. *Economy of motion.* This is the oxygen cost required to maintain a specific speed. By using better technique, the elite endurance athletes use up to 15% less oxygen to maintain a pace than recreational athletes. Technique is critical in improving economy. For example, runners ideally should have a relaxed upper body, swimmers recover the arms in a relaxed manner or not sweep arms across the body under the water, and cyclists should not throw their upper body around and keep relaxed in the upper body. These wasted activities use up valuable fuel and oxygen but don't produce speed. Longer, slower runs, cycles, swims and rows improve economy as does race-pace training using intervals where technique can be concentrated on while working hard for shorter periods.

5. *Fuel usage.* At high race speeds there is a greater reliance on carbohydrate than fats as a fuel for energy production. However, well-trained endurance athletes can make greater use of fats as a fuel during racing than less-trained athletes, thereby conserving valuable liver and muscle carbohydrate (glycogen) stores.

Through the correct training techniques, we can adapt our bodies to maximize each of these above factors.

**Training techniques for successful endurance performance**

A common practice of many athletes is to adopt the prevailing training methods of current world-class athletes in their sports. This approach has not only led to many aging athletes burning out but also has fostered the belief that more is better with an emphasis on "big mileage" being seen as the key to successful endurance performance. In a classic study on young swimmers, well-respected USA sports scientist and masters swimmer, Dr David

Costill, halved the volume of training being undertaken by a swim squad and found no change in swim performance compared to a squad who maintained twice the volume. This research strongly argues against the belief that more is better. Indeed, the prevailing training research recommends a combination of both quantity and quality as the keys to endurance performance.

When training to develop endurance, one of the most common and scientifically correct ways to improve performance is to use heart rate monitoring and the heart rate zones concept. Taking the heart rate manually on the thumb side of the wrist or at the neck beside the windpipe is the easiest and most convenient way to monitor training intensity. However, I'd recommend the use of a heart rate monitor (I suggest *Polar* brand as they were the original and from my experience, are the most robust for use by athletes) is more preferable because of the errors involved in taking manual heart rates. Heart rate monitors can be expensive if you go to the top of the range models that will give you temperature and altitude if you want! Check out the *Polar* website at: http://www.polar.fi/ or see your run or bike store who generally have experience and carry a small range. However, before we examine the heart rate zones concept, let's examine ways we can determine our own maximum heart rate.

## Determining maximum heart rate

To use a heart rate monitor and the heart rate training zones outlined below, you MUST know your maximum heart rate (MHR). Historically, to estimate your MHR, we used:

$$MHR = 220 - age \pm 10 \text{ beats/min}$$

Such a formula would give the MHR for a 60 year-old as anywhere between 150 and 170 beats/min, a large variation. Recently, a new formula has been developed and validated for use by healthy adults:

$$MHR = 208 - (0.7 \times age) \text{ beats/min}$$

Again, this formula suggests a 60 year-old athlete would have a MHR of 166 beats/min.

However, research and experience tells us that the MHR of individuals varies enormously. For example, in people over 60 years of age, MHR can vary anywhere between 200 to as low as 105 beats/min. Thus, not knowing your MHR exactly will see you either under- or overestimating your training intensities. Apart from individual differences, few people realize that maximum heart rate can vary within a person depending on:

- *Amount of muscle mass used*. In general, the larger the muscle mass, the higher the MHR. For example, a triathlete's MHR for swim, bike, and run may be different with the run generally the highest, then the bike, then the swim. Again, in a swimmer, MHR for each stroke may be different with butterfly having the highest MHR and freestyle the lowest.
- *Body position*. In general, the more an athlete's heart works against gravity, the higher the MHR. This is due to the fact that the amount of blood returning to the heart is enhanced in a flatter position (e.g. swimming, cycling on aero bars), whereas the more

upright (e.g. running, cycling on brakehoods), the less blood returns to the heart meaning the amount of blood pumped per beat is reduced and thus the heart has to beat faster to get the same volume of blood to the muscles.

- *Water pressure.* Swimming or water running generally exhibit a reduced MHR compared to the same action on land. Why? The water pressure on the body encourages the return of blood to the heart, meaning the heart can pump less number of times to get the same volume of blood to the muscles as the same intensity of training on land.
- *Drugs.* For example, a type of blood pressure drug called beta-blockers reduces the ability of the heart to beat quickly. With hypertension affecting many aging athletes, an awareness of this limiting factor on the use of heart rate training zones is important.

Thus, a number of factors influence an individual's MHR. While a sport-specific MHR test under the watchful eyes of a doctor and/or qualified exercise physiologist at a hospital or laboratory at a University is the safest and recommended method for determining MHR in aging endurance athletes, the following tests have been widely used in young athletes to determine MHR.

While it is strongly recommended that maximum heart rates for an older (>40 years) athlete be determined within a sports science laboratory with a doctor in attendance, the experienced and healthy endurance athletes may decide to determine maximum heart rate themselves. There are two possible methods available to a coach to establish maximum heart rates - a step test or the 2 x 4 minute effort method.

1. *Step Test*

    This can be done by warming up well, then doing 10 continuous one minute increases in intensity starting easy then gradually building till the last minute is all out.

    Examples might be:
    - Runners: 8-10 x 400m
    - Swimmers: 8-10 x 100m
    - Cyclists: Start in 42/39:19/21 gears then increase gearing every minute on a windtrainer. If you run out of gears, increase the resistance on the flywheel.
    - Rowers/kayaker: 8-10 increases in ergometer ratings / wattage / time per 500m or gradual increases in rating and pressure within the boat.

2. *2 x 4 Minute Efforts*

    This method requires the athlete, after a warm-up, to do an all out 4 minute effort (e.g. 1km run, 300m swim, timed effort on bike, windtrainer, rowing ergometer), have a two minute recovery, then go again. Not easy and only recommended for the experienced, highly motivated and competitive aging endurance athlete with no medical complications.

    Each of the above maximum heart rate tests should be done wearing a heart rate monitor and be followed by a 10-15 minute warm down. The manual palpation method at the neck or wrist is fraught with errors when heart rates are high. For example, if one or two beats are missed at the beginning of a six- or ten-second pulse count, this may mean 10-20 beats over a minute. If you are a triathlete, you should establish maximum heart rate for swim, bike and run separately. They are *usually* different with running generally the highest, cycling approximately 10 beats per minute lower, and swimming the lowest at 10-20 beats lower than running.

Now that we have established our maximum heart rate directly or by using the more cautious formula method, knowledge of the different heart rate zones is crucial.

### Endurance training heart rate zones

Sport science has shown that as we exercise harder, the heart rate increases in direct proportion to the speed. Thus, due to the straight line relationship between training intensity (speed) and heart rate being a straight line (Figure 6.1), we can use heart rates as a means of determining training intensity.

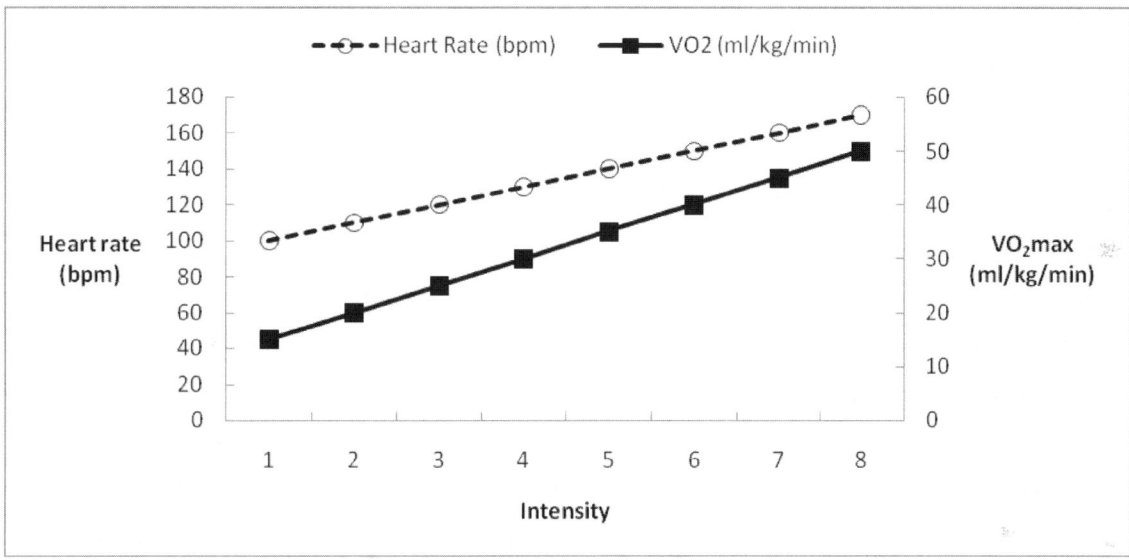

*Figure 6.1:* The straight line relationships between exercise intensity and both heart rate and oxygen consumption.

Once maximum heart rate has been determined using the methods referred to above, the following table can be used to establish heart rate training zones:

*Table 6.2:* Endurance training intensities based on percentages of maximum heart rate (MHR).

| Zone | Name | Intensity |
|---|---|---|
| 1 | Recovery | < 65% MHR |
| 2 | Aerobic | 65-75% MHR |
| 3 | Extensive endurance | 75-80% MHR |
| 4 | Intensive endurance | 80-85% MHR |
| 5 | Anaerobic threshold | 85-90% MHR |
| 6 | Maximum aerobic | > 90% MHR |
| 7 | Speed | Not applicable |

These heart rate zones are scientifically based guidelines but they are only guidelines. Too many endurance athletes become slaves to a heart rate monitor or a heart rate that they saw in one of the many heart rate training books available. Many of these books assume each person has a maximum heart rate of 220-age, or that the zone 2 training zone can be determined by taking your age from 180. The only real way to determine your maximum heart rate is in a laboratory or using the all out or incremental test referred to earlier.

When using these heart rate zones and a heart rate monitor, it is also important to remember that heart rates will be higher when exercising in hot and / or humid conditions. This is due to the fact that when you train in the heat, you may dehydrate slightly through sweat loss. This lowers your blood volume that results in the heart having to pump more quickly and harder to get the same amount of blood and oxygen to the working muscles. Secondly, when training in the heat, blood is diverted to the skin to help off load the heat generated in the muscles. Again, the heart has to work harder to keep the amount of blood pumping to the muscles to give them the oxygen they require to maintain speed.

Research suggests that heart rates increase by 1.4% for each degree above 21 degrees Celsius. For example, at a constant pace, a heart rate of 140 at 21 degrees will become 160 at 31 degrees.

Bearing these considerations in mind, let us now discuss each of these training zones individually.

1. *Heart Rate Zone 1* is the recovery zone. The important factor here is that intensity is low and the duration generally short. This type of "training" is useful after competition, after hard training sessions such as those in levels 5, 6, or 7 or when the body tells you it's time to lighten the load. Inexperienced aging endurance athletes or those with low endurance fitness levels generally recover more quickly from doing nothing, rather than zone 1 work.

2. *Heart Rate Zone 2* is the minimum intensity required to give an endurance training adaption. The beginner endurance athlete might start out at 65% of MHR but as fitness improves or the years accumulate, the intensity required to gain adaptations will increase to 70-75% of MHR. This is commonly called LSD (long, slow distance) or "conversation pace". The adaptations that occur with this level of training include:
   - increased stroke volume (amount of blood pumped per heartbeat)
   - increased oxygen transport in the blood
   - increased blood volume
   - increased ability of the muscles to use oxygen
   - increased capillary (blood vessel) density within the trained muscles
   - improved use of fat as a fuel, thus teaching the muscles to conserve the limited carbohydrate (glycogen) supply

This type of training, together with level 3 extensive endurance training, forms the basis of endurance training and should be performed for a minimum of 30 minutes depending on the event being trained for. Obviously an Ironman (person!) triathlete would need to spend many more hours of level 2 training if they need to swim for 1-1.5 hours, ride for 5-8 hours, and then run a 42.2 km marathon. Aging endurance athletes should aim for a minimum frequency of three training sessions per week, with longer and more frequent sessions for the more competitive and experienced aging endurance athlete. This level of training should be emphasised during the preparation (pre-season) phase (see Periodisation section in this chapter) of the training season but never forgotten during the other training phases.

3. *Heart Rate Zone 3* training is done at 75-80% of maximum heart rate for long periods (hence it is sometimes called extensive endurance). Examples are 10-30k runs, 40-120k rides, 5-15k rows or paddles, or 1500-3000m swims or longer sets of intervals. This type of training also takes place during the preparation phase of training and induces similar adaptations to those noted above for level 2 training.

4. *Heart Rate Zone 4* training is performed just below anaerobic threshold (80-85% of MHR) and because intensity is lifted, duration is reduced. Examples are 5-20k runs, 30-80k rides, 5-10k rows or paddles, or more intense intervals. Importantly, this intensive endurance intensity is just below "hurt but hold" anaerobic threshold intensity and is thus "strong but comfortable". The adaptations that occur with this training include:
   - elevation of $VO_2max$
   - elevation of anaerobic threshold
   - improvement in economy or efficiency

Like the previous zone, this type of training takes place during the preparation phase of training and also induces similar adaptations to those noted above for level 2 and 3 training.

5. *Heart Rate Zone 5.* It is difficult to understand how training at large volumes below planned race pace can possibly prepare you for endurance racing (zones 5-6), unless you are a marathoner or long distance triathlete who generally race at intensive endurance pace. It is therefore crucial for most endurance athletes to undertake some training at anaerobic threshold (85-90% of MHR). This type of training aims to expose the body to sustained exercise corresponding to the endurance athlete's highest current steady state pace. In general, this intensity can be described as the "hurt but hold" intensity. The adaptations that take place with this type of training are:
   - elevation of $VO_2max$
   - raising of the anaerobic threshold
   - increased removal of lactic acid
   - decreased production of lactic acid
   - increased tolerance of the pain of lactic acid being in the muscles
   - specific nervous system patterning of the muscle fibers needed during racing.

The intensity of training is elevated to 85-90% of maximum heart rate and can be done through continuous work of at least 20 minutes duration but no longer than 60-90 minutes (5-20k runs; 20-60k rides; 1500m swims) because after this time our muscles will run out of energy in the form of carbohydrate. Another form of zone 5 training is interval training with short recoveries that are half or less of the work time (10-15 x 100m swims; 15-20 x 1k cycles; 8-10 x 400m runs) (Figure 6.2 overleaf).

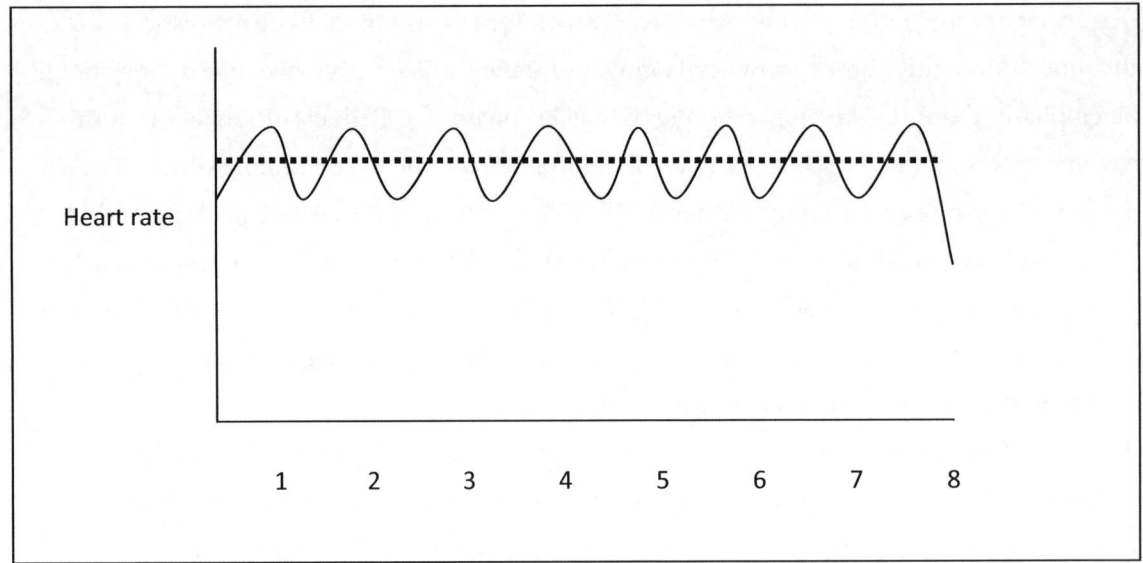

*Figure 6.2:* An example of heart rates during work and rest intervals when performing anaerobic threshold (zone 5) interval training.

It is important with anaerobic threshold training intervals that the quality of the last interval should be as good as the quality of the first interval and the recovery relatively short compared to the interval duration. This type of training should be performed at the most twice per week, should be preceded by a good warm-up, followed by a good warm-down, and generally be preceded and followed by an easier (zones 1 / 2) day so that the quality of the workout can be high.

During anaerobic threshold training periods, recovery is critical and base-training intensities (zones 1-4) should not be forgotten. Recovery can also be enhanced by eating or drinking carbohydrate-rich foods since both levels 5 and 6 training mainly use muscle and liver carbohydrate as their energy source and supplies will be depleted after such training. The carbohydrates should have a high glycemic index (see Chapter 16) and be consumed ideally within the first 30 minutes after training but critically within the two hours after training.

To highlight the importance of zone 5 training and interval training for the aging endurance athlete, a section of this chapter is devoted to interval training for improvements in the anaerobic threshold.

6. *Heart Rate Zone 6* or maximum aerobic training employs intervals with speeds that are greater than planned race pace but with long recoveries. The overall training volume during such a session is reduced, but the intensity is lifted, during this final pre-competition phase that lasts 4-6 weeks (see section on Periodisation later in this chapter). Again, recovery (zones 1-2) training the days before and after these sessions is critical. Heart rate zones 2-5 training intensities should not be forgotten during this training phase. Examples of this type of zone 6 training are 3-8 minute (300-400m swims; 5k reps on the bike; 1k reps on the run track) repeats with 3-6 minute active (easy swim, spinning or jog) recoveries. Intensity is 90-100% of maximum heart rate for each interval but recovery intensity is down to 60-70% of maximum heart rate. Athletes should be

well warmed up and build into the first ten seconds of each interval. Repetitions depend on individual tolerances but 4-10 reps would be suggested depending on the individual athlete, their training age (years of training), fitness level, predisposition to injury, and whether you swim, bike or run which have an increasing "tear-down" factor. At the most, two sessions of zone 6 per week should be used with easy recovery work in between. Adaptations that take place with this type of training include:
- increased tolerance to lactic acid
- elevated VO$_2$max
- improved endurance speed.

7. **Speed** training for the aging athlete is far more important than it is for the younger endurance athlete for a number of reasons. First, aging athletes tend to train with decreased intensities, suggesting that the fast twitch b fibers (the pure speed fibers found in large amounts in sprinters) are not activated at any time. If they are not activated, they decrease in size and possibly number – use it or lose it – and lead to decreased muscle size, thus muscle strength, and thus speed and power. Secondly, aging muscles that are used to contracting slowly as a result of slow training over longer distances, forget to turn over fast when in a race. Speed work (e.g. 3-20 second all out-efforts with long recoveries) done in short bursts once to twice a week depending on the training phase, can help the aging muscle and nerves to fire quickly. Thus, when faced with racing at a slower than sprint pace, the muscle scan cope. Two or more days of recovery at low intensity zones are needed to recover from these sessions as muscle damage is likely. Measuring heart rates during or at the end of all-out sprint work. However, they may be useful to see when you are recovered enough to sprint again.

For the aging endurance athlete, the vast majority of training should be in zones 2-4 with spikes of zones 5-7 depending upon the training phase.

## Measuring intensity in endurance training

Having discussed the importance of knowing the seven different zones for endurance development, let us now turn our attention to ways we can measure intensity in endurance sports. Apart from measuring heart rate, there are a number of ways we can measure intensity. Some require equipment, some considerable skill and experience, and other methods requiring basic skills and knowledge.

1. **Pace.** When I first became involved seriously with running in the early 70s, pace was everything. Four-, five-, six- or seven-minute mile pace were the gold standards used. These days we use time/400m run or time/100m swim and base these off goal 10k run or 1500m swim pace or current best 5000m run or 1500m swim times. The problem is that the feedback doesn't come until you've finished the distance and looked at the time. In cycling the feedback can be instant if you have a bike computer but is affected by wind direction, hills, or where you are in the bunch. However, for the experienced

aging endurance athlete, pace is great for swim and run workouts and tables are found in the endurance literature to help you. I personally use tables found in Joe Friel's excellent triathlon training book called *The Triathletes Training Bible* (www.velogear.com). The pacing method takes experience, a strong awareness of your body and how it feels in the various heart rate training zones, and a wristwatch, bike computer or pace clock.

2. ***Rating of Perceived Exertion (RPE).*** The experienced aging athlete has a well-developed ability to know how hard they are exercising based on things such as breathing rate and depth, sweat rate, muscle sensations, and overall body sensations. This perceived exertion requires no equipment just a sense of body awareness. Two scales exist for the RPE scale that is sometimes called the *Borg Scale* after the person that developed it. The original 6-20 scale was developed to represent 60-200 heart beats per minute in younger university students. However, aging people can still use it although a newer 1-10 scale has been developed. 6 on the old scale (1on the new scale) represents rest while 20 (10 on the new scale) represents very, very hard intensity.

The RPE scale is commonly used for novice or recreational athletes, aging people getting into exercise for the first time, or people rehabilitating from a medical condition.

*Table 6.3:* Rating of Perceived Exertion (RPE): A subjective method of monitoring intensity or pain levels.

| OLD 6-20 SCALE | | | NEW 1-10 SCALE | | |
|---|---|---|---|---|---|
| Rating | Description | HR Zone | Rating | Description | HR Zone |
| 6 | No exertion | 1 | 1 | Very, very light | 1 |
| 7 | Extremely light | 1 | 2 | Very light | 1 |
| 8 | | 1 | 3 | Fairly light | 2 |
| 9 | Very light | 2 | 4 | Light | 3 |
| 10 | | 2 | 5 | Somewhat hard | 3 |
| 11 | Light | 3 | 6 | Moderately hard | 4 |
| 12 | | 3 | 7 | Hard | 5 |
| 13 | Somewhat hard | 4 | 8 | Very hard | 6 |
| 14 | | 4 | 9 | Very, very hard | 6 |
| 15 | Hard | 5 | 10 | Extremely hard | 7 |
| 16 | | 5 | | | |
| 17 | Very hard | 6 | | | |
| 18 | | 6 | | | |
| 19 | Extremely hard | 6 | | | |
| 20 | Maximal exertion | 7 | | | |

3. ***Power.*** Sport scientists use measures of power when prescribing from or describing test results. We generally talk in terms of units called *watts* but to use this measure, you need

access to expensive gear such as a *RacerMate Computrainer*, *SRM* crank set, or one of the new *Polar* products, all of which enable a cyclist to use power as the measure of intensity. However, these devices are expensive, require a knowledge of basic sport science and are generally out of the reach of most aging athletes.

## Methods for determination of anaerobic threshold (AnT)

As you may have gathered from the above discussion, anaerobic threshold (AnT) training is critical for strong performances in endurance events. There are a number of methods commonly used to determine this important training zone for endurance athletes of any age. They include:

1. *AnT as a percentage of maximum heart rate.* The easiest way to determine anaerobic threshold is to work at 85-90% of your maximum heart rate. This obviously requires us to determine our own maximum heart rate since using the equation 220-age is fraught with errors when used with athletes. If you are a triathlete, you will need to know your maximum heart rate for swim, bike and run; they are *usually* different with running generally the highest, cycling approximately 10 beats per minute lower, and swimming the lowest at 10-20 beats lower than running (Table 6.4).

*Table 6.4:* Training heart rates for a 50 year old triathlete when swimming (MHR 155 bpm), cycling (160 bpm) and running (170 bpm).

| Heart rate zone | Swimming | Cycling | Running |
|---|---|---|---|
| Recovery | < 100 | < 104 | < 110 |
| Aerobic | 100-116 | 104-120 | 110-128 |
| Extensive endurance | 116-124 | 120-128 | 128-136 |
| Intensive endurance | 124-132 | 128-136 | 136-145 |
| Anaerobic threshold | 132-140 | 136-144 | 145-153 |
| Maximum aerobic | > 140 | > 144 | > 153 |

My extensive experience in lactate curve testing (see below) many young and masters endurance athletes tells me that novice or unfit athletes of any age are usually at the 85% end of the range and fitter more experienced athletes at the 90% or even up to 92% of maximum heart rate range for high performance endurance athletes.

2. *A lactate curve* is usually done in a sports science laboratory under the supervision of an exercise physiologist and/or doctor. This test involves working progressively harder (running or swimming faster, pushing bigger gears, increasing time per 500m on a rowing ergometer) every 3-5 minutes while blood is taken and heart rates recorded. Lactate is produced in relatively large amounts when the muscles begin working anaerobically (in the absence of enough oxygen). Once produced in the muscles, the lactate moves into the blood where it is removed via the heart, liver, and other muscles. When the concentration of lactate rises dramatically in the blood, scientists have suggested the

athlete is at anaerobic threshold (Figure 6.3).

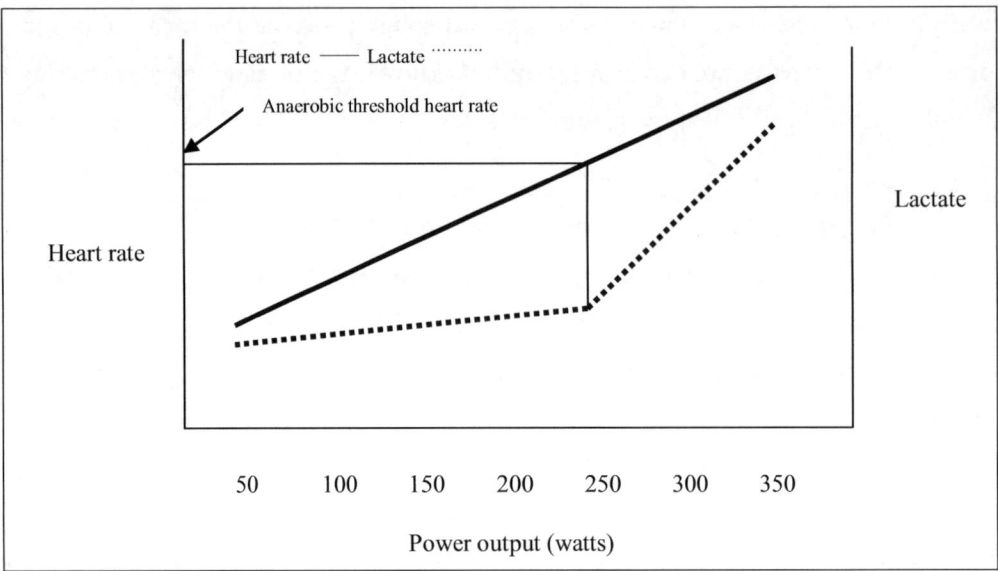

*Figure 6.3:* Blood lactate responses of a masters rower to increased exercise intensity (watts) on a rowing ergometer.

Because we know the running speed, gearing, or (wattage) time per 500m at which lactate began to rise, we can determine the heart rate at which anaerobic threshold occurred. While it is the most valid method for threshold determination, it generally requires sports scientists and quite expensive equipment.

3. ***The Conconi method*** for anaerobic threshold determination was developed by an Italian sports scientist named Conconi who worked with former world one-hour cycling champion, Francesco Moser. The principle of this test is that work rate (speed, power) is increased every 30-60 seconds and heart rate recorded at the end of each period using a heart rate monitor. You then plot a graph of speed against heart rate (Figure 6.4).

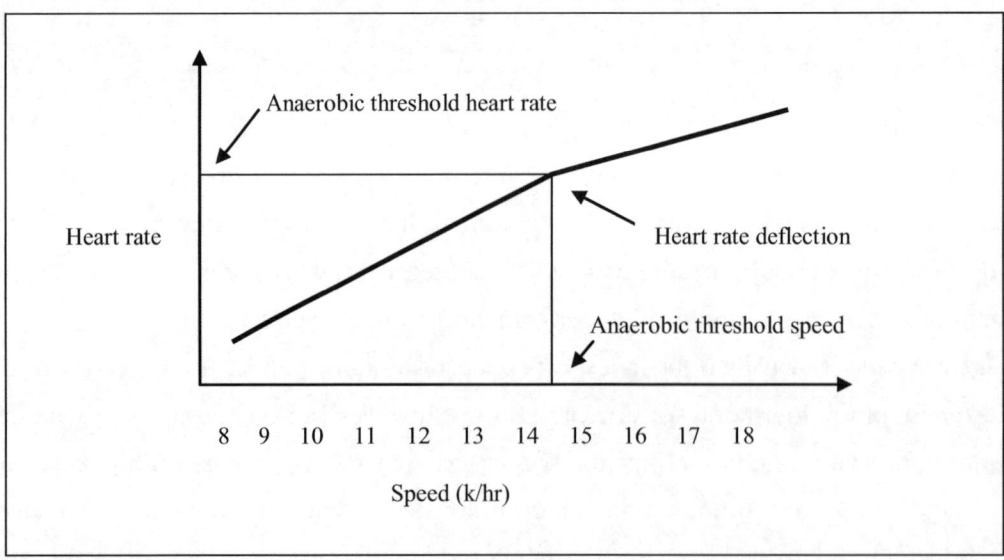

*Figure 6.4:* Diagram of the velocity of heart rate deflection (Vd) and associated anaerobic threshold heart rate and speed determined using the Conconi method.

Conconi believes that heart rate increases in a straight line until a particular speed (anaerobic threshold) at which the line curves downwards. My experience with this method is that it works with some athletes but not with most. However, the beauty of the test is its simplicity; all you need is a heart rate monitor and a pen and paper. You can also look at an online calculator at: http://www.brianmac.co.uk/coni.htm for more details on the Conconi test.

4. *Time trial.* This should be done over at least 30-40 minutes on an uninterrupted course (pool early on a Saturday morning, windtrainer, rowing ergometer, or run track) and at a steady state pace with no sprint at the end. The aim is to self-select a pace you can maintain continuously for the time trial with no sprints or change in pace. The heart rate and average speed is going to be very close to your anaerobic threshold. Again, the beauty of this test is its simplicity. However, my experience is that this test is most useful for experienced aging athletes who know how to hold pace well.

One of my past postgraduates undertook a study on 14 young, high performance cyclists. We were investigating whether high performance athletes could self-select anaerobic threshold. On two occasions, the cyclists were tested. During the first test they did 10 x 4 minute increases in work on a windtrainer and we took blood out of their earlobes in order to do a lactate curve as described above. We determined the anaerobic threshold at 285 watts of power using the lactate curve method. On the second occasion, we asked the cyclists to ride at the highest but most consistent power output (watts) they could hold for 40 minutes. The cyclists self-selected 287 watts - so close to what the blood lactate curve showed anaerobic threshold to be that the difference is negligible. We concluded that *high-performance athletes* appear to be able to self-select threshold during a 40-minute time trial.

Once determined, the AnT heart rate, like all training heart rates, will be subject to increases due to dehydration and training in hot and humid conditions. The smart coach and athlete must teach or learn what this "feeling" of AnT is like and listen to the body rather than becoming a slave to a heart rate monitor. I cannot emphasise enough how AnT training, when used in a planned and periodised endurance training program, will improve endurance performance.

**The importance of anaerobic threshold interval training for aging endurance athletes**

I'm getting older but refuse to believe I have to get slower. However, I have to face the facts - the 10km run time isn't what it used to be and the 40k bike time trial and 400m swim times are dropping. Sure, as a sports scientist I'm aware my ability to pump blood and oxygen is reduced and I'm losing strength - both of which will contribute to reduced endurance speed. However, as a sports scientist I also am aware there is something I can do to try and hold my endurance speed - interval training.

The few studies that have examined training habits of older athletes have shown that the older we become, the more we do mileage and the less we focus on intensity or how hard we train. Maybe this is due to us losing a little motivation, having family and career commitments, not being interested in hurting any more, or we're just training for enjoyment and health rather than performance. Unfortunately, training slower means racing slower. To race fast we must train fast. Research that has examined training practices of endurance athletes has conclusively shown that improvements in endurance performance are directly related to the intensity of training.

From a physiological standpoint, muscles are made up of small fibers. These muscle fibers are basically of three types - slow twitch, fast twitch a, and fast twitch b. The *slow twitch fibers* are endurance fibers - they contract relatively slowly, are great at using oxygen for energy production and are fatigue resistant. The *fast twitch a fibers* are speed fibers but are also quite fatigue resistant. In contrast, the *fast twitch b fibers* are also speed fibers but fatigue very quickly. Thus, research has shown that sprinters of all ages have high percentages of fast twitch fibers with predominantly fast twitch b fibers. In contrast, older endurance athletes have a high percentage of slow twitch fibers. Genetics primarily determines the percentage of these fibers we are born with so blame mum and dad if you're not fast or don't have endurance. Research also suggests we cannot turn the slow twitch fibers into fast twitch fibers but we can train the fast twitch fibers to move between b and a or a and b, depending on what type of training we do. Sprint training will hold the b fibers as sprint fibers. The right type of training, anaerobic threshold interval training, can help the aging endurance athlete turn those fast twitch b fibers into the more fatigue resistant fast twitch a fibers, thus improving endurance performance.

So why are we discussing muscle structure? Well the important point is that when we train slowly, we only train the slow twitch fibers and therefore will have good fatigue resistance. This is obviously important for *Ironman* triathletes, road cyclists, marathon runners and marathon swimmers, but what about the shorter endurance events. The faster we train, the more fast twitch fibers we use to generate force and speed (see Figure 6.5).

The important point is that if we train hard enough to use the fast twitch b fibers that fatigue easily, we can convert them into fast twitch a fibers that give us speed but are resistant to fatigue - just what we need for endurance speed. However, if we do speed training too hard or too long using the fast twitch b fibers, we will produce lactic acid which leads to fatigue during training. The answer is therefore to train a particular way that uses those fast twitch b fibers but does not produce high levels of lactic acid that will slow us down. That is, interval training – harder efforts with easy or rest recovery.

*The keys to endurance interval training*

While endurance interval training can be used in a wide variety of ways, interval training to improve speed for endurance events should consist of relatively short (e.g. 30-90 second intervals with short rests - half or less of the interval time). Examples of intervals in a variety of sports are shown in Table 6.5 opposite:

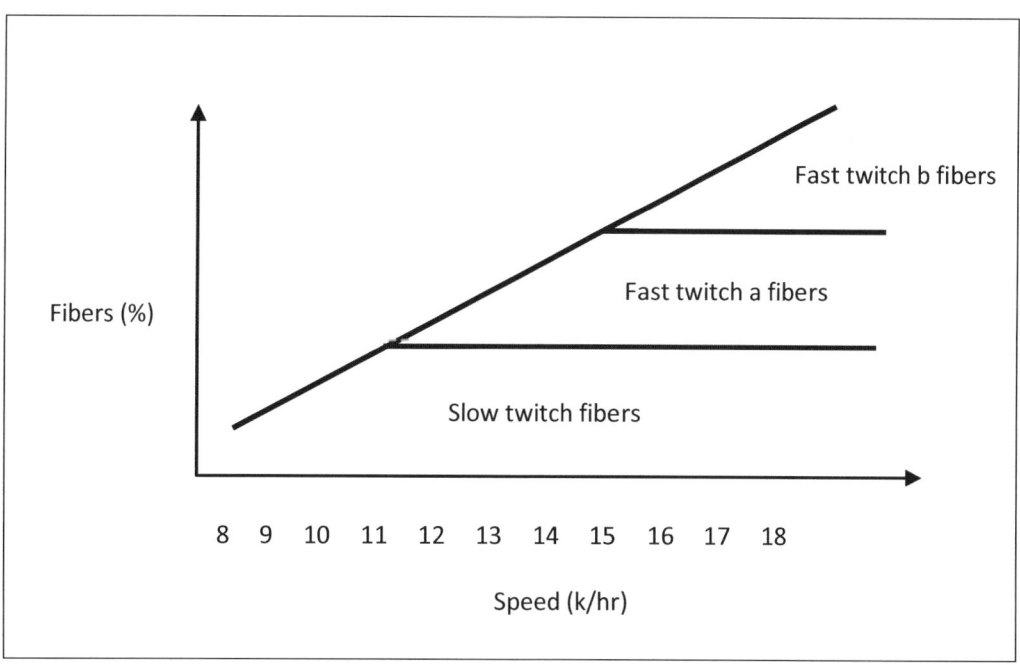

*Figure 6.5:* As intensity of exercise increases, more fibers are recruited for use in a graduated manner.

*Table 6.5:* Examples of swim, bike and run interval training sessions for older athletes. (MHR = maximum heart rate).

| Variable | Swim | Bike | Run |
|---|---|---|---|
| Set | 10 x 100m | 15 x 1k | 8 x 400m |
| Time | 90 sec | 90 sec | 100 sec |
| Rest | 30 sec | 30 sec | 40 sec |
| Intensity (% MHR) | 85-90% | 85-90% | 85-90% |

The key to anaerobic threshold interval training is that the quality of the last interval is as good as the first. If we go too hard in the first interval, we'll have to recover for longer than we should, or the speed of the rest of the intervals won't be as good. I see too many athletes (young and old) who either go too hard too early (generally the young bucks!) or take too long a rest. The key is to have fluctuations of 10-20 beats above and below this 85-90% of maximum heart rate during the interval and recovery, respectively, as shown in Figure 6.2 earlier in this chapter.

### A word of caution

For aging endurance athletes, interval training is the answer to improving your speed over longer distances. In the aging endurance athlete, this type of training becomes very important because muscle biopsy studies have shown that as we age we lose both the size and number of these all-important fast twitch fibers we need for speed. I'd suggest the reason is that these fibers are rarely stimulated due to aging athletes training with less intensity.

Although not scientifically proven, interval training may go a long way to preventing this decline in fast twitch fiber size by stimulating them regularly. However, a word of caution! Interval training is hard work. It should be done when we are fresh, after we have developed a good aerobic base of easier work, after a good warm-up, be followed by a warm-down and stretching, and be followed the next day by recovery training such as an easy 20-30 min of training at the recovery or aerobic levels shown in Table 6.2 earlier in this chapter. I would also suggest that only two sessions per week of this type of work be done, especially in runners. It can lead to injuries and visits to physiotherapists for athletes that do too much of it, have poor technique, or have not built their training program progressively to the point where they can cope with this type of training.

## Developing the endurance capacities

Whether we're running 10k on the road, swimming 1500m in a lake or pool, rowing or paddling 90k down a river, or riding a 40k time trial, we need endurance. So what does it take to race well at endurance events? Apart from relying on mum and dad to have given us the right genes (hopefully Levi 501's), we need three qualities - a high aerobic capacity or VO$_2$max, a high anaerobic threshold, and great economy or efficiency of movement. Even if our folks didn't give us the right Levi's, we can do something about these other three qualities - with the right training! Below are suggested training strategies to develop the capacities required for successful endurance performance in masters athletes.

### 1. Aerobic capacity or VO$_2$max

This is the maximum volume of oxygen that can be transported to, and used by, the working tissues. Obviously, the higher the aerobic capacity, the more oxygen we can use compared to our opponents. Elite runners have had figures for VO$_2$max of around 70-80 ml/kg/min with older runners would have figures of 35-55 ml/kg/min with women (generally) having 10% lower figures than men.

*Training to increase VO$_2$max*

Aerobic capacity is theoretically able to be increased by about 25% if we start from scratch with no fitness at all. However, for most endurance athletes who are reasonably fit most of the time, we might be able to increase it by 10%.

Elevating VO$_2$max can be done in three ways:

a. *Reducing body (fat) weight.* Reducing body fat means we've got less body weight to carry through a race, meaning more oxygen is available to the working muscles. In Table 6.1 you will notice that the units are expressed in milliliters of oxygen *per kilogram* (of body weight) per minute (ml/kg/min), so the lower the body weight, the higher the figure.

b. *Increasing distance covered per session or week.* <u>Gradually</u> increasing how far or often we train will also elevate our aerobic capacity. If we are an "ultra-beast" such as the across-America masochists or Triple-Ironman animals, then just covering greater and greater distances at a low intensity is what it's about. However, most of us mere mortals cover less distance in hopefully less time. Progressively increasing distances allows our heart to develop its ability to pump more blood, the muscles to develop more capillaries, and more fuels (carbohydrate and fat) to be stored and used more efficiently by our muscles.

The 30-minute plus workouts, three times a week in heart rate zones 2-4 (65-85% of maximum heart rate) are what we need initially. However, we need to gradually increase either the number of sessions per week or how far we go per workout to keep elevating VO$_2$max. Of course, the added benefit, on the assumption we hold diet constant, is that we burn up fat and lose weight.

c. *Increasing training intensity.* There will come a point at which regular, long, easy workouts will not benefit VO$_2$max. This is when it's time to elevate intensity by training at the higher heart rates for shorter distances that gradually become longer. So if our regular swims, ride, runs, rows were 30-40 minutes at 65-85% of maximum heart rate, once a week we might start to go 20 minutes at 85-90% maximum heart rate. As intensity lifts, distances drop. This prevents overtraining and tiredness, enabling the astute aging athlete to be fresh for those quality workouts. As we progressively increase intensity through anaerobic threshold training, there will come a time, generally 6-10 weeks out from race day, where we need to just top up our VO$_2$max. This is done with 3-8 minute intervals at 90% plus maximum heart rate and long (2-4 minutes), easy (60-70% MHR) recoveries. Depending on what sport we are doing (runners less than swimmers or cyclists), our state of heart health, and our experience, for the aging endurance athlete I'd suggest only 4-8 of these "gutbusters" in a session and at the most twice in a hard week. These are damn hard work and require commitment and mental toughness. Be fresh when you do them and have a recovery session the next day.

## 2. Anaerobic threshold (AnT)

The second and most important capacity for an endurance athlete is AnT. While numerous ways exist to determine this intensity or heart rate, the higher your anaerobic threshold relative to your VO$_2$max, the better you'll race. Generally anaerobic threshold occurs at 85-90% of MHR with my experience from lab tests telling me the better and fitter the athlete, the closer to 90% it is. Put simply, this pace or heart rate is one where you can "hurt but hold" for 30 minutes or so - about race pace or just under.

*Training to increase anaerobic threshold*

Research has shown that both interval training and medium-long continuous sessions at 85-90% MHR elevate both anaerobic threshold and VO$_2$max. As shown in Figure 6.2, anaerobic threshold intervals should have the heart rate elevating 5-10 beats above the anaerobic threshold heart rate (approx 85-90% maximum heart rate) during the interval and recovering to 10-20 beats below during recovery. Intervals are a nice way to be introduced to threshold training because you get recoveries and can control the number you do. Examples of anaerobic threshold intervals are shown in Table 6.6 earlier in this chapter.

The training principle of specificity says you should train the way you want to race and that generally means continuous workouts for endurance athletes. Continuous anaerobic threshold workouts should be 15 minutes plus in length and intensity held at that "hurt but hold" pace. Theoretically, there is not enough carbohydrate in the muscles and liver to go longer than 60-90 minutes or so at this pace, unless we are really fit or use sports drinks or gels to keep up our carbohydrate energy supply.

Whether you chose intervals or continuous anaerobic threshold workouts, be careful. These workouts are hard. At the most once a week is suggested for most recreational aging endurance athletes with two-three per fortnight for the aging athlete with years of training behind them. Again, be fresh for anaerobic threshold work, be well warmed-up and focus on warming-down, stretching, and using recovery techniques (massage, spas, hot/cold showers, high glycemic index foods) after the workout (see the recovery chapter). This type of training should be done after the $VO_2$max has been developed.

### 3. Economy

Assuming we have developed a high $VO_2$max and an elevated anaerobic threshold which both give our racing muscles plenty of oxygen, we now need to use that increased available oxygen efficiently. Most of us are about 20-25% efficient with more experienced athletes with great technique, at the lower end of this range. That is, of the available oxygen burned to create energy, only a quarter is used to race - the rest is lost as heat!

*Training to improve economy*

Improving economy means reducing all the factors that use oxygen but don't generate speed as well as training at goal race pace. That is, ensure that our technique is close to perfect. Swimmers need to body roll, recover with relaxed arms, and streamline their bodies through the water. Runners and cyclists need to be relaxed in the upper body and have strong lower back and abdominal muscles to enable the pistons (legs) to work off that solid base. Rowers need to be relaxed during the recovery phase and time the catch, drive and release in the correct sequence.

Drills, coaching, and concentration on correct form during training and racing enable us to develop economy. For older athletes, don't believe that old dogs can't learn new tricks. It might take longer, but it can be done. Training at goal race pace can also develop economy. For example, if a 10k run wants to be completed in 40 minutes, then a training set of 400 or 800m runs should be completed at four-minute kilometer pace as you approach the major event you are training for.

### Pacing the race

How often do you see youngsters or inexperienced aging athletes at the start of a triathlon, open water swim, or particularly fun run, go out hard then die? What is the best pacing strategy? Go hard and try and hold on, even split or build the race? Very little has been written on the area of pacing so let's try and take a scientific look at the concept and see if we can come up with some answers.

*The physiology of pacing*

Going out too hard at the start of an endurance race leads to a rapid accumulation of lactic acid that has three negative consequences for racing:

- It stops muscles contracting properly thus slowing us down
- It slows down the breakdown of carbohydrate and thus energy supply
- It hurts which encourages us to slow down

If the lactic acid is produced in high concentrations at the start of an event, the lactic acid will take longer to remove, even when we slow down. Putting this theory into practice would suggest that aging endurance athletes that head out too hard, "die" later in the race.

Going out slower in the earlier parts of a race reduces the amount of lactic acid produced and prevents the negative outcomes above from slowing us down. A slower start also allows the heart, lungs and blood vessels to get moving and deliver that all-important oxygen. The more oxygen available to the working muscles, the less lactic acid produced. This allows the middle and latter stages of the race to be done at a faster rate without any of the negative consequences outlined above.

Another trick of the trade is to be as warmed up as possible just before the start of the event so that the heart rate and delivery of oxygen to the muscles is optimal before the gun goes. This means that the muscles are already aerobic so they will not produce as much lactic acid, thus enabling us to go harder.

*The research on pacing*

Studies have compared the three possible pacing methods - even-pacing, fast-slow and slow-fast (negative splitting) pacing. The research has shown that fast-slow pacing that the inexperienced youngsters use is the least effective method of racing. However, the research is relatively inconclusive as to whether even-paced or slow-fast pacing is the best way to go. One study looked at three strategies to run 1245 meters as fast as possible. The first run was started at 13.9 mph and that pace was held till the end - a time of 3min 20secs. The second run was done starting at 13.5 mph and running at 14.9 mph till the finish - the result the same 3 min 20 sec time for the 1245 meter run. This run produced the least lactic acid and the lowest oxygen consumption. The third run was a disaster for the runners. They ran at 14.9 mph at the start and came home at 13.5 mph, the head out hard and die method!! Performances plummeted and both lactic levels and oxygen consumption skyrocketed. In 1993, a study from Wisconsin, USA, studied nine-well trained cyclists and came up with strong support for the slow-fast method of pacing in a 2km time -trial. The first kilometer was covered at 56, 53, 51, 50 and 48% of their best 2km times. The final kilometre was to be completed as fast as possible. The moderately slow 51% method produced the best performance times and fastest second km. None of the nine cyclists performed well with the fast (48%) starting km.

*What the elite use*

Years of watching elite swimmers and runners have also revealed that most use the even or slow-fast slow pacing methods. While there are always exceptions in elite sport (e.g. Perkins in the 1500 free or Peter Robinson in Triathlons), the fast-slow method has seldom proved successful in endurance sport. In support of the even-paced and slow-fast methods we can learn a lot by looking at runners like Daniel Komen (held the world record for 5km run - 12:39) or Paul Tergat (held the world record for 10km run - 26:27). Komen ran the following 1km splits in his world-record run - 2:32, 2:32, 2:31, 2:31 and 2:31 (slow bugger eh!). Tergat, on the other hand, used the slow - fast method of pacing in his world record 10km run. He ran 13:17 for the first 5km then came home in 13:10 for the final 5K.

*How to prevent dying in a race?*

Obviously a strong aerobic base, high aerobic capacity, anaerobic threshold and economical technique are crucial and come with training. However, four strategies are crucial when preparing for and actually racing.

1. When preparing for racing, ensure you do *goal pace training* leading into the major event. That is, doing repeats in the pool, on the track, road or river that are at the pace you want to race at.
2. At race start, warm-up well before the race. An effective warm-up should include moderate pace work, small amounts of above race-pace work and race-pace work. I see far too many endurance athletes cruising in warm-up or not warming up at all and wondering why they perform poorly when the gun goes.
3. If you are a triathlete or duathlete, practice your transitions from swim to bike and bike to run. This type of training will teach the blood vessels in the required muscles to open up more quickly and teach the nervous system to get used to a new action.
4. Finally, take the advice from the research outlined above, even-pace or negative split an endurance race. Give those muscles a chance to get the blood and oxygen in so they don't produce that acid that slows us down and makes us hurt.

## Concurrent Sprint, Strength and Endurance Training

Most team sports such as the footballs, hockey, netball and basketball require the development of different physical capacities for optimal performance. For example, the physical capacity of speed is required to 'beat' opponents, strength for body collisions and physical contacts and endurance capacity to allow the player to recover and repeat sprint efforts. For athletes to perform at their best, speed, strength and endurance need to be developed to optimal levels. However, often development of one of these components can inhibit the development of another. Therefore, the coach and athlete need to find 'middle ground' where training is periodised so that each physical component can be optimally developed.

The purpose of this section is to present a summary of the available research on concurrent training and suggest the practical implications from this research on how a coach or athlete might maximize team sport fitness.

*Research Findings*

The training adaptations to endurance training has been well described and include increases in the chemicals that produce aerobic energy, increased density of the small blood vessels that deliver blood and thus oxygen and nutrients, and increased VO$_2$max, with the result being an increased capacity to perform prolonged exercise with little or no increase in strength. Conversely, most studies have shown that strength training either does not change VO$_2$max or has little positive effect. Moreover, strength training has been shown to increase force production through increasing muscle size and increase the concentration of chemicals that produce anaerobic energy. While a small number of studies have suggested otherwise, the majority of research strongly suggests that doing strength and endurance training together has been found to reduce the development in strength with no effects on endurance performance.

Few studies have been published that have examined the combination of sprint and endurance training. While one of the limitations of many of these studies was the subjects used were college-based recreational athletes who may have overtrained, the study did show up some interesting results. In one study, three groups were studied over an eight-week training period. The first group was a sprint-group who trained three times per week and did two sets of sprints with each set consisting of 3x100m efforts (3 min break) and 3x50m efforts (90 seconds break) at 95% of maximum speed and a 5 minute break between sets. The second group was an endurance-group who also trained three times a week on alternate days and covered 30 minutes continuous aerobic work at or above 85% of age-predicted maximum heart rate. The third group combined sprint and endurance training six days per week alternating sprint and endurance training as above. The table below shows the results of the study.

*Table 6.6:* Effects of training on performance measures. Results are averages only and * denotes statistical differences from pre-training values.

| Measure | Sprint-Training | | Endurance-Training | | Concurrent Training | |
|---|---|---|---|---|---|---|
| | Before | After | Before | After | Before | After |
| 30 min run (meters) | 5890 | 5932 | 5465 | 6152 * | 6731 | 7397 * |
| Aerobic Power (ml·kg-1·min-1) | 55 | 54 | 50 | 53 * | 57 | 62 * |
| 50m sprint (seconds) | 6.94 | 6.77 * | 8.00 | 7.83 * | 7.04 | 6.87 * |
| 100m sprint (seconds) | 13.50 | 12.89 * | 15.97 | 15.56 * | 13.26 | 12.80 * |

The results strongly suggest, as we would expect, that improvements in performance are independent of combined performance of both sprint and endurance training. For team players, the results strongly suggest that a combination of both sprint and endurance training leads to not only good gains in speed, but importantly when having to recover between efforts, higher gains in aerobic capacity than endurance training alone. Importantly for coaches, the results also show that sprint training with long rest intervals does not increase aerobic power, but distance running may produce some improvement in sprint performance. The significant gains in sprint and endurance performance with combined sprint and endurance training may be due to increased strength, increased running (leg) speed through nervous system adaptations, and improved anaerobic capacity, all of which have previously been shown to enhance endurance performance.

From a practical point of view, these results suggest that physical training in highly aerobic team sports such as hockey, touch, soccer and rugby league, and depending on player position, rugby union and netball, should be placing a strong emphasis on endurance development through a combination of sprint and endurance training.

*Practical Implications*

Based on the above results plus knowledge of physiology and training theory, when an aging team sport athlete is faced with maximizing speed, endurance and strength, the following guidelines are suggested:

- Sprint training should either be done in the afternoon when athletes are warmer or at the commencement of a training session when the athletes are fresher.
- Strength training should be completed in the evening with at least 48 hours rest from the previous session on the particular muscle groups used.
- Endurance training should be periodised so that the time between endurance training sessions and strength or speed sessions are maximum to allow appropriate recovery / regeneration between sessions.

Understanding these points, the proposed weekly training plans (Tables 6.7 and 6.8) may be appropriate for a periodised weekly plan for an aging team sport player completing speed, strength and endurance training.

*Table 6.7:* A sample model of periodised weekly training plan for a highly motivated and/or competitive aging team sport player completing speed, strength and endurance training concurrently.

|    | Mon | Tues | Wed | Thurs | Fri | Sat | Sun |
|----|-----|------|-----|-------|-----|-----|-----|
| AM | Endurance | Rest | Endurance | Rest | Endurance | Rest | Rest |
| PM | Strength | Flexibility/Speed/Skill | Strength | Flexibility/Speed/Skill | Strength | Endurance or Flexibility & Speed | Rest |

*Table 6.8:* A sample model of periodised weekly training plan for a recreational aging team sport player completing speed, strength and endurance training concurrently.

|    | Mon | Tues | Wed | Thurs | Fri | Sat | Sun |
|----|-----|------|-----|-------|-----|-----|-----|
| AM | Rest | Rest | Endurance | Rest | Rest | Rest | Rest |
| PM | Speed/ Skill/ Endurance | Flexibility/ Strength | Rest | Flexibility / Strength | Speed/ Skill/ Endurance | Game | Rest |

### Periodisation of endurance training

Now that we have examined the different endurance training intensities and methods of developing endurance capacity, we need to make decisions on how we put these training intensities together - the concept of *PERIODISATION* that will be discussed in detail in a later chapter.

The art of training correctly is putting these training intensities together during a week (microcycle), 3-4 week block (mesocycle) or 12-14 week block (macrocycle) to maximize training time and prevent overtraining. Hard, medium, and easy days, weeks or three to four-week blocks are manipulated to stress the body at times and then to allow the body to adapt to that stress. Below we will give some specific examples on how we might periodise the training periods for endurance athletes.

A microcycle of a week might consist of six training sessions with a day off but with two periods of easy, medium, hard days. During the base development or *general preparation phase* where we are getting the "miles in the legs" or "kilometers into the arms", the terms easy, medium and hard might be distances covered getting longer or heart rate zones 2-4 being manipulated and distances held constant. During the *specific preparation* or mid-season phase, the same easy, medium, hard schedule might be in place, but hard might be zones 5-6, medium level 3-4, and easy level 2.

A mesocycle for endurance might be a 3-4 week period where a hard week is followed by an easy week, then a medium week. Again assuming six sessions a week, a hard week mid-season might be 2 x HR zone 2-3, 1 x HR zone 4, 1 x HR zone 5, and 1 x HR zone 6 with an easy week being 1 x HR zone 6, 1 x HR zone 1, 3 x HR zone 2, 1 x HR zone 5. Remember the objective of each phase (developing VO$_2$max or AnT) but as a rule of thumb increase volume through early season phases, lift intensity and drop volume during mid-season, and do the same during the *competition* phase.

The endurance training year or season can be broken up into four main phases:
1. *Aerobic endurance base / foundation training* is performed during the non-competitive period of the training year and builds the aerobic base on which more intense training is built. HR zones 2-4 are emphasised with kilometers gradually built up. This phase may last up to 12-16 weeks depending on the time lag between the athlete's last competitive phase and their experience. For the aging endurance athlete, it is also the time to build muscle mass get strong with weight training under the guidance of

a strength specialist (see Strength Chapter). Late in this phase, the strength work in the gym should be converted to power and power endurance by lowering the weight, doing the exercises faster, and doing more repetitions.

2. *Specific endurance and aerobic endurance training* or mid-season training can last 6-8 weeks and is done by introducing HR zones 4-5 while maintaining the lower intensity HR zones. Recovery between HR zone 5 sessions is important so as to allow quality work to be done during those sessions. Volume (km) drops but intensity is lifted during this phase. Races should be entered and considered to be HR zone 5-6 training. Weight training should be maintained 2-3 times per fortnight – one for strength maintenance, and 1-2 sessions for power endurance development.

3. *Specific endurance training* is undertaken in the last 4-6 weeks where, although all other levels are maintained, HR zone 6 training is introduced to give endurance speed. Volumes are reduced as a result of the intensity being high. Injuries may occur during the transition and speed / power phases because intensities are so high. Listening to the body during these phases is essential and recovery methods (see Chapter 15) should be used extensively. Importantly, both anaerobic threshold and maximum aerobic power training are difficult and should only be undertaken by healthy aging athletes who have no cardiac risk factors, a training age of 2-3 years, are not prone to overuse injuries, and who have undertaken an extensive foundation phase. As a general rule, when doing quality work (HR zones 5-6), be fresh; quality counts! Again, power endurance and strength training should be maintained in the gym 1-2 times per 7-10 days.

4. *Tapering or peaking* is a highly individual matter but usually takes place during the last 7-10 days prior to major competition and involves a gradual or dramatic reduction in training volume (km). Frequency and intensity of training should be maintained. A recent study found that middle distance runners significantly improved their performance by sharply reducing their training volume while maintaining their training intensity seven days before a race. This taper method was superior to both a reduction in training intensity and total rest in the week prior to competition. It is generally accepted that the longer the athlete has been training, the longer the taper can be. However, if training duration has been short, then a "drop dead" taper of 2-3 days where volume is dropped dramatically might be recommended.

## Conclusion

A correctly planned endurance training program that emphasises a strong base followed by "hits" of higher quality anaerobic threshold and maximum aerobic intervals, will allow the healthy aging endurance athlete to optimize their genetic potential. However, because endurance training involves long and sometimes intense training, the training program needs to be periodised to allow for adequate recovery times both within a week and from week to week.

While the principles of training such as specificity, progressive overload and recovery discussed in Chapter 4 are important, the smart aging endurance athlete must obey the most important training principle of all - listen to your body!

# CHAPTER 7

# Strength and Power Training for the Masters Athlete

*Age is a myth. Guys in their seventies can be just as strong as younger guys if they work at it. I no longer have the boundaries I once did. In my early thirties, I thought I was at my peak, and that it would be impossible to improve in the forties. Well, I'm in my forties and improving and now I think that progress will be difficult but not impossible in my fifties.*

**Al Oerter**

*Don't worry about upgrading your equipment. Upgrade your body.*

**Anonymous**

## Introduction

This chapter is one of the most important in the book. Strength development for the aging athlete is essential due to an age-related decrease in muscle mass and strength observed in not only aging non-athletes but also masters athletes who have maintained hard training into older age. My own research suggests that this decrease in strength and muscle mass begins to occur at around 45-50 years but accelerates after age 65-70 years of age. Thus, the older the athlete, the more important strength training becomes.

Loss of muscle mass is one of the major factors affecting reduced performance in aging athletes. In aging non-athletes, research has shown that muscle mass decreases by nearly 50% between the ages of 20 and 90 years. This appears to occur in four stages.

1. Muscle size peaks between 16-19 years of age for females and 18-24 years for males.
2. Between 25 and 50 years there is a 5-10% decline in muscle size.
3. Between 50 and 65-70 years there is another 15% decline,
4. After 65-70 years there is another accelerated loss of a further 25%.

This decrease in muscle mass is due to a number of age-related factors including:
- Decreased muscle fibre size, particularly in the fast twitch muscle fibres.
- Decreased number of muscle fibres (less muscle per unit volume), especially the strength and power producing fast twitch fibre (at age 30, about 60% of muscle fibres are fast twitch, at age 80, it's about 30%).

These changes in muscle mass are even more marked in women. Apart from these changes, the reasons for the decline in muscle mass with age have been suggested to be due to impairment of the nerve-muscle junction function and a lack of activation of the fast twitch fibres with age through inactivity. Given that the fast twitch fibres are activated with speed, power and strength training, it makes sense that the aging athlete should be placing a strong emphasis on strength and power training as well as high intensity endurance and sprint training, all of which can activate the all important fast twitch fibres.

Taken together, the age-related decrease in muscle size and strength impacts all aspects of athletic performance in masters athlete, in particular events or sports that demand speed and power. In non athletes, research has shown that strength increases up to age 30 years, plateaus between 30 and 50 years, then decreases by about 30% between ages 50 and 70 years and then dramatically declines after 70 years of age. Indeed, research has shown that after the age of 74 years, 28% of men and 66% of women cannot lift objects weighing more than 4.5 kilograms. In world class masters weightlifters, strength and power also decrease but the decrease appears linear with increased age (Figure 7.1)

*Figure 7.1:* Male and female weightlifting records (combined 'clean and jerk' and 'snatch') for different age groups.

Importantly, a strong relationship has been observed between walking speed and strength in both aging men and women. Extending this finding to aging athletes, it would suggest that muscular strength and power (strength exerted quickly) are vitally important for the aging athlete to maintain or develop speed. However, even in elite masters weightlifters we see a decrease in muscle strength and power into older age (Figure 7.1).

Thus, weight training should be seen as vital for the older person, not only to remain independent into older age, but for health and sports performance reasons. Before we examine the specifics of developing a weight-training program, let's examine the benefits of strength training for the older person with particular focus on the aging athlete.

## Benefits of Strength Training

Numerous health and sports performance benefits arise as a result of an effective strength-training program in aging male and female athletes.

Increasingly, weight training is being used in older non-athletes because of its great health benefits that include:

- Increased strength increases independence into older age.
- Increases bone density thus helping prevent and treat osteoporosis.
- Normalises blood pressure in people with high blood pressure.
- Reduces resistance to insulin so helps control diabetes in type II diabetics.
- Decreases both total and abdominal fat that are linked to increased cardiovascular disease risk.
- Increases resting metabolic rate in older men so helps burn Calories or kilojoules at rest.
- Reduced falls risk.
- May reduce pain and improve function in people with knee osteoarthritis.
- Improves posture.
- As a form of exercise it reduces stress.

For masters athletes, the sports performance benefits include:

- Increased muscle mass so important for strength and power development in sport.
- Increased fast twitch fibre area for speed and power generation.
- Increased muscle strength for sports performance and daily living (e.g. lifting, carrying, climbing stairs).
- Increased muscle power for speed and power generation.
- More muscle to take up oxygen and improve endurance performance following endurance training.
- Stronger connective tissue (ligaments, tendons, cartilage) to increase joint stability and help prevent injury in sport.
- Increased bone density and thus bone strength helping to prevent injury and osteoporosis.
- Reduced risk of falls in older age.
- Increased daily energy expenditure and loss of body fat as a result of the increased muscle mass using up more Calories or kilojoules.
- Improved self-confidence and self-esteem in training and competition.

For aging female athletes who are more at risk of osteoporosis than aging males, there is the additional benefit to including strength training - enhanced bone remodelling to increase bone strength and reduce the risk of osteoporosis and falls in older age. While this is important in both aging men and women, it is especially important to post-menopausal aging female athletes since the decreased oestrogen hormone levels lead to decreased bone density.

Numerous studies have confirmed that strength training, as long as it overloads the aging muscle, can lead to huge gains in strength. For example, one study of 90+ year olds in a nursing home showed that 8 weeks of strength training lead to a 174% increase in strength. More recently, a Finnish study examined the effects of 6-months of twice-a-week weight training on strength and power in healthy middle-aged (39-40±3 years) men and women and older (67-72±3 years) men and women who had a history of recreational, low intensity physical activity including walking, jogging, cross-country skiing, aerobics or cycling. After the 6 months of strength and power training, the following changes were observed:

- Maximal leg strength values increased in all groups by between 21-35%.
- Leg power improved by between 21-32%.
- The electrical activity of the leg muscles significantly increased suggesting that nervous system changes occurred to enhance strength and power development.
- Fast twitch fibre area increased in all groups.
- Slow twitch fibre area increased in the older women.
- Muscle mass increased, particularly in the older women.

Thus, the results suggest that older people benefit greatly from weight training and the improvements in strength and power are due to both nervous system and muscle size changes. There is every reason to suggest that a similar weight training program that initially focuses on strength and later focuses on power, can lead to increases in the strength and power of aging male and female athletes.

## Definitions

1. ***Strength*** is the maximum force that can be generated by a muscle group with one maximum effort. Strength can be further divided into three areas:
   a. ***Absolute strength*** refers to the maximum force or weight that can be lifted once. It is generally measured as 1 RM (repetition maximum). Thus, an aging athlete's 1 RM for the squat exercise in a gym may be 100 kg.
   b. ***Relative strength*** refers to the 1 RM strength *relative to body weight*. Thus, if two aging athletes have a 1 RM squat of 100 kg but one is 100 kg and another 75 kg in weight, the 75 kg athlete has much greater relative strength and theoretically should perform better.
   c. ***Strength endurance*** or muscular endurance is the ability to sustain a high level of muscular force for a relatively long period under conditions of fatigue. Sports such as rowing demand strength endurance where 50% of 1RM may be required to be sustained for 4-6 minutes.
2. ***Power*** is the *rate* of applying force or strength. A powerful movement is one that involves speed. Most sporting events requiring speed, demand power. As with strength, the *power-weight ratio* is of major importance in sport. That is, if two athletes have the same power output but one is 25 kg lighter than the other, the lighter athlete has a far greater power-weight ratio. Most sports demand ***power endurance*** or the ability to sustain powerful contractions over a period of time. Sprint running, swimming and cycling are sports demanding power endurance.

## Determining 1 RM

The maximum amount of weight we can lift in one (not two) lift is called a 1 RM (Repetition Maximum). Similarly, 10 RM stands for the maximum weight we can lift 10 times – not 9 or 11. The importance of this is that when strength specialists develop weight-training programs, they use either of two terms in general to determine intensity or what load you lift or push or pull. First, they may use the RM method above. That is 3 RM or 12 RM. Secondly; they may use the percentage of 1 RM method. That is 50% 1 RM or 80% 1 RM.

Thus, determination of the 1 RM for every exercise is important to determine your exercise intensity when you do your weight training session. Here are the steps to safely determine your 1 RM:

1. Have some familiarisation sessions in the gym using a wide variety of exercises.
2. Select the exercise for 1 RM testing.
3. Warm-up with 10 repetitions of a light weight.
4. Rest
5. Do 5 repetitions with a medium weight
6. Taking 2-3 minutes between lifts, take 3-8 attempts to determine the heaviest lift you can do for that exercise.

Research has shown there is minimal risk in older healthy people determining a 1 RM. However, the research was conducted on people who had two key concerns covered:

1. Prior medical screening according to the procedures outlined in Chapter 2.
2. Supervision of the 1 RM testing by qualified staff.

It must be emphasised that a professionally run fitness centre or gym should insist on these two guidelines being met. If you are in doubt about your own health or ability to undertake maximal lifts to determine your 1 RM, ensure you see your family doctor for a medical clearance.

## Strength Training Methods

I cannot emphasise enough that these methods are based on both science and art and must be developed under the supervision of a trained strength specialist that you should find within your sport at a high performance level or at a gym that younger athletes from your sport go to. Talk to coaches and high-level younger athletes to see whom they recommend.

While this chapter will outline the basic principles of developing a program for your sport, event and individual needs, it is beyond the scope of this book to give specific details for every aging athlete in every sport or event. Get to that specialist and tell them I sent you!

There are many different ways to develop the different types of strength and power outlined above. These include:

1. *Hypertrophy Training.* This type of training develops muscle size. Given that one of the most dramatic declines that occurs after 50 years of age (and more so after 65-70 years of age) is a loss of muscle mass, this type of weight training becomes the most important. The weights are medium weights and the repetitions relatively high.

2. *Maximal Strength.* This type of training occurs after hypertrophy training and develops the ability of the increased muscle size to develop strength. The weights are heavy and the number of repetitions is low.

3. *Isometric Training.* This type of training involves pushing against an immovable object with the muscle contracting but not moving. For example, in rock climbers and racquet players who need to develop isometric strength in the forearms for gripping, squeezing a tennis ball is an example of isometric training. Given that most sports demand muscles move, this type of strength training has limited application in sport except when coming back from injury or in some specific sports and positions (e.g. Rugby front-row forward's neck strength). For aging athletes with blood pressure problems, isometric training should not be undertaken as it closes down blood vessels within muscles and increases blood pressure.

4. *Eccentric Training.* This type of training involves the muscle lengthening while it exerts force. Examples might be squats where the quadriceps at the front of the thighs is lengthening while the body is being lowered. This type if training is a must for athletes where running or sprinting is involved. It is also the type of muscle contraction that has been shown to lead to the most muscle damage and soreness so gradually introduce it into your program.

5. *Power Training.* This type of training should be done after developing strength as the greater the strength, the greater the power that can be developed after this type of training. It involves rapid movements of lighter weights and just a few repetitions. For sprinters in all sports, this type of training is a must. However, it should be done after hypertrophy and maximal strength work and must be done with correct technique as it can easily lead to injuries if poor form is used. Again, get professional help to ensure correct program development and correct technique.

6. *Power Endurance Training.* This type of training is what most sport is all about – contracting muscles fast to generate powerful contractions to get speed. It is certainly something I focus on for my triathlon training. It has helped my bike hill-climbing in particular. Like power training, correct form is essential. Because it is developing endurance, fairly light weights are used but repetitions are high and done fast to train the nervous system.

7. *Pliometrics.* This type of training is great for developing power. It involves lifting light weights or body weight with rapid movements such as hopping, jumping, bounding or leaping. It is obviously required for sports or events such as sprint running and jump events in athletics. Examples can be seen on the web at: http://exrx.net/Lists/PowerExercises.html

8. *Core Stability Training.* The body's core is the abdominals and lower back. If it is not strong and stable during sport, the legs are not pumping off a stable base, the upper body will move unnecessarily off line if the hips wobble. Lack of strength in this area is one of the commonest causes of lower back pain.

## Variables in a weight training program

In any weight training program there are a number of variables that must be considered. Let us examine each in turn.

*Table 7.1:* Sample exercise selection table.

| Muscle group | Exercise | Equipment |
|---|---|---|
| Chest | Bench press<br>Incline bench press<br>Dumbbell bench press<br>Dumbbell incline bench press | Barbell or machine<br>Barbell<br>Dumbbell<br>Dumbbell |
| Shoulders | Military press<br>Dumbbell shoulder press<br>Shoulder raises | Barbell or machine<br>Dumbbell<br>Dumbbell or barbell |
| Upper back | Lateral pulldown<br>Seated row<br>Chin-up or pull-up | High cable pulley<br>Low cable pulley<br>Chin-up bar |
| Triceps | Triceps press-down<br>Dips | High cable pulley<br>Dip station |
| Biceps | Arm curl | Barbell, dumbbell, low cable pulley |
| Quadriceps | Leg press<br>Squat<br>Leg extension | Machine<br>Barbell or machine<br>Machine |
| Hamstrings | Leg curl | Machine |
| Calves | Calf raise/leg press<br>Standing heel raise<br>Seated heel raise | Machine<br>Machine or barbell<br>Machine |
| Lower abdominals | Vertical leg raise<br>Supine leg raise | Vertical leg raise<br>Lying on floor |
| Upper abdominals | Crunch<br>Sit-up | Lying on floor |
| Lower back | Back extension | Machine |

1. *Exercise selection.* There are hundreds of exercise choices available. While Table 7.1 gives a selection of the most common exercises, more are available at the website http://exrx.net/Lists/Directory.html Athletes must be aware that over time they should move from general exercises that strengthen muscles generally to more specific actions and speed of actions as the goal approaches. The beginner strength trainer should be focussed on developing a foundation of general strength and good technique as well as developing core (abdominals and lower back) stability and strength. Once developed over a long period (months – off season for experienced athletes, years for a novice), this foundation of general strength should move to specific exercises that are movement specific for the sport or event training for. Crucially, the choice of exercises should also focus on exercises that prevent injury. For example, team players may need to focus on exercises

that strengthen the knee joint while throwers or racquet sport players may need to focus on strengthening the trunk stability and rotation muscles.

2. *Order of exercises.* Four principles need to be adhered to:
   a. Do the priority exercises early in the training session before fatigue sets in.
   b. When training all muscle groups in a session, do the large muscle groups (e.g. bench press) before small muscle groups (e.g. triceps press-down), multi-joint exercises before single joint, or rotate upper and lower body exercises.
   c. When training upper body one day and lower body the next, do the large muscle groups (e.g. bench press) before small muscle groups (e.g. triceps press-down), multi-joint exercises before single joint, or rotate opposing exercises (e.g. triceps and biceps, quadriceps and hamstrings).
   d. When training individual muscle groups, do the multi-joint exercises before single joint and higher intensity exercises before lower intensity exercises.

3. *Number of repetitions* (reps) is the number of times each exercise is done. In general, the higher the number of repetitions, the lower the load or weight lifted. For muscle endurance development, the higher the number of repetitions; for strength, the lower the number of repetitions. Thus, the beginner should be focussed on higher numbers of repetitions to develop strength with low to moderate loads. This enables the development of good technique while developing some strength, muscle endurance and hypertrophy at the same time. Good technique means less likelihood of injury when the weights increase over time.

4. *Sets* are the specific number of repetitions done as a group without resting. In general, the greater the number of sets, the greater the benefit but the greater the fatigue. For beginners, two sets per exercise will suffice for the first 2-4 weeks, as the repetitions will be high (and fatiguing) with the load low. Gradually the number of sets can be increased.

5. *Load* is the amount of weight lifted, pushed or pulled. The higher the load (and therefore the lower the number of repetitions), the greater the strength gains; the lower the load (and therefore the higher the number of repetitions), the greater the endurance gains. 2.5-5% increases in load per week are suggested.

6. *Tempo.* This is the rate at which you work the muscles. For example, if we use the bench press exercise, 2-1-2 means out (push) for 2 seconds, rest for 1 second, in (back) for 2 seconds.

7. *Intensity* is generally expressed as a percentage of 1 RM or in terms of number of repetition maximums (RMs).

8. *Speed* at which the exercise is done. Generally expressed as seconds such as 2-1-2 that is 2 seconds up, hold for 1 second, 2 seconds down. Research has shown that the more time a muscle is under tension, the greater the muscle hypertrophy so the larger the muscle becomes. An increased speed of lifting influences muscular power. For beginning aging athletes, a slow speed not only allows for muscle hypertrophy, it allows good technique to be developed.

9. *Recovery* is the amount of rest between sets. In general, the less the rest, the greater the endurance gains; the longer the rest, the better the strength gains when lifting heavy loads or doing power exercises, both of which are fatiguing and require longer rest.
10. *Frequency* is the number of times the strength training is done per week. In general, the more experienced the athlete, the more frequent the number of sessions per week.

**Factors in weight training program design**

As in every facet of an aging athlete undertaking any safe and scientifically based training program, strength training has a number of factors that must be incorporated into the strength training program design. These include:

1. *Progressive Overload*. This principle is based on the concept that an aging athlete must adapt to the demands of greater physiological challenges to the muscular and nervous system. That is, progressively over time, the aging athlete and/or their strength specialist can manipulate the following variables to enable the greatest adaptation to take place:
   a. Load may be increased.
   b. Repetitions may be increased.
   c. Repetition speed may be altered.
   d. Sets may be increased.
   e. Frequency of training may be increased.
   f. Rest periods may be shortened for endurance improvements or lengthened for strength and power training.
   g. Any combination of the above but the American College of Sports Medicine suggests only 2.5-5% increases in training volume to prevent overtraining.
2. *Specificity*. This training principle says that the weight training must relate to the actions and demands of the sport. While non-specific strength programs may enhance speed and power and help to prevent injury in the aging athlete, over time, the athlete and strength specialist should match:
   a. The movement patterns of the sport.
   b. The muscles used in the sport.
   c. The joint velocities of the sport.
   d. The range of motion of the sport.
   e. The loads of the sport.
   f. The metabolic demands of the sport (power or strength, speed or endurance).
3. *Periodisation*. There is a complete chapter in this book devoted to this topic and the general principles surrounding this systematic process of varying the volume and intensity of training over time. However, there are a number of well-researched ways of developing strength and power over time. These include:
   a. *Classic or linear model of periodisation.* This model is characterised by high initial training volumes (sets and repetitions) and low intensity (weight lifted) to develop

muscle endurance and moves towards decreases in volume and increases in intensity in order to maximise strength and power. Each training phase is characterised by an emphasis on a particular physiological adaptation (e.g. hypertrophy, strength then power). The classic model progresses systematically through the following training phases:

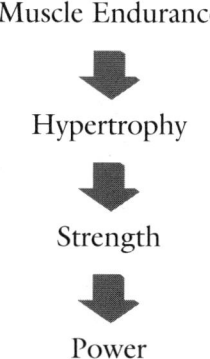

The linear model varies the intensity over time. For example, a 16-week program might have weeks 1-4 as light (endurance), weeks 5-8 moderate (hypertrophy), weeks 9-12 heavy (strength), and weeks 13-16 (power) as very heavy.

b. *Undulating or non-linear model of periodisation.* This model enables variation in intensity and volume within each 7-10 day cycle of training. That is, this model attempts to train endurance, strength, hypertrophy and power within this time block but emphasises only one of these characteristics within any one training session. For example, if an athlete is training three days a week, Monday might be 3-5 RM loads (power), Wednesday 8-10 RM loads (strength) and Friday 12-15 RM loads (endurance).

Comparisons between these two models of periodising strength and power development have suggested that the classic linear model is superior in developing strength, cycling power and leg power over the long term. However, it appears that the non-linear or undulating model where intensity and volume are manipulated within a week is superior in a short-term (e.g. 4 week) training period.

## Developing muscle strength

Strength is the foundation of power, power endurance and muscular endurance – all the factors required for sport. Strength is highly dependent upon the size of the muscle as well as the quality of nerve stimulation that muscle receives. Table 7.2 overleaf summarises the key factors to be considered when developing strength.

*Table 7.2:* Factors relevant to strength development.

| Factor | Novice | Advanced |
|---|---|---|
| Muscle Action | Concentric – muscle shortening<br>Eccentric – muscle lengthening | Concentric – muscle shortening<br>Eccentric – muscle lengthening |
| Loads | 60-70% 1 RM | 80-100% 1 RM |
| Repetitions | 8-12 | 1-6 |
| Progression | Reassess 1RM every 2-4 weeks<br>Increase load 2-10% | Reassess 1RM every 2-3 weeks or drop reps and increase intensity 2-10% |
| Sets | 1-3 | 2-3 |
| Exercise Selection | Single and multi-joint exercises | Multi-joint exercises |
| Free-Weights or Machines | Free weights and machines | Free weights |
| Speed of Movement | Slow to moderate with good technique | Slow to moderate to fast depending on sport or event and with good technique |
| Rest between Sets | 3-5 minutes for multi-joint exercises (e.g. bench press)<br>2-3 minutes for single joint exercises (e.g. leg curl) | 3-5 minutes for multi-joint exercises (e.g. bench press)<br>2-3 minutes for single joint exercises (e.g. leg curl) |
| Frequency | 2-3 times/week with 48 hrs between sessions | 4-5 times/week depending on sport/event/training phase |
| Range of Motion | Complete or to individual tolerance | Complete or to individual tolerance |

### Developing muscle hypertrophy

One of the most important facets of training for aging athletes should be to hold on to muscle mass. Research has conclusively shown that in both aging non-athletes and aging athletes, muscle mass decreases with increasing age. Thus, hypertrophy weight training should become crucial for the aging competitive athlete. Moreover, the older the athlete, the more importance should be placed on this type of training.

Following heavy weight training, the body increases the rate of protein synthesis for 36-48 hours, thus building increased muscle mass. People with faster twitch fibres such as sprinters appear to hypertrophy more than the slow twitch fibre endurance athletes. Muscle damage, seen more with eccentric (muscle lengthening) exercises (e.g. the downward action in squats) than concentric muscle shortening exercises (e.g. the upward action in squats) appears to stimulate muscle hypertrophy, suggesting that the tempo of the eccentric action in any exercise should be longer than the shortening of the muscle phase (e.g 3-1-2). It also appears that hypertrophy takes place after nervous system changes that are seen with strength training. Thus, it can take up to 6-8 weeks of strength training before any increase in muscle size is seen. Table 7.3 summarises the key factors to be considered when planning a muscular hypertrophy weight training program.

*Table 7.3:* Factors relevant to the development of muscular hypertrophy.

| Factor | Novice | Advanced |
|---|---|---|
| Muscle Action | Concentric – muscle shortening<br>Eccentric – muscle lengthening | Concentric – muscle shortening<br>Eccentric – muscle lengthening |
| Loads | 70-85% 1 RM | 70-100% 1 RM |
| Repetitions | 8-12 | 1-12 with majority 6-12 |
| Progression | Reassess 1RM every 2-4 weeks<br>Increase load 2-10% | Reassess 1RM every 2-3 weeks or drop reps and increase intensity 2-10% |
| Sets | 1-3 | 3-6 |
| Exercise Selection | Single and multi-joint exercises | Multi-joint exercises |
| Free-Weights or Machines | Free weights and machines | Free weights |
| Speed of Movement | Slow to moderate with good technique | Slow to moderate depending on sport or event and with good technique |
| Rest between Sets | 1-2 minutes | 2-3 minutes for 1-6 RM<br>1-2 minutes for 7-12 RM |
| Frequency | 2-3 times/week with 48 hrs between sessions | 4-6 times/week depending on sport/event/training phase |
| Range of Motion | Complete or to individual tolerance | Complete or to individual tolerance |

Apart from undertaking muscle hypertrophy weight training, there a number of other positive and negative factors that will affect the gains in muscle mass. These are shown in Table 7.4 below.

*Table 7.4:* Positive and negative factors affecting muscle mass development.

| Positive Factors | Negative Factors |
|---|---|
| Testosterone | Cortisol stress hormone |
| Growth hormone | Negative energy balance |
| Insulin | Fasting after exercise |
| Positive energy balance | Too much exercise |
| Post-exercise carbohydrate and protein | Inadequate recovery between workouts |
| Resistance training | |
| Adequate recovery between workouts | |

Thus, research suggests the following strategies be undertaken to increase muscle mass by minimising the negative factors and maximising the positive factors above:

1. Stress the major muscle groups with repeat sets of 8-12 RM loads with relatively short rests between sets and exercises.
2. Ensure adequate recovery between training sessions.

3. Positive energy balance (food intake) to allow the energy to be used for building muscle.
4. Frequent feeding is preferable to a few meals. More frequent meals helps maintain blood amino acid levels and thus uptake of these for muscle building.
5. Extra protein intake may help promote muscle building. A well-balanced athlete diet will ensure enough protein intake if snacks such as protein bars or tuna salads etc are taken. There is no need for protein supplements.
6. Post-exercise feeding is important. Eating protein and carbohydrate immediately after weight training increases the effect of exercise alone on stimulating muscle growth.

### Developing muscle power

Muscular power (speed-strength) is the key to sports performance. Developing power in the gym means doing fast actions so that a muscle's *rate* of force development is increased. Given that the greater the strength, the more power we can develop, it is crucial that strength be developed first with heavier loads, then the load lightened and the speed of contraction be increased progressively. However, once we have developed strength and then start developing power (speed-strength), we must continue to maintain strength by 1-2 sessions per week of strength training. Table 7.5 summarises the key factors to be considered when developing muscular power.

*Table 7.5:* Factors relevant to muscular power development.

| Factor | Novice | Advanced |
|---|---|---|
| Muscle Action | Sport-specific | Sport-specific |
| Loads | 30-60% 1 RM | 30-60% 1 RM |
| Repetitions | 3-6 | 1-6 |
| Progression | Reassess 1RM every 2-4 weeks Increase load 2-10% | Reassess 1RM every 2-3 weeks or drop reps and increase intensity 2-10% |
| Sets | 1-3 | 3-6 |
| Exercise Selection | Multi-joint exercises | Multi-joint exercises |
| Free-Weights or Machines | Free weights and machines | Free weights |
| Speed of Movement | Fast with good technique | Fast with good technique |
| Rest between Sets | 2-3 minutes for multi-joint exercises (e.g. bench press) 1-2 minutes for single joint exercises (e.g. leg curl) | 2-3 minutes for multi-joint exercises (e.g. bench press) 1-2 minutes for single joint exercises (e.g. leg curl) |
| Frequency | 2-3 times/week with 48 hrs between sessions | 4-6 times/week depending on sport/event/training phase |
| Range of Motion | Complete or to individual tolerance | Complete or to individual tolerance |

## Developing muscular endurance

Most sports demand some level of muscular endurance or the number of repetitions performed with a specific load. While aerobic or cardiovascular endurance is a factor in muscular endurance, sprint runners still need to contract their muscles maximally many times over 100 meters with little contribution from the aerobic system. While strength training itself can improve muscular endurance, research has shown that specificity of training produces the greatest increase in muscular endurance. Training to improve muscular endurance demands high numbers of repetitions and/or short recovery times between sets. Table 7.6 summarises the key factors to be considered when developing muscular endurance.

*Table 7.6:* Factors relevant to muscular endurance development.

| Factor | Novice | Advanced |
|---|---|---|
| Muscle Action | Sport-specific | Sport-specific |
| Loads | 40-60% 1 RM | 30-80% 1 RM |
| Repetitions | 15 | 15-25 |
| Progression | Reassess 1RM every 2-4 weeks Increase load 2-10% | Reassess 1RM every 2-3 weeks or drop reps and increase intensity 2-10% |
| Sets | 1-3 | 3-6 |
| Exercise Selection | Multi-joint exercises | Multi-joint exercises |
| Free-Weights or Machines | Free weights and machines | Free weights |
| Speed of Movement | Moderate with good technique | Fast with good technique for low reps Moderate for high reps |
| Rest between Sets | < 90 seconds | < 90 seconds |
| Frequency | 2-3 times/week with 48 hrs between sessions | 4-6 times/week depending on sport/event/training phase |
| Range of Motion | Complete or to individual tolerance | Complete or to individual tolerance |

## Development of strength-endurance and power-endurance

Following the development of strength using the above methods under the supervision of a strength and conditioning specialist, if the sport or event being trained for demands strength-endurance or power-endurance, and most do, there are a number of ways to develop these qualities. These include:

- *Body-weight exercises* such as push ups, sit-ups, squats etc can be done easily at home with minimal equipment but the choices of exercises are limited and the resistance cannot be controlled that easily.
- *Weight training* to develop strength-endurance or power-endurance should follow the guidelines in Table 7.7 overleaf:

*Table 7.7:* Factors relevant to developing strength or power endurance.

| Factor | Value |
|---|---|
| Sets | 2-3 |
| Repetitions | 20-40 |
| Load (RM) | 20-40 |
| Tempo | 0.5-0-0.5 |
| Rest between sets (mins) | 1-2 |
| Frequency (x/week) | 2-3 |

- *Circuit training.* This involves either body weight or weight training devices being used and one exercise being done then immediately followed by another exercise using a different body part. Circuits can be based on time (e.g. 30 seconds at each work station) or number of repetitions (e.g. 20 squats). The exercises chosen should be sport-specific and aimed at performance improvement or injury prevention. If in doubt of which exercises, pay the money and join a gym or get professional advice from a strength and conditioning specialist.
- *Resisted sports movements.* These methods include uphill running, stair running, sand dune running, water running, weighted vest running, tethered swimming, towing a parachute or sled, placing a tube on the front of a row boat, or cycling into a wind, cycling up hills, or doing low cadence, high resistance work on the wind-trainer. These training methods are for experienced aging athletes with good form, balance and strength and should be initially done with supervision.

## Strength-training aids

Numerous general and sport-specific strength-training aids are available on the market. Many are a gimmick and many have strong applications in strength training. Let's examine some of the more common ones.

- *Stretch Cords* are commonly used in swimmers. They are cheap and available from swimshops/pools with the tubing available from surgical supply company chemists/pharmacists or dive shops. The greater the thickness, the greater the resistance. They are portable, light, and exact movements can be replicated on land as they are done in the pool.
- *Free weights or dumbbells* are relatively inexpensive, available from fitness suppliers or sports stores and can be used at home in so many ways to develop and maintain strength. Again, get advice from a strength professional in developing a home-based strength program.
- *Sport-specific aids.* These include:
  - *Tethers* are used by swimmers and are fixed to a point (e.g. starting block) while the swimmer works against the water to hold a position. They are great for strength and power development, but very stressful on the heart and blood pressure.

- *Drag suits* with pockets to catch water and make the swimmer work harder, thus developing strength and power endurance.
- *Paddles* vary in size and shape and are used to develop strength in swimmers. Small paddles should be used initially with speed slow and distances short. Distance, speed and paddle size can be increased over time.
- *Resistance Aids* include swimmers wearing shoes or towing a bucket, runners pulling sleds or small parachutes, rowers attaching a small tube to the front of the boat.

- *Medicine Balls* are highly-effective in developing strength and power endurance. They are also great for developing core body strength and action-specific strength such as that for throwers. See the website: http://exrx.net/Lists/PowerExercises.html for examples of exercises.
- *Swiss Balls (Medi-balls, Fit-balls)* are increasingly gaining favour for developing core strength. For aging athletes with lower back pain or the need to develop strength in the abdomen and lower back, this type of training is essential and the *Swiss ball* is a fun way to doing it. Do a *Google* search re core stability exercises (e.g. http://www.acefitness.org/exerciselibrary/default.aspx) for great examples for different body parts or visit a sports physiotherapist or *Pilates* specialist for advice on a core strengthening program.

## Minimising risk of injury

There is no evidence to suggest that older people suffer weight-training injuries at any greater rate than younger people. In fact, studies have shown that older people doing weight training suffer far less injuries that prevent them training than people doing walk-jog training programs. However, the following guidelines should be followed to minimise the risk of injury during weight training:

- Warm-up (cycle or jog then stretch the joints and muscles about to be used).
- Use correct technique for each exercise.
- Learn from a trained strength and conditioning specialist.
- Use "spotters" as partners for heavy lifts.
- Once fatigued, do minimal more repetitions.
- Ensure equipment is in working order.
- Ensure you have space around you.
- Concentrate on major muscle groups (e.g. hips, knees, shoulder and elbow muscles).
- Start at low intensity and build the intensity slowly.
- Start with machine weights (e.g. *Universal*) then move to free-weights (bars and free-weights).
- The order of exercises should progress from large to small muscle groups (e.g. squat before leg curls).

- Use dynamic exercises rather than isometric exercises where muscles contract against a solid object but don't change length.
- Do the exercise through the full range of motion.
- Breathing rhythm is essential to prevent dramatic rises in blood pressure. Exhale while lifting and inhale slowly while lowering the weight.
- The older the athlete, the longer (2-4 days) between weight training sessions as it appears older people take longer to adapt to weight training and longer to recover after hard exercise.

## Weight training warm-up principles

As in speed or endurance training, to prevent injury and maximise the training workout, the following principles should be adhered to when doing a warm-up for weight training at home or in the gym:

- 12 to 15 repetitions performed before the workout sets.
- Load approximately 50% of workout weight.
- 30 seconds to 3 minutes rest before workout set.

The benefits of such a specific warm-up include:

- the muscles and joint can be warmed up with the exact mechanics which will be performed during the workout set(s)
- The muscle and joint(s) is less susceptible to injury
- Muscle can contract with greater intensity
- Technique and breathing can be rehearsed

No warm-up set is required for high repetition exercises as high repetition sets (>20) are not as intense and serves as a warm-up in its self.

## Free-weights or machine-weights?

From a safety perspective, particularly in the aging athlete who has little or no experience with weight training, variable resistance machines that use weight stacks are recommended for a number of reasons:

- They reduce the risk of injury to hands, feet and lower back.
- They reduce the risk of exercise-induced high blood pressure.
- Weights can be increased in small and time-efficient ways.
- Resistance can be applied through the full range of motion, thus developing strength through the range and developing or maintaining flexibility of the joint(s) involved.
- More time-efficient than free weights.

## Women and strength training

Traditional gender roles and differences in peak strength values have resulted in many misconceptions about the role of strength training for women. Historically, strength was seen as a male 'thing' and women discouraged from doing weight training as it was seen as unfeminine. Thus, aging female athletes may have never achieved their potential physically and athletically. Thankfully, times have changes and many younger female athletes and non-athletes are actively involved in sport and strength training.

It is true that men are generally stronger than women when it comes to absolute 1 RM strength because men have a greater muscle mass. However, when we compare the strength per cross-sectional area of muscle, the strength is almost identical. The differences in absolute strength are due to not only hormonal differences (men have 10 times the amount of the anabolic hormone testosterone), but also other physiological differences between men and women including body size and structure with men generally taller and heavier and with longer arms and legs that help act as levers when exerting force.

When it comes to strength and power training, women are able to develop strength just as much as men can. Indeed, a recent study showed that women in their 70s are able to develop their strength to a greater extent than men of the same age. While women may not be able to lift the same weights as men, they can lift the same relative amounts (% of maximum lift) as men. It appears that, just like older men, the increases in strength are due to both nervous system changes and increased muscle size. Testosterone levels in the aging women appear to strongly influence the amount of strength and power development, suggesting a strong argument for the possibility of some testosterone supplementation if undertaking hormone replacement therapy.

Let's now dispel some of the common myths that surround women and strength training including:

1. *Strength training causes women to become larger and heavier.* The truth is strength training helps reduce body fat and increase muscle mass. While this may result in a small increase in overall body weight, the reason is that same volume of muscle weighs more than fat. Research has shown that strength training increases strength with little or no change in lower body girths, and a very small change in upper body girths. Only women with genetic predisposition for muscle enlargement and who do high volume, high intensity weight training will see substantial increases in muscle size.

2. *Women should use different training methods than men.* Historically women were encouraged to use weight machines and slow, controlled movements for fear of injury from using free weights and barbells, power exercises, or body weight exercises. The truth is that research has shown that women are no more predisposed to injury than men in this area as long as correct technique and a progressive increase in intensity is used in the program.

3. *Women should avoid high intensity or high-load strength training.* Most women are able to train at high volumes and high intensities similar to men. Like men, these should be well structured and overseen by a strength-training specialist.

## Conclusion

The area of strength training is a science unto itself. As you can see from the above discussion, numerous factors need to go into planning a periodised and sport-specific strength program, making the successful program as much art as it is science. Be aware of the importance of the principles outlined in this chapter but make every effort to contact a strength and conditioning specialist through your local gym, a high performance coach in your sport, or the *National Strength and Conditioning Association* (http://www.nsca-lift.org/trainers/locator/). They will have the expertise and knowledge to assist you. Finally, take my and every expert in the field of aging and sport's advice – take up weight training to improve your strength and power for sports performance but also to hold onto good health and independence into older age.

# CHAPTER 8

## SPEED AND POWER DEVELOPMENT IN THE MASTERS ATHLETE

*Running occurs on the ground, sprinting occurs over it.*

Percy Duncan

*A champion quality is to go deeper into pain.*

Eddie Merckx

*Simply put, the most profound training responses will occur when you train faster.*

Rick Niles

## Introduction

One of the most obvious things masters athletes notice as we age is that we get slower. While some aging athletes I know may be faster than when they were younger through training smarter or through using a more scientific approach to their training, in general the frustration of slowing down hits us all. An examination of the 50m freestyle swimming world records (see Figure 8.1) emphasises this slow down.

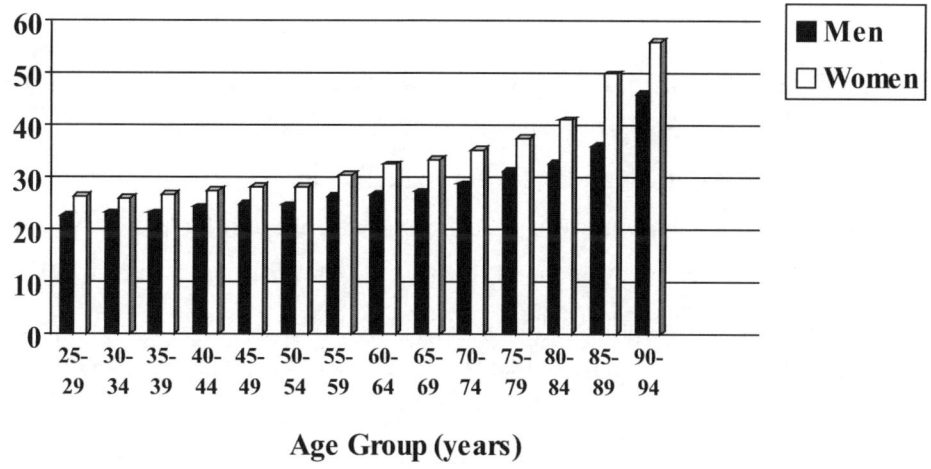

*Figure 8.1:* 50m freestyle male and female world records (sec) for various age groups.

With few exceptions, my experience in masters swimming, veteran cycling, distance running and triathlon over many years is that too many aging athletes use endurance-training methods and expect to go fast. According to the training principle of specificity, this is not possible. The purpose of this chapter is to suggest a more scientific approach to speed and power training in the aging athlete.

Throughout this book it has been emphasised how important weight or resistance training is for the aging athlete, regardless of whether for endurance events, middle distance events or pure speed events. This is due to the fact that one of the major changes that occurs with aging is a loss of muscle mass, particularly after the age of 50 years and even more so after the age of 65-70 years. A loss of muscle mass means decreased strength, decreased force production, and thus decreased speed and power. Muscular speed and power are important for success in sprinting in every sport, jumping and throwing events in athletics, hitting, kicking and punching movements in other sports.

## Definitions

In order to get the most out of this chapter, a number of definitions must be understood.

1. *Speed* is the distance covered divided by the time it takes to cover that distance. In sports such as swimming or running, the speed is covered in a straight line. However, speed for a football, basketball, netball or water polo player may mean changing direction while moving. Thus, a number of types of speed training need to be defined:

   a. *Maximum speed* is the highest speed an aging athlete can reach. This normally occurs three to five seconds after the start of a race from a stationary position.

   b. *Acceleration speed* in sports such as team sports or tennis is crucial. These are sports where short sprints are done but maximum speed may not be reached. The ability to get into a space or take a gap are more important in team sports than maximum speed.

   c. *Speed endurance* is the ability to sustain maximum speed or near maximum speed and to withstand the effects of fatigue. Events longer than five seconds in duration (e.g. 100-400m runs, 25-100m swims), team (e.g. team sports) or individual (e.g. tennis, squash, badminton) sports where recovery between sprints isn't long enough to recover all require high levels of speed endurance.

   d. *Change of direction speed* is crucial in most team and racquet sports. The ability to evade or chase an opponent in team sports, or change directions quickly in racquet sports requires agility as well as acceleration speed.

   The following table suggests which of the types of speed are important for which sports.

*Table 8.1:* The relative importance of types of speed for common sports. 3= highest.

| Sport | Maximum Speed | Acceleration Speed | Speed Endurance | Change of Direction Speed |
|---|---|---|---|---|
| Tennis, Squash, Badminton | 1 | 3 | 2 | 3 |
| Basketball, Netball, Touch | 1 | 3 | 3 | 3 |
| Soccer, Rugby, Rugby League, Australian Rules | 3 | 3 | 3 | 3 |
| Swimming, Cycling, Running | 3 | 2 | 3 | NA |

## Relationships between speed, strength and power

The greater the resistance needed to be overcome to achieve the sporting movement, the greater the need for strength. For example, a veteran shot putter demands strength-dominated power compared to a javelin thrower who demands speed-dominated power. Why? Because the shot putter needs to throw a shot weighing 4-6 kg at around 10-14 m/sec whereas a javelin thrower throws their 600 g implement at around twice that speed.

Strength is also required for strength-endurance events. For example, if masters rowers are required to apply 50% of maximum strength to an oar over a 4-minute period and rower A can apply 200 kg of force to an oar in one pull compared to rower B who can only apply 100 kg, then athlete A will be able to produce more total work during the duration of the event and thus perform better.

It is thus crucial that aging athletes understand what type of speed, strength or power is required for their chosen sport or event and train that capacity. However, most sporting events demand power or power endurance. Power is strength done at speed. Thus, for most athletes, and in particular aging athletes who lose both strength and power with age, it is crucial that strength is first developed then that strength turned into fast strength (power) or power endurance, either in the gym or on the training track. The previous highlights the methods used to develop strength and power in the gym. This chapter will focus on developing speed and power qualities in a sport-specific way on the training field.

## Factors affecting acceleration and speed

Contrary to popular opinion, no one body design is perfect for sprinting in sport. Numerous body types and variations in height, weight and lever lengths of arms, trunks and legs have proven effective. Some sprinters are short and turn legs or arms over quickly, others are tall and take longer strides or strokes than the shorter athletes. However, there are a number of physiological factors that affect speed and acceleration in sport:

1. *Muscle fiber type.* In general, three types of muscle fiber exist in an athlete's body

    *a. Slow-twitch* fibers that rely on oxygen to produce energy (aerobic). These fibers develop force slowly, are fatigue resistant, and contract relatively slowly with low power output and relatively low anaerobic capacity.
    *b. Fast-twitch a* fibers are an intermediate fiber that can contribute to both speed and endurance. They develop force moderately fast and have moderate fatigability, contraction time, power output and aerobic and anaerobic capacity.
    *c. Fast-twitch b* fibers do not rely on oxygen to produce energy and are thus highly anaerobic. They produce force quickly, fatigue quickly, and have high power outputs, low aerobic and high anaerobic capacities.

Thus, muscles with a high percentage of fast twitch fibers, especially the fast twitch b fibers, contract more quickly and powerfully. Aging athletes born with a high percentage of these fibers make better sprinters while aging athletes born with high percentages of slow twitch fibers make the better distance athletes. Inherited percentages of these fiber types are similar in both men and women but research has shown that the size of the fast twitch fibers drops with age in both male and female masters athletes. This decrease in the size of the power producing fast twitch fiber is one of the reasons why both muscle mass and speed drop with age. Thus, hypertrophy weight training that builds muscle mass will help develop the size of these fibers and thus help to maintain speed or at least slow the decline in speed with age. Crucially, research has shown that low intensity exercise typical of many aging athletes, recruits and uses only the slow twitch fibers. High intensity (heavy load) training recruits and uses the all important speed and power-producing fast-twitch muscle fibers. Thus, *it is the intensity or load, not the speed that activates the fast-twitch fibers.* As we will see later, there are many ways to load the muscles of aging sprinters to develop and maintain the size of these fibers.

1. ***Body Fat.*** One of the more important factors in sport is the power-weight ratio. An athlete carrying excess body weight (fat) that does not produce power will not, all other things being equal, perform as well as another aging athlete who can produce the same force but carries less body fat. Thus, aging sprint athletes should focus on low body fat for not only health reasons, but for performance reasons. The weight control chapter in this book outlines the scientifically correct ways for an aging athlete to lose and maintain body weight for sports performance.
2. ***Gender.*** Figure 8.1 at the start of this chapter shows the gender differences in 50m-swim performance that reflects sprint performance in any sport. It appears the major difference is that women have less power-producing muscle and carry more non-power-producing fat than men. Together with males possessing longer force-producing levers, these factors contribute to males being faster in sport.
3. ***Anaerobic Capacity.*** While this factor will not contribute to acceleration and speed, it will affect speed endurance or the ability to last at speed. Sprint athletes primarily produce energy from two anaerobic energy sources in the body. Firstly, the initial 6-10 seconds of any sprint rely on the alactic phosphagen energy system that sits in the muscles waiting to

break down rapidly to produce anaerobic energy. Secondly, muscle carbohydrate breaks down in the absence of oxygen to produce lactic acid, this process also creating rapid energy for muscle contractions via what is called the lactic acid energy system. However, if the level of lactic acid rises too much, it not only slows down the energy-producing reactions in the muscles, it inhibits muscles contracting properly, leading to poor form and a drop in performance and the reason 100m swimmers or 400m runners 'hit the wall' close to the end of a race. The longer the sprint, the more the need for this type of energy to maintain speed. Thus, sprint training needs to develop the rate at which anaerobic energy comes from both these energy systems and, depending upon the length of the sprint, needs to focus on developing a tolerance to the painful lactic acid build-up.

4. *Age*. As shown in Figure 8.1, age leads to decreased speed. The major reason appears to be an inevitable age-related loss of muscle mass secondary to a loss of the size and number of fast twitch muscle fibers. However, increasing levels of body fat and thus lowering power-weight ratios, slower nerve conduction velocities, and decreased reaction times also play a part.

Apart from the need to undertake strength training in the gym to increase muscle mass, the aging athlete should be making every effort to undertake high load sprint-type training to stimulate the fast-twitch muscle fibers that determine speed. By doing that, they may also help prevent the age-related loss of muscle mass and performance.

## Development of speed

In most sports, aging athletes involved with speed events start from a stationary position or partially moving position (e.g. field games) and must reach maximum speed as fast as possible. This is referred to as acceleration or the rate of change of speed. Speed refers to the point where the aging athlete cannot accelerate any more and have maximum velocity. At this point, the aging athlete tries to hold onto that speed as long as possible without slowing down due to fatigue, friction or air or water resistance. Sprint times in sports can thus be improved in these three areas – acceleration, speed development, speed endurance development, plus both starting and finishing technique. In aging team sport athletes, change of direction speed is also crucial. While change of direction speed and the technique of starting and finishing is sports-specific and beyond the scope of this book, methods of developing speed, acceleration and speed endurance will now be discussed.

### Guidelines for speed development

It is beyond the scope of this chapter and book to give a specific formula for developing speed in every athlete of every age and gender for every sport. The competitive aging athlete should make every effort to obtain some of the excellent books available that outline specific programs for speed development in specific sports. I recommend the publishers Human Kinetics as the best source (*www.humankinetics.com*). However, there are a number of guidelines that should be adhered to develop speed in any athlete of any age or ability. These include:

1. *Be fresh.* All speed training must be performed when the body is fully recovered from a previous event or training session. A tired, sore or overtrained aging athlete cannot improve their speed when fatigued from previous training or work.
2. *Master correct technique.* Correct sprinting technique through many repetitions to reinforce skill development. Initially this should be done at slower speeds but then the speed is gradually increased while correct form is held. Sport-specific drills are an excellent means of developing correct sprint technique (*www.humankinetics.com*).
3. *Warm-up with intensity.* Too few aging athletes warm-up correctly. A warm-up should include low intensity work that develops a light sweat, stretching the specific joints and muscles being used in the sport or event, and then some technique-specific drills followed by gradual increases in intensity to event-specific intensity.
4. *Rest between efforts.* All sets and repetitions of a speed training session must be followed by adequate recovery so the next effort is high quality. The shorter the effort in time, the shorter the rest. As a general rule, a 1:4-6 work-to-rest ratio is recommended.
5. *Vary the training.* Speed training sessions should be varied between light, medium and heavy days. For example, back-to-back hard days would not benefit speed development.
6. *Monitor training volume.* Aging athletes should track the total distance covered during each maximum speed training session to see that there is a gradual progression in distance.
7. *Speed endurance is developed with longer intervals.* Doing longer intervals (e.g. 150-400m runs, 50-100m swims, 30-60 second bike efforts) or decreasing the rest between shorter intervals (10-20m runs, 12.5-25m swims, or 5-10 second bike efforts) develops speed endurance. The aim should be sport-specificity. Obviously a team player needs to do short sprints up and back with short recoveries, but after say 6 x 10m efforts, a long rest of 2-3 minutes might be taken so the quality of the next set of 6 x 10m is high.
8. *Strength and power development in the gym.* The aging sprint athlete MUST focus on developing muscle mass, strength and power in the gym. To do this, use the guidelines given in the previous chapter of this book but then enlist the help of a strength specialist at a local gym, through connections you may have in your sport, or through the *National Strength and Conditioning Association* (http://www.nsca-lift.org/trainers/locator/). The money will be well spent. The older the competitive aging athlete, the more important this becomes.
9. *Include flexibility training.* Apart from an age-related loss of muscle mass, strength and thus the need for strength training, one of the other major declines that occur with age is a decreased range of motion about a joint. This loss of flexibility will obviously mean that speed will decrease due to the stride or stroke length decreasing. While may aging athletes stretch before and after training sessions, too few do flexibility training using the principles outlined in Chapter 9 of this book and stretch at home 2-3 times per week.

## Phases of speed training

With the above principles in mind, let us now examine a six-step progressive model for developing speed in competitive aging athletes:

1. *Base Training.* Developing a training base early in a season or in the transition phase or off-season enables an aging athlete to have a foundation upon which to develop speed and power without getting injured. Stretching, strengthening, drills for skills, and development of some endurance should be keys.

2. *Functional Strength and Power.* Developing muscle mass, strength and power in the gym under the guidance of a strength specialist should be a priority. Chapter 7 outlines the guidelines for developing the qualities of strength, muscle mass (hypertrophy) and power.

3. *Pliometrics.* This step focuses on hopping, jumping, bounding, hitting, kicking exercises that must be explosive and sport-specific. Donald Chu's book *Explosive power and strength* or Lee Brown's *Training for speed, agility and quickness* are excellent resources for sport-specific exercises such as this with great diagrams and descriptions of exercises and drills (www.humankinetics.com). While such training should only be undertaken with aging sprint athletes with a large training age or with a well-developed base of strength and power training in the gym, there is no reason aging athletes cannot undertake such training. Indeed, recent research is suggesting power training is more important than strength training for preventing falls and undertaking the tasks of daily living. Moreover, such training does show remarkable improvements in power of older people without the fear of injury, as long as the program is progressive and supervised closely. Later in this chapter we will examine in detail the principles of pliometrics training.

4. *Sport Loading.* This step focuses on sport- or event-specific speed and loading the athlete with relatively light resistance that develops speed and power without changing sprinting form. Speeds should be 85-100% of maximum. The ways to increase resistance include weighted vests, harnesses, parachutes, uphill sprinting, stairs, sand, and weighted sleds for runners, drag suits, leg ties, buckets, or tethers for swimmers, large gears, slow cadences, headwinds, hills for cyclists, and tire tubes for rowers.

5. *Sprinting Form and Speed Endurance.* This phase develops sprinting technique and the ability to hold the speed for longer.

6. *Overspeed Training.* This phase involves applying excess 5-10% extra speed through the use of overspeed training techniques such as those referred to below in the section on sprint-assisted training. The aim of such training is to train the nervous system to increase stride or stroke rate or in cyclists, cadence.

## Speed training methods

Numerous training methods have been developed to develop speed, acceleration, speed endurance and change of direction speed for aging athletes involved with team sports or racquet sports. These are summarized in Table 8.2 below. The book by Lee Brown and others (2000) titled *Training for speed, agility and quickness* (www.humankinetics.com) has some excellent drills for each of these methods but in particular the change of direction drills.

*Table 8.2:* Program variables for developing maximum speed, acceleration, speed endurance and change of direction speed in aging athletes.

| Variable | Maximum speed | Acceleration speed | Speed endurance | | Change of direction speed |
|---|---|---|---|---|---|
| Intensity (%) | 95-105 | 100 | 95-100 | | 100 |
| Interval length (seconds) | 2-5 | 2-5 | 2-5 | 10-60 | 2-5 |
| Rest between intervals | Complete (2-3 mins) | Complete (2-3 mins) | 30-90 secs | 3-8 mins | Complete (2-3 mins) |
| Number of intervals | 6-12 | 6-12 | 3-10 | | 6-12 |
| Start method | Flying | Stationary or slow walk | Not applicable | | Various but sport-specific |
| Frequency (times per week) | 2 | 2-3 | 2-3 | | 2-3 |
| Base qualities needed | Aerobic and power | Strength and aerobic | Speed and aerobic | | Speed and aerobic |

1. ***Sprint-assisted training (Overspeed training).*** For sprint runners, downhill running (<3% grade), being towed by a partner attached to an elastic or inelastic cord, treadmill sprinting or high speed stationary cycling; for cyclists drafting behind a motor-bike or high cadence work on the track or ergo; for swimmer having coach pulling a hip harness or using elastic tubing all appear to lead to increases in leg or arm frequency and thus speed. Speed should only be increased by approximately 5% as injury risks are increased, as are the risks of poor technique. Thus distances should be short, warm-up and stretching and cool downs longer, and the number of intervals reduced. This type of training is recommended for aging athletes with a longer training age and who are very experienced and with good technique, balance and strength. The guidelines for this type of training are:
    - Warm-up with walk (cycle)-jog-stride-sprint cycles then specific stretches then repeat the walk-jog-stride-sprint cycle again.
    - Focus on correct technique.
    - Focus on strong communication with your partner or coach.
    - Use towing on a grassy surface.
    - Expect to be sore 24-48 hours after the first overspeed workout, even if sprint fit.

- Use overspeed training at the start of the training session when fresh.

The *Sports Speed* book by Dintiman and Ward (2003) (www.humankinetics.com) is an excellent resource for suggested training programs for overspeed training in runners.

2. *Acceleration sprints* gradually increase from a rolling start, through jogging, to striding out and eventually sprinting at maximum pace. This type of training is useful for emphasizing maintenance of sprint technique as speed increases.

3. *Sprint-resisted training (Sport loading training)* such as uphill running, stair running, sand/sand dune running, water running, weighted vest running, tethered swimming, or towing a parachute or sled to increase strength and speed endurance. As with sprint-assisted training, these training methods are for experienced aging athletes with good form, balance and strength. Again, the *Sports Speed* book by Dintiman and Ward (2003) is an excellent resource for suggested training programs for sprint-resisted training in runners. However, briefly, the following methods and guidelines are suggested:
   - *Weighted vests* in young runners have been shown to increase leg power dramatically. 3-8 sprints of up to 40-120m with complete recoveries are suggested.
   - *Harnesses* where a partner of similar body weight and power holds back the runner who tries to run at about 90% effort. Progressively increasing repetitions of 3-10 short efforts (10-60m) with complete recoveries are recommended.
   - *Parachutes* can be bought in various sizes and again run at about 90% effort with short efforts (10-60m) and complete recoveries are recommended.
   - *Uphill sprinting* develops starting speed and acceleration speed (steep grades – 8%) or starts and speed endurance (1-3%). The *Sports Speed* book by Dintiman and Ward (2003) is an excellent resource for suggested training programs for uphill and downhill sprinting in runners.
   - *Stair climbs* must be safe (non-slip) and well spread to allow correct technique. Ideally the inclines should be between 3-8% grades.
   - *Sand running* places high loads on runner's knees, ankles and hips. Use it sparingly.
   - *Weighted sleds* or pulling tires develops power and strength. It is important to hold correct form so choose a weight that allows correct form over 5-40m.

4. *Hollow sprints* are accelerations and brief sprints interrupted by periods of recovery in the form of jogging or walking. For example, accelerate for 30m, jog for 30m, accelerate for 30m, and walk for 150m. This form of sprint training is appropriate to masters team games players as it offers a variation in speed and tempo within each sequence.

5. *Repetition sprints* involve running distances at a constant speed (75-100%) with recovery periods of sufficient length to allow the athlete to maintain form and the required quality. They are good for development of speed endurance and allow a sprinter to "finish on" in a sprint race or team players recover quickly for the next effort rather than dying in the last of 5 sprints. The following guidelines are recommended for developing speed endurance:
   - Sprint up to 30 seconds at 90-95% maximum speed, OR

- Maximum sprints of 10-60 seconds.
- Rest periods of 1-5 minutes to recover for the next maximum effort of 10-60 seconds.
- Team players should use distances covered in their sport.
- Over time increase the distances or shorten the recovery time.

6. ***Resistance or weight training*** involves the strengthening and then power development of the muscles used in the sport or event. In sprint running the gluteals, hamstrings, quadriceps, calf, abdominals, lower back, and hip flexor muscle are critical. In sprint freestyle swimming the latissimus dorsi, triceps, and pectorals are important.

As a guide, Table 8.3 below summarizes the training phases and specific exercises that a masters sprint runner might undertake leading up to a major event.

*Table 8.3:* Training phases and resistance/weight training exercises for masters sprint runners.

| Training Phase | Specificity | Objective(s) | Exercises |
| --- | --- | --- | --- |
| General Preparation | Low | Injury prevention, hypertrophy | Squats, deadlifts, hip extensions, hip flexion, bench press, trunk stabilization |
| Specific Preparation | Medium | Strength development | Half-quarter squat, lungs, power cleans, push press |
| Pre-Competition | High | Power development | Sled sprints, inclined sprints, speed bounding, vest sprinting, hopping, double leg drops-jumps |
| Competition | Very high | Specific power | Sled sprints, inclined sprints, speed bounding, vest sprinting |
| Transition | Low | Recovery, rehabilitation | |

As discussed in earlier chapters and at the beginning of this chapter, it is STRONGLY RECOMMENDED that the older speed and power athlete undertake resistance training. A strength and conditioning specialist from the *National Strength and Conditioning Association* (http://www.nsca-lift.org/trainers/locator/) should be consulted to develop a specific program for you. Before seeing them, read this and the previous chapter to make informed decisions. Point the chapters out to them as few may have experience with masters athletes.

7. ***Pliometrics*** involves the athlete moving small resistances (such as body weight) with speed. Examples are hopping, jumps, and bounding for the lower body and swinging, quick-action push-offs, catching and throwing weighted objects (medicine balls, shot puts, sandbags), arm swings, and pulley throws for the upper body. Table 8.4 describes the four types of movements commonly used in pliometrics.

*Table 8.4:* Types of pliometrics and examples of exercises for each.

| Jumps (one- or two-legged) | Hops (start or land on 1 leg) | Bounds (going for distance 1 leg to the other) | Shock (depth jumps, jumps for height) |
|---|---|---|---|
| Jumps in place (tuck, pike, split squat, squat, jump squat, skipping) | < 10 repeats (double- or single-leg, speed hop, lateral hop) | > 10 repeats (going for distance e.g. 30-100m) | Depth jumps off a box |
| Standing Jumps (long, triple or lateral jumps) | > 10 repeats (double- or single-leg, speed hop, lateral hop, hopping cones) | < 10 repeats (going for distance e.g. 20m) | |

The books by Dintiman and Ward (2003) and Lee Brown and others (2000) contain great diagrams and descriptions of over 50 such exercises. Exercises that simulate specific movements of the sport or event should be chosen and are a great way to develop strength and power in the muscles involved in sprinting. While many athletes may be strong, it is the speed of the movement(s) in pliometrics that develops power. Thus, the key objective in pliometrics is to generate maximum force in the shortest time.

Even for the aging power athlete, such exercises are recommended as long as general strength, core stability has been developed, and the pliometrics program is developed by and initially overseen by a strength and conditioning specialist or coach who monitors the progression of the program.

The major myth about such training is that injury rates are high. However, the research data suggests that the cause of injury is not performing explosive actions or lifting heavy, it is performing such exercises with incorrect technique. At the age of 52, and after six weeks of developing strength and core (lower back and abdominal strength), I commenced doing some simple pliometrics 1-2 times per week (step-ups, lunges, jump squats). I have already noticed my bike hill climbing power has increased significantly as a result. The strength and conditioning specialist who helped me spent two sessions with me initially showing me correct technique and discussing how I could progressively overload myself and where to fit the pliometrics into my overall training program so as to minimize fatigue and maximize the pliometrics.

Here are the scientific guidelines under which he and I work when doing pliometrics:

1. *The exercises correspond to the form, muscle actions and range of motion of the sport.* As a developing cyclist, I use step-ups, lunges, and jump squats where I power into or out of each action.
2. *The exercises should correspond to the correct direction of movement.* Because hill climbing in cycling depends greatly on hip and knee extension, the above exercises are perfect.
3. *The rate of stretch is tied to the effectiveness of pliometrics.* The higher the rate of stretch, the greater the resultant muscle contraction. Initially, in order to prevent injury, I

stretched the muscles relatively slowly in each action. However, over time, I am now able to stretch faster to get a more powerful muscle contraction and thus more power.

4. *Explode at the beginning of the action and let inertia move the limbs through the range of motion.*
5. *Too much extra weight (vests, ankle weights) may increase strength without increases in power.* It also increases the risk of injury. The body is the resistance. Weights less than 5% of body weight (e.g. < 5 kg) are enough resistance.
6. *Have as little wall, implement or ground contact time as possible.* The faster a muscle is forced to lengthen, the stronger the resulting muscle contraction.
7. *When landing or pushing, handle the forces with as little joint bending as possible.* This reduces contact time making the resultant muscle contraction more powerful.
8. *Master correct form.*
9. *Focus mentally on speed and form.*

Apart from these guidelines, a number of safety precautions are suggested with pliometrics. While injury surveys, even in older non-athletes, have shown that power exercises are not likely to produce injuries, well-put together and supervised programs must adhere to the following safety precautions:

- Limit pliometrics to two sessions a week, 48 hours at least apart and not immediately after or the day after heavy strength training unless lower-body strength training is combined with upper-body pliometrics training.
- Number of jumps etc should not exceed 80-100 per session in a beginner.
- Ensure complete recovery between sets (e.g. 2-4 minutes) so the quality of each set is maintained at a high level.
- Intensity should begin with low intensity (e.g. skipping, wall-pushes) and progress to two-foot jumps in place, to standing jumps (standing long or triple jumps or jumps over cones) to multiple jumps and hops (double leg hops, single leg hops, cone hops, repeat triple jumps) to depth jumps or box jumps double leg, to depth jumps or box jumps single leg, to bounding for distance.
- Ensure a strength training base before commencing pliometrics.
- Use a strength and conditioning specialist initially to help with correct form and program design.
- Warm-up with walk (cycle)-jog-stride- sprint cycles then specific stretches.
- Use footwear with ankle and arch support, and a non-slip sole.
- Use a surface that is shock absorbing such as grassy areas, artificial turf, mats. Never do them on asphalt, cement or hard gym floors.
- If using boxes, ensure they have a non-slip top and ideally rounded edges.
- If using depth jumping (e.g. jumping off one box and onto another), the heights should be less than 0.75 meter or for heavy people (>100 kg) less than 0.5 meters.

## Periodisation of speed training

While all the above training methods are useful in maximizing speed, they will be of minimal benefit if not sequenced correctly into your training program. A number of basic principles must be adhered to in the quest for speed:

1. To develop speed (as opposed to speed endurance), training must be performed in a state of minimal fatigue. That is, when you are fresh.
2. The intensity of the speed training must be maximal.
3. The total amount of speed work must be kept small so as to minimize fatigue while maintaining good technique.

Table 8.5 shows an example of a periodised training plan for a 50-year old masters sprint runner.

*Table 8.5:* A yearly periodised plan for a 50-year-old 100m sprint runner.

| | Transition Phase | | General Preparation | | | Specific Preparation | | | Pre-Competition | | | Competition |
|---|---|---|---|---|---|---|---|---|---|---|---|---|
| Months | 1 | 2 | 3 | 4 | 5 | 6 | 7 | 8 | 9 | 10 | 11 | 12 (major goal) |
| Training Emphasis | Mental and physical recovery | | Hypertrophy and neural strength training, Endurance | | | Acceleration, maximum strength, power | | | Maximum speed, power | | | Maintenance |
| Acceleration | | | | ▓ | | ▓ | | | | | | |
| Maximum Speed | | | | | | | | | ▓ | | | |
| Speed Endurance | | | | | | | | | | ▓ | | |
| Hypertrophy | | | ▓ | | | | | | | | | |
| Maximum Strength | | | | | ▓ | | ▓ | | | | | |
| Power | | | | | | ▓ | | ▓ | ▓ | | | |
| Power Endurance | | | | | | | | | | ▓ | | |

A number of factors must be taken into account when planning speed training. Firstly, when during the session should speed training be done? The aim of speed training is to develop the nervous and muscular systems together. It is therefore important that neither of these systems is fatigued when developing speed. The best way to ensure this is to do the speed work at the beginning of the training session. Speed drills can be included in the warm-up and followed directly by the speed development work.

The second question is when to place the speed sessions during the week? The important rule here is that you should do speed training after a minimum of 24-48 hours of rest or active recovery. This ensures that you are fresh and not tight from the previous training session. An example of a week is shown in Table 8.6 overleaf:

*Table 8.6:* Example of a week allowing recovery for maximal speed development.

|    | Mon  | Tues   | Wed    | Thurs | Fri    | Sat  | Sun    |
|----|------|--------|--------|-------|--------|------|--------|
| am | Rest | Speed  | Drills | Speed | Drills | Rest | Drills |
| pm |      | Weights |       |       | Weights |    |        |

The reason for the strength sessions being held on the same day is that heavy strength training creates significant nervous system and muscle fatigue. Thus, if done the day before a speed session, you may be fatigued from weights and not have good sprint form for your speed workout.

The third commonly asked question is what other training methods inhibit speed development? Short duration endurance work has no effect on speed. However, longer runs, swims, or cycles do turn some of those fast twitch muscle fibers into fibers that are more like the slow twitch endurance type. As a sprinter you need all those fast twitch fibers for speed and power generation.

When during the training phase (preparation or competition) should speed work be performed? The consensus these days is all year round. The difference between the preparation and competition phases is in the intensity and volume of work performed. Speed running volume should be high all year round, but because the intensity of speed training during the preparation phase is lower than during the competition phase, the volume can be greater. The emphasis during preparation is on technique and developing acceleration through quality runs and power-speed drills (pliometrics or accelerations). These sprints are at 95% with strong emphasis on technique and fast, relaxed form. Recovery can be reduced to develop some aerobic endurance but not to the point where form is compromised. During the competition phase, the intensity of speed work is high (95%+) for most sessions. As a result, the recovery between repeats is longer and the volume per session reduced.

As you may have gathered, the method of periodizing speed development where low intensity, high volume training was followed by high intensity, low volume is now outdated. This approach can lead to great losses in explosive speed that cannot be recovered during the competition phase of the year. Thus, to maximize speed potential, speed work should be carried out throughout the whole season. The emphasis is on quality, not quantity. This means that you need to be fresh for your quality speed sessions and highlights the importance of recovery..

### Recovery between sprints (within a session)

Recovery between sprints is a critical factor that can be altered depending on whether an athlete wants to develop maximal speed (in, for example, a one-off, all-out sprint) or speed endurance. The key consideration in developing and improving maximal speed is for the muscles to have near-full reserves of creatine phosphate, the major energy source for creating short-term (<10 seconds) speed. Prior to a one-off sprint, creatine phosphate levels within a muscle are likely to be close to maximum. However, following even a brief sprint of 6-10 seconds, it may take three-five minutes for creatine phosphate to be resynthesised. So, if during training, an athlete is forced to repeat a sprint before creatine phosphate has had sufficient time to resynthesise, that sprint will be slower - which is not desirable if the aging athlete wants to improve maximal speed by having all sprints done at maximal speed.

Sometimes, anaerobic capacity or 'lactate tolerance' is trained (particularly when the games-player wants to mimic match conditions). In this type of training, the recovery between sprint bouts is deliberately kept short - to progressively reduce the levels (and thus the contribution) of creatine phosphate in helping the muscles contract. This puts an ever-greater responsibility on the lactic acid energy system in meeting the energy needs of the sprint. This in turn leads to a significant accumulation of lactic acid and accelerated fatigue. The purpose of this type of training is to deliberately induce fatigue to cause the muscles to adapt to 'game-like' situations.

A golden rule is that when maximal speed is being trained, a full recovery (often perhaps up to and even longer than five minutes) is necessary between sprints. An active (low intensity exercise such as jogging) recovery is known to be more effective than a passive recovery such as sitting or standing. For improving anaerobic capacity or lactate tolerance, keep the recovery periods brief and experience fatigue.

## Recovery between sprint sessions

As stated above, for maximal speed to be improved, the masters athlete needs to be rested and fresh. Careful periodisation within each microcycle (i.e., a seven to ten day block such as in Table 8.6) will help protect sprinters from unwanted fatigue and promote improvements in speed.

Following a hard sprint session, the lactic acid in blood and muscle will disperse and return to 'normal' levels within 30-45 minutes. Moreover, muscle glycogen (carbohydrate) stores can be replenished within 24 hours provided a high carbohydrate diet with some protein is consumed soon after training. However, despite near full recovery of fuel reserves within 24 hours, sprint training on consecutive days will prove counter-productive for most athletes. It is likely that after each hard training session, microscopic damage to the muscle fibers is caused and that 24 hours is simply not long enough for repairs to take place. There is also something coaches refer to as 'central nervous system fatigue'. Although little scientific evidence is available on this phenomenon, it seems reasonable that the nervous system (which is responsible for controlling maximal efforts during sprint exercise) may need an extended time to recover from an intense sprint session. However, aging athletes should normally avoid more than three well-spaced sprint or high intensity training sessions each week.

## Planning the speed and power program

If aging sprint athletes are to achieve faster performances, they must achieve higher maximum speed levels so as to allow greater speeds at less than maximal efforts. They must therefore develop both maximal speed and speed endurance. It thus makes sense to develop maximal speed throughout the training year or season in parallel with speed endurance training. Historically, speed endurance at below maximal speeds was developed prior to maximal speed that was developed in the last 4-6 weeks prior to major competition. A proper progression to develop speed should be:

- Develop proper sprint mechanics – drills.
- Introduce higher intensity sprints over shorter distances that maintain technique.
- Work on speed development over distances less than 5-7 seconds in duration.
- Work on speed development over distances 7-20 seconds in duration.
- Maintain intensity of work between maximum and sub-maximum; and,
- Only allow the athlete to run as far as technique will allow.

As a general rule, the following factors need to be taken into account when developing a speed or power program.

- The shorter the event, the greater the reliance on strength or power (e.g. shot put).
- Where there are large resistances to movement such as body mass or other athletes- rugby union or league, rowing, weightlifting, then power development relies on strength and power.
- Acceleration relies heavily on strength per kilogram of body weight.
- Where resistance to movement is small, speed is more important than strength
- While speed is dependent upon genetics, speed can be developed through maximal speed training.
- Speed and power training should be sequenced to optimize performance. For example, to develop power, the masters athlete should firstly hypertrophy (enlarge) muscles, then develop strength, then power.

## Conclusion

Three basic concepts appear important for speed. Firstly, it is true that "sprinters are born". Unless mum and dad have given us the right (and I know mine didn't!) fiber type, body build, strength, and nervous system, we will find it hard to be quick. Secondly, "speed only comes from speed work". Speed will only be developed through fast training where we teach our muscles to contract maximally and our nervous system to co-ordinate the movements. Too many aging athletes don't adhere to this concept and train slow to race fast. The final concept is "too much speed work makes you stale". It would appear that speed is developed when we are fresh and our muscles and nervous systems are not tired. This strongly suggests that speed training should be done twice a week and at maximum three times with active rest in between. It also suggests that speed training be done at the start of a training session and not, as I often see in the pool or on the playing fields, at the end of a training session.

**Recommended Books**

- Brown, L., Ferrigno, V. and Santana, J. (Eds). (2000). *Training for speed, agility and quickness.* Champaign, IL, Human Kinetics. ISBN: 0-7360-0239-1. Available from Human Kinetics (http://www.humankinetics.com/). Contains numerous drills and exercises for sprint runners and team players. A classic book.
- Chu, D. (1998). Jumping into pliometrics. Champaign, IL, Human Kinetics. ISBN: 13- 9780-8801-18460. Available from Human Kinetics (http://www.humankinetics.com/). A classic book for sprint runners and the most complete book ever written on this form of explosive power training.
- Dintiman, G., Ward, R. and Tellez, T. (1998). *Sports Speed.* Champaign, IL, Human Kinetics. ISBN: 0-88011-607-2. Available from Human Kinetics (http://www.humankinetics.com/). A classic book for sprint runners.

## CHAPTER 9

# DEVELOPING FLEXIBILITY IN MASTERS ATHLETES

*A little push in the right direction can make a big difference.*

**Anonymous**

*Stretching is not stressful. It is peaceful, relaxing and non-competitive.*

**Bob Anderson**

## Introduction

Apart from an age-related reduction in muscle mass and thus strength, power and speed, the loss of flexibility with age is another important factor explaining drops in performance in masters athletes, especially in the speed and power athletes.

To give specific stretches for specific sports is well beyond the scope of this book and chapter. However, this chapter will highlight the science behind aging and flexibility and present the key principles on flexibility training for masters athletes as well as recommend some great websites and books to help with this area of training.

## Definitions

*Flexibility* is the range of motion of single or multiple joints. For example, in freestyle swimmers, a high degree of shoulder and hip rotation flexibility is required to get a high elbow recovery, a good catch, good length of stroke and body roll. Runners need a good stride length so hip flexibility becomes crucial. *Stretching* is the process of elongating connective tissues (ligaments, tendons, joint capsules – the case around the joint that holds in the fluid), muscles and other tissues.

There a number of types of stretching:

1. *Static flexibility* is the range of motion about a joint typically measured in degrees at the end of the joint's movement. Once the muscle and joint are stretched to the point of tension, the stretch is held to allow the connective tissue around the muscle and joint to stretch. No external force is applied to the body. The advantages of static stretching are:
   - Very safe
   - Limited risk of injury
   - Good for overall flexibility
   - Good for beginners
2. *Partner or Object Stretching* is similar to static stretching except another person or object

(e.g. Door, wall, post) is used to increase the degree of stretch. For safety reasons, the object should be immovable and the partner a trusted person who listens and responds to your commands. The advantages of this type of stretching are:
- An increased range of movement
- Good for specific problem areas
- Great for cool-downs when muscles are shortened

3. *Ballistic flexibility* is associated with bouncing or bobbing in a rhythmic motion. The momentum of the limbs or body forcibly increases the range of motion but the risk of injury is higher as is the likelihood of muscle soreness. Thus, ballistic stretching has received very little support from coaches or sport scientist.

4. *Dynamic or functional flexibility* is the opposition or resistance of a joint to motion. It is the actual ability to use the range of joint movement during an activity and is thus very sport-specific. A controlled, soft bounce or swinging motion is used to force the joint past it's normal range of movement. The force of the bounce or swing is gradually increased but always controlled. This type of flexibility correlates most strongly with sports performance. This type of stretching:
- Should only be used by well-trained and conditioned athletes.
- Is very beneficial for athletes who use full-range of motion while moving (e.g. gymnasts, divers).
- Has a high risk of injury.
- Should only be used after a period of static stretching.

5. *Proprioceptive Neuromuscular Facilitation (PNF)* stretching consists of alternating an isometric muscle contraction and static stretching. The area to be stretched is positioned so that the muscle is under tension while in a static stretch. The athlete then contracts the stretched muscle group for six-seconds or more while a partner applies resistance against the contraction to stop the joint moving. The muscle is then relaxed and a controlled stretch applied for the standard 30 seconds. After a 30 second recovery, the process is repeated 2-3 times. While this type of stretches is advanced and should be taught by a qualified sports trainer or physiotherapist and are easier done with a partner, they have been shown to give the greatest benefit compared to static, ballistic or functional flexibility exercises. The advantages of this type of stretching are:
- A greatly increased range of movement.
- Excellent for specific muscle groups.
- Great for rehabilitation.
- Promotes both flexibility and muscle strength.
- Is very useful for athletes who need strength at the end of range of motion (e.g. Rugby forwards, divers, sprinters).

For the best discussion available on the science and methods of stretching mentioned above, see the excellent books at the end of chapter that also give great sport-specific diagrams.

## Benefits of flexibility training

The benefits below only accrue if the exercises are done with correct technique, regularly, and the stretches are done slowly and gradually. The benefits include:

1. Improved performance by a better range of motion (e.g. increased stride or stroke length).
2. Relaxation – both mental and physical.
3. Improved body awareness.
4. Reduced risk of joint sprain or muscle strains.
5. Reduced risk of back problems.
6. Improved postural alignment.
7. Prevention and treatment of many sports-related injuries.
8. Reduced muscle soreness.
9. Reduced muscle tension.
10. Improved strength by lightening the load on opposing muscle groups.

Research has also shown a relationship between poor flexibility and subsequent injury in the Achilles tendon, plantar fascia (arch of the feet), and the hamstring tendons. Stretching programs have been shown to be effective in reducing the severity and frequency of injuries as well as reducing the symptoms of musculoskeletal injuries and regaining the range of motion about an injured joint. For the masters athlete that needs to optimise performance while preventing injury and preventing an age-related decline in flexibility, stretching programs should therefore be essential.

## Factors affecting flexibility

Flexibility is not a general characteristic and is specific to a particular joint, a particular joint action, a particular speed, a particular side of the body and to a given sport or position in that sport. For example, a tennis player or baseball pitcher will be far more flexible in their serving or pitching shoulder than their non-dominant shoulder. Thus, stretching exercises need to be tailored to meet the specific needs of the individual athlete and the sport they play or position they play in. However, regardless of the range of motion about a joint that an individual may have, the following factors influence flexibility:

- *Gender* - typically women are more flexible than men. This is most likely due to hormonal factors and the decreased muscle mass of women.
- *Body temperature* - flexibility increases with heat (about 10-20%) and decreases with cold (about 10%). Hence an aerobic warm-up that elevates the muscle temperature will enhance a stretch.
- *Activity levels* - typically, more physically active people are more flexible.
- *Pain tolerance* - in general, people that can tolerate some pain for extended periods may develop better flexibility.
- *Disease pathology* (eg arthritis or damage to joints) - such pathologies may limit flexibility and stretching.

- *Connective and muscle tissue* - the relative contributions to flexibility are
  - Joint capsule (capsule that hold fluid in the joint) - 47%
  - Muscle and its covering fascia - 41%
  - Tendons and ligaments - 10%
  - Skin - 2%
- *Age* - an age-related decrease in the range of motion about all joints is typically observed. Table 9.1 below shows some of the typical age-related declines in flexibility observed in some joints.

*Table 9.1:* Typical age-related decreases in flexibility of various joints.

| Joint-Action | Decrease from youth (%) |
|---|---|
| Spine extension (arching back) | 50 |
| Hip extension | 20 |
| Hip flexion | 25 |
| Knee flexion | 2 |
| Shoulder flexion | 25 |
| Hip rotation | 10 |
| Ankle flexion | 30 |

### Aging and flexibility

The range of motion about a joint depends primarily on bone, muscle and connective tissue structure and function. Aging affects the structure of the muscle and connective tissue in particular. The major changes that occur with aging are changes to collagen, the primary component of the fibres that make up the covering of muscles, the ligaments, the joint capsule and the tendons that surround a joint. It appears that the water content of these fibres decreases which alters their elasticity. Furthermore, crystals form in all the fibres that make up these structures which also reduces flexibility. Moreover, there is an age-related increase in the cross-linking of these fibres that increase the rigidity of the connective tissue. Finally, degenerative joint disease may further limit the range of motion about a joint. Thus, flexibility declines with age, with the maximum range of motion occurring in the mid- to late twenties.

However, the good news is that older people can improve flexibility with specific stretching exercises. Indeed, a number of studies on older non-athletes have observed improvements in spinal flexibility of between 25 and 40% holding stretches for 10 seconds each, doing them three times each, three times per week.

As with all forms of physical training, the principle of *specificity* is paramount. That is, stretch to prevent sport specific injuries or develop flexibility in the joints that are required for your specific sport, event or position. In this regard, for older athletes, I strongly recommend the book called *Sports Stretch* by Michael J. Alter (www.humankinetics.com) that describes and shows 311 stretches for 41 sports (see details at end of chapter). I also suggest a visit to a specialist sports physiotherapist or at least a physiotherapist who understands your sport. Talk to the high performance coaches or athletes you know about who they might be. When you visit them, ask them to do a *musculoskeletal screening* on you. If you have private health insurance, this is allowable under most schemes so cost will be minimal. The screening will identify any sport-specific weaknesses or imbalances in flexibility and/or strength you may have. They should then prescribe a stretching and/or strengthening program specific to your and your sports needs.

**Principles of flexibility training**

The following principles should be adhered to for a safe and effective static stretching program:

1. *Warm-up* for 10 minutes to increase body temperature and increase blood flow to muscles and connective tissue that limit flexibility (ligaments, tendons). Stretching itself will not warm-up these tissues while a warm-up (light calisthentics, jog, swim or cycle followed by joint rotations, twisting, bending) will enhance muscle and connective tissue extensibility. In cold weather, the warm-up might be more intense and more clothes worn to stay warm during the stretching routine. I do my stretching routines immediately after (and in!) a shower at night and in front of the TV.
2. *Isolate the muscle group to be stretched*. Alter's book gives excellent examples for 41 sports.
3. *Use correct alignment and technique*. Again, Alter's book is excellent for this with great diagrams and dot-pointed explanations.
4. *Exhale going into the stretch* to facilitate relaxation during the stretch.
5. *Breathe normally during the stretch* but accentuate exhaling when going deeper into the stretch.
6. *Hold the stretch at the point of tension, not pain.*
7. *Hold the stretch for 10 to 30 seconds.* A study has found holding a hamstring stretch for 60 seconds just as effective as a 30-second stretch.
8. *Come out of the stretch as carefully as you go into it.*
9. *Do 2-3 repetitions of a 10-second stretch or one of a 30-second stretch.* Given that the lack of flexibility is due to connective tissue tightness, research has shown that low force, long duration stretching is the most effective to get increased range of motion about a joint.
10. *Stretch 3-5 days per week.*
11. *If your sport demands dynamic flexibility, incorporate a progressively-increasing velocity flexibility strategy.* That is, stretch in the following order:
    a. Static
    b. Slow, short of end of range stretching (below 75% of actual sport speed)
    c. Slow, full range stretching (again below 75% of actual sport speed)
    d. Fast, short of end of range stretching

e. Fast, full range stretching

A pre-stretching warm-up does give an added benefit over stretching alone in improving long term flexibility, although a warm-up (e.g. easy cycling, warm-shower) has been shown to help maximise a stretch in the short term and minimise injury during stretching.

In summary, the American College of Sports Medicine (ACSM) recommends that static stretches should be held for 10 to 30 seconds, whereas, PNF techniques should include a six-second contraction of the muscle followed by a 10- to 30-second assisted stretch. The ACSM also recommends at least four repetitions per muscle group should be completed a minimum of 2-3 days per week while Alter suggests 3-5 days per week and 1-3 repetitions per stretch depending on the length of time the stretch is held.

## Effects of flexibility training

An effective stretching program will improve the factors that limit our flexibility. These changes include:

- The stretch reflex (a reflex that makes a muscle contract if stretched too far) is reset to a longer muscle length allowing the muscle to be stretched further before resistance of the muscle contracting.
- Muscles increase their length by adding more sarcomeres, the small working units in a muscle that when they contract in series, cause a muscle to contract. This theoretically also means an increase in strength.
- The connective tissue around the muscle fibres and muscle itself get longer.
- Other connective tissues that surround a joint also get longer (ligaments, tendons and joint capsules - they keep the fluid enclosed around a joint).
- Scar tissue developed over years of small or large tears have their cross-links broken down.
- Stretching stimulates the production of gel-like substances that help lubricate the connective tissue making them freer to move.

All of the above help improve our range of motion that in older athletes is crucial for maintaining or improving the range of motion about a joint and in turn minimising the risk of injury while helping to maximise performance.

## Retention of flexibility

Until recently, little was known about the retention of flexibility after stopping training. A recent study recruited 33 University students and divided them into three groups – a control group who did nothing different, a group who did flexibility training for 5 consecutive days doing three 30-second stretches, and a third group who did the same stretching but with heat applied. Each person was tested before and after the 5-day program, then 25 days after stopping the training. Flexibility improved in the flexibility groups and was retained for the whole 25 days at levels greater than before the training began.

## Concurrent weight and flexibility training

Doing both weight training and flexibility training is thought to increase flexibility levels more than just flexibility training alone. This assumes that when doing the weight training, we emphasise the full range of motion of the joint(s) involved in the weight training exercise. It also assumes that stretching exercises are included in the training program, and that the muscles surrounding the front and back of the joint are trained.

A number of studies have also shown that peak strength and power can be increased by flexibility training. It is suggested that the stretching programs reduced the elastic stiffness of the muscles and joints, and may increase the number of individual structural elements within a muscle fibre.

## Precautions when flexibility training

Alter's book *Sports Stretch* suggests stretching should never be done if:
- A bone blocks the motion.
- You recently fractured a bone.
- You have an inflammation in or around a joint.
- You have osteoporosis.
- You experience sharp pain with joint movement or muscle elongation.
- You've had a recent sprain or strain.
- Your joint lacks stability.
- You suffer vascular (blood vessel) disorders or skin diseases.
- You suffer a loss of function or decrease in range of joint motion.
- Are hypermobile (large range of motion) in a joint.

If you have any of the above see a sports physiotherapist or sports physician for advice.

## Contraindicated stretches

All stretches present some risk if done with incorrect technique or by not following the above guidelines or precautions. While the stretches listed below may be seen as advanced stretches and of use to those who need them for specific sports (e.g. martial arts, dancing, wrestling, yoga) or who have developed the flexibility over years to do them safely, in general they should not be used by the average athlete. I have also included some exercises that are commonly used but that can be detrimental to athlete conditioning programs. The contraindicated stretches and exercises include:

- *The Plough* - lying on your back then bringing your knees over your head and placing them beside your head with arms extended on the floor behind you. It places enormous pressure on the neck, lower back and intervertebral discs and compresses the lungs and heart making breathing difficult.
- *Knee Sitting* - kneeling down on your knees with your bottom on your calves. This places stress on the patellar tendon and ligaments of the knee and should be avoided,

especially by aging athletes with a history of knee injury.
- *Hurdler's Stretch* - this stretch does help with hamstring and lower back flexibility but also stretches the medial (inside) ligament on the inside of the knee promoting knee instability.
- *Deep Knee Bend* - can endanger the lateral (outside) ligament of the knee and compress the cartilage in the middle of the knee joint. Obviously weight lifters, gymnasts and baseball catchers need it.
- *Back Hyperextension* - lying flat on your stomach and grabbing the ankles with your hands creating an arch in your back. This places great stress on the lower spine.
- *Trunk Twist* - particularly done with weights, it places strain on the knee ligaments. In sports such as tennis, golf or throwing sports it is obviously important and bending the knees slightly can help reduce the strain.
- *Standing Straight Leg Toe Touch* - forces the knee to hyperextend to the back and places great pressure on the lumbar spine. Obviously, divers and gymnasts who pike and weightlifters need it.
- *The Bridge* - lying on your back them arching your back up so much you have your weight on the hands and feet only. This places enormous pressure on the spinal discs and pinches nerve fibres between these discs. In sports such as wresting, judo and gymnastics it is important.
- *Inversion* - hanging from a bar or wearing boots and hanging raises blood pressure and may rupture blood vessels.
- *Double-Leg Lifts* - lying on your back and then lifting straight legs off the floor for 10-20 centimetres. This exercise places great stress on the lower back. Athletes with heavy legs and weak abdominal muscles are at greatest risk.
- *Straight-Leg Sit-Ups* - also places great stress on the lower back.

## Acute effects of stretching on strength and power

Stretching prior to an event has long been a part of warm-up in sport. The belief has long been that by increasing the range of motion about the joint we reduce the risk of injury and improve our performance. There is no doubt that stretching anecdotally and theoretically reduces injury, although no scientific evidence suggests it does.

However, recent research is suggesting that stretching immediately prior to strength and power events may reduce power output and force production and thus performance in power events. For example, one study showed decreased vertical jump performance after three different stretches of the hip and knee extensor muscles while another study showed decreased maximum lifts in leg curl and leg extensions following both static or ballistic stretching. The reduced strength performance prompted the researchers to recommend at least 20 minutes between static stretching and strength or power performance.

## Conclusion

With increased age comes a reduction in flexibility. Given that the range of motion about a joint is crucial for sports performance, a flexibility training program should become, like weight training, essential for masters athletes.

A sports physiotherapist should be consulted by the competitive masters athlete as they have the skills to conduct a musculoskeletal screening to identify sport-specific muscle strength imbalances, sport-specific joint flexibility problems, and then to prescribe a flexibility program specific to your sport and event.

## Recommended Books

- Alter, M. (1998). *Sport Stretch* (2$^{nd}$ Edn). Champaign, Illinois, Human Kinetics. ISBN: 0-88011-823-7. Available from Human Kinetics (www.humankinetics.com). Contains 311 stretches for 41 sports. The classic book for sports stretching.
- Frederick, A. and Frederick, C. (2006). *Stretch to Win*. Champaign, Illinois, Human Kinetics. ISBN: 0-73605-529-0. Available from Human Kinetics (www.humankinetics.com). Covers the science and practice of flexibility training with a large variety of stretching methods specific to many sports.

# CHAPTER 10

## PERIODISATION AND PEAKING FOR THE MASTERS ATHLETE

*The thinking must be done first, before the training begins.*

Peter Coe

*Failing to plan means planning to fail.*

Lawrie Lawrence

*Step by step. I can't see any other way of accomplishing anything.*

Michael Jordon

*If you don't know where you are going, every road will get you nowhere.*

Henry Kissinger

*If I had nine hours to cut down a tree,
I would spend six hours sharpening my axe.*

Abraham Lincoln

*The quality of the finished product cannot be better than
the quality of the raw materials placed in process.*

Broom and Longenecker

## Introduction

Peaking at the right time of a season demands preparation and planning. I see too many aging athletes that train the house down but cannot get it together on the race day. Creating that "peak" takes not only months of blood sweat and tears but working hard at times and easy at times (a concept called *periodisation*) and maximising all that work through tapering of that training (a concept called *peaking*). The purpose of this chapter is to introduce both these concepts and outline the guiding principles behind each.

## Periodisation

Periodisation is no more than a technical term for adopting a sensible and well-planned approach to training. A well-planned season maximises training gains and performance improvement.

Periodisation involves dividing the training year (or season) into different phases. During each phase of the training year, one or more of the physical demands (e.g. endurance, strength, speed etc.) of the event or game is *emphasised*. In general, lower intensity base training is performed several months before important event. As the competition draws closer, higher intensity and more specific training must be done. While having to plan ahead might seem difficult, the alternative is usually an *ad hoc* approach to training which guarantees less than optimal improvement in performance. Sadly, most masters athletes I know take this *ad hoc* approach to their training rather than having a goal for each workout (e.g. speed or endurance development, <u>not</u> both), each week of training (e.g. speed development with endurance maintenance), or each month or similar block of time.

The key to success is a well-organised training program, sometimes formulated years in advance of a major competition (e.g. World Masters Games or State, National or World Championships). A well-thought out and periodised plan acts as the framework for the training workouts on a daily, weekly, monthly and perhaps yearly basis. This approach allows a logical and sensible progression in an athlete's training load such that the factors of frequency, duration and intensity are blended into a comprehensive plan. Exactly how this should be done for each individual is beyond the capability of science and is more an art based on personal experience, knowledge of your strengths and weaknesses and knowledge of the guiding principles discussed in this chapter for each training phase.

## Planning the Yearly Training Program

As shown in Table 10.1 below, there are three main training phases in any annual training plan:

1. The preparation (pre-season) phase
2. The competition (in-season) phase
3. The transition (off-season) phase

*Table 10.1:* Division of the annual training plan into its sub-phases, macrocycles (3-6 weeks) and microcycles (weeks).

| Phases of Training | Preparation Phase | | Competition Phase | | Transition Phase |
|---|---|---|---|---|---|
| Sub-Phases | General Preparation | Specific Preparation | Pre-Competition | Competition | Transition |
| Macrocycles | | | | | |
| Microcycles | 1 2 3　1 2 3 | 1 2　1 2　1 2 | 1 2　1 2 | 1 2 3 4 5 6　1 2　1 1　1 2 | 1 2 3 4 |

The *preparation phase* is normally divided into *general* and *specific* preparation sub-phases.

Similarly, the *competition phase* is further divided into *pre-competitive* and *competitive* sub-phases. The types of training performed and the overall training load for each of the sub-phases must vary depending on forthcoming competition demands. Each of the phases and sub-phases is composed of smaller cycles (periods of time) in order to make the organization and planning of the training program more systematic and manageable. These cycles are called *macrocycles* and *microcycles*. A macrocycle is usually one month (3-6 weeks) in length while a microcycle is typically one week in length, such that four to five microcycles make up one macrocycle.

The basic premise of all periodised training programs is that training should move from general to specific and emphasise the unique needs of each athlete. For example, during the general preparation phase, a masters road cyclist needing strength (that sounds like me!) should work out with weights in the gym to develop general strength (heh, I'm doing that!). However, during the pre-competition phase, more time should be spent doing hills or simulating race pace and less time spent in the gym.

Each of the macrocycles and microcycles has specific objectives for the development of certain abilities in the athlete (e.g. speed, strength, flexibility, skill, etc.), which fit with the overall objectives for each of the training phases. It should be noted that the length of the respective phases and sub-phases would vary between different sports and depend greatly on an individual athlete's strengths, weaknesses and years of training. For example, a masters rower with 30-40 years of consistent rowing behind them may not need a long general preparation phase because of their training age.

Periodisation also involves arranging training workouts in such a way that the fitness elements (e.g. endurance, speed, strength) developed during the general preparation period are maintained while new ones are focused on and gradually emphasised more during the specific preparation phase. Small changes are introduced during the 3-6 week macrocycles. The targeted fitness element is gradually developed and is then maintained as a new element is then focused on.

When planning the yearly training program it is wise to work backwards from the date of the most important competition, and organise the phases and cycles of the training year according to this calendar date. As a general rule, and following the principle of progressive overload, volume and intensity are gradually increased during the preparation phases and when the competition phase is entered, volume drops while intensity is increased (see Figure 10.1 overleaf).

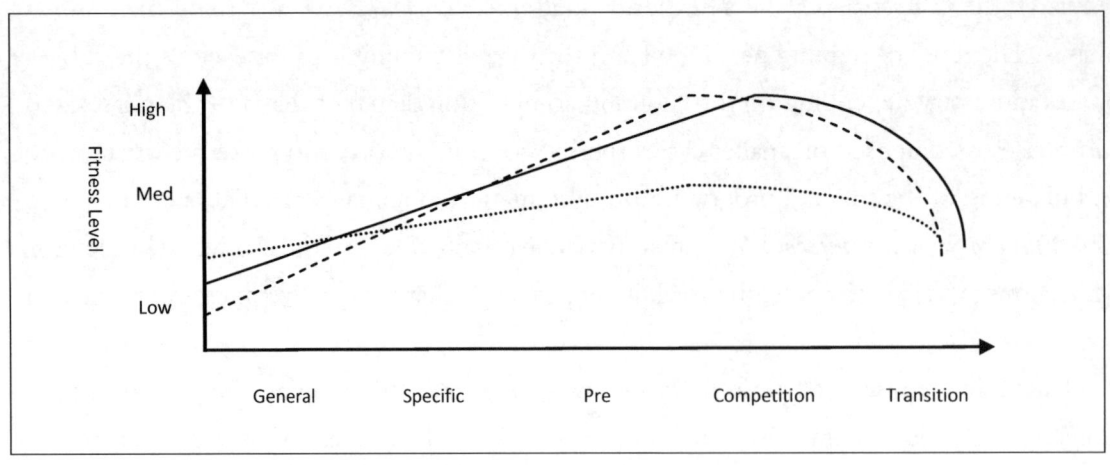

*Figure 10.1:* General principle of varying training volume and intensity to produce a peak.
───── *Fitness*   ------- *Intensity*   ··········· *Volume*

## Training Load Progression

Improvements in sports performance for an athlete of any age are a direct result of the amount and quantity of work the athlete achieves during training. Workload must increase gradually according to each aging athletes' physiological and psychological abilities, their ability to adapt to the training load, and their motivation to succeed. The physiological basis of this principle of progressive overload is that the body adapts to the training stimulus and improves its efficiency and capacity to do the work being demanded of it. The rate of improvement will depend on the structure of the annual plan and how well the athlete structures their macrocycles and microcycles to incorporate periods of hard work with periods of rest and recovery.

According to the leading authority on training methodology, Dr Tudor Bompa, four theories have been proposed to progressively overload an athlete.

1. ***Standard Loading.***

   In most team sports, the number of training sessions per week is usually 2-3, the games are once a week, the pre-season training is 4-12 weeks depending upon the level of competition, and the season is a prescribed length. Training for sports that demand week in - week out competition means early season fitness must be developed early and then maintained throughout the season as shown in Figure 10.2. Because of limits on the available time for training, it is difficult to develop fitness during the competition phase of the year.

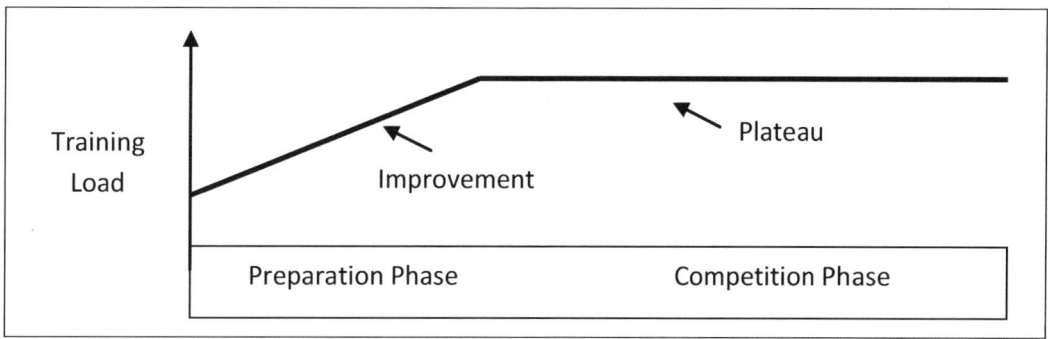

*Figure 10.2:* Standard loading typical of team players who show improvement only in the preparation and pre-competition phases of training.

2. *Overloading*

Historically, it was believed that athletes only developed their fitness if they were overloaded with training load greater than those normally experienced. This method was developed from short-term training studies completed in the early days of sport science and suggested that athletes need to be continually overloaded with more frequent, greater intensity, or greater volumes of training in order to gain benefits (Figure 10.3).

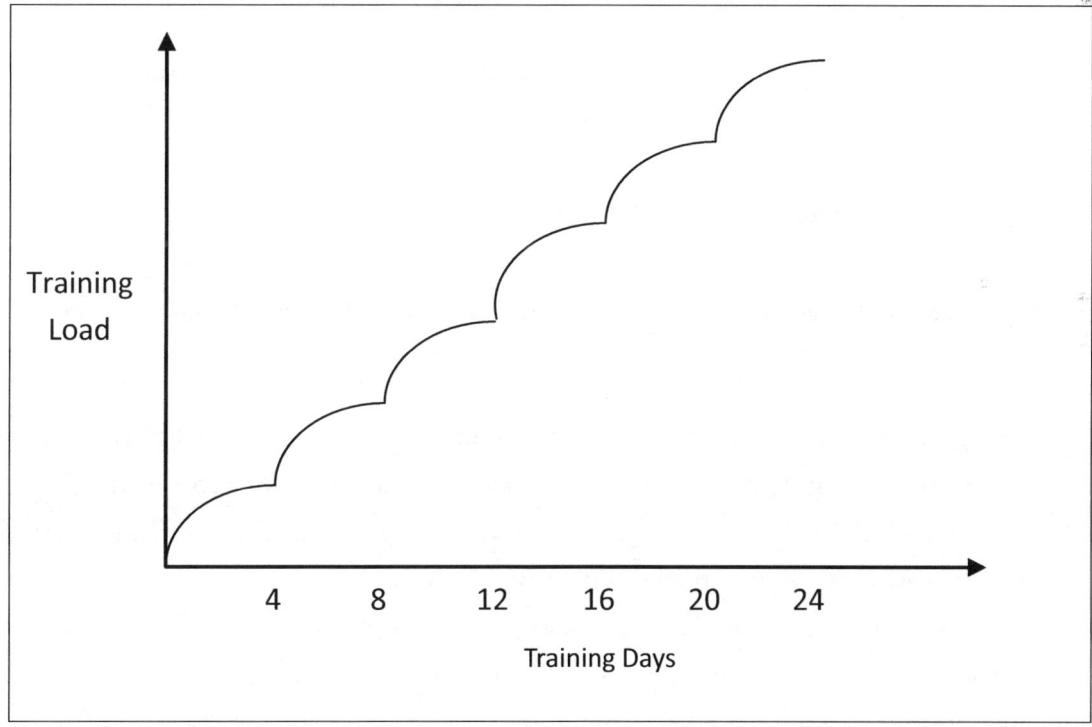

*Figure 10.3:* Progressive overloading model of periodisation.

The standard loading curve suggests that the athlete is continually being loaded with no time for recovery or regeneration. This was the old "no pain, no gain" principle – just keep pushing and you (hopefully!) will come out the other end a better athlete. In the short-term, such a method of loading may work, but longer term it leads to staleness, fatigue, burnout and overtraining.

### 3. Flat Loading

For the highly developed and experienced, world class masters athlete who might be competing regularly at a high level (there aren't too many of them around folks!), flat loading might be suggested. It involves three microcycles of high intensity or high volume training followed by a regeneration or recovery microcyle. The training is the highest the athlete can tolerate without getting injured or ill and the recovery week consists of low volume, high intensity training with plenty of rest and recovery using the methods outlined in Chapter 15.

### 4. Step Loading

Research has conclusively shown that an athlete under the physiological stress of training needs time to adapt to the imposed training stress. It is now widely accepted by elite coaches and younger athletes that this model shown in Figure 10.4 applies to any athlete of any age. That is, training induces fatigue. When rest or recovery training follows this training fatigue, adaptation and fitness improvements take place.

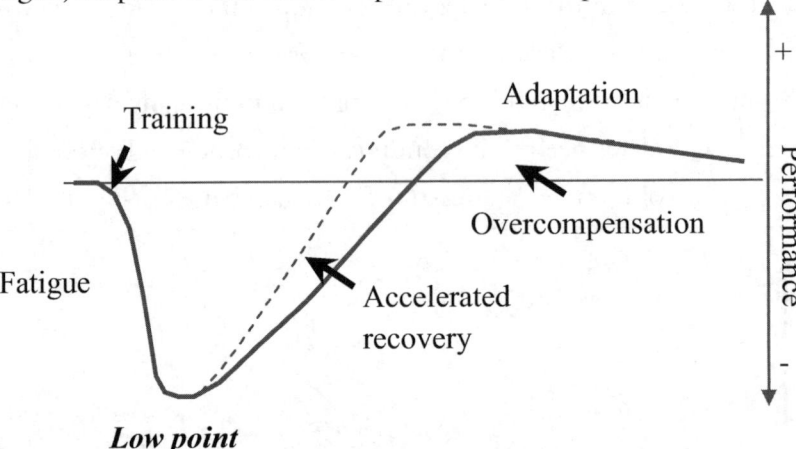

*Figure 10.4:* Training-adaptation model widely accepted as the model for optimising an athlete's performance.

Thus, the *Step Loading Model* of overloading an athlete demands two key components. Firstly, ever increasing training stress and secondly, time to adapt and recover. In accordance with the principle of progressive overload discussed in Chapter 4, there are a number of ways that training stress can be increased including:

- Increasing the number of training sessions per microcycle or macrocycle (e.g. week 1 = 4 sessions, week 2 = 5 sessions, week 3 = 6 sessions, week 4 = 4/5 sessions)
- Increasing the number of hours training per cycle (e.g. week 1 = 4 hours, week 2 = 6 hours, week 3 = 8 hours, week 4 = 6 hours)
- Increasing the number of high intensity training sessions per cycle (e.g. week 1 = 1 session, week 2 = 2 sessions, week 3 = 3 sessions, week 4 = 1 session)
- Increasing the total number of drills, repeats or distance covered per cycle (e.g. week 1 = 8 x 100m swims, week 2 = 10 x 100m swims, week 3 = 15 x 100m swims, week 4 = 10 x 100m swims)

Any of these variables can be manipulated to induce step loading that is simply demonstrated in Figure 10.5 below. As the figure suggests, the vertical lines suggest an increased loading that progresses in a stepwise fashion from easy to medium to hard then back to a relatively easy week. The horizontal lines represent the period of adaptation. The first three microcycles (weeks) suggest an increased training load (e.g. kilometres run, number of hard intervals, weight lifted) while the last microcycle (week 4) is an unloading period where the weights are lowered, the distance run decreased, or the number of intervals cut.

There is a direct relationship between the length and height of each step in Figure 10.5. The longer the length of adaptation, the greater the increase in either or both the volume and intensity of training.

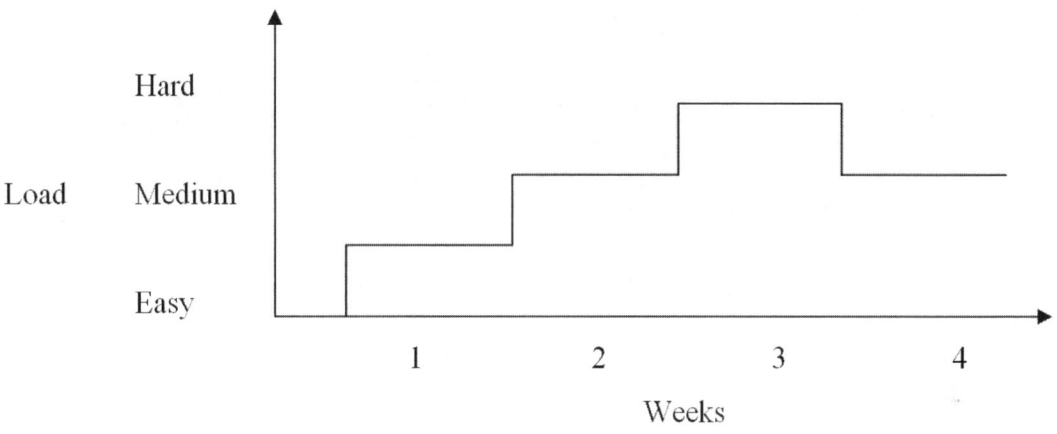

*Figure 10.5:* Increasing training load using the Step Loading Model.

While the step loading model might suggest a mathematically equal increase in the training load, this is not the case. One training session is not enough to induce an adaptation. The same training stimulus needs to be applied a number of times over a microcycle or macrocycle to gain adaptations. Sport scientists suggest a 3-6% increase in training intensity per microcycle or 5-10% increase in training volume (distance, number of repeats, total weight) per microcycle. If the increase in either is greater, then other factors such as intensity or duration should be dropped to compensate.

## A Typical Macrocycle

Figure 10.5 above demonstrates a four week macrocycle with four one-week microcycles. Importantly, each microcycle is emphasising a particular fitness component (e.g. strength, speed or endurance) or training intensity (e.g. heart rate zone, running speed). Indeed, each macrocycle should also be emphasizing a component or element of fitness. We start with general training but as we get closer to the major goal, the training should become more race or event specific in duration and intensity. Over the period of a macrocycle, any number of training variables can be changed including the number of training sessions per week, the distance covered per week, the number of high intensity sessions per week, or the number of repeats completed per session.

Table 10.2 below shows an example of four-week macrocycle that manipulates the number of high intensity training sessions per week. The gridded cells represent high intensity sessions with week 4's high intensity session being of shorter duration, having less intervals, and having longer rest between intervals.

*Table 10.2:* Increasing training load by increasing the number of high intensity training sessions per microcycle (week). Gridded cells are high intensity sessions.
R = Recovery, L = Low intensity, M = Medium intensity, H = High intensity.

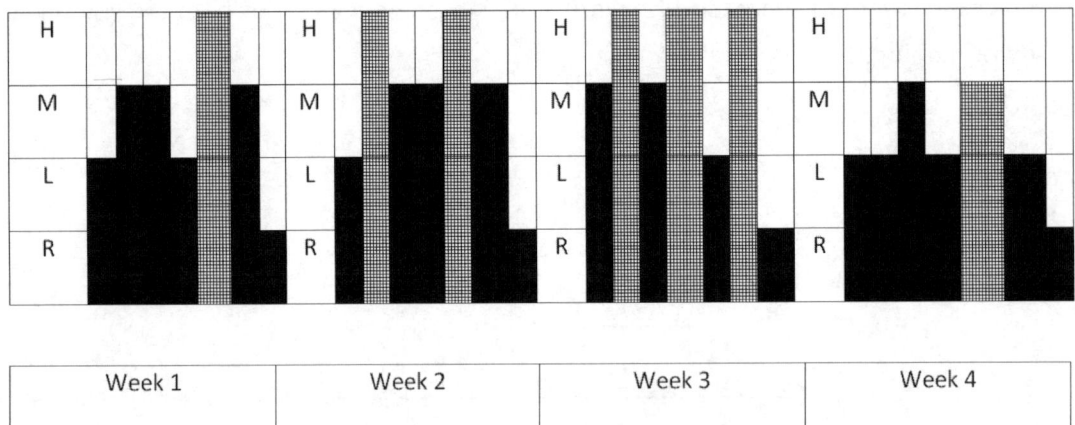

| Week 1 | Week 2 | Week 3 | Week 4 |

Table 10.3 below presents an example of a four-week macrocycle for an endurance runner who is just beginning the general preparation sub-phase of training. As can be seen, there are six training sessions (four running and two weights sessions) planned for each microcycle, and four microcycles make up the macrocycle.

*Table 10.3:* A typical macrocycle for an endurance runner at the beginning of the general preparation sub-phase of training.

| Type of Training | M | T | W | Th | F | S | S | M | T | W | Th | F | S | S | M | T | W | Th | F | S | S | M | T | W | Th | F | S | S |
|---|---|---|---|---|---|---|---|---|---|---|---|---|---|---|---|---|---|---|---|---|---|---|---|---|---|---|---|---|
| Low Intensity Continuous Aerobic | X |  | X | X |  | X |  | X |  | X | X |  | X |  | X |  |  | X |  | X |  | X |  |  |  | X |  |  |
| Aerobic Intervals |  |  |  |  |  |  |  |  |  |  |  |  |  |  |  |  | X |  | X |  |  |  |  | X |  |  |  |  |
| Anaerobic Threshold Intervals |  |  |  |  |  |  |  |  |  |  |  |  |  |  |  |  |  |  |  |  |  |  |  |  | X |  |  |  |
| Weight Training |  | X |  | X |  |  |  |  | X | X |  |  |  |  |  | X | X |  |  |  |  |  | X | X |  |  |  |  |
| Recovery Days |  |  |  |  |  |  | X |  |  |  |  |  |  | X |  |  |  |  |  |  | X |  |  |  |  |  |  | X |
| Objectives | Develop Endurance Base  Minimise Soreness in Week 1 | | | | | | | Develop Endurance Base  Increase Weekly km by 10% | | | | | | | Develop Endurance Base  Introduce Aerobic Intervals  Increase Reps in Weights | | | | | | | Develop Endurance Base  Intro AnT Intervals | | | | | | |
|  | Microcycle 1 | | | | | | | Microcycle 2 | | | | | | | Microcycle 3 | | | | | | | Microcycle 4 | | | | | | |

The types of training used reflect the phase of training; here the athlete is just beginning to prepare for the next competitive season, therefore the objective of this macrocycle would be to develop an endurance base of fitness. Hence, endurance base training is programmed and emphasised.

After the first two microcycles (weeks) where aerobic endurance is emphasised, more intense (aerobic intervals and anaerobic threshold intervals) training workouts are gradually introduced, in preparation for future macrocycles. The training sessions are spaced over the week such that there is no more than one session per day and the athlete has to run only once on consecutive days (Friday and Saturday). This is designed to allow for sufficient recovery time between run training sessions, so that the athlete does not become tired and stale from too much training. With this in mind, the seventh "training session" for the week is a planned recovery day, where the athlete does no formal training or may use massage, spa, and/or other recovery techniques (see Chapter 15) in order to overcome the fatigue induced by the training sessions, and start "fresh" for the next week's training.

## A Typical Microcycle

The microcycle is the hub of the training program as it involves all the training sessions for the week. As a general rule, only one or two microcycles should be planned in advance, as the rate and degree of improvement by different athletes cannot always be accurately predicted. In contrast, the macrocycle should be planned in advance, although more or less microcycles than originally thought may be needed to meet its objectives (e.g. speed or strength or endurance development). Here the athlete and coach need to be flexible and sensible in conducting the training program.

Table 10.4 overleaf presents an example of a microcycle for a 50-year old 100 metre sprinter in the competition phase of training who has a weekend club meet. The objective of this microcycle is to maintain the athlete's speed and power developed in the previous macrocycles and microcycles, and also to improve start, relay changeover and running technique, while allowing sufficient recovery pre-competition.

There are two morning weight training sessions, with the heavier loads and greater volume occurring earlier in the week (Tuesday), and the lighter loads and lesser volume being programmed later in the week (Thursday), which is closer to the competition day. The Monday and Wednesday afternoon sessions are the harder track workouts, with the Tuesday and Thursday afternoon sessions emphasising skill and technique more than conditioning. There are three half-day recovery sessions programmed (Monday, Wednesday and Friday mornings), with a full day of recovery both preceding and following the competition day. Also, the harder afternoon sessions are separated by an easier afternoon Tuesday workout as it is inappropriate to program high intensity workouts on consecutive days.

To allow sufficient recovery and enable athletes to perform quality workouts without being restricted by fatigue from earlier training sessions, at least one day of recovery or easier training should always separate the hardest training workouts in a microcycle. Furthermore, no more than two high intensity sessions should be programmed in any one microcycle, as this may overload the athlete and reduce the expected improvement in performance.

Dr Tudor Bompa, the guru of the concept of periodisation, has suggested that the

*Table 10.4:* A typical microcycle for a veteran 100 metre sprinter during the competition phase of training.

|      | Monday | Tuesday | Wednesday | Thursday | Friday | Saturday | Sunday |
|------|--------|---------|-----------|----------|--------|----------|--------|
| AM   | Recovery | Gym – Power<br>3 x 4 squats<br>85% 1RM<br>2 x 10 step-ups with bar<br>3 x 4 bench press 85% 1RM<br>3 x 10 hip extensions 85% 1RM<br>3 x 6 seated row 85% 1RM<br>3 x 8 leg curls 75% 1RM | Recovery | Gym-Power<br>3 x 8 squats 60% 1RM<br>3 x 6 box jumps<br>3 x 6 cleans at 60% 1RM<br>2 x 12 medicine ball catch and throws – 5 kg | Recovery | Recovery | Recovery<br>Low Intensity Aerobic Intervals |
| PM   |        | Low intensity aerobic training<br>Jog curves, stride straights for 4 laps<br>Sprint Training<br>4 x 60m on 5 mins at 100% speed<br>3 x 150m on 8 mins at 90% speed | Sprint Training<br>2 x (4 x 75m) at max speed with 5 mins between reps and 10 mins between sets<br>Technique drills 15-20 mins at 75% max speed<br>4 lap easy jog | Sprint Training<br>6 x 30m starts at max speed with 3 mins between reps<br>4 x 50m sprints on curves at max speed on 4 mins<br>4 lap easy jog | Recovery | Compete | Recovery |

Pliometrics
2 x 4 double leg long jumps
2 x 4 low hurdle jumps
2 x 20m bounding

following principles be adhered to when developing a microcycle:
- If doing both speed (or strength) and endurance training, an endurance training session should be *after* a speed or strength session
- For quality work (speed, strength or high intensity endurance training), be fresh
- Learn and perfect technique with medium intensity
- Then perfect technique at below maximum and then maximum intensity
- Then develop your general fitness then your specific fitness
- Maximum intensity training should be done only twice in a week
- Submaximal endurance training should be done a minimum of three times per week
- Two sessions per week maintains strength, flexibility and speed
- Two-three sessions per week are needed to develop power
- Rest and recovery should be a minimum of once per week
- Follow intense training sessions with easier sessions

When doing the actual planning for a microcycle, the following factors must be considered:
- Establish the objectives of the microcycle (e.g. develop endurance base, develop strength)
- Plan the number of training sessions, the volume (distance covered, number of repeats, total weight), and the intensity
- Decide how many easy, moderate and hard sessions in the week
- Decide where to put them in the week – see examples in Figures 10.6 - 10.9 below
- Decide the type of training (speed, intervals, continuous, pliometrics etc)
- Start the microcycle with low- or moderate-intensity sessions and gradually increase the intensity
- Before an important competition, use a one-peak microcycle that occurs 3-5 days before the event.

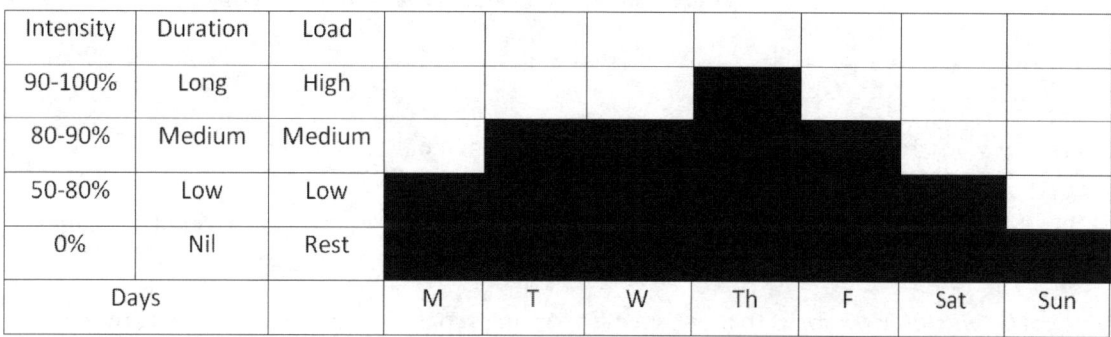

*Figure 10.6:* Microcycle (week) with one peak.

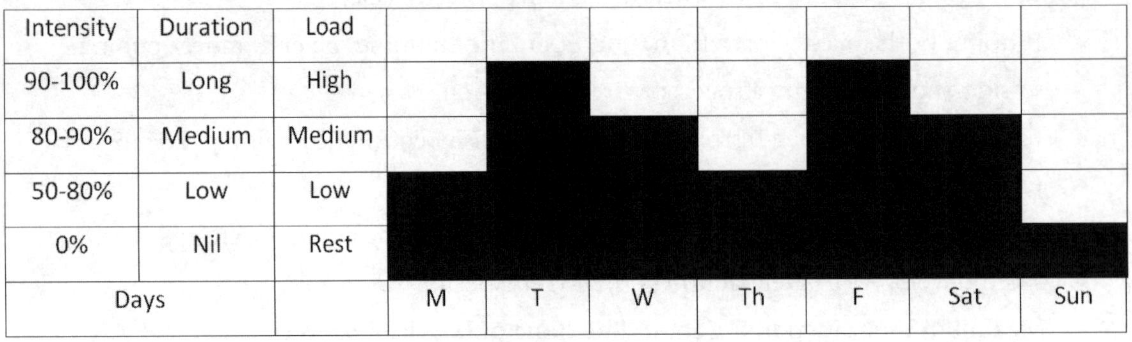

| Intensity | Duration | Load | | | | | | | |
|---|---|---|---|---|---|---|---|---|---|
| 90-100% | Long | High | | | | | | | |
| 80-90% | Medium | Medium | | | | | | | |
| 50-80% | Low | Low | | | | | | | |
| 0% | Nil | Rest | | | | | | | |
| Days | | | M | T | W | Th | F | Sat | Sun |

*Figure 10.7:* Microcycle (week) with two peaks.

| Intensity | Duration | Load | | | | | | | |
|---|---|---|---|---|---|---|---|---|---|
| 90-100% | Long | High | | | | | | | |
| 80-90% | Medium | Medium | | | | | | | |
| 50-80% | Low | Low | | | | | | | |
| 0% | Nil | Rest | | | | | | | |
| Days | | | M | T | W | Th | F | Sat | Sun |

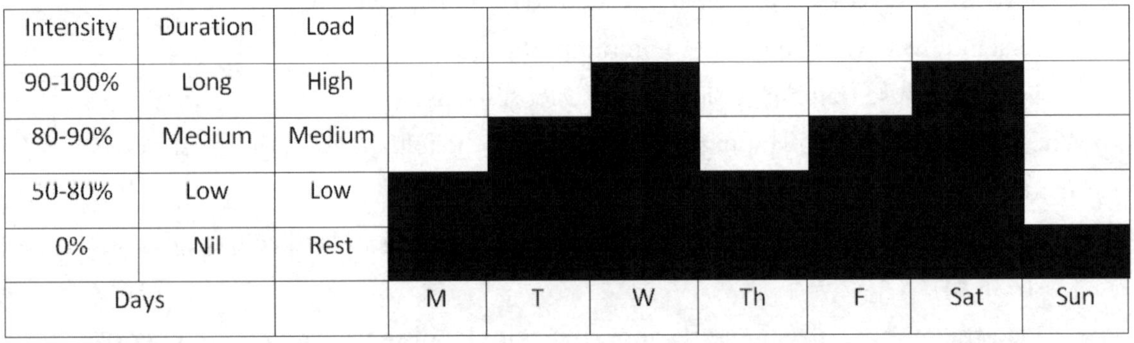

*Figure 10.8:* Another example of a microcycle (week) with two peaks.

| Intensity | Duration | Load | | | | | | | |
|---|---|---|---|---|---|---|---|---|---|
| 90-100% | Long | High | | | | | | | |
| 80-90% | Medium | Medium | | | | | | | |
| 50-80% | Low | Low | | | | | | | |
| 0% | Nil | Rest | | | | | | | |
| Days | | | M | T | W | Th | F | Sat | Sun |

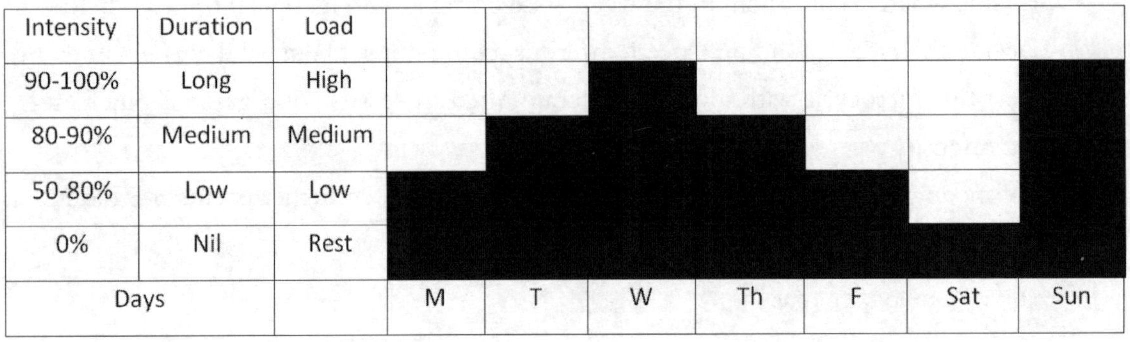

*Figure 10.9:* Microcycle (week) with two peaks, Sunday being a competition.

Dr Bompa refers to four types of microcycles that each depend on the overall training objective and where they sit in the overall annual plan:

1. *Developmental Microcycles* that are specific to the preparation phase. The aims are to develop skills, technique, weaknesses, and general endurance. For example, Figure 10.8 might be for a masters triathlete in early season training who might do a long run on the Wednesday and a long ride on the Saturday.
2. *Shock Microcycles* that suddenly increase training demands beyond those previously experienced. These are often used during the preparation phase and may have three peaks of long and/or hard work. Such a microcycle became famous here in Queensland

with legendary swim coach Lawrie Lawrence who would have week-long swim camps on the Gold Coast early season where he pushed young swimmers beyond their normal boundaries with surf swims, beach runs and 2-3 swim sessions a day. Such shock microcycles are taxing mentally and physically and should be followed by a regeneration microcycle.

3. *Regeneration Microcycles* remove fatigue from the body and mind and restore energy levels to levels that enable the athlete to work hard again. Low intensity or low volume training is suggested. These microcycles are used after shock microcycles, periods of heavy training or after a series of competitions and are effective in preventing overtraining.

4. *Peaking and Unloading Microcycles* are microcycles where the overall volume of training is dropped but intensity is maintained and frequency of training is reduced or maintained. It sets up the athlete for a major performance by reducing fatigue and priming all the systems for a maximum effort. Such a cycle will be discussed later in this chapter in the section on tapering and peaking.

In general, it appears from the available research that different components of fitness are developed at different rates. For example, it has been suggested that regular flexibility training shows benefits within days, strength within weeks, speed from month to month, but cardiovascular endurance may take years to develop to a competitive level. Thus, the increases in loads (frequency, duration, intensity) are generally smaller for endurance development than they are for strength development where gains are relatively fast compared to those seen with endurance training.

I see too many masters athletes doing the same program, generally developed in an ad hoc manner, year after year and never improve. They wonder what they need to do to get better. The answer is to try something new. Try planning the season based on the above principles of periodisation, try a new type of training stimulus (this book is pushing flexibility training, speed work, and in particular weight training for the masters athlete), or try higher intensity training that is followed by a period of adaptation.

## Planning a Training Session

To achieve maximum benefits, each training session must be planned in advance and designed to fit into the overall objectives of the current microcycle. This, however, does not mean that each training session directly promotes the main objective of the microcycle. For example, a low intensity aerobic training session, separating two maximal sprint training sessions, does not directly work to improve speed and power for a sprinter, which may be the main objective of the microcycle. The easy aerobic session is just as important as the more specific sprint workouts in achieving the overall objectives of the microcycle, as it helps to facilitate good recovery between the intense training sessions, without which the same degree of improvement could occur.

Once again, it is important to understand that easier training sessions and recovery

sessions are fundamental to improvement in an aging athlete's performance. High intensity training workouts cannot be performed every day and should not be programmed more than twice a week for the recreational aging athlete or three times for the more experienced aging athlete with a large training age. Therefore, in planning a training session, the type of training to be performed should be determined by considering:
- Objectives of the microcycle
- Date of the next competition
- Yesterday's training
- Tomorrow's training.

## The Structure of a Training Session

Each training session can be split into various segments and should be conducted in a logical sequence. The correct ordering of training activities is important in order to avoid one training activity (e.g. endurance) reducing the effectiveness of another (e.g. speed). An example of incorrect ordering would be the programming of skill work for a touch player immediately after completing an intense period of repeated short sprints that produce fatigue. A suggested order of training activities for a team game player might be:
1. Team briefing - to set the tone for the training session
2. General warm-up - easy aerobic exercise, then stretching, then some speed drills
3. Speed or power training - best done while fresh
4. Individual and team skill drills - incorporating tactics and strategies
5. Specialised fitness and/or skill work - depending on individual player requirements
6. Cool down - easy aerobic exercise, then stretching.

For aging speed athletes the order of training activities may be simplified even further:
1. General warm-up
2. Speed and power training
3. Technique training
4. Specific fitness and conditioning training
5. Cool down.

For aging endurance athletes only three training activities may be required:
1. General warm-up
2. Specific fitness and conditioning training
3. Cool down.

## Periodisation of Training for Team Game Masters Athletes

*1. The Preparation (Pre-Season) Phase*

The prime objective of the preparation phase for any athlete is to develop a sound fitness base on which the more intense and specialised training for competition can be built. The longer the base period of training the easier it should be for athletes to adapt and respond to the later high intensity training. Furthermore, the longer the period of base training, the longer an athlete should be able to perform consistently at her/his peak during the competition phase. Hence, the preparation phase usually involves two to three macrocycles, one or two in the general preparation sub-phase and one in the specific preparation sub-phase. The first macrocycle typically involves a high volume of low to moderate intensity training, which is progressively and gradually reversed in nature over the remainder of this phase (i.e. lower volume and higher intensity training).

While team game athletes all have different specific competition requirements, they can all benefit from developing a good endurance base of fitness. Because this is directly related to performance, team game athletes will find that good endurance fitness will enhance their recovery from high intensity training efforts, which will be performed in future macrocycles. A greater number of quality repeats in a training set should also be possible before fatigue occurs. Team game players such as aging footballers may cover 4-8 km in total distance during a game, which may last from 40-120 min, further emphasising the need to develop good endurance fitness.

However, the training methods used to build endurance will vary with the position played on the field. While continuous aerobic training is appropriate for mid-field player, the speed athletes who play on the wings should use higher intensity interval training, where the fast twitch muscle fibres that are more specific to their competition requirements will be used. If the endurance base is achieved mostly by lower intensity continuous aerobic training, the slow twitch muscle fibres will be used, which may be counterproductive to the speed and power development of a sprint athlete. Team game players should use a mix of continuous and interval training, as this is more suited to their specific game requirements.

For the aging team athlete who is losing fast twitch fibre number and size, speed training becomes essential. Too many aging athletes train with low intensity and wonder why performances or PB's are not happening. A focus on some speed work, even for the aging endurance team athlete, is essential in helping to keep the muscles activated and the nerves firing.

As well as developing an endurance base of fitness, team game players must also develop strength and power by appropriate weight training during the preparation phase. While power development is the ultimate goal for speed athletes, increases in strength are fundamental to improvements in power, which will then be emphasised in the competition phase. As emphasised many times throughout this book, strength training, particularly hypertrophy (muscle enlargement) training, is essential for male and female masters athletes. This is due to the fact that age-related declines in strength, speed, power, and endurance can be related to the age-related decline in muscle mass that accompanies aging. The preparation phase of an annual plan is the time to emphasise this type of training. For specifics on hypertrophy and weight training, see Chapter 7.

Masters athletes should also be aware that concurrent strength (or speed) and endurance training might interfere with each other. That is, if both of these capacities are trained together, then the overall improvement in each of them is likely to be less than if they were trained separately. This is most likely due to differences in the pattern and efficiency of muscle fibre recruitment, as endurance training mostly stresses slow twitch fibres, while high intensity strength (or speed) training utilises fast twitch fibres. In practice, to avoid seriously compromising the degree of improvement in either capacity, the following points should be borne in mind:

- Don't attempt to train strength/speed and endurance in the same session or day
- Train one capacity (speed or endurance) at a time
- Emphasise one capacity in a microcyle (week)
- In any macrocycle, the development of either strength/speed or endurance should be emphasised, while the other capacity is maintained by lesser amounts of training.

Lastly, team game players must also develop their basic skills during the preparation phase. Simple, individual skills should first be trained, before progressing to more complex and tactically oriented skills.

2. *The Competition (In-Season) Phase*

The objective of the competition phase is to develop the masters athlete's specific fitness and readiness for competition to their maximum levels. Training during this phase is high intensity with a gradually reduction in volume as the competition date draws near. The pre-competition sub-phase (usually one four-week macrocycle), which immediately follows the specific preparation sub-phase, is possibly the most demanding period of training in the year. High intensity, quality training (at or near race or game intensity) of moderate volume is performed in this macrocycle, to bring the aging athletes' specific fitness and skill requirements to their peak. For team game athletes, strategies and tactics to be used in competition must be emphasised and practised. The strength developed in the preparation phase for both team game and speed athletes must be converted into power by performing pliometric and power weight training as described in Chapters 7 and 8.

This sub-phase of training is, therefore, a potentially stressful period for the athlete. During this phase, the responses to, and recovery from the training, must be considered by both coaches and athletes. Injuries and chronic fatigue must be avoided. The advice of Forbes Carlisle, the well-respected Australian swimming coach of the 1950s, 1960s and 1970s should be heeded - *it is better to under-train than to over-train*. Chapters 13 and 14 focus on practical ways an older athlete can prevent overtraining and stay well.

The competitive sub-phase may last some months and therefore incorporate several macrocycles. Fitness should be maintained in this period by specific high intensity training of relatively low volume. Re-development of specific fitness may be required for athletes who suffer injury. As fitness should be at its peak when entering this sub-phase, the focus of training can be directed more to skill, technique, tactics and psychology, and special attention should be paid to ensuring a good preparation for each competition.

The final microcycle before every competition should allow peaking to occur. Training workouts should be at or close to competition intensity, but be brief in duration and few in number, such that a low volume of training is performed. More recovery sessions should also be programmed and nutritional procedures such as carbohydrate loading emphasised. This type of macrocycle works well for aging endurance and speed athletes, who may have infrequent competitions scheduled, or are planning for major events such as State or National titles.

The masters team game player is quite different; they usually must compete each week, with only a five to eight day break between games. Recovery and lower intensity training sessions should be programmed early in the week to allow sufficient recovery from the previous game. The main training session is performed midweek (moderate to high intensity and volume), with a brief, quality workout occurring one or two days prior to the next game. Recovery and nutritional procedures (carbohydrate loading) should also be emphasised at this stage of the week. Microcycles of this nature are designed to allow a "mini peak" for each game throughout the competition phase, but it is no easy matter to achieve this during weekly competition.

3. *The Transition (Off-Season) Phase*

The main objectives of this phase are to prevent "detraining" or the complete loss of fitness, maintain a reasonable level of endurance fitness, while accepting that some reduction in peak condition will occur. The transition phase is also a time when nagging injuries can recover, and athletes can psychologically benefit from a break in the normal training routine, especially after the additional stresses of the competition phase. Specific weaknesses in an athlete's fitness profile (e.g. lack of flexibility, upper body strength or skill on non-preferred side) can also receive special attention without interference from other types of training.

To maintain some degree of endurance fitness and provide a break from normal training, the masters athlete should cross-train during the transition phase. Cycling, swimming, running, water running, rowing and team or individual games (basketball, touch, squash and tennis) are examples of activities that can assist in maintaining endurance fitness and limiting any weight gain. These sorts of activities are most appropriate for endurance and team game athletes, and while speed athletes may also use them, they should also perform some interval training (perhaps once a week) at reduced intensity (60-80% of max speed) to prevent total detraining (loss of fitness) of their fast twitch muscle fibres. Endurance and/or strength weight training should also be performed once a week by aging speed and team game athletes to limit the decline in specific muscle conditioning.

## Periodisation of Strength Training

As with all periodised plans, the objectives, content and method of strength training changes depending on the phase of training. These changes should reflect the type of strength required for the sport, the event(s) or an individual athlete's weaknesses and strengths. For the aging athlete it is STRONGLY recommended that specialist expertise be sought to help with planning a strength-training program. There is no doubt in my mind that weight training to increase muscle mass and develop strength and power is crucial for the masters athlete. The inevitable age-related decline in muscle mass occurs slowly after 50 years of age and rapidly after 65-70 years of age. This age-related drop in muscle mass is primarily due to a loss of size and number of the fast twitch fibres, the force and speed producing fibres. Weight training will go a long way to helping prevent or slow this decline. There is also no doubt in mind, even as a former Health and Physical Education teacher and now sport scientist, that developing a weight training program is an art and a science requiring very specific knowledge and expertise. Speak to coaches and younger athletes in your sport to find out who these local experts are and seek them out.

*Table 10.5:* Possible periodised plan for strength, endurance and speed training for masters athletes.

| Phases | Preparation | | Competition | | Transition |
|---|---|---|---|---|---|
| **Sub-Phases** | General Preparation | Specific Preparation | Precompetition | Competition(s) | Transition |
| **Strength** | Anatomical adaptation | Maximum strength | Conversion to:<br>• Power<br>• Muscle endurance | Maintenance of power or muscle endurance<br>Peaking | Compensation |
| **Endurance** | Aerobic endurance | Aerobic endurance<br>Specific endurance | Specific endurance | | Aerobic endurance |
| **Speed** | Aerobic and anaerobic endurance | Specific speed<br>Anaerobic endurance | Specific speed<br>Agility<br>Reaction time<br>Speed endurance | | Games |

From Table 10.5 above we can see that a periodised plan demands examining six stages:

1. *Anatatomical Adaptation Phase*

    After taking a break during the transition phase to allow the body to regenerate after a season of hard work, we must prepare the body's joints and muscles for the hard work that will come. The main objective of this phase is to involve most muscle groups and

thus prepare the muscles, ligaments, tendons, and joints for the upcoming harder training. Training should involve the following:
- 9-12 exercises
- load of 40-60% of maximum lift (called 1 RM – <u>R</u>epetition <u>M</u>aximum)
- 8-12 repetitions of each exercise
- 2-3 sets of each exercise
- Done at slow-medium speed
- 60-90 seconds between each set and exercise
- 4-6 weeks duration for experienced weight trainers, 6-12 weeks for masters athletes new to weight training.
- 2-3 times per week

2. *Maximum Strength Phase*

   Most sports require power (strength done quickly) (e.g. sprinting, field events), muscular endurance (middle distance swimming, cycling and running), or both (running, cycling, rowing, swimming). Both power and muscle endurance are affected by the level of maximum strength. In masters athletes wanting to hold on to performance or improve, improving strength will develop not only strength (the ability to lift one heavy weight), but also the power and endurance of muscles. For the aging athlete, the goal of this phase is to develop muscle mass (women will develop little if any mass because of lack of enough male hormone testosterone) and strength. Once strength has been developed, it can be turned into power by a different type of weight training. The duration of this strength phase might be 6-12 weeks depending on the aging athlete's needs. For an aging power or speed athlete, longer should be spent during this stage, for an aging endurance athlete or team player, 6-8 weeks may be enough. Be guided by your strength specialist.

3. *Conversion Phase*

   Once muscle mass and strength have been developed using the principles outlined in Chapter 7, to be sport-specific we must gradually convert that strength into power, muscle endurance, or power endurance, whatever the demands of the event we are training for are. This phase is relatively short (4-8 weeks) and the emphasis is gradually placed on doing the exercises quickly (for power development) or doing more repetitions (endurance) or both (power endurance). However, strength also needs to be maintained so once or twice a week, depending on the sport or event, strength training alone should be done.

4. *Maintenance Phase*

   Once strength, power, muscle endurance or power endurance have been developed, during the preparation and pre-competition phases, they need to be maintained. A shot-putter may do two strength and two power sessions a week where a high- or long-jumper may do one strength and two power sessions. A middle distance runner or swimmer may do one strength, one power and one power endurance session over a period of 10 days. The number of exercises done may be very small and very specific thus reducing the time demand. For example, at the time of writing this (late specific preparation phase) I do three exercises only (lunges, squats, and step-ups – aimed at developing my cycling power) with an emphasis on speed and power endurance.

5. *Peaking Phase*

   Five to seven days before a major event, strength training should cease. Why? Because the type of training you should be doing should be focussed on specific speed or power (e.g. sprint running, cycling, rowing, or swimming) and you should be freshening up and peaking for the event(s).

6. *Compensation Phase*

   After the major competition(s), we need time to refresh both mentally and physically. If injured, this is the time to get those niggles looked at and rehabilitated. It might also be a time to develop your weaknesses in the gym. For example, a masters swimmer with "swimmer's shoulder" might do some work on the external rotators of the shoulder, a sprint runner might do some work on hamstrings if they are susceptible to injuring them.

**Periodisation of Endurance**

An annual plan for endurance development requires three main phases:

1. *Aerobic Endurance*

   Progressively over this period, training volume should be gradually increased using distance as the stimulus, rather than intensity. Intensity should be low to moderate (heart rate zones 1-3 as discussed in Chapter 6) during this phase which can last 4-12 weeks depending upon the fitness level and training age of the athlete as they enter this phase from the transition phase. During the transition phase they should have done some strength training with an emphasis on building muscle mass plus some aerobic work similar in nature to their chosen sport. I never recommend taking longer than 10-14 days off completely. It is just too hard to get any endurance fitness back. Do something different maybe but don't stop completely even if it is 1-2 times per week.

   This is also the time that a masters endurance athlete should be doing strength training. The older the athlete, the more the emphasis should be on muscle enlargement (hypertrophy) and strength training. This should be done the day after an easy endurance session and should be followed by an easy-moderate endurance session.

2. *Aerobic Endurance-Specific Endurance*

   Once developed during the general preparation phase, aerobic endurance (heart rate zones 1-3) should always be maintained during this phase. The intensity of the training is progressively lifted (heart rate zones 4-6) over this period till goal race-pace is achieved. The volume of training is relatively high during this phase that may last 6-10 weeks.

   This is the time where the strength developed in the earlier phase is gradually converted to power endurance by doing more weights repetitions but at a faster speed with lighter weights. Again, be fresh for the weights session by having an easy endurance session before the weights session. Strength can be maintained with one session per week in the gym.

3. *Specific Endurance*

    During the pre-competitive and competitive phases, all training intensities, including those above goal race-pace, should be used to stress the capacities of the athlete, but also maintain the capacities developed in the earlier phases. Weight training (strength and power endurance) should be maintained 2-3 times per 10-14 days with at least one strength session done.

## Periodisation of Speed

Similar to endurance development, the periodisation of speed depends upon the training age of the athlete, the event or sport being trained for, the level of athlete, and the competition schedule. Team players will require a different plan to a pure sprinter. However, the following phases are general to both (see Table 10.5).

1. *Aerobic and Anaerobic Endurance*

    A solid foundation of aerobic work or moderate intensity, short-long tempo runs builds endurance, strengthens muscles, joint ligaments and tendons, and prepares the body for the upcoming harder phases. Fartlek (speed play) work is aerobic work interspersed with faster efforts and should be used initially, followed by intervals and repetitions that build anaerobic endurance. Technique drills and sport-specific skills can be incorporated. Pliometrics can also be introduced using the principles outlined in Chapter 8. Specifically, two-legged jumps initially moving to hopping, jumping then bounding.

    For the aging sprinter in particular, strength and hypertrophy weight training should be done during this phase. Not only will it help with preventing injuries by strengthening ligaments, tendons and joints, it will develop the muscle size and strength that the next phases can turn into sprinting power.

2. *Speed and Anaerobic Endurance*

    As the competition phase approaches, speed training should become more intense, specific and focussed on technique done at speed. Maximum velocity efforts with long recoveries should be used. For more on speed development, see Chapter 8. Pliometrics can start to focus on single-legged activities such as hopping, jumping or bounding.

    The aging sprint athlete should be converting that strength gained during the transition and general preparation phase into power by progressively lowering the weights being lifted, do more sport-specific exercises and doing them at increasing speed. While doing this, muscle mass and strength need to be maintained with 1-2 weights sessions per week focussed on strength and hypertrophy.

3. *Specific Speed*

    Event-specific training is focussed on during this phase. Short-term (e.g. 100m run, 25m swim speed,) or longer-term speed (200-400m run or 50-100m swim speed) should be focussed on. Again, maximal single efforts with long recoveries develop race speed. Speed endurance comes with lower intensity efforts and shorter rests, the type of training a team player needs. Pliometrics should be focussed on single-legged activities such as hopping, jumping or bounding that mimic the sport or event.

Again, the aging sprint athlete should be maintaining that strength and power gained during the previous phases with 2-3 sessions per week (one focussed on strength and 1-2 focussed on power).

4. *Specific Speed, Agility and Reaction Time*

Race-specific drills and workouts should be used during the competitive phase. Starts are crucial and for team players, agility drills that mimic the demands of the sport, event, or playing position are paramount.

As with the previous phases, maintenance of strength and power through visits to the gym and pliometrics can be done with regular sessions of each.

In summary, an annual plan should be broken up into a number of phases and sub-phases where the strength, power, speed and endurance demands are emphasised at different times of the plan. Such a plan demands time, patience and motivation to stick to but will bring about far greater gains than the standard ad hoc approach I see most masters athletes take. Emphasise something (speed, endurance, strength, power) within each session, don't try and confuse the body by doing bits and pieces of each. Moreover, within a microcycle or macrocycle, emphasise a capacity or endurance training heart rate zone and watch the body adapt. Crucially, always remember that once you have developed something (e.g. strength) maintain it with 1-2 sessions in a microcycle while emphasising another capacity.

## Tapering

Tapering is the term used to describe a reduction in training before competition. The exact length of a taper depends on two major factors. First, how fit you are coming into your major event and secondly, what type of event you have trained for. If you have a large base of months of uninterrupted training and have your endurance, speed and power levels at high levels, the taper can be longer. The more unfit you are, the more important it is to keep training until maybe three days out from the event when you have a "drop-dead" taper that will be discussed later. The longer the event for which you are tapering, the longer the taper should be. This allows time for accumulated fatigue to disappear and possible muscle damage to be repaired.

Most coaches and athletes design a taper through trial and error since few scientific studies have actually compared performance before and after a period of reduced training. This section will examine some of the available research studies and, more importantly, their implications for aging athletes and their coaches. The aim is to give a scientific basis to the "art" of tapering - an "art" developed through trial and error on the part of the athlete, the experienced "eye" of the coach, and the verbal communication that comes from a strong coach-athlete relationship.

A summary of some of the available research appears in Table 10.6 below. The most important point to note is that it is a gradual lowering of training volume *with* a maintenance of both training intensity and frequency that appears to produce the greatest improvement in performance.

*Table 10.6:* Summary of a number of studies examining the effects of tapering on performance. TTE = Time to Exhaustion.

| Athletes | Taper | Measure | Change |
| --- | --- | --- | --- |
| Runners | 5 days of high intensity intervals | Leg strength | 33% increase |
| Runners | 5 days of low intensity running | Leg strength | 33% increase |
| Runners | 7 days of no running | Leg strength | 37% increase |
| Runners | 5 days of high intensity intervals | TTE | 22% increase |
| Runners | 5 days of low intensity running | TTE | 6% increase |
| Runners | 7 days of no running | TTE | 3% decrease |
| Runners | 14 days of no running | TTE | 9.2% decrease |
| Runners | 7 days high intensity intervals | 5 k run times | 3% decrease |
| Swimmers | 14 days reduced volume (53%) | Swim times | 3.1% increase |
| Swimmers | 10 day reduced volume (76%) | Swim power | 5% increase |
| Cyclists | 4-8 days reduced volume | Cycling power | 8% increase |

When tapering for major events, we can manipulate the following variables:
- Taper length or duration
- Training volume
- Training intensity
- Training frequency

1. *Taper Length*

Studies done on swimmers in the late 1980s examined blood variables like haemoglobin and red blood cell number rather than performance. These studies suggested that a seven-day taper was optimal, with longer tapers negatively affecting a number of blood parameters. More recent studies have shown that tapers between 7 and 21 days, as long as they are *stepwise* (volume gradually reduced over time), will result in improved performance, with tapers longer than 21 days leading to only maintenance of performance and not improvements. In general, the fitter the person and the longer the event, the longer the taper. For the person who has done little training for an event, a *"drop-dead"* taper of three days might be used where no training or minimal training is done in the days leading up to an event.

2. *Training Volume*

A stepwise reduction in training volume leading to an event appears critical to improved performance. Studies done on swimmers have shown that this gradual reduction in training volume leads to both improved swim performance and swim bench power output. In contrast, a study done on runners in 1990 reduced training volume straight away to 70% of normal volume for three weeks and found no improvement in 5k run performance. Taken together, it appears that an incremental, stepwise decrease in training volume results in improved performance. Reducing the training volume gradually by up to 60% of normal distances appears to lead to the best gains in performance.

3. *Exercise Intensity*

Training during tapering is usually done with interval work with enough recovery between intervals to maximise intensity. In endurance athletes, a number of studies have shown that reducing training intensity below 70% of $VO_2max$ (about 80% of maximal heart rate) either maintains or reduces performance. In contrast, tapers that use high intensity intervals have lead to significant performance improvements as long as the volume is reduced at the same time. This suggests that if you are used to say 15 x 100m swims or 400m runs that you might reduce this to 12 > 10 > 8 > 6 > 4 over time. However, the important point is that the intensity of these efforts is maintained.

4. *Exercise Frequency*

The number of training sessions per week for athletes varies greatly between individuals depending on work and family commitments, level of motivation, holidays etc. A great reduction in training frequency is not recommended. A study on swimmers in the late 1980s found that a 50-85% reduction in training frequency, combined with the standard reduction in training volume lead to decreases in performance. In contrast, a number of studies on cyclists and runners only reduced training frequency by 20-40 % and observed improved performance as long as training intensity was maintained. These results suggest that training frequency should be maintained and a great reduction in training frequency should be avoided, particularly in the "feel" sports such as swimming and rowing.

## Practical Peaking Recommendations

From these principles above, a number of practical recommendations are suggested:
- Athletes should gradually reduce the volume (kilometers, minutes) of training by up to 60% in the 7-14 days leading up to a major event.
- Highly-trained athletes should taper for no longer than 14 days.
- Moderately trained athletes need only taper for 3-5 days to improve performance.
- The longer the training age (years of training), the longer the taper can be.
- While gradually reducing the training volume, the intensity of each workout should be maintained.
- Training frequency should be maintained or not be reduced by more than 40%.

- Some athletes may feel "heavy" during the taper, possibly due to increased carbohydrate storage in muscles as a result of not training as often or as hard. A possible solution is to do a small volume of intense work right up to the day of competition.
- Tapering is highly individual and each athlete "psychs" themselves in different ways during this period. Some athletes feel they "need" days of rest, some "need" a small hit out the day before a race. Listen to your body and learn what works for you. If you're a coach, listen and observe your athlete's repeat times.

# CHAPTER 11

## EXERCISING IN THE HEAT AND COLD

*The time will come when winter will ask what you did all summer.*

**Anonymous**

*Dig the well before you are thirsty.*

**Chinese Proverb**

### Introduction

Not all of us live in my home state of sunny Queensland, Australia where the weather is fine one day and perfect the next! Many masters athletes have to train and compete in hot and/or humid summers or cold winters. If you live in Melbourne, Australia, you'll enjoy all of these conditions within a 24 hour period! The purpose of this chapter is to examine the body's responses to exercise in both hot and cold conditions, what changes occur in these responses with age, and how the aging athlete can maximize training and competition performance in these extremes of climate.

### Basic Thermal Physiology

Thermoregulation is an essential bodily function defined as the ability to maintain a normal body temperature (about 37°C) by balancing heat loss and heat generating mechanisms. This optimal temperature is important because the body's physiology is designed to be optimal within a narrow temperature range.

The body's temperature during exercise is dependent on what is called the *heat balance*. That is, the balance between what heat is generated and gained during exercise and how much heat the body loses through the heat loss mechanisms. Table 11.1 on the following page summarizes these heat gaining and heat losing mechanisms.

It is the balance of these mechanisms that determines the body's responses to exercise in the heat and cold. In cold, wet and windy conditions, it is likely that the heat loss mechanisms will predominate causing the body temperature to drop. In hot and humid conditions, the heat gaining mechanisms may predominate, causing the body temperature to increase. When these mechanisms fail to hold the body temperature within its preferred narrow range, sports performance deteriorates. Independent of age, this drop in performance is enhanced if an athlete starts the training or competition dehydrated, sick, hung-over, tired, unacclimatised, or with a poor level of aerobic fitness. Overheating of the body leads to heat injuries such as heat cramps, heat exhaustion, or heat stroke while a lowering of the body temperature can lead to frostbite or hypothermia.

*Table 11.1:* Heat gain and heat loss mechanisms in the human body.

| Heat Gain Mechanisms | Heat Loss Mechanisms |
|---|---|
| Exercise (can increase heat production up to 20 times) | Evaporation (turning sweat into a gas) |
| Digesting food (contributes about 10% to our metabolic rate) | Conduction (skin contact with cooler surfaces or fluids) |
| Resting metabolic rate (over a day, about 60% of heat generated) | Radiation (electromagnetic heat from the body surface) |
| Radiation (electromagnetic heat from sun or hotter surfaces) | Convection (movement of heat from a hot to a cold area) |
| Conduction (skin contact with hotter surfaces or fluids) | |

**Aging and Exercise in the Heat**

When we exercise in the heat, we generate large amounts of heat as our resting metabolism increases heat (energy) production by up to 20 times normal. There are two major mechanisms by which we lose this heat. Firstly by increasing skin blood flow (why our face or skin turns red!) we take heat away from the body core to the skin which allows us to lose heat via radiation and convection (the hot air molecules beside the skin are replaced by the cooler ones as wind passes by or we move through the air when we move). The second and most important mechanism of heat loss is producing, and more importantly, evaporating sweat. The evaporation of the sweat is the major avenue of heat loss from our bodies to the environment. However, what is not often understood is that the sweat we produce MUST turn from the liquid that appears on our skin to a gas as it evaporates into the air. It is this process of turning liquid sweat into a gas that loses heat, not the sweating process itself. If the air is humid, there is little space left for the sweat to evaporate into, so we struggle to lose heat and thus making it more dangerous when exercising in hot and humid conditions such as the Hawaii Ironman. In contrast, in dry conditions, the sweat evaporates so quickly we may not even be aware we are sweating, making us more likely to dehydrate without being aware of it.

In general, the available research suggests that with age there is a:
- Reduced sweat rate compared to younger people
- Reduced sense of heat and cold
- Slower initial sweat response time
- Reduced thirst sensation
- Reduced fluid intake for a given level of dehydration
- Reduced fluid intake during recovery from exercise

Taken together, these findings suggest that older people might be more susceptible to heat injury than younger people.

For years it has been thought that the aging process is accompanied by a decreased ability to effectively regulate body temperature while exercising in the heat. This belief has been perpetrated by the observation that older people suffer heat injuries or death during heat waves. Furthermore, many laboratory studies have shown that older, untrained men and women respond to heat stress with higher body temperatures, higher heart rates, lower sweat rates, and greater loss of body fluid than younger untrained people. But what about masters athletes?

## Masters Athlete and Exercise in the Heat

Research suggests that older male and female endurance athletes may be at an advantage in coping with exercise in the heat compared to aging non-athletes. Research from Pennsylvania State University in the USA examined a group of 55-70 year old male and female endurance athletes and compared their responses to exercise in the heat with younger athletes matched for aerobic fitness level, body size, and body fat. The major finding was that the older athletes generate the same body heat as the younger athletes, thus suggesting that we masters athletes respond to heat better than older non-exercisers. However, the same researchers found that the older athletes had a 25-40% lower skin blood flow and that while the older athletes activated the same number of sweat glands; each sweat gland had a significantly lower sweat output compared to the younger athletes. However, this diminished sweat rate in the older athlete was only observed in a hot and dry environment. In a hot and humid environment, the older athletes produced the same sweat volumes as their younger counterparts. These findings strongly suggest that the older athlete needs to take care when exercising in the heat.

An aging athlete may also be at increased risk of heat injury due to having a reduced total body water reserve compared to younger people. A number of research studies have shown that older people have about 65% of their body weight as water at age 25 but that this drops to about 53% by age 75 years. Put another way, an average 30 year old weighing 70 kg has about 7-8 liters more body water than a 75 year old of the same weight. Combined with an age-related reduction in thirst sensation, aging athletes competing in hot and dry environments where the sensation of fluid loss via sweating is dampened due to the sweat evaporating so quickly, it appears aging athletes may become dehydrated prior to sensing thirst. Given that thirst is a sign that a person is already dehydrated, aging athletes may again be at greater risk of heat injury.

Can the older athlete acclimatize to the heat? The research suggests yes. In 1988, a study was undertaken that matched a group of middle-aged male runners (46±5yr) and a group of 20-year-old runners. The researchers acclimatized both groups to the heat in the same way and observed no age-related differences between the athletes in their response to running in the heat. Whether the same response would be observed in 60 plus year olds remains to be seen.

Each of the heat studies above observed great variability in each of the older athlete's response. The researchers strongly suggested that, regardless of age, the level of aerobic capacity ($VO_2max$), acclimatization, and hydration level of the individual athlete are far more important in determining a masters athlete's ability to exercise in the heat than age itself.

## Preventing Heat Injuries in Masters Athletes

The following guidelines are strongly recommended for the aging athlete when exercising in the heat:

1. *Acclimatize.* Most heat-related injuries occur during the first few exercise sessions in the heat. Shorten the duration or lower the intensity of the training sessions for the first few days. Acclimatization leads to reduced heart rates at any exercise intensity, lower body temperatures, lower glycogen (stored carbohydrate) use, greater skin blood flow, increased blood volume, increased sweat rates, an earlier onset of sweating, and lower electrolyte losses in sweat, all very positive adaptations to increasing exercise intensity or duration in the heat. Research suggests 10-14 days to acclimatize with 75% of the adaptations taking place within the first 5 days. The following standard guidelines may help if you plan to use an acclimatization strategy:
   a. Attain your fitness in a cool environment *before* attempting to acclimatize
   b. Exercise at intensities above 60% of maximum heart rate and gradually increase the intensity, and duration from 15-30 minutes to 90 minutes over the 14 days
   c. Do the high quality work during the early morning or evening hours, the easier work at other times
   d. Monitor body weight to ensure you're hydrated (1 kg lost = 1 L of fluid lost)
   e. Start acclimatizing at home by wearing insulated clothing (tracksuits, extra layers).

2. *Fluid Replacement.* Drink as much fluid (suggested is 500 ml) as tolerable 30-45 minutes *before* training or racing. Drink a cup of fluid (100-300 ml every 15 minutes *during* exercise to ideally replace what you lose. The gut appears to maximally absorb 1-1.2 litres of fluid per hour so drinking any more than this is not recommended. *After* exercise, drink about 150% more fluid than the amount that quenches your thirst, eat meals high in water content (fruit and vegetables), and to replace the sodium lost in sweat, a sports drink such as *Gatorade* (see Nutrition chapter) is recommended during and after exercise longer than one hour. Drinking water alone during exercise may lower the concentration of electrolytes in the blood that may lead to a reduced desire to drink, thus not restoring our blood volume lost through excessive sweating. Sports drinks that contain 6-8% (6-8 grams /100 ml) carbohydrate and sodium are best. Given that fructose has been linked to gut upsets, it may pay to avoid any sports drink that contains it.

3. *Consider hyperhydrating.* That is, storing more water in your body before racing. Glycerol is a hyperhydrating agent available from chemists that has been shown to benefit endurance performance in endurance athletes racing in hot and humid conditions. It is taken at the rate of 1-1.2 grams per kilogram of body weight with a large amount of fluid (20-25 ml of diet cordial – to hide taste! - per kilogram of body weight) in the 1-2 hours prior to racing and has been shown to help the body hold extra water. Having tried this before a half-ironman triathlon, I now regularly use it when racing in hot and humid condition. While the books say it can lead to headaches and a feeling of bloating, I never had any of those symptoms but took it over a 2 hour period and at the lowest recommended dosage.

4. *Monitor Urine Colour.* Dark yellow urine is concentrated and indicates the need to drink more fluid.
5. *Use common sense.* If you are concerned that it's too hot to exercise at a certain time of the day, it probably is. Train in the early morning, late evening, or go swimming or water running instead.
6. *Maintain a high aerobic fitness level.* Research has shown that the best predictor of heat tolerance in older athletes exercising at a given pace is aerobic capacity.
7. *Know the early warning signs of heat injury.* Primarily due to dehydration and less often salt depletion, the warning signs of heat injury are higher heart rates, muscle cramps, light-headedness, dizziness, headache, nausea, chills, excessive thirst, cooler and paler skin, profuse sweating, weakness and fatigue. Slow down, stop, get to a well-ventilated shaded area and drink cool fluids.
8. *Pay attention to health status or use of prescription drugs.* Diabetes, asthma, epilepsy, pregnancy and hypertension can lower the ability to exercise in the heat. Some prescription drugs associated with some of these conditions (diuretics, vasodilators, adrenergic blockers, anticholinergics) may affect the ability to tolerate exercise in the heat. Ask your family doctor or a Sports Physician if in doubt.
9. *Use a sunscreen.* While little research has examined this factor, particularly in aging athletes, suggests the use of water soluble sunscreen at the rate of 30 ml/m$^2$ of skin (we have approximately 1.8-2.0 m$^2$ of skin) will (compared to no sunscreen):
    a. Reduce skin temperature
    b. Allow greater conduction of heat from muscles to skin
    c. Help lower body temperature
10. *Watch what you wear.* Fabrics (e.g. *Gor-Tex* or cotton NOT nylons, rayons, lycra) that don't hold heat and allow evaporation via wicking (sweat moves into fabric and evaporates such as when wearing a tight cotton T-shirt) are best. White or light colors and designs that maximize skin exposure are best. A well-ventilated white hat makes sense, and possibly packing it with ice to cool the head is worth trying.
11. *Watch where you exercise.* Training or racing in windier or shadier parts of the course or training area makes sense in order to reduce incoming heat and increase heat loss. Grassy areas don't hold the heat like bitumen roads so look to an oval for a run or get out the mountain bike and hit the bush tracks instead of the road.
12. *Precooling.* Cool water immersion (bath, shower, pool, ocean) for 30-60 minutes at 23-25$^0$C, wearing an ice vest, or sitting in front of a fan with wet-shirts or being sprayed has been shown to benefit endurance performance in the heat. The theory is that the skin blood flow is diverted to the muscles and the temperature gradient from the muscles to the cooler skin allows for greater heat loss. However, the benefits may be lost with too long and/or hard a warm-up.

Older female athletes may be more at risk of heat injury than men. They generally have a larger surface area to body mass ratio, lower total body water, generally have greater heat insulating fat deposits, a lower rate of sweat production than men and, if not menopausal or post-menopausal, have a menstrual cycle that at times can elevate body temperature. Body temperature is elevated during the luteal (time between ovulation and menstrual flow) phase of the menstrual cycle meaning that female endurance athletes will have an elevated threshold body temperature to turn on the sweat response. During this phase, skin blood flow is also elevated meaning less blood is available to working muscles and the temperature gradient between skin and muscle is lower meaning heat loss via conduction is reduced. The increased body fat will compromise the ability to lose heat compared to leaner men or women but is a plus in the cold. The larger body surface area to mass ratio may mean increased heat entering the body from the environment. The lower rate of sweat production means a poorer ability to lose heat via evaporation.

Thus, exercise tolerance time in the heat is less in women than men because of the reduced ability to lose heat and increased ability to store heat. Female masters athletes thus need to pay stricter attention to the factors above that help prevent heat injuries.

### Aging and Exercise in the Cold

Many masters athletes live and train in a cold climate. Indeed, even sunny Queensland experiences mid-winter cold when the temptation on a Sunday morning is to pull the bedcovers up and forget that long run. Or the Tuesday and Thursday morning rides mean layers of gear, beanies and booties and getting up 10 minutes earlier to gear up – not easy when it's 4.30am, cold and dark, and you're trying not to wake the kids up. This section will firstly examine the mechanisms of heat loss in a cold environment, then examine how age affects these mechanisms, and finally make recommendations on how masters athletes can prevent injury when training in the cold.

Heat is transferred from a higher to a lower temperature. Normal body temperature is $37^0C$ with skin temperature $31^0C$. If the air or water temperature is less than $31^0C$, heat will be lost from the body. The amount of heat loss will depend on a number of factors:

- Air or water temperature - the colder the temperature, the greater the heat loss
- Amount of body fat - the higher the body fat, the less the heat loss
- Wind velocity - the stronger the wind, the greater the heat loss
- Athlete's body surface area - taller, thinner people have a greater surface area per kilogram of body weight and are more susceptible to feeling the cold
- Age of the athlete - older groups have less ability to cope with cold
- Athlete's fitness level - the fitter the aging athlete, the greater the ability to produce more heat during exercise
- Intensity of exercise - the slower we exercise, the less heat is produced
- Amount of external insulation - layers of clothing, swim cap, grease, or wetsuits hold heat into the body
- Duration of the exercise - the longer we exercise for, the greater the risk.

- Gender - females generally have lower VO₂max values and lower heat generating muscle mass than males, plus a higher surface area-to-mass ratio that increases the rate of heat loss. However, greater body fat stores in women appear to balance these negatives with the limited research to date suggesting females and males are equally susceptible to cold injury.

A lower body temperature during exposure to the cold causes two major responses in the body. Firstly, heat to increase the body temperature is generated through shivering which raises the metabolic rate (heat production) by three or more times. This mechanism is bought on by both decreases in both skin and core (body) temperature. Aging athletes have a decreased muscle mass able to generate as much heat from shivering as youngsters. Decreases in skin and body temperature stimulate the second response to cold - vasoconstriction or narrowing of the blood vessels, particularly those below the skin. This decreases skin blood flow and increases the insulating effect of the body tissues. In addition, warm blood is redirected to the deeper tissues that promote heat conservation because the deeper veins of the arms and legs lie close to the major arteries. The heat from the warmer arteries can then warm-up the cooler veins. However, the narrowing of blood vessels that occurs in the arms and legs does not occur in the surface vessels of the head. This means that up to 25 percent of the total heat loss to the air or water can occur from the head. This is the reason why woolen hats or bathing caps are strongly recommended when exercising in cold air or water.

It is generally believed that older people are less able to maintain body temperature during cold compared to younger people. Recent research in Canada compared exercise responses to both resting for 30 minutes and exercising for 30 minutes in the cold ($5^0$C) in eight young adults (26.5±2.6yr), eight well-trained older athletes (59.5±3.4yr) matched with the youngsters for aerobic capacity, and 11 untrained seniors (63.5±4.0yr). The researchers observed a greater rate of decrease in body temperature in both the older groups compared to the youngsters. The research also supported the previous research on aging and exercise in the cold and suggested that the older groups had a lower resting metabolic rate (heat production) due to an age-related reduction in heat-producing muscle mass, a resultant decreased ability to shiver to produce heat, and a decreased ability to vasoconstrict (make the blood vessels narrower) compared to the younger group. Older athletes therefore appear to lose heat more than younger athletes and have a reduced ability to produce heat when they get cold, thus making us more susceptible to cold injuries than younger athletes. However, in older women, studies have shown, at least in older non-athletes, this group appears to be able to tolerate the cold slightly better, possibly due to increased body fat. Whether this is seen in older endurance-trained females who are in general leaner than older non-athletic women, remains to be researched.

Exercise in the cold has been shown to lower the aerobic capacity (VO₂max), muscular strength and power and thus speed. The slower speed has been suggested to be due to a slowing of energy production, slowing of the nerve conduction velocity, and increased muscle and connective tissue (ligaments, tendons) viscosity or stiffness. However, endurance exercise in the cold may be enhanced by cool environmental temperatures or by treatments such as brief, pre-exercise cold-water immersions, cold showers, or cold packs. This is probably due to maintenance of the all-important muscle blood flow in cold conditions where the demand for skin blood flow is low.

While it has been well documented that we can acclimatize to exercise in the heat, no such evidence exists that we can do the same in the cold. However, it might be suggested that continuous exposure may lead to increased narrowing of the skin blood vessels, increased insulation secondary to increases in body fat, or that our resting metabolic heat production increases after prolonged exposure to the cold.

## Swimming and the Cold

Swimming in cold water, particularly for older swimmers and triathletes, is worthy of discussion. Water has 200 times the conductivity of heat than air. Thus heat is lost from the body much more rapidly during cold water immersion than exposure to air of the same temperature. The ideal water temperature for swimming is 26-28$^0$C. Wetsuits should be worn in water 20$^0$C or below and no swim events should be held if the water temperature is 16$^0$C or below (FINA rules).

For the masters athlete at risk of coronary heart disease, even greater caution is needed in the cold. As noted above, the cold causes blood vessels to constrict. This narrowing of the blood vessels raises blood pressure, thus causing the heart to work harder and need more oxygen. However, the blood vessels carrying blood and oxygen to the heart may also constrict and reduce oxygen delivery to the heart, thus causing chest pain, and the likelihood of a heart attack. Research has shown that arm work such as swimming has a greater effect on raising blood pressure than legwork. Thus, aging swimmers, particularly those at risk, should take extra caution in water below 24$^0$C and consider wetsuits, greasing up or at least wearing a couple of bathing caps. Increasing body fat might also be suggested as it both increases buoyancy and acts as an excellent insulator.

## Preventing Cold Injuries in Masters Athletes

With the special considerations for aging swimmers noted above, the following guidelines are strongly recommended for the masters athlete when exercising in the cold:

1. *Correct warm-up.* In cold conditions, particularly for speed and power events, warm-up may require wearing heavier clothing, exercising and stretching for longer and / or more intensely, and warming up immediately before the event.
2. *Wear appropriate clothing.* The goal is to provide adequate insulation while avoiding accumulation of sweat. Multiple layers are suggested. The innermost layer should carry moisture away from the skin (polypropylene, wool, cotton, *Gore-Tex* or synthetic fibers are suggested). The middle layers should include good insulation materials such as down or synthetics. In windy or rainy conditions the outer layer should be water and wind

resistant. Zippered clothes are excellent in that they insulate at the start of exercise but can be opened up to allow heat loss as we warm-up. Proper head covering is a must. Similarly, the ears, fingers, and toes need to be protected so beanies, gloves and boots or shoe covers are recommended.

3. *Guage the wind.* Rapid air movement markedly increases convective heat loss as warm air close to the skin is replaced by colder air. Wind direction can affect comfort in the cold. Runners, cross-country skiers, kayak or ski-paddlers are well advised to "head out" facing the wind and to "come home" with the wind. This avoids the high wind chill while wearing sweat-soaked clothes.

4. *Avoid damp and windy conditions.* The combination of cold, wet and windy conditions dramatically increases heat loss and thus the risk of cold injury. Wearing water proof clothing or *Gore-Tex* material helps prevent the underlying clothing getting wet.

5. *Avoid rapid cooling after exercise.* Add clothing soon after finishing a cold weather endurance event, get out of the wind, and find a warm spot in the sun or indoors.

6. *Prevent frostbite.* The fingers, toes, ears and face are susceptible to frostbite because of the reduced blood flow to these tissues during cold exposure. Avoiding the wind, wearing gloves, beanies, boot covers and creams and reducing the duration of skin exposure is recommended. Importantly, athletes may not be aware of frostbite because extreme cold blocks the sensation of pain.

7. *Awareness of the signs of cold injury.* Early signs of hypothermia are weakness, fatigue, numbness, poor judgment, drowsiness, blurred vision and a decreased shivering rate then followed by collapse and unconsciousness.

## Conclusion

The human body operates to maintain its optimal temperature at around 37-38 degrees. Exercising in the hot, humid or cold conditions will see the body's heat loss and heat gain mechanisms operate to maintain this optimal temperature. Older people appear more susceptible to heat and cold injuries for a variety of reasons. In contrast, older endurance athletes appear to be able to tolerate both heat and cold conditions well compared to older untrained people. However, masters athletes, especially those not endurance trained or with cardiac risk factors, need to adhere to the many suggestions discussed above on how to safely exercise in both the heat and cold.

# CHAPTER 12

## INJURY PREVENTION AND MANAGEMENT FOR THE MASTERS ATHLETE

*In nature there are neither rewards, nor punishments – there are consequences.*

Robert Ingersoll

*The ideal man bears the accidents of life with dignity and grace, making the best of circumstances.*

Aristotle

*I always felt that there was longevity in me. As for size, I was 204 pounds when I was 16 years old and that's the weight I played at throughout my career. You've got one body, so you'd better take care of it, and that takes sacrifice. You've got to love what you're doing. If you love it, you can overcome any handicap or the soreness or all the aches and pains, and continue to play for a long, long time.*

Gordie Howe

*Success is getting up one more time than you fall down.*

Anonymous

*To race and suffer, that is hard, but that is not being laid out on a hospital bed in Indianapolis with a catheter hanging out of my chest, with platinum pumping into my veins, throwing up for 24 hours straight for five days. We have all heard the saying "What does not kill you makes you stronger" and that is exactly it.*

Lance Armstrong

## Introduction

Apart from a traumatic incident occurring to my family, one of my biggest fears is getting injured and not being able to exercise regularly! Apart from a couple of broken bones and joint dislocations playing Rugby in my teens and twenties, and self-inflicted shin splints leading up to a national aquathon (5k run, 800m swim) championship in 1982, I have to date remained injury-free.

While we all make every attempt to train injury-free, some of us either overtrain or are pre-disposed to sports injuries due to our anatomical structure and/or poor training technique practices. A number of age-related changes occur in bone, cartilage, tendons, muscles and ligaments that theoretically make masters athletes more susceptible to sports-related injuries. Stiffer tendons, muscles, joint capsules and ligaments, a reduced rate of tissue repair, decreased joint flexibility and a loss of bone mineral density all contribute to an increased vulnerability to sports injuries with advancing age.

The purpose of this chapter is to examine the possible causes of these injuries, ways we can prevent them, and if we suffer an injury what we can do about managing our injuries.

## Rate and Risk of Injury

Aging athletes are susceptible to two types of sports injury; those resulting from current training or competition, and those that occurred as youngsters that have come back to haunt us. When faced with diagnosing an injury, a sports physician or physiotherapist must be aware that what they are being presented with may be signs and symptoms resulting from earlier injuries and/or are the result of degenerative disease.

There is no evidence to suggest that aging athletes suffer injuries at a greater rate than younger athletes. Indeed, a study undertaken at Stanford University in the United States observed that aging people who engage in vigorous running and other aerobic activities have lower mortality (death) and slower development of disability than do members of the general population who are the same age. Research on injury and training patterns in the aging athlete has also suggested that masters athletes tend to avoid sports with body contact or potential for injury, train at a slower pace with greater "mileage", and tend to enter longer distance races than the younger athlete. This may make the aging athlete more susceptible to overuse injuries than the younger athletes, particularly if the masters athlete is doing those longer distances with poor technique.

Research has confirmed that when injuries do occur in the aging athlete, they are generally due to overuse and most often observed in the lower extremity. A study published in the British Journal of Sports Medicine examined sports-related injuries in 97 male athletes (70-81 years) from a variety of primarily endurance sports over a ten-year period. The researchers observed that 75% of the injuries occurred in the legs with most injuries being observed in the knee (20%). Sprains of the knee and thigh were the most common acute injury. A classic study from the mid-1980s by DeHaven and Littner indicated that the incidence of inflammatory problems increased significantly with aging, until by the age of 70 years, the top five injuries were all inflammatory in nature including arthritis, tenosynovitis, fasciitis, capsulitis, and tendonitis. Thus, these conditions need to be identified early and treated or managed. If ignored or poorly managed, these minor problems manifest as major injuries and may mean cessation of sports involvement or a lengthy time off training and competing.

Research clearly shows that the majority of injuries in athletes (both young and old) can be tracked to a certain cause such as overtraining. Thus, with a little planning of the training program, masters athletes can avoid most common injuries.

Most injuries in aging athletes are caused by overuse, faulty biomechanics (technique) or poor flexibility.

1. *Overuse*

    Aging athletes experience natural decreases in the physical capacities (endurance, strength, speed, flexibility) needed in sport plus a reduced capacity to recover from training and racing. Competing too often, training too intensely too often and/or for too long, failing to rest and recover, ignoring flexibility training and avoiding strength training will eventually catch up with a masters athlete. These problems can be exaggerated in athletes with heavy work or family commitments and tend to train inconsistently or squeeze training in and not warm-up or cool down as effectively as they should. The masters athlete who makes these mistakes opens themselves up to overtraining injuries.

    The majority of aches and pains are due to overuse. For example, in runners, each running step requires your body to absorb three to four times its weight for many kilometers, cyclists complete 90-100 revolutions of the legs each minute for hours on end, with swimmers completing 40-50 strokes per 50 meters for lap after lap. The repetitious nature of such exercise can lead to breakdown and injury. Use of the following guidelines can help reduce your risk of overuse injury:

    - Build kilometers/miles slowly. As a rule of thumb, increase distance by no more than 10% a week
    - Do not routinely increase distance by 10% per week. Have easy weeks and hard weeks by varying intensity, distance, and frequency of training
    - Follow hard days (either intensity or distance) by easy days
    - Incorporate some cross-training. Replace a running day with swimming, cycling, or walking. This will still give you an aerobic workout while giving the trained muscles a rest.
    - The risk of overuse injuries increases dramatically the more kilometers undertaken. Learn your limits and maintain that limit if you start getting aches and pains. Increase intensity and recoveries to keep enhancing performance if kilometers become limiting
    - Racing places enormous stress on your body. Plan a racing schedule that allows adequate recovery between events. Train easy for a few days after an event.

2. *Biomechanics*

   Faulty technique places abnormal forces on muscles, bones or joints. For example, in running, a common problem is pronation (rolling in of the ankle joint) as the foot lands. If you feel you have faulty running technique, see a sports physiotherapist or sports podiatrist who is trained to analyse technique and foot function. In aging swimmers a common injury is swimmers shoulder. While this complaint may be due to overtraining, it is often due to poor technique (not enough body roll) or inadequate shoulder flexibility. In veteran cyclists, knee pain behind the knee cap is often experienced due to pushing big gears too often or too long or poor bike set up.

   Prevention of biomechanical problems can often be prevented by visiting a sports physiotherapist before commencing training and having them conduct a musculo-skeletal profile. This profile examines both your strength and flexibility characteristics in relation to the demands of your sport or event. Talk to other athletes from your sport(s) as to a sports physiotherapist who knows your sport(s). A good coach will also ensure you are training with correct technique prior to commencing harder training where the risk of injury increases. Finally, ensure you are using the correct equipment (e.g. running shoes, bike set-up) that suits your body type and style. A reputable bike dealer or specialist running shop will be able to assist here.

3. *Flexibility*

   Training and competing regularly have many performance benefits, but increased flexibility is not one of them. As training increases muscle strength, it also shortens and tightens muscles. Tight muscles and tendons restrict your range of motion around a joint. Thus, stretching before and after training and competition is extremely important for masters athletes. If you have concerns in this area, see a sports physiotherapist who will prescribe a stretching program for your specific needs. The following guidelines are important when stretching are discussed at length in Chapter 9:

   - Warm-up before stretching with an easy jog or cycle.
   - Isolate the muscle group to be stretched.
   - Use correct alignment and technique.
   - Exhale going into the stretch to facilitate relaxation during the stretch.
   - Breathe normally during the stretch but accentuate exhaling when going deeper into the stretch.
   - Hold the stretch at the point of tension, not pain.
   - Hold the stretch for 10 to 30 seconds.
   - Come out of the stretch as carefully as you go into it.
   - Do 2-3 repetitions of a 10-second stretch or one of a 30-second stretch.
   - Stretch 3-5 days per week.
   - If your sport demands dynamic flexibility, incorporate a progressively-increasing velocity flexibility strategy. That is, stretch in the following order:
     - Static

- Slow, short of end of range stretching (below 75% of actual sport speed)
- Slow, full range stretching (again below 75% of actual sport speed)
- Fast, short of end of range stretching
- Fast, full range stretching

I also strongly recommend a book titled *Sports Stretch* by Michael Alter (www.humankinetics.com) that describes and gives diagrams of 311 stretches for 41 sports.

4. *Maintain high levels of strength*

   As discussed throughout this book, one of the most common causes of age-related decreases in performance is loss of muscle mass and strength and the older we become the more strength and muscle mass we lose. Strength training is thus strongly recommended for the masters athlete. In terms of injury prevention, strong muscles and joints are less likely to be damaged. The strength training exercises should be sport specific for the higher performance aging athlete but general strengthening exercises also appear to work to prevent injuries.

## Injury, Healing and Aging

Despite using good technique, gradually increasing our training load and doing strength and flexibility programs, injuries can still occur. The body's normal response to an injury occurs in three phases:

1. Inflammatory phase
2. Proliferation phase
3. Remodeling phase

Each of these phases of injury healing is affected by aging. Once an injury occurs, there is an inflammatory response where the body gets all the raw materials needed to prevent infection, remove debris, and begin repair to the site of injury. These processes are slowed with age. The proliferation phase is also dampened with the migration, replicating and growth of various cells delayed with aging. Finally, when remodeling of the damaged tissue takes place, it is well documented that the collagen connective tissue is laid down more slowly, in smaller amounts, and with less effective binding patterns than seen in younger people. Thus, repair to muscle, ligament, tendon and cartilage appears delayed with aging. However, there is no evidence to suggest that bone repair following fractures is delayed.

## Treatment Considerations for Aging Athletes

While the healing process may take longer in aging athletes, there is no reason why a medical practitioner or physiotherapist should treat an aging athlete any different to a younger athlete. Some of the issues that a health care professional needs to be aware of or should be made aware of by an injured masters athlete seeking treatment are:

- *Ageism*. Never accept the statement "what do you expect for someone your age?" or "aren't you too old for this?" Aging athletes are entitled to participate in sport as much as younger people. In light of the health benefits that accrue from physical fitness into old age, an enlightened sports medicine professional should be encouraging your involvement.

- *Don't give in to being told to stop.* Aging athletes, just like younger athletes, will want to get back to training and competing as soon as possible. Being fit and athletic is an important component of their self-image and this is threatened when sports involvement is restricted.

- *Accept or encourage time out.* Masters athletes should accept, and medical professionals encourage, a short time out to recover from the injury as the break will mean long term involvement in the future. Alternative strategies (e.g. water running, cross-training, stretching, weight lifting) might be suggested to maintain or develop alternative fitness aimed at minimizing the time it takes to come back to full training. The more sport-specific the alternative without further damaging the injury the better.

- *Encourage technique modification.* Many sports injuries are due to poor technique being done repetitively. If bracing cannot help correct a technique, encourage a coach's involvement to alter technique.

- *Rehabilitate quickly.* Sports physicians and sports physiotherapists are highly aware of the need to begin rehabilitation from injury back to normal functioning in as short as possible time as soon as possible after injury. Given that aging athletes take longer to heal but are, in general, just as committed to performance as younger athletes, it is crucial that rehabilitation commence quickly and with all available treatment modalities. As with younger athletes, the longer an aging athlete is away from training, the longer it will take to regain that hard-worked-for, sport-specific fitness.

As a general rule, for athletes and sports medicine professionals, it has been suggested that rehabilitation will take twice as long for a 60 year-old athlete as it does a 20 year old. Athletes aged 75 or older may take three times as long due to the significant age-related changes that occur after this age.

## Rehabilitation from Injury

Recovery from injury is often more complex and difficult for both the patient and the treatment team. After initial first-aid treatment with RICE (Rest, Ice, Compression, Elevation), the rehabilitation process begins with an adequate and thorough diagnosis that needs to be specific so that the best treatment plan can be implemented. A comprehensive medical/injury history and thorough examination should be done by a sports physician or sports physiotherapist with an excellent knowledge of anatomy and the sport. Special tests such as a bone scan, CT scan or MRI may help the early diagnosis and loss of condition in the athlete.

Acute injuries such as fractures may take 6 (upper limb) to 12 weeks (lower limb) to heal. Soft tissue injuries of the lower limb may take longer to heal than those of the upper body because of weight-bearing.

Aging athletes with overuse injuries (e.g. shin splints, tennis elbow, plantar fasciitis, tendonitis, swimmer's shoulder, rower's back) need to hasten slowly. Ideally, treatment should be undertaken early rather than keeping on playing or competing that may exacerbate the problem. After several weeks of treatment and relative rest doing other activities, athletes can commence training again at a lighter load, gradually increasing training volume by about 10% per week.

Figure 12.1 below shows a typical rehabilitation plan called the pyramid of recovery and should be monitored closely by the treatment team.

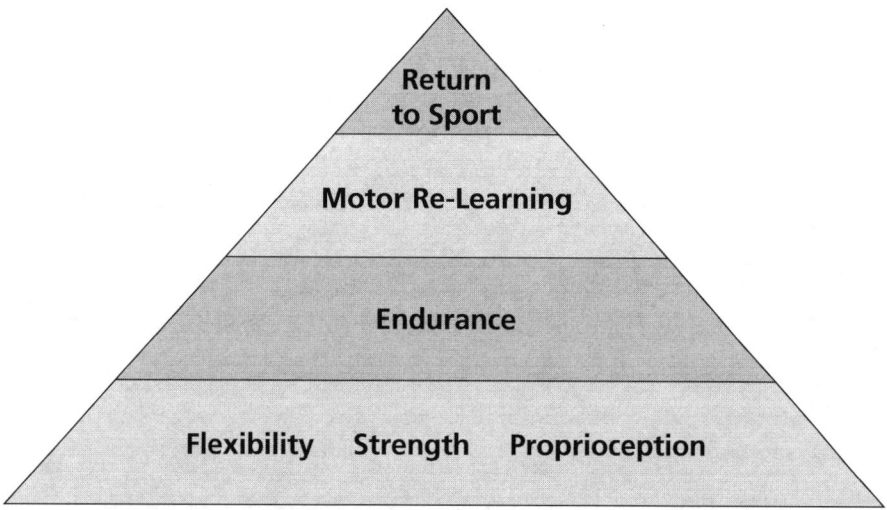

*Figure 12.1:* Pyramid of recovery.

Full range of joint motion should be gained with minimal aggravation of symptoms and healing structures. The muscles and connective tissues surrounding the injury should also be strengthened using the same principles. Proprioception is the term used to describe the muscle, joint and tendon nerve impulses that tell the brain about joint position, joint motion, vibration and pressure. Balance and coordination activities help retrain the muscles and nerves to help proprioception so activities such as balance boards, mini trampolines, and agility and coordination exercises assist this process. Endurance takes two forms. Firstly, muscle endurance such as specific, low load, high repetition exercises in the gym or at home; and secondly, cardiovascular endurance exercise such as swimming, cycling or water running. Motor re-learning involves exercises such as advanced coordination and agility drills, progressive running, throwing or racquet drills and then sport-specific drills that increase in frequency, intensity and duration until full return to activity.

## Typical Rehabilitation Protocol

Whenever an injury occurs the first priority is immediate treatment using sound first aid principles. A general guideline for injury rehabilitation, including the phases and general rehabilitation techniques used in each phase are shown in Table 12.1. In practice, these phases may overlap and should always be conducted with sports physiotherapist supervision and ideally the involvement of a strength and conditioning specialist who works with the sports physiotherapist.

*Table 12.1:* Phases of injury rehabilitation and techniques recommended.

| Phase | Rehabilitation Techniques |
|---|---|
| 1<br>PRICE protocol to protect and control inflammation | Protection – to avoid further injury<br>Rest – to allow healing<br>Ice – to control swelling and inflammation<br>Compression - to control swelling and inflammation<br>Elevation - to control swelling and inflammation |
| 2<br>Restore range of motion and promote healing | Active and passive movement<br>Therapeutic modalities (e.g. ultrasound, hot-cold, electrotherapy, diathermy, laser) |
| 3<br>Restore strength | Need to consider the following<br>type of exercise<br>type of resistance<br>type of contraction |
| 4<br>Restore power and functional ability | Pliometrics<br>Sport-specific conditioning |
| 5<br>Return to competition | Medical clearance<br>Controlled and progressive training |

## Medications and the Masters Athlete

The use of medications is a concern for athletes of all ages but in particular the aging athlete who may have pathology (e.g. osteoarthritis, hypertension or diabetes). In general, the older a person becomes, the more medication they consume. Combined with the physiological and pathological changes that occur with aging, it is not surprising to see an increase in adverse drug reactions in older people.

As far as the effectiveness of pharmaceutical drugs in aging people goes, the following age-related changes may affect the response of aging people to medications:

1. *Reduced absorption* of medication due to the decreased gastric acid production, increased stomach-emptying time, reduced intestine absorption surface area, and decreased intestinal blood flow

2. *Altered distribution through the body.* With aging there is a reduction in total body water, an increase in body fat, and a loss of muscle and bone mass. Water-soluble medications will therefore be distributed over a smaller volume and will have a greater effect per dose. In contrast, fat-soluble medications will be dispersed over a larger body volume and have diminished effect per dose

3. *Reduced liver clearance.* The liver gets smaller and has a reduced blood flow with aging. Thus, medications requiring liver metabolism will be handled more slowly

4. *Reduced cell receptors*. Medications, like hormones, can bind with special receptors on the walls of cells. The number of receptors can decrease with aging thus reducing the amount of the medication that actually enters a cell, thus reducing its effectiveness.

In athletes, one of the more common medications used are NSAIDS (non-steroidal anti-inflammatory drugs) such as *ibobrufen, acetylsalicylic acid, naproxen* and *indomethacin*. In all athletes, but particularly masters athletes, they should be used with caution for several reasons. First, they can induce gastrointestinal problems such as ulcers. Secondly, aging is associated with an increased incidence of adverse reactions to NSAIDS. Finally, while NSAIDS may take away the pain, they do not take away the cause so an aging athlete may keep training and do more serious damage. In sufferers of osteoarthritis where NSAIDS are commonly prescribed, this is a concern. A safer approach may be to take a smaller dose or none prior to exercise, and then a full dose afterwards to limit pain and inflammation.

## Drug Testing and Aging Athletes

Drug testing in younger athletes was introduced for two reasons. Firstly, some drugs endangered the health of the athletes; and secondly, because many drugs were performance enhancing, their use contravened the spirit of fair play and equal competition most of we masters athletes value.

The growth and increasing competitiveness of masters sport has lead to the introduction of random drug testing at major masters events around the world. The dilemma facing aging sports administrators is that many IOC-banned drugs are prescribed or regularly used by aging athletes for health maintenance or treatment of diseases. However, in most cases where a product contains a banned drug, there are alternative drugs to treat the problem. If in doubt, look at the World Anti-Doping Code 2009 *Prohibited List* and *Therapeutic Use Exemptions* at: http://www.asada.gov.au/WAD_code09/index.htm then discuss your therapy with your family doctor or sports physician.

In 1991, the Australian Sports Drug Agency (ASDA) was established to provide both education programs on the drugs in sport issue and to conduct independent testing of Australian athletes. However, its primary focus was at the elite and open level of competition. At the World Masters Games in Brisbane, 1994 the Board of Directors of the games insisted on drug testing through ASDA and developed the following position statement:

> *World Masters Games condemns the use of performance enhancing substances as potentially dangerous to health, contrary to the ethics of sport and incompatible with the philosophy of Masters Sport.*

The list of IOC-banned substances was adopted by the World Masters Games Board. However, the games organisers also stated that any aging athlete who tested positive and who had a medical certificate from a qualified medical practitioner may refer that certificate to an appointed tribunal hearing or provide evidence that the use of the banned substance was for therapeutic and / or medication purposes only. The games organisers also informed competitors that they should not cease medication to compete in the games.

The 1995 Australian Masters Games drugs policy states that the organisers view the use of drugs as *detrimental to sport and the spirit of the Australian Masters Games*. While these organisers did not organise random drug testing, they reserved the right of ASDA or individual sports to conduct their own testing at their own expense. The games organisers also stated that they will recognize the sports imposed sanctions and may retrieve awards and ban guilty competitors from further participation at those games.

The following groups of drugs have been banned by the IOC and World Anti-Doping Agency (WADA).

*Table 12.2:* Substances and methods prohibited by the World Anti-Doping Agency (2009).
\* Aeronautic, automobile, karate, motorcycling, powerboating, shooting, archery, tenpin bowling.
# Same sports as in \* plus bobsleigh, golf, bridge, skiing and snowboarding, billiards and snooker, curling, gymnastics, wrestling.

| Prohibited at all times | Prohibited in-competition only |
|---|---|
| **Substances** | |
| Anabolic agents | Stimulants |
| Hormones or related substances | Narcotics |
| Beta-2 agonists | Cannabinoids |
| Hormone antagonists and modulators | Glucocorticosteroids |
| Diuretics and masking agents | Alcohol \* |
|  | Beta-blockers # |
| **Methods** | |
| Enhancement of oxygen transfer | |
| Chemical and physical manipulation | |
| Gene doping | |

1. *Anabolic agents* are artificial versions of the hormone testosterone that helps build muscle and aid recovery from both training and injury. Examples include *Deca-Durabolin, Stanazol,* and *Primobolan.*
2. *Stimulants* refer to a group of drugs that boost alertness and physical activity by increasing heart and breathing rates and brain functions. By acting on the central nervous system, stimulants can stimulate the body both mentally and physically. These include cocaine, amphetamines, *Sudafed, Orthoxicol, Actifed,* and *Demazin.*
3. *Hormones or related substances* are substances that are produced by glands in the body and that, after circulating through blood, can affect other organs and tissues to change bodily functions. Examples are erythropoietin, human growth hormones, insulin, and corticotrophins. Athletes use them to: stimulate the production of naturally occurring hormones, increase muscle growth and strength, and increase the production of red blood cells to improve the blood's ability to carry oxygen.

4. **Narcotic** are usually taken in the form of painkillers that act on the brain and spinal cord to treat pain associated with painful stimuli. They decrease the amount of pain felt from injuries or illness, thus allowing the athlete to maintain training or competing. Examples are heroin, morphine, pethidine, *Palfium* and *Di-gesic, Codeine, Panadeine. Codral*, and *Dymadon*.

5. **Beta-2 Antagonists** are drugs commonly used to treat asthma by relaxing the muscles that surround the airway and opening up the air passages. They can provide the same advantages of a stimulant or, if administered into the bloodstream, have anabolic effects. To increase their muscle size and reduce body fat. When taken orally or by injection, Beta-2 can have powerful stimulatory effects. *Formoterol, salubutamol, salmeterol* and *terbutaline* are permitted by inhalation only to prevent and/or treat asthma and exercise-related respiratory problems. However, athletes need to provide a medical note in order to attain a therapeutic-use exemption.

6. **Cannabinoids** are psychoactive chemicals derived from the cannabis plant that cause a feeling of relaxation. Hashish and marijuana are the most common. While not considered performance enhancing, it is banned because its use is damaging to the image of sport. There are also safety factors involved as the use of marijuana could weaken the athlete's ability to perform, thereby compromising the safety of the athlete and other competitors.

7. **Hormone antagonsists and modulators** that act as chemical messengers in the body. Examples are human growth hormone, human chorionic gonadotrophin and corticotrophin, all of which are responsible for growth in the human body. Athletes may use these hormones to increase size and strength of muscles or spare glycogen as an energy source.

8. **Glucocorticosteroids** are used mainly as anti-inflammatory drugs and to relieve pain. They are commonly used to treat asthma, hay fever, tissue inflammation and rheumatoid arthritis. Examples are *dexamethasone, fluticasone, prednisone, triamcinolone acetonide* and *rofleponide*. When administered systemically (into the blood), they can produce a feeling of euphoria, potentially giving athletes an unfair advantage by masking pain felt from injury and illness. They are prohibited when administered orally, rectally, or by intravenous or intramuscular administration. All other administrations require the athlete to provide a medical note in order to attain a therapeutic-use exemption.

9. **Diuretics and masking agents** are products that can potentially conceal the presence of a prohibited substance in urine or other samples. They help the body lose water and salt, thus causing weight loss and making the urine so weak that other drugs may not show up in a drug test. Examples are *Lasix* and *Aldactone*.

10. **Blood doping** involves removing blood several weeks before competition and then replacing it 5-7 days before competition to increase the number of red blood cells and therefore oxygen carrying capacity of the blood.

11. **Beta-Blockers** are cardiac medications most often used to treat high blood pressure by reducing heart rate and reducing fine tremor, thus resulting in a "steadier hand".

In sports such as pistol shooting and archery these drugs can have obvious benefits. Examples include *Betaloc, Inderal, Lopresor*, and *Tenormin*. These drugs should not be stopped suddenly unless on doctors advice.

## Gut upsets in athletes

Runners, cyclists, swimmers, triathletes and team players have all experienced the "tummy upset" at some stage in training or competition. Sometimes it might be some nausea, belching, a stitch, and at worst can be diarrhea midway through a race. Studies on gut upsets suggest that the incidence is between 10 and 81% depending on the type, duration, and intensity of the exercise studies. Running produces the highest rate and the longer the event, the higher the incidence.

Scientists break gut upsets into two areas. First, the upper part of the gastrointestinal (GI) tract symptoms that include nausea, vomiting, belching, heartburn that appear more common in cyclists or swimmers compared to runners. Secondly, lower GI tract symptoms (bloating, passing wind, stomach cramps, stitch, busting to "poo" or diarrhoea) that are far more in runners, particularly those that are younger (inexperienced), unfit, or doing longer races.

The myths suggest it "must be something you ate" or "you drank too much". However, the scientific facts suggest otherwise with numerous factors being suggested as possible causes of gut upsets:

- High intensity exercise versus low intensity
- Long duration exercise tends to bring on lower GI tract symptoms versus shorter bouts which tend to bring on upper GI tract symptoms
- Energy depletion - the need to ensure race nutrition
- Carbohydrate malabsorption - the need for low GI foods and sports drinks
- Training age (years of training) - evaluating what may have caused the upset
- Dehydration - this has been suggested as **the major** factor in gut upsets and highlights the need to prevent it
- Reduced blood flow to the gut with a 60-70% reduction being observed during hard exercise - this upsets the ability to absorb food/fluid
- Hormonal influences - high aerobic fitness levels minimize changes in these
- Infections - being healthy prior to and staying away from polluted water
- Stress - psychological strategies to remain calm before racing
- Not clearing the bowels before training / racing - I find a bowl of muesli and plenty of water the night before does the trick first thing in the morning of a race
- Too much fiber in the pre-race diet - fiber encourages quick transit time through the gut
- Too much fat and / or protein in the pre-race diet - these food types sit in the gut longer than carbohydrate
- Eating within 30 minutes of training/racing - not enough time to clear food through the gut

- Drinking hypertonic (particle dense) drinks (sports drinks are isotonic) - such drinks pull water into the gut and encourage diarrhea
- Mechanical trauma - the bouncing up and down of running.

Given these factors, there are some we can do something about and some we can't. However, it is obvious that diet (food and fluid) is a major influence since that is what the gut is all about. So, before we examine how we can prevent or minimize the likelihood of gut upsets, let's examine the physiology of the gut in a little detail to help us understand why certain preventative measures have been suggested.

Food and drink are *stored* in the stomach and then move from the stomach into the intestine for *absorption* into the blood. A number of factors affect the rate at which a solution leaves the stomach (see Table 12.3 for summary).

*Table 12.3:* Factors affecting the rate at which a solution leaves the stomach.

| Solution characteristic | Rate of stomach emptying |
|---|---|
| Volume | Increases with larger volume |
| Energy content (kJ/Cals) | Decreases with increased kJ/Cals |
| Osmolarity (particles in solution) | Increasing osmolality slows rate |
| Temperature | Faster with cooler fluids |
| Acidity level (pH) | Decreases the more acidic |
| Exercise | > 80-90% max heart rate slows rate |
| Stress | Anxiety slows emptying |

Once the mix is out of the stomach and into the small intestine for *absorption*, again a number of factors affect the rate of absorption (see Table 12.4).

*Table 12.4:* Factors affecting the rate of absorption of food and fluids from the small intestine.

| Factor | Rate of absorption |
|---|---|
| Carbohydrate | 6-10% (6-8g/100mL) of carbohydrate maximizes |
| Osmolality (particles in solution) | Isotonic (same as blood) or hypotonic maximize |
| Sodium | Increases absorption of fluid |
| Anions (negative ions) | Chloride maximizes absorption |

Thus, taken together, if the aim is to maximize stomach emptying and intestinal absorption, the food/fluid we take in before and during exercise should adhere to the following guidelines to prevent gut upsets:

- Take in a relatively large and tolerable volume of fluid before racing/training (500 mL 30-60 minutes prior to training or racing)
- Ensure the solution is cool
- Prevent dehydration through regular drinking during training/competing (up to 800-1000 mL/hr)

- Use sports drinks that meet the guideline requirements of carbohydrate and sodium concentrations
- Try and remain calm (easier said than done when competing)
- Try not to eat-drink high energy foods before racing.

Apart from these factors, sport scientists have suggested other ways to prevent gut upsets including:

- Vitamin E supplementation (1000 International units/day for two weeks) has been shown to reduce gut upset incidence in marathon runners
- Stay away from training in or drinking from polluted waters
- Train using the strategies you plan to use in racing
- Practice before and during race drinking and eating routines in training
- Avoid dramatic changes in pre-competition meals that you usually have
- Avoid high fat / high protein foods pre-race/training as they slow emptying and absorption
- Avoid high fiber foods before racing/training
- Don't ingest extra caffeine, high doses of vitamin C, sodium bicarbonate, or dubious and untried nutritional aids just prior to or during racing or training
- Try to defecate and urinate prior to exercise. Two strategies I use. First, I eat my normal muesli bowl and drink a glass of water before I go to bed the night before I race. Second, I hold my first urination (unless busting) until after another glass of water first thing after getting up. The extra pressure in the bladder seems to push on the bowels to help get rid of that load! Getting down to it I know, but it works for me!
- Avoid fructose (fruit sugar) in pre-race meals and during-race nutrition as it is absorbed slowly and has been linked to gut upsets.

The factors affecting gut upsets are numerous but if preventative measures are in place through good coaching and athlete self-evaluation, then they should be minimized. However, if all else fails, do as I do on the long runs - tuck 6-10 sheets of toilet paper under the top laces, find a quiet spot, and pray it doesn't rain!

## "Stitch"

Abdominal side-pain during exercise, particularly in runners, swimmers and horseriders, is another relatively common complaint often experienced by athletes. The pain is sharp and stabbing when severe and aching or pulling when less severe. It appears "stitches" are more common in sports where repetitive torso movement is present and is exacerbated after meals. Like cramping, several theories but no one cause have been put forward to explain "stitches" including:

1. loss of blood supply to the diaphragm (breathing muscle)
2. stress on the ligaments that extend from the diaphragm to hold up the gut

3. rubbing and irritation of the abdominal wall by the stomach or intestine folds.

Risk factors for the onset of "stitches" include:
- eating a meal too close to training or racing
- high carbohydrate rich fluids (gels, energy drinks such as *Sustagen*) taken too close to the event
- hypertonic (energy drinks such as *Lucozade*, fruit juices, soft drinks) or hypotonic (water) taken too close to the event
- high intensity racing or training.

Avoiding "stitches" involves:
- Drink isotonic fluids (e.g sports drinks) during activity
- Eat a normal, quickly digested meal 2-3 hours before the activity
- Avoid exercise after a large drink or meal
- Avoid sugary foods and drinks before and during the activity
- Avoid large volumes of fluid that may distend the stomach and press against the abdominal wall. Drinking regular, smaller volumes is suggested.

Immediate treatment of "stitches" can involve:
- leaning forward
- tightening the abdominal muscles
- breathing in and out deeper

Over the years of training, two methods have worked for me – one when stationery, the other when running. One method was taught to me by an ex swimming coach of mine, now deceased, named Cyrus Weld. He represented Australia at the 1952 Commonwealth (then Empire) Games in Vancouver, Canada. He told us as young swimmers that between intervals, bring the relevant side knee up to our chest, and take some deep breaths. It works. However, when doing running races, it's not too practical to stop. Thus, the second method has proven the best method when running and was taught to me by Dr Andrew Semple, pioneer of the Queensland Marathon Road Runners Club in Brisbane, Australia and mentor to many older runners in Brisbane during the 70s and 80s. He taught me to keep running, slow down if necessary, but to breathe in deeply while leaning back, then blow out forcefully and deeply while leaning forward. This method also works.

## Muscle Cramps

These are defined as painful, spasmodic, involuntary contractions of muscles that occur during or immediately after exercise. The incidence of muscle cramps is very high with 30-70% of endurance athletes having experienced them at some stage in their career. While no one cause of muscle cramps has been identified, the following theories have been put forward:

1. *Fluid and electrolyte imbalances.* Cramps seem to occur more often during endurance events in hot and humid conditions when dehydration and loss of electrolytes in sweat are

common. Because sodium is the most common and abundant electrolyte lost in sweat, it is the one implicated in muscle cramps due to its major role in the muscle contraction process.

2. *Depletion of calcium, potassium and magnesium.* These electrolytes are not lost from muscles and the blood in the same quantities as sodium but may play a minor role in muscle cramping. While sweat losses of these are small, a recent study of magnesium's role in cramping did show a reduced rate of muscle cramping in endurance athletes who took *Magonate* (magnesium gluconate) the night before and during races, suggesting that magnesium may play a protective role in muscle cramping.

3. *Muscle fatigue.* Cramps appear to occur early season or when the levels of fitness can't match the demands of the event.

4. *Contraction of the muscle in a shortened position.* For example, swimmers calves are contracting during normal swimming in a shortened position.

5. *Other causes.* Diabetes, blood vessel disorders, and nervous system conditions may also predispose an aging athlete to muscle cramps. Creatine, a relatively new product being used by body builders or team players to enhance body mass and help recover between sprints (it has no application for endurance athletes), has been linked to a higher incidence of muscle cramping.

From a study of 1,300 marathon runners, risk factors that have been identified for exercise-induced muscle cramping include:

- older age
- longer history of running
- higher body mass
- shorter daily stretching time
- irregular stretching habits
- family history

The same group of 1,300 runners identified the following exercise-related conditions that were associated with muscle cramping during or after exercise:

- higher race pace
- longer duration events
- hill running
- poor race performances
- muscle fatigue.

From all the above discussion, prevention of muscle cramps thus involves:

1. Drinking adequate fluids and electrolytes (NB sodium) during events.
2. Replenish sodium during and after heavy training, especially after profuse sweating. This may mean adding salt to the post-exercise meal.
3. Possibly use magnesium supplementation before and during events.
4. Ensure adequate conditioning for the event to prevent muscle fatigue, particularly regular stretching.

The immediate treatment for muscle cramps involves:
1. *Stretching.* The muscle should be stretched immediately.
2. *Massage.* While stretched, the area should be massaged to alleviate the pain and encourage blood flow to the affected muscle(s).
3. *Stimulate recovery.* Rest and rehydration with fluids containing electrolytes, particularly sodium.

Chronic cramping may indicate a metabolic disturbance and suggest a visit to a sports physician if the above preventative strategies do not work.

## Delayed-Onset Muscle Soreness

To increase strength, speed or endurance, masters athletes need to place greater loads on the muscles and cardiovascular system with progressively increasing frequency, intensity or duration of training. When the muscles cannot cope with the increased load, muscle pain and stiffness can occur in the 24-48 hours after training or racing at this higher intensity than we are used to.

Eccentric (muscle lengthening while producing force) muscle actions such as downhill running, pliometrics (jumping, bounding, hopping) or the downward phase of weights exercises such as the bench press cause damage to the muscle fibers that lead to decreased flexibility, muscle soreness, loss of strength, and decreases in muscle performance. There would be few aging athletes who have not experienced this delayed-onset muscle soreness (DOMS).

A number of possible causes have been suggested to cause DOMS:
1. *Lactic acid accumulation.* This is the most common belief but has no basis whatsoever because lactic acid levels fall back to normal between 30-60 minutes after exercise.
2. *Muscle and connective tissue damage.* The higher intensity or unaccustomed exercise causes muscle and connective tissue structure damage that causes muscle inflammation and pain.
3. *Muscle swelling.* Some researchers believe that the muscle and connective tissue damage causes inflammation that then leads to muscle swelling as a result of fluid accumulation that in turn reduces the range of motion and pain as a result of increased intramuscular pressure.

The muscle and connective tissue damage theory leading to increased swelling and pain of the muscles appears to be the most popular theory behind DOMS.

Bearing these theories in mind, the following methods have been proposed to reduce or avoid DOMS:
1. *Warm-up.* Increasing the muscles temperature by increasing muscle blood flow leads to more relaxed muscles, increased flexibility of the connective tissues within and around the muscles, decreased muscle viscosity, all of which improve muscle function

and performance. The warm-up needs to raise the body's temperature and prepare the specific muscles for the specific speed and action about to be completed. Thus, a general (e.g. cycling, jogging) warm-up increases the body temperature while the specific action (e.g. bench press) done at the specific speed but with lower weights will help prepare the muscle(s) for the heavier load about to be completed.

2. ***Repeat the load soon after DOMS sets in.*** The inflammation response mentioned earlier leads the muscle and connective tissue structures to adapt and strengthen. Doing a lighter load but of the same action as that that caused the DOMS, has been shown to help alleviate the pain.

3. ***Warm-down and stretch***. Both these actions will help reduce the swelling and lengthen the tightened structures that occur with DOMS.

4. ***Gradually increase training intensity***. A 10% increase in training load per week is suggested.

5. ***Cold application.*** May help reduce the pain, swelling and inflammation. Ice packs or cold-water immersion are suggested.

6. ***NSAIDs.*** Nonsteroidal anti-inflammatories such as *aspirin* or *ibobrufen* may reduce soreness temporarily but they won't help healing.

7. ***Compression Garments.*** These reduce muscle swelling, a possible cause of DOMS.

## Injury Prevention Strategies

While this chapter has focused on injury management, it is obviously crucial for the aging competitive athlete to focus on injury prevention. A successful training program is one that provides regular improvement in sports performance <u>without</u> injuries. While the issue of *staying well* is discussed in detail in Chapter 14, below are a number of key strategies to prevent injuries in aging athletes:

- Always include a warm-up and cool-down
- Start hydrated, stay hydrated and end hydrated
- Acclimatize to environmental stress
- Use protective equipment
- Don't use poorly fitted or worn footwear
- Use equipment that fits well
- Integrate exercises that work the core stabilizing muscles of the stomach and lower back
- Develop correct technique
- Check biomechanical and anatomical imbalances with a sports physiotherapist
- Develop a sound base of endurance and strength before intense training
- Emphasise periodisation into the training program
- Avoid dramatic increases in training load
- Eat a well-balanced diet with healthy snacks

- Get plenty of rest and sleep
- Get fit to play sports, don't play sports to get fit

Table 12.5 below provides some excellent and well-respected websites to bookmark or look at for specific advice on specific injuries. Such a discussion of common injuries in specific sports is well beyond the scope of this book.

| Table 12.5: Recommended Websites for Injury Prevention and Management |
|---|
| • http://www.physsportsmed.com/index.php?page=home is the home page of one of the best free on-line journals for any matter pertaining to Sports Injuries - *The Physician and Sports Medicine Journal*. It has a great search engine. |
| • http://www.acsm.org/health%2Bfitness/comments.htm is a website run by the American College of Sports Medicine, the premier sport and exercise science organization in the world, and has a wide range of sport and exercise-related topics to peruse. It has a great search engine. |
| • http://www.nlm.nih.gov/medlineplus/sportsinjuries.html is maintained by the highly respected National Library of Medicine in the United States. It has a huge range of sports-injury topics. |
| • http://www.sportsinjuryclinic.net is a self-diagnosis site with information on over 90 sports-related injuries. |
| • http://www.injuryupdate.com.au is an Australian website providing as much public information as possible regarding typical sports injuries in major sports. |

# CHAPTER 13

## OVERTRAINING AND THE MASTERS ATHLETE

*Everything in excess is opposed by nature.*

Hippocrates

*In everything the middle course is best:
all things in excess bring trouble to men.*

Plautus

*Listen to your body, not your conscience.*

Anonymous

*Many dedicated endurance athletes don't need to be told what to do –
they need to be told what not to do.*

Scott Tinley

### Introduction

A smart athlete or coach plans their training program to gradually increase training load. This slow progression in frequency, duration and/or intensity of training leads to positive adaptations and improved performances. Conversely, overtraining by doing too much hard work too often for too long will lead to negative adaptation and overtraining.

Research has identified many signs of *overtraining*. *Burnout* occurs when an athlete is so psychologically drained they lose motivation and often also lose interest in their training. The onset of these conditions is diverse and varied. No two athletes will respond to training loads in the same way. Adaptation rates vary from one individual to another so it is not always appropriate to prescribe the same workloads for all athletes but it is essential to monitor their responses to training so that workloads can be varied accordingly. Workloads need to be adjusted to the adaptation rates exhibited by each individual and the wise coach or masters athlete will monitor the responses of their athletes or themselves through cues or signs that are indicative of overtraining (Table 13.1).

*Table 13.1:* Typical observations of an athlete's poor adaptation to training.

| Coaching observations | Signs and symptoms of non-adaptation |
|---|---|
| Direct communication | • they have heavy arms or legs<br>• they don't feel good<br>• their arms or legs are sore<br>• they are tired. |
| Body language | • Facial expression and colour<br>• The look in their eyes<br>• Bending over to recover after an effort<br>• Bad technique compared to normal |
| Physiological | • Increase in resting heart rate<br>• Loss of body weight<br>• Loss of appetite |
| Psychological | • Low motivation<br>• Low concentration<br>• Aggressiveness<br>• No self confidence |
| Others | • Poor eating habits<br>• Poor sleep patterns |

The experienced masters athlete should monitor their training adaptations through regular recordings in a training diary or logbook. This is an essential tool for competitive masters athletes so that they learn how to *listen to their own bodies*. Learning to *listen* to the body's signs and cues is one of the most important skills any athlete young or old can acquire. Recordings of the quality of sleep, morning resting heart rate and body weight, and a daily rating of fatigue levels are four critical markers that should be recorded every day by athletes.

One of the first signs of overtraining is a consistently poor sleep pattern. Also an elevated resting heart rate recorded first thing in the morning (i.e. > 6-10 beats per minute above the normal range) is an indication that any training undertaken should be minimal if at all. Body weight is best recorded each morning before eating and after going to the toilet. Rapid weight loss or rapid weight gain is not advisable, and unexplained weight loss may be indicative of overtraining. Feeling tired after training is a normal response but feeling fatigued all the time is a sign that the body has not adapted to the training load being placed on it. These four variables take two minutes a day to record and may be the first indication of maladaptation or non-adaptation to training recognised by an athlete.

Personally, I have a habit of pushing the envelope when it comes to training for big events, a common problem in competitive triathletes, particularly when working in a stressful job and with family responsibilities. The signs that I'm doing too much work without enough recovery have been picked up over many years of training and include:

- 2-3 successive days of muscle soreness, despite recovery strategies being used
- A mildly sore throat
- Swollen lymph glands in the neck
- Falling asleep in front of the TV watching a favourite program

- "Shortness" with my family over "little things".

When I see these things coming on, rarely these days because I practice what I preach, I hit the vitamin C, multivitamin and multiminerals, eat heaps of fruit and vegetables mixing the colours, take a day or two off completely, get an early night or two, then do a very easy active recovery session (e.g. water running or one hour ride in small gears on the flat) first session back. It works for me.

## Causes of overtraining

Numerous studies have been conducted in the area of overtraining in young elite athletes. This research has shown that there is no one sign or symptom that can be used to identify if an athlete is overtrained. However, the common cause appears to be too much training stress without enough recovery. Given that training stress is a combination of the physical and psychological load placed on our body and recovery is affected by our lifestyle, social environment and health, the following table summarises the activities that may cause overtraining in an athlete of any age.

*Table 13.2:* Common causes of overtraining in athletes.

| Training Errors | Athlete Lifestyle | Social Environment | Athlete Health |
|---|---|---|---|
| Overlooking recovery | Lack of enough sleep | Too many family responsibilities | Illness |
| Training too hard too often | Unorganised daily plan | Frustration with family, workmates or peers | High Fever |
| Abrupt increases in training load | Smoking, alcohol, coffee | Job dissatisfaction | Nausea |
| Coming back from injury or illness too quickly | Inadequate living space | Stressful work activities | Niggling injury |
| Not listening to your body | Arguments with peers or loved ones | Excessive emotional activities (noisy music, social life) | Menopause |
| | Poor diet | Lack of support for sports involvement from significant others | Medical condition (diabetes, hypertension etc) |
| | Stressful lifestyle (financial, work) | | |
| | Loss of partner or loved ones | | |

## Symptoms of overtraining

In the late 1980s and throughout the 1990s numerous European, American and Australian sport scientists conducted many studies on overtraining in elite athletes. Despite the vast number of studies published, no one sign or symptom of overtraining has been identified that suits every athlete at all levels in every sport, except one – <u>consistently poor training and competition performance</u>. From the literature, a group of Australian sport scientists came up with an extensive list of symptoms that may be useful in helping you diagnose whether you have overtraining syndrome (see Table 13.3 below).

*Table 13.3:* Signs and symptoms suggestive of overtraining syndrome in athletes.

| Physiological/Performance | Psychological/Information Processing |
|---|---|
| Decreased competition performance | Depression |
| Decreased training performance | Apathy |
| Prolonged recovery | Emotional instability |
| Reduced tolerance to loading | Difficulty concentrating |
| Decreased strength and power | Decreased ability to cope with large amounts of information |
| Decreased maximum working capacity | |
| Decreased body fat | Immunological |
| Changes in resting heart rate greater than 6-8 beats/min | Increased susceptibility to illness/colds/flu |
| Increased breathing frequency | Swelling of lymph glands |
| Increased breathing and heart rate at low exercise intensities | One-day colds |
| Chronic fatigue | Decreased lymphocyte counts |
| Insomnia (poor sleep for more than 2 nights) | |
| Loss of appetite | Biochemical |
| Loss of menstruation | Decreased haemoglobin |
| Increased soreness, aches and pains | Decreased serum ferritin (iron stores) |
| Body weight variation greater than 1 kg in a day | Mineral depletion (zinc, magnesium, selenium, copper) |
| | Elevated cortisol hormone (stress hormone) |
| | Low free testosterone levels |
| | Decreased ratio of free testosterone/cortisol ratio of more than 30% |
| | Increased uric acid production |

**Treatment of overtraining**

If you feel you have developed overtraining syndrome, reduce or cease training immediately, irrespective of the cause. Consult a sports physician or sports medicine specialist with a reputation for working with athletes in your sport or experience in working with tired or overtrained athletes. They should take a history and do some blood tests similar to some of the ones mentioned in Table 13.3. If you have mild overtraining that doesn't warrant a visit to the sports doctor, reduce the training load, especially high intensity sessions and focus on active recovery methods discussed in detail in Chapter 15 of this book. Avoid competing and any other source of emotional or physical stress.

**How far can we push ourselves? A personal journey.**

In discussions with many athletes and coaches over the years, I often hear that there is little practical advice on determining how hard we can push our body's limits to gain fitness whilst still maintaining the ability to "bounce back" with planned rest or taper. As an aging athlete and sport scientist, I am also continually developing my understanding of my own body's ability to cope with the stress of high training loads.

I recently successfully completed a four-month preparation for a Half-Ironman triathlon (1.9k swim, 90k ride, 21.1k run) in Yeppoon, Central Queensland. This particular preparation added another dimension to my understanding of how far I can push myself as a competitive masters athlete. Like most preparations for an age-group triathlete, there was the continual juggling of the stressors of work, family, and training together with dietary needs, recovery strategies, and the periodising of training by listening to my body (seems to be getting louder the older I get!). I'd like to combine these personal experiences with some research one of my former PhD students, now Dr Aaron Coutts recently completed on overreaching-overtraining in team sport athletes to examine some practical and theoretical views on *how low can we go?*

Researchers have produced many theories on the principles of training with the diagram below summarising many of them for me.

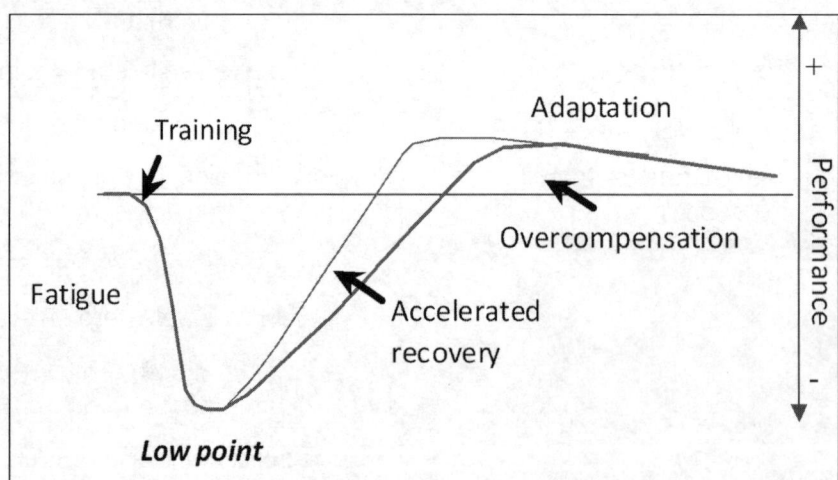

*Figure 13.1:* Training-adaptation model showing low point below which overtraining may occur.

The *low point* in Figure 13.1 is the key area that a smart athlete or coach needs to monitor – just how far (how long, how hard, how often) can we push that low point before we overtrain ourselves or the athlete we might be coaching? My experience in the recent triathlon preparation taught me some valuable lessons in answering this question. I need to acknowledge the many interesting discussions I have had on this matter with Mr Ken Tucker, coach and father of former Commonwealth Games cycling champion, Kenrick Tucker. More recently Ken has become coach of the female cycling stars of the world, Kerrie and Anna Meares, and also his own son Russell who recently won a cycling gold medal in world record time at the World Masters Games. My personal responses to that half-ironman preparation concur strongly with Ken Tucker's belief and Dr Aaron Coutts' research findings on team players. That is, the further down we can push that low point *without getting sick or injured*, the better we will bounce back. However, before we look at my experiences, let's look at what the books say.

## Overtraining theories

Two leading researchers in the overtraining area, Carl Foster and Manfred Lehmann, have produced an excellent theoretical overview of overtraining. They suggested that overtraining is linked to a number of different causes:

1. *Neuroendocrine dysfunction:* In simple terms this means that hormones important to performance and training adaptation (growth hormone, cortisol, testosterone etc.) that are controlled by the brain and nervous system, are compromised in their release from endocrine glands or uptake by the target organs they affect.
2. *Sympathetic/parasympathetic imbalance:* The balance between these two parts of the nervous system determines our actual response to anything. In overtrained athletes, Table 13.4 below summarises sport scientist's findings on the signs of overtraining in this area.

*Table 13.4:* Nervous system signs and symptoms of overtraining.

| Sympathetic | Parasympathetic |
|---|---|
| Impaired performance | Impaired performance |
| Easily fatigued | Easily fatigued |
| Disturbed sleep | Sleep easily/depressed |
| Increased resting heart rate | Very low resting heart rate |
| Postural hypotension (poor blood pressure adjustments when going from lying to standing etc) | Decreased libido (men) or amenorrhea (periods loss) in women |
|  | Loss of competitive desire |
| Increased incidence of infections | Increased incidence of infections |

3. *Catabolic/anabolic imbalance:* Endurance athletes such as long distance triathletes have problems maintaining nutritional intake and thus body weight. Classically, the ratio between testosterone (an anabolic or protein-building hormone) and cortisol (a catabolic or breaking down hormone) determines this type of overtraining.
4. *Amino acid imbalance:* Researchers have shown that an increased uptake of branched-chain amino acids (isoleucine, leucine, valine) by muscle during prolonged exercise – usually associated with carbohydrate depletion – may lead to an increase in the production of a neurotransmitter substance in the brain called 5-hydroxytryptamine (5-HT) that leads

to sleepiness, tiredness and thus fatigue.

5. ***Carbohydrate deficit:*** This is one of the commonest theories on overtraining and is widely recognised by coaches and athletes, hence the emphasis on a high carbohydrate diet in athletes. Low carbohydrate levels in muscle leads to low blood lactate levels and coaches and sport scientists commonly use a RPE (Rating of Perceived Exertion) to lactate graph to identify it. A higher RPE (e.g. 14 vs 12) for a set level of blood lactate (e.g. 2 mmol/L) may indicate overreaching.

6. ***Other abnormalities:*** Two other factors are consistently seen in overtrained athletes – changes in mood states and immune system suppression. Tired athletes often say "I need a break", "I'm grumpy", "I'm tired". They also seem more susceptible to illness. While moderate exercise enhances the immune system, hard training seems to lead to a greater ability to "get the flu", "a sore throat", "a runny nose" etc.

## The personal experience

Being a sport scientist, I was acutely aware of the above factors impacting on how far I could push myself daily, weekly or monthly. While it was impractical (cost, time, availability) to monitor blood parameters such as cortisol, testosterone, growth hormone, lactate, it was easy to *listen to the body* by using cues such as RPE-Heart Rate relationships, muscle soreness, sore throats, "grumpiness", and my responses mentally (motivation, concentration levels in particular) and physically (actual performance or heart rates) to standard exercise sessions completed each week (e.g. regular Wednesday 70 km ride). The cues were there to be monitored with the most important principle being to go with the body's reaction on the day rather than the planned session but with one important caveat – keep pushing to that low point.

Recovery strategies for me included eating high glycemic index foods (bread was cheap and easy), hot-cold contrasts in the shower, weekly deep water running, stretching, self-massage and use of the hard-easy principle where active recovery became the easy. These strategies maximised my ability to be able to train hard or long again without "getting sick" or injured.

Although I caught a dose of the "flu" three weeks out from the race as a result of one of my children bringing it home from school, I fought it off for a week by dosing up on multi-vitamins and multi-minerals, vitamin C and a few days of complete rest. While it took a gradual lift in volume and intensity over the next week to get the "feel" and confidence to think I was "back", the fact that I was at a low point prior to the enforced break actually ensured I was able to bounce back better than ever.

I then embarked on a plan to "push the envelope" again for a week with a large increase in volume and intensity then taper according to the principles outlines in Chapter 10 of this book. The seven-day taper worked well with maintenance in frequency and intensity of training but a dramatic drop in volume.

It all worked well during the event with a PB, success in my age-group and one of the best races I'd ever had – it all came together! The lesson learnt? Push the envelope but *always listen to the body* to know how low to go, and then recover hard.

## What about team sport players?

Dr Aaron Coutts, now a recognised world leader in monitoring training loads in athletes, completed his PhD study with me in 2002. He examined the effects of overtraining in semi-elite (State League) rugby league players during a preseason preparation. During six weeks of progressive overload training, the group who completed 28.3% more training (endurance, interval, speed and resistance training) than a control group displayed significantly reduced aerobic capacity, poorer sleep quality, lower feelings of self-worth and lower sub-maximal heart rates before the taper. Generally the overtrained group felt worse and had decreased performance compared to the group who completed normal training. Interestingly, the typical blood and urine markers (e.g. testosterone, cortisol) did not show differences between groups.

As with my personal endurance experience, during a recovery week before the competitive season commenced, the performance rebound of the players commonly associated with taper was significantly greater in the overtrained group who had done more work and gotten closer to the low point. The results again suggest that there is a role for pushing an athlete to a low point but ensuring they get a chance to recover and bounce back. The art of training smart and coaching, is knowing how low to push each individual athlete.

## Practical Tips

Personal experience plus a sport science background suggests that the following factors be considered when deliberately overreaching before an event or wanting to prevent overtraining:

- Proper nutrition with emphasis on carbohydrate
- Minimise other life stressors and get quality rest
- Regular quality sleep patterns maintained
- Avoid sick people and large crowds
- Avoid putting hands to the eyes and nose
- Use multivitamins and mineral supplements during intensified training
- Space the quality workouts
- Get a "flu" shot if training during winter
- Maintain hydration and avoid excessive alcohol
- Plenty of stretching, massage & hydrotherapy
- Develop a strong fitness base before training hard

## Conclusion

Preparing for a sporting goal is an adventure where lessons are learnt and new experiences unfold. While sport science might alert us of the warning signs of overtraining and give us the guiding principles in terms of nutrition, recovery and program planning, nothing can assist the athlete more than *listening to their body* in terms of knowing how low to go. Push the envelope knowing the limits. I hope the above helps you with your own adventures.

# CHAPTER 14

## STAYING HEALTHY AND ILLNESS-FREE

*One of the reasons I've lasted so long is that I take care of myself. I don't smoke. And I keep in shape during the off-season doing a lot of hard work. You can play the game for a long time if you take good care of your body.*

**Gaylord Perry**

*If you don't do what's best for your body, you're the one who comes up on the short end.*

**Julius Irving**

*Refuse to be ill. Never tell people you are ill; never own it to yourself. Illness is one of those things which a man should resist on principle at the onset.*

**Bulwer-Lytton**

*Health is not a condition of matter, but of mind.*

**Mary Baker-Eddy**

*Health lies in labor, and there is no royal road to it but through toil.*

**Wendell Phillips**

### Introduction

Training hard is what it takes to reach the top or achieve those hard-sought-after PB's. Research has conclusively shown that the intensity of training is the key to better performance. However, if we train too hard for too long without resting or recovering well, we can overtrain, become injured or get sick. Many masters athletes I know have not learnt to listen to their bodies and have an easy day or rest day when those aching muscles are telling them it's time to ease off. Furthermore, many don't plan training programs to include recovery strategies and/or rest days. Many just keep pushing till they get sick.

The purpose of this chapter is to examine the age-related changes that occur in our immune system that may make masters athletes more susceptible to illness when training hard. More importantly, this chapter examines nutritional and other strategies that the smart aging athlete can incorporate into their daily lives to stay well while training hard.

## The Immune System

There are two lines of defense against invading cells. Firstly, the mucosal system that consists of the tear glands, the nasal and salivary glands, mammary glands during lactation in women, mucus from the urino-genital tract, and the fluid within joints. This defense system produces cells called immunoglobulins such as IgA and IgG. Secondly, the blood contains numerous white cells that are produced in different parts of the body (thymus gland, lymph gland) and transported within the blood to fight and neutralize invading cells. The major cells involved with this component are T-cells (from the thymus gland), B-cells, and Natural Killer (NK) cells.

The immune system is a complex system influenced strongly by the nervous system and the endocrine (hormone) system. The physical stress of exercise affects both the immune system response and the hormone response. When we exercise long and/or hard, the stress hormones cortisol and adrenalin increase. Hard and long exercise sessions also lead to body temperature increases, protein metabolism increases, drops in blood glucose levels, and blood oxygen levels decrease. All these changes lower the activity of the immune system during and after exercise when these factors gradually return to normal.

Psychological stress also causes a depression in the immune system. The stress of exams, depression, work or family stress, lack of sleep, divorce and deaths have all been shown to reduce the activity of the immunoglobulins and blood immune system cells that fight infection, making athletes more susceptible to illness and infection during such times, particularly if training hard at the same time. In contrast, relaxation and recovery strategies have been shown to increase the activity of these infection fighters, strongly supporting the need to ensure recovery strategies are part of the normal training program.

## The Aging Immune System

Aging is associated with a functional decline in several components of the immune system, suggesting that the elderly are more vulnerable to obtaining infectious diseases, cancers and autoimmune (body fighting itself) disorders such as rheumatoid arthritis. Aging has been shown to lead to the following changes in the immune system:

- *T-cells* from the thymus gland have been shown to decrease in both number and their responsiveness to invading cells. Moreover, the thymus gland has been shown to significantly decline in size after adolescence to the point where it is one-tenth the size in older age as it was in childhood.
- *B-cells* decrease in number with advancing years.
- *NK-cells* have been shown to be maintained or decrease slightly with advancing age. Limited research has been conducted on the effect of exercise on the aging immune

system. To date, it appears the immune system response to a single bout of exercise is maintained with age. With long-term training in masters athletes, limited research has been conducted. In older non-athletes, the effect of 12 weeks of walking five days a week at 60% of heart rate reserve ([220-age] – resting heart rate) showed no effect on the immune system of a group of inactive women 73±1 years old. However, immune system function was observed to be greater in a group of 73±2 years old female endurance athletes compared to age-matched non-exercisers of the same age. Thus, while limited research has been conducted on aging athletes, it appears that light physical activity may retard the normal age-related decline in the immune system. Moreover, it appears it is only the very highly conditioned aging athlete who appears to gain benefits in terms of illness prevention.

## The effects of training on the immune system

In a nutshell, research to date suggests that the harder and / or longer we train for, the more at risk we are of getting sick by reducing the functioning of our immune system. In contrast, regular moderate exercise appears to boost our immune system's ability to fight infection. However, research in the area of exercise and the immune system is relatively new. Clinical trials suggest that training before getting an infection has either no effect or decreases the incidence of illness. However, if exercise is done while the infection is incubating in the body but not displaying symptoms, the research suggests training has no effect or may increase the severity of infection.

For most athletes, the first sign of sickness is an upper respiratory tract infection – affectionately known by the medical profession as URTI. Studies that have surveyed athletes' rates of developing URTI suggest an increase in URTI in the 3-72 hours after heavy training or competition whereas moderate training has been claimed to reduce the incidence and severity of URTI symptoms. Thus, there appears to be an "open window" period after hard training where there is a decline in the number of blood natural killer cells that can kill viruses. A decline in their number makes athletes more susceptible to viral infection 3-72 hours after hard training. Thus, staying away from sick people and large groups of people during this period is suggested. Endurance exercise longer than one hour such as cross-country skiing, cycling, swimming and running can also cause a temporary fall in the levels of nasal and salivary mucosal antibodies immediately after training, again supporting this "open window" hypothesis.

It appears that only those athletes undertaking longer competitive events, or suffering from the consequences of excessive training volume or intensity coupled with inadequate recovery, may be at increased risk of URTI. Thus, exercise scientists have come up with the "J-Curve" to describe the relationship between the amount and intensity of exercise and the risk of URTI (see Figure 14.1 overleaf).

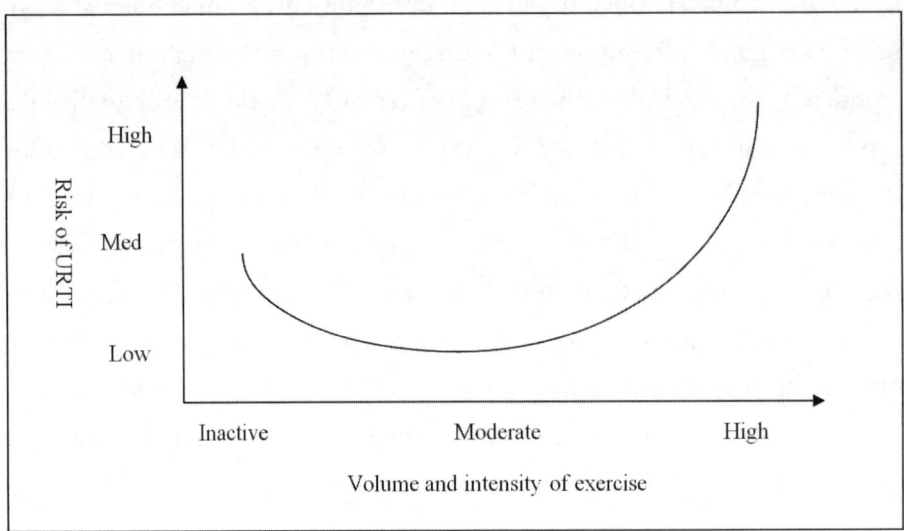

*Figure 14.1:* The "J-Curve" model showing the relationship between varying amounts of exercise and the risk of upper respiratory tract infection (URTI).

## Risks of Exercising with Viral or Bacterial Infection

No training should be done when athletes are suffering from myocarditis, infectious mononucleosis, viral infections or when showing signs of elevated body temperature. One reason why the medical profession advises against performing hard training during acute viral infections is the potential of developing myocarditis, an inflammation of the heart muscle. Training while infected with a virus has been shown to increase viral cell numbers, increase inflammation, lead to death of part of the heart muscle, and possible sudden death. Warning signs of a systemic infection where such a risk may be present include a fever, muscle soreness, fatigue, coughing, vomiting, diarrhea, and swollen glands. A medical opinion should be sought immediately and all exercise ceased.

## Boosting the Immune System

A number of strategies have been suggested to maintain or boost the immune system. These include nutritional strategies, monitoring training volume and intensity, limiting and controlling environmental factors, considering psychological stressors, developing behavioral and self-management skills, and medical screening and management.

1. *Nutritional Strategies to Maintain or Boost the Immune System*

   As noted above, a heavy schedule of training and competition can lead to suppression of the immune system and increased risk of infection, particularly of the upper respiratory tract. Diets high in carbohydrate and protein, low in energy (trying to lose weight), and large doses of vitamins and minerals are commonly used in the diets of athletes of any age. Such dietary practices may compromise immune function. For example, diets excessively high in carbohydrate, favored by athletes to keep their energy levels up, are typically low in meat products and thus low in protein and vitamin $B_{12}$, both important components of the immune system. Long or short-term dieting and thus energy-restricted diets can also influence the immune system with one study showing that loss of 2 kilograms of body mass over 2 weeks adversely affected the immune system.

Recent scientific evidence suggests that nutrition may play a crucial role in preventing URTI. Research has focused on vitamins and minerals, an amino acid called glutamine, oils, protein, and carbohydrate and their role in maintaining or boosting the immune system's response to prolonged or intense exercise.

a. *Vitamins and Minerals*

Vitamins are essential nutrients that cannot be made by the body and must be obtained from food. They are essential co-factors in many energy making reactions and the making of tissues such as muscle and bone. The vitamins essential for the immune system are vitamins A, $B_{12}$, C and D. Vitamins $B_6$ and folic acid are also important but deficiencies in these are rare.

Vitamins A (β-carotene), C and E are antioxidants and are important for endurance athletes who produce damaging molecules called "free-radicals" when training long and hard. Vitamin A deficiency in humans results in the immune-cell producing thymus gland getting smaller, increased binding of bacteria to respiratory linings, and impaired production of the mucosal immunoglobulin IgA, all of which will result in a higher incidence of infection.

A South African study of young ultra marathon runners demonstrated a strong association between vitamin C supplementation (600mg per day – 10 times the recommended daily allowance - for 3 weeks) and fewer URTI symptoms. It must be noted that not all studies have shown such a positive response. However, for those of us involved with heavy endurance training, it may be worth a try. Vitamin E supplementation in older non-athletes has been shown to boost the immune system so may have a role in helping maintain the immune system in aging athletes, although this remains to be researched. Indeed, a 1992 study of 96 healthy older people examined the effect of 12 months of vitamin and mineral supplementation on the immune system and the likelihood of illness due to infections. Not only were the blood and salivary markers of the immune system up, the supplementation group were only ill due to infection for 28 days versus the non-supplemented group who were ill for 48 days. Again, this finding suggests that aging athletes should consider vitamin and mineral supplementation on a daily basis.

The trace element selenium is a co-factor in antioxidant defense. Thus, it is possible that the requirement for selenium is increased in aging athletes in heavy training. However, large doses appear to have safety risks with intakes of 25 mg per day (about 40 times that recommended) associated with vomiting, abdominal pain, hair loss and fatigue. Food sources of selenium include cereals (e.g. corn, wheat, and rice), nuts (brazil nuts and walnuts), legumes (soybeans), animal products (beef, chicken, egg, cheese), and seafood (tuna).

The research supports the obtaining of these extra vitamins and minerals by eating more fruit and vegetables or simple supplementation by taking a multivitamin-multimineral supplement emphasizing these vitamins and minerals. Megadoses of them have been shown to have a negative impact on the immune system.

b. *Fish and Linseed Oil*

Following hard or long training, there is a period after exercise where the immune system function is suppressed making us more susceptible to infection. Fish and linseed oils, at least in animal studies, have been shown to reduce the incidence of infection after exercise.

c. *Protein and Amino Acids*

The daily protein requirement for athletes of any age is approximately double that of non-athletes. An intake of 1.2-1.6 grams of protein per kilogram of body weight per day is recommended for endurance and power athletes training daily. Inadequate intakes of protein have been shown to lower the T-cell system activity and increase the incidence of infections. In contrast, too much protein in the diet has also been shown to lower glutamine levels and thus energy supply for the immune system cells, increasing the risk of infection.

d. *Glutamine*

Glutamine and glucose that we get from eating carbohydrates are both important fuels for immune system cells called lymphocytes and monocytes that kill invading cells that may cause illness. Lowering the availability of the fuels glutamine and glucose through intense or prolonged exercise lowers the rate of immune system cell production, thus making us more susceptible to illness. Thus, the amino acid glutamine (at about 5 gm per day or 0.1 gm per kilogram of body weight) is being suggested as a supplement worth trying in athletes susceptible to illness.

e. *Carbohydrates*

It is currently recommended that athletes in heavy training consume about 60% of their daily energy intake (Calories or kilojoules) as carbohydrate at the rate of between 5-10 grams of carbohydrate per kilogram of body weight per day depending on whether they train hard and/or long. This recommendation is aimed at restoring the liver and muscle stores of carbohydrate to allow for effective muscle contractions for training on successive days or even twice a day.

When we exercise hard and / or long, we reduce the blood glucose levels, especially if we don't eat or drink carbohydrates during training (gels, sports drinks). This has the effect of increasing the release of a couple of stress hormones (adrenalin and cortisol), increasing growth hormone release, and decreasing blood insulin levels. Together these hormones act to increase blood glucose levels through a number of mechanisms including using proteins to create glucose.

This model strongly suggests that if we carbohydrate supplement (eat/drink) during endurance exercise or hard training / racing we can maintain or elevate blood glucose levels which prevent the release of the stress hormones which in turn counteract the negative immune system changes associated with URTI.

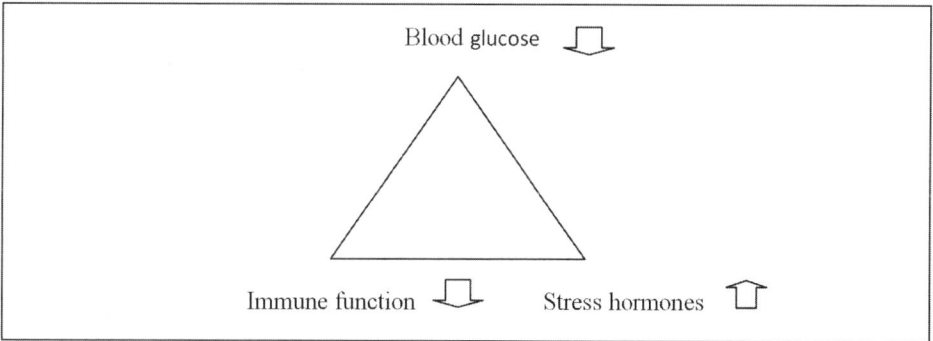

*Figure 14.2:* The effect of low blood glucose levels on stress hormones and the immune system.

Research strongly suggests that lowered blood glucose levels lowers the immune system response and makes us more susceptible to URTI. Two recent studies on runners and triathletes have strongly supported this suggestion. Both studies had the young athletes running or running and cycling for 2.5 hrs at close to race pace. The athletes either drank a placebo (dummy fluid) or a sports drink. The results of these studies showed that, in the sports drinking condition, the athletes maintained blood glucose levels, reduced the stress hormone concentrations in their blood and most importantly reduced their immune system response, a good thing in terms of stopping the athletes getting sick. These results strongly suggest that keeping blood glucose levels up in training or racing by eating or drinking is the way to go to try and hold off URTI.

The following guidelines for consumption of carbohydrate before, during and after exercise have recently been suggested by the *Gatorade Sports Science Institute*.

*Table 14.1:* Guidelines for consumption of carbohydrate before, during and after exercise.

| Food Source | Before | During | After |
|---|---|---|---|
| Sports Drink | 500 ml 1hr before | 150-300 ml every 15-20 min | 1500 ml for every kg of weight lost |
| Sports Bar | 1 bar 2 hr before | Not recommended | 1-2 bars immediately after |
| Sports Gels | 1 packet before with water | 30-60 gm CHO / hr | Immediately after to deliver 1 gm CHO / kg of bodyweight |
| High CHO Drink | 500 ml 2-5 hrs before | Not recommended | Immediately after to deliver 1 gm CHO / kg of bodyweight |

### 2. Monitoring Training to Maintain or Boost the Immune System

In most sports, improvement in performance is related to a progressive increase in training volume and intensity with a resultant need to focus on recovery to regenerate.

An imbalance between training load and recovery is a major contributor to fatigue, overtraining and illness in athletes of all ages. A recent study conclusively showed that over a 6-month to 3-year period, 84% of illnesses in young highly-trained athletes were preceded by an upwards spike in the training load of the athletes above their normal training threshold. In particular, high intensity training appears to place the athlete at most risk. Thus, the following guidelines are suggested to maintain wellness in the aging athlete:

- Commence training with a low to moderate load
- Develop an initial endurance base with gradual increases in volume *before* intensity
- Develop intensity after volume and in a progressive and periodised approach
- Incorporate variety and cross-training (e.g. water running, weights, cycling) to reduce staleness and monotony
- Incorporate rest and recovery strategies such as those suggested in chapter 15 of this book
- Avoid overtraining by a gradual (10% / week) increase in training load, having rest days or periodizing training. Declining training performances, loss of motivation, excessive fatigue, muscle soreness and depression suggest overtraining
- Space out the hard workouts
- Work on the hard-easy principle (a hard training session is *always* followed by an easy training session
- Implement regular testing to monitor performance. If performance is declining, despite training longer and / or harder, re-examine the training program, nutritional or recovery practices
- Use daily monitoring in a log book to record training activities and loads, heart rate responses, feelings and health status

3. ***Controlling Environmental Factors to Maintain or Boost the Immune System***
   Aging athletes are often required to train or compete in environmental conditions such as heat and humidity (tell me about it I say as I swelter during summer months in Rockhampton, Central Queensland, Australia as I swim, ride and run!), cold, altitude, or the air pollution of larger cities or open highways. Extremes of heat and cold act as a "double threat" to the aging athlete when doing quality training as both conditions have been shown to compromise the immune system. The following guidelines are suggested to maintain health in the aging athlete when training or competing in adverse environmental conditions:
   - limit the duration and intensity of training
   - In hot and humid conditions do the intense training during the cooler parts of the day
   - In hot and humid conditions, acclimatize over 7-10 days starting with low intensity exercise
   - In hot and humid conditions, replace fluids regularly during exercise
   - In hot and humid conditions, wear appropriate clothing (cotton, minimal and loose)
   - In cold conditions, limit skin exposure

- In cold conditions, wear layers of clothing and remove or add them as required
- In cold conditions, move training indoors if too cold
- In cold conditions, be aware of the windchill in cold conditions – exercise *with* the wind when tired
- At altitude, acclimatize over 10-21 days at altitude (above 2000m) starting with low intensity training
- At altitude, "Live high, train low" if possible
- Avoid polluted areas or conditions by training during less-polluted times of the day or in less-polluted areas.

4. *Limiting Psychological Stressors to Maintain or Boost the Immune System*

There is convincing scientific evidence that psychological stress increases the risk of upper respiratory tract infections in non-athletes. While every individual is different in how they handle stress, there is no doubt that personality has an outcome on infectious illness outcomes with the optimist and more relaxed person showing faster recovery from illness and injury than the pessimist or highly stressed personality.

In masters athletes training regularly, hard and / or for long periods, psychological stressors (family, work or competition stress) may exaggerate the immune response and make the aging athlete more susceptible to illness or make the recovery process take longer. Thus, during periods of high stress, training loads should be monitored and the other strategies examined here need to be focused upon. The following guidelines are suggested to maintain health in the masters athlete when training or competing in during periods of high stress:

- Implement a support network of family and friends
- Develop ways of coping with work or family pressures
- Develop time management strategies (I personally have found training in the mornings before my girls and wife get up has reduced family stress levels significantly. I also sometimes squeeze a short, sharp session in at work lunch times)
- Seek professional help if needed
- Use relaxation and recovery strategies as suggested in the next chapter of this book
- If stressed from other factors, avoid hard or long training sessions, especially in the heat. Lower the training intensity or duration or just take the day off!

5. *Developing Behavioral and Self-Management Skills to Maintain or Boost the Immune System*

Apart from the nutritional strategies suggested earlier, there are numerous other behavioral strategies the aging athlete can use to avoid getting ill. These include:

- Avoiding exposure to infected people or large crowds, particularly after hard or long training in the heat
- Avoid physical contact with these people
- Avoid or limit long waits in departure lounges, aircraft cabins, or trains and buses

- Avoid or limit communal living and dining or large shopping malls and restaurants
- Avoid or limit exposure to public facilities such as change rooms or toilets
- Attend to personal hygiene such as:
  - Washing hands before meals
  - Avoid sharing towels
  - Avoid sharing water bottles or buckets of ice or water
  - Use your own sporting clothes or gear
  - Avoid sharing eating utensils
  - Keep the hands away from eyes and nose as they are routes for infection
- Get enough sleep, especially when traveling overseas against time zones
- Avoid rapid weight loss – it negatively impacts on the immune system
- Use disposable and individual cups, not shared cups.

6. *Medical Screening and Management to Maintain or Boost the Immune System*

   The sports medicine specialist plays a major role in preventing and / or treating a sick aging athlete. Signs and symptoms such as elevated temperature, elevated heart rate, fatigue, muscle pain, sore joints, and swollen glands suggest the need for a visit to the doctor. There are a number of ways the sports medicine specialist can help or be used by the aging athlete to avoid getting ill. These include:
   - Screening for immune system function if becoming ill regularly
   - Obtaining the traditional winter "flu" shot
   - Ensuring known medical conditions are medicated
   - Determining the origin of infection (virus, bacteria or inflammatory)
   - Prescribing medications such as antihistamines or decongestants
   - Managing viral illnesses – exercise should be avoided during fever, myocarditis, infectious mononucleosis, or related viral syndromes
   - Immunizing according to recommended guidelines when traveling overseas

## Curing the Common Cold

The common cold is a viral infection of the upper respiratory tract caused by a bug called the rhinovirus. While there is no known cure for the cold, various nutrition-related strategies have been used to manage them. Three of the more common supplements (Vitamin C, Zinc lozenges and Echinacea) will be examined in light of what the research says about their effect on overcoming the common cold.

1. *Vitamin C* has been shown to not only prevent colds but reduce its duration and symptoms when taken in doses that exceed the recommended daily allowance of 60 mg/day. Studies have shown that it is safe to take supplement doses of between 500-1000 mg/day. Older athletes susceptible to kidney stones and gout should avoid these large doses. Vitamin C supplements have also been associated with "runners diarrhea" so be warned!

2. *Zinc Lozenges* have also been shown to not only prevent colds but reduce its duration and symptoms when taken in short-term doses that exceed the recommended daily allowance of 12-15 mg/day for older females and males. However, prolonged zinc supplementation of 75 mg/day has been shown to lead to copper deficiency. People with hemochromatosis (iron overload in the body) should avoid zinc supplementation. The recommended dose at the onset of cold symptoms is 1-2 days of zinc gluconate lozenges taken at 13.3 mg every two hours when awake. Indeed, combination throat lozenges containing vitamin C and zinc should be considered the first line treatment for athletes with an upper respiratory tract infection.
3. *Echinacea* is derived from native Indian medicinal plants and was the top selling herbal medicine in the United States from 1995-1998. Like zinc lozenges, it has been shown to not only prevent colds but reduce their duration and symptoms when taken in short-term doses. It can be taken orally at 900 mg of root per day or 90 drops of 1:5 (grams/ml) per day with 50% ethanol but for no longer than eight weeks.

Most of us who have trained regularly over many years have had minor or serious injuries, been tired as a result of training too hard too often, or possible even been victims of overtraining. Training can have both positive and negative effects on the older athlete's body. However, both young and older athletes are strongly advised against training when feeling ill (particularly with a fever / high temperature), after excessive alcohol, if training is aggravating an injury, for consecutive hard weeks or periods, or when feeling very tired or stressed.

## To Train or Not to Train? The Neck Check

Often when an athlete of any age gets "sick", we wonder whether it is safe to train or race or not. A sport scientist called Randy Eichner, a specialist in immune function and sport, has developed a wonderfully easy test called the *Neck Check* that makes the decision on whether to train with a cold or illness simple.

1. *Above the Neck* symptoms (stuffy or runny nose, sneezing, watery eyes, scratchy throat) suggests head out easy. If you feel better after 10 minutes, up the pace and do the usual workout.
2. *Below the Neck* symptoms (aching muscles, productive cough, hacking cough, nausea, vomiting, diarrhea, fever) suggest no training. Recovery will be faster with complete rest.

## Preventing Fatigue

An ideal training program causes fatigue that the body has time to adapt to so it can be stressed again at a higher level. As the training load is progressively increased, fatigue increases but should not be allowed to override the positive benefits of the body's adaptation. To avoid fatigue which comprises the ability to continue training effectively, the following should be followed:

- Increase training loads gradually - no dramatic increases in intensity, frequency or duration of workouts. The rule of thumb is 10% per week increase in any one of these variables
- Get enough recovery and rest (see the next chapter for more detail)
- Have regular days off training and chill out
- Change the daily routine sometimes (e.g. a different training venue, training partner or group)
- Include regeneration and relaxation techniques whenever possible (e.g. massage, spas)
- Eat well and drink plenty of fluids (see the Nutrition chapter for more detail)
- Consider additive effects of stressors other than training (e.g. emotional and work stress, climate, lack of time).
- Keep a log book to monitor training loads, your body's response to this, muscle soreness and how you're feeling - this will help you LISTEN TO YOUR BODY.
- Watch for warning signs of overtraining (see below).

## Signs of Overtraining

Research has shown that there is no one sign of overtraining in athletes. It appears that when training loads are too great and/or the body does not have enough time to adapt, that any of the following signs might be seen in different individuals.

*Physical Signs*
- Performance decrements
- Decreased ability to train effectively
- Elevated resting heart rate
- Slower heart rate recovery
- Gastrointestinal disturbances
- Muscle soreness
- Headaches
- Increased susceptibility to colds, cold sores, infections
- Menstrual disturbances
- Loss of appetite
- "Heavy Legged" feeling
- Elevated blood pressure
- Deterioration in sporting skill

*Emotional & Behavioural Signs*
- Chronic Fatigue
- Apathy
- Depression
- Anxiety
- Irritability

- Sleep Disturbances
- Boredom
- Low Motivation
- Inability to Relax
- Mood Changes
- Poor Coordination
- Decreased Self Confidence

Listen to the body and watch for these signs of overtraining. If observed, act quickly to reduce the symptoms of overtraining by using some of the strategies outlined in the Recovery chapter. If overtraining symptoms persists, contact a sports physician for professional advice.

# CHAPTER 15

## RECOVERY STRATEGIES FOR THE MASTERS ATHLETE

*The cool-down should not be performed after training,
it should be the last part of training.*

**Martin Dowson**

*Take rest; a field that has rested gives a beautiful crop.*

**Ovid**

*I do everything intense. I play intense, I work out hard, then I relax hard.*

**Andre Agassi**

*The purpose of training is to stress the body, so when you rest it will grow stronger and more tolerant of the demands....*

**David Costill**

*I've learned to back off when I need to.*

**Mark Allen**

### Introduction

Whether you want to be the best at your sport or beat that PB, there is no alternative to hard training. One thing I have learnt the hard way via the best teacher I have ever had, experience, is that *training hard* and *training smart* are not always the same thing. To train smart, we must allow time for our body to adapt to the training undertaken. Pushing the training without enough time to recover can lead to overtraining, overuse injuries or burnout problems. For many athletes the question becomes "How can I train hard without falling apart or getting injured?" If you want to perform at your best and optimize your training without experiencing these problems you need to follow the formula for success:

### *Train Hard + Recover Harder = Better Performance*

Too many aging athletes work hard but often ignore recovery strategies except when they get sick or injured. From my experience and knowledge, together with progressive training overload and specificity of training, recovery is one of the most important principles of training. However, it is the one training principle most frequently forgotten in training programs.

Quality training breaks down muscle and connective tissue, tires the nervous system, and uses up valuable muscle carbohydrate that we need to provide us with the energy to train. We must allow the body sufficient time to repair, replace, and strengthen damaged tissue. The masters athlete who doesn't allow enough time to rest and recover often experiences tissue breakdown at a faster rate than the rate of repair, ultimately leading to decreased training performance and / or injury.

The rate of recovery between athletes is highly variable. Given that the physiologies, training age, genetics, and environmental influences on aging athletes is even greater than younger athletes, it is not surprising that the rate of recovery in aging athletes is even more variable than in younger athletes. Thus, some aging athletes can train intensely twice per week and require easier training sessions the other training days in the week while another athlete the same age might be able to train for five days in a row hard, then take one day off and go hard again. Regardless, research and anecdotal evidence strongly suggests that aging athletes need longer to recover. Personally, when just swimming (summer) or running (winter) alone I always used the *hard-easy principle* of alternating hard and easy intensities on alternate days. While I am still able to do this, doing triathlon's now makes it easier because swimming or cycling don't tear me down like running does. Regardless, I still find I can only handle 2-3 hard (Level 4-6 – see Chapter 6) training sessions in a week now, whereas as a 20 year-old athlete I could go hard most days and still cope – at least I thought I did!!

## Barriers to Effective Recovery

For aging athletes, a number of barriers affect the optimal use of recovery and rest in training and competition. These include:

- *Athletes and coaches underestimate the value of recovery.* There is no doubt that effective recovery strategies and practices work – the science says so!
- *Athlete subculture.* In my current sport of triathlon, it's never a matter of how well you trained and recovered, it's always how far or long you went that appears important in chats with mates. The harder or longer you trained, the better light you are seen in. How wrong these people are!
- *Poor training or competition performances.* Such efforts lead to an athlete wanting to train harder and / or longer to achieve better performances. Maybe it is just more rest and recovery they need?
- *Time constraints.* For the majority of masters athletes with family and work commitments this presents a problem in as much as training time is limited so time for recovery takes a back seat to time to train.

The smart aging athlete will prioritize recovery strategies into their normal day. They will realize that quality training requires quality recovery and plan their training schedule to incorporate active recovery sessions into their training week. They will adopt nutrition and fluid intake strategies into their daily life to maximize recovery without it becoming all time-consuming. They will use the real world recovery strategies discussed in this chapter.

## Recovery and Aging

Little research has examined the ability of aging muscles and tissues to recover from training. What research has been done has tended to focus on aging non-athletes, rather than aging athletes. A number of studies on both rats and humans have suggested that there are age-related differences in both the susceptibility of muscle to exercise-induced muscle damage and the ability of this muscle to repair. It appears that for the same relative intensity (%) of exercise, older muscles are damaged more, at least in older non-athletes. A recent study, however, found that after eight weeks of strength training, younger (20-30 years) and older (65-75 years) men displayed similar muscle damage when examined under an electron microscope. This suggests that training may help prevent muscle damage in older people. To my knowledge, no studies have examined differences in muscle damage in masters versus younger athletes.

Most human and rat studies suggest that recovery from a training session that induces muscle damage is impaired in aging people. Certainly my own anecdotal evidence based on years of observing my own response to training and listening and observing other aging athletes from endurance sports, is that recovery takes longer from intense training sessions. A number of reasons have been put forward for this increased muscle damage and longer recovery. They include:

- The age-related decrease in muscle size and strength. Strength training is thus an obvious solution to overcome this issue as it can increase both the size and strength of muscle
- The age-related decrease in flexibility or range of motion about a joint means that when an aging person exercises less elastic connective tissue, damage is more likely to occur in that connective tissue that is less elastic, less lubricated, and less pliable. The solution is to ensure that flexibility training become a vital part of a masters training program
- The age-related decrease in antioxidant and antioxidant agents (enzymes) within most tissues including muscle and connective tissue. This suggests the need for antioxidant supplementation and / or multivitamin – multimineral supplementation
- The age-related decrease in the inflammatory response within muscle means that the appearance of cells to remove damaged cells is compromised, delaying the repair of muscle and connective tissue. Both warm-down and active recovery as well as following hard training with easy training may address this issue
- The age-related decrease in muscle protein synthesis (building) rates may slow the

rebuilding of muscle and connective tissue after training-induced damage. Protein intake following training sessions may enhance this process.

## The Principles of Recovery

Quality training in itself will not achieve the best results for a masters athlete. All athletes need time to adapt to the quality training if they want to maximize performance. The principle of recovery refers to that part of the training process where the benefits of training are maximized through practices that encourage natural adaptation to the training stimulus.

Training sessions are designed to bring about improvements in athletic performance. This is achieved in part through progressively overloading the body and the fuel stores that underpin each of the five S's of training (stamina, strength, speed, suppleness, and skill). Underlying this progressive overload principle is the understanding that in order to develop a particular capacity or system, that capacity must first be challenged or stressed. The training load that represents the stimulus for change to occur provides this stress. The training undertaken results in a degree of fatigue or depletion of the physical or psychological systems involved with that training. Adaptation to training is accelerated when fatigued systems are restored to normal operating levels as quickly as possible after training.

Adaptation to the increased workload is evidenced by improved performance that is the goal of every training program. Positive adaptation to a training stimulus is sometimes referred to as *overcompensation*. The principle of recovery relates to the encouragement of adaptive processes after the presentation of the training stimulus. If there is sufficient recovery before the next workload the underlying system or fuel store stressed during training can improve its capacity to cope with the next stressor. Planning appropriate recovery activities as part of the training program accelerates adaptation to the training stimulus by reducing the time it takes for an athlete to reach the overcompensated state shown in Figure 15.1.

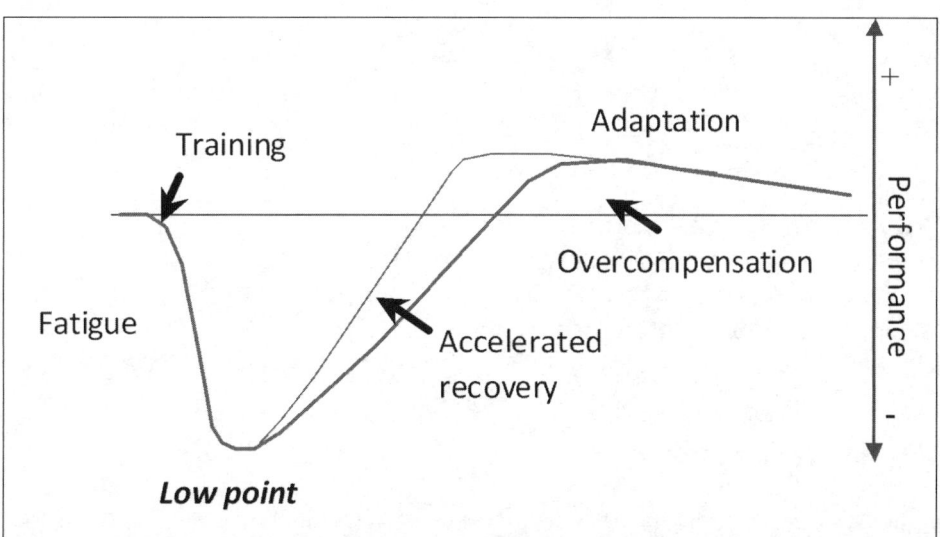

*Figure 15.1:* Accelerated adaptation through accelerated recovery.

The following principles are recommended when implementing recovery training:
1. ***Total recovery time depends on the type and duration of the training.*** Thus, the longer or harder the training, the longer and harder the recovery. When tapering for an event and training volume drops significantly, recovery strategies need not be as long or intense.
2. ***Begin recovering immediately after training or competition.*** Begin with a cool down and stretch while drinking and/or eating the correct amounts of food and fluids. More details on this will be discussed later in this chapter.
3. ***Remove all other forms of possible stress.*** The stress response from psychological factors is the same as it is with the physical stress of training and competing. Thus, a masters athlete facing work and / or family pressure and trying to train might want to consider lowering training volume or intensity to compensate for these other stressors in their life.
4. ***Recovery is specific to the individual.*** Just as individuals respond to physical or psychological stressors differently, so also do different athletes respond to the different recovery strategies. Try them, evaluate them, and then hold onto the ones that suit you and your lifestyle.

A recent book called *Enhancing recovery: preventing underperformance in athletes* edited by German Sports Scientist, Dr Martin Kellman *(www.humankinetics.com)*, has prioritized some of the recovery strategies that we are about to discuss by allocating them RP's or Recovery Points as shown in Table 15.1 below.

*Table 15.1:* Recovery Points (RP) ratings of commonly-used recovery strategies.

| Recovery Strategy | Recovery Points (out of 10) |
|---|---|
| **Nutrition and Hydration** | 10 |
| • Excellence in breakfast | 1 |
| • Excellence in lunch | 2 |
| • Excellence in dinner | 2 |
| • Excellence in snacks between meals | 1 each snack |
| • Excellence in fast refueling after training | 2 |
| • Excellence in hydration | 2 |
| **Sleep and Rest** | 4 |
| • High quality sleep | 3 |
| • Rest or "power nap" | 1 |
| **Relaxation and Emotional Support** | 3 |
| • Any form of relaxation done as soon as possible after training (hydrotherapies, imagery, visualization, music, meditation, listening to music, watching a movie) | 2 |
| • Staying mentally relaxed | 1 |
| **Stretching and Cooling Down** | 3 |
| • Cooling down | 2 |
| • Stretching | 1 |

Obviously, the above list shows us a list of priorities that the smart masters athlete needs to consider. Let us now turn our attention to discussing the recovery strategies mentioned in this list and how to best apply and use them.

## Types of Recovery

When an athlete of any age trains, they challenge four functions within the body – nutritional, physiological, neurological, and psychological. Thus, it makes sense that recovery strategies are designed to match the type of training with the type of recovery. One of Australia's leading recovery experts is Angie Calder who used to work as the recovery consultant with elite athletes at the Australian Institute of Sport and now acts as a private consultant in recovery methods. Angie ranked these four functions in order of importance for both endurance and speed and power athletes (see Tables 15.2 and 15.3 below). The ranking is based on the sites of fatigue for each type of athlete.

*Table 15.2:* Order of importance of different modes of recovery for endurance athletes.

| Rank | Function | Site of Fatigue |
|---|---|---|
| 1 | Nutritional | Fuel and fluid stores |
| 2 | Physiological | Muscles |
| 3 | Neurological | Peripheral nervous system |
| 4 | Psychological | Brain |

*Table 15.3:* Order of importance of different modes of recovery for speed and power athletes.

| Rank | Function | Site of Fatigue |
|---|---|---|
| 1 | Neurological | Peripheral nervous system |
| 2 | Physiological | Muscles |
| 3 | Nutritional | Fuel and fluid stores |
| 4 | Psychological | Brain |

Each of the four functions has separate recovery strategies that aim to restore that function back to pre-training or pre-competition levels as quickly as possible. Table 15.4 below shows the actual recovery strategies relevant to each of the functions.

Thus, for endurance athletes, drinking and eating, active recovery and stretching, contrast showers and spas, massage and rest are recommended. For speed and power athletes, contrast hot and cold showers and spas, active recovery and stretching, drinking and eating and massage and rest are recommended.

The recovery scientist at the Australian Institute of Sport, Dr Shona Halson, conducted a benchmark study examining the effectiveness of all the major forms of recovery used by elite coaches and athletes across the world. Her study consisted of looking at what research said about these methods, what actual recovery practices were being used by leading coaches and athletes, and what the sport scientists within sports institutes felt worked. Table 15.5 summarizes her results and findings.

*Table 15.4:* Actual recovery strategies used for different modes of recovery.

| Function | Nutritional | Physiological | Neurological | Psychological |
|---|---|---|---|---|
| **Guideline** | Restore fluid and fuel stores | Increase blood supply to fatigued muscles | Promote muscle relaxation | Promote psychological recovery |
| **Activity** | • Rehydrate<br>• Nutrition (high GI foods and protein) | • Active recovery<br>• Hydrotherapy<br>• Massage<br>• Compression garments | • Active recovery<br>• Stretching<br>• Hydrotherapy<br>• Massage<br>• Rest/Sleep | • Visualization<br>• Breathing<br>• Massage<br>• Meditation<br>• Rest/Sleep |

*Table 15.5:* Ratings (low to high) of commonly-used recovery strategies as rated by an Australian Institute of Sport benchmarking study.

| Recovery Strategy | Rating |
|---|---|
| Active recovery | Medium-High |
| Acupuncture | Medium |
| Anti-inflammatories | Medium |
| Compression garments | High |
| Contrast water therapy | High |
| Food and fluids | High |
| Hyperbaric chambers | Low-Medium |
| Ice therapy / cold water immersion | High |
| Massage | Medium-High |
| Pool recovery / deep water running | Medium-High |
| Sauna | Low |
| Spas with jets | Medium-High |
| Stretching | High |
| Ultrasound | Low |

Thus, Dr Halson's research suggests that athletes should focus their efforts on active recovery, compression garments, contrast water therapy, food and fluids, ice and / or cold water therapy, massage, deep water running / poolwork, spas with jets and stretching. The details on each of these strategies will now be discussed.

### Recovery Strategy 1: Fluid and Fuel for Recovery

Planning is required in order to prepare for an event or training session and provide afterwards for the replenishment of fluid and fuel stores used during training. Replacing fluid and glycogen (carbohydrate) stores after training is important for most sports. Carbohydrate loading pre-event is designed to maximize the storage of glycogen and minimize the onset of fatigue. Our metabolism is increased during and after exercise with an increased blood supply going to the training muscles 30-45 minutes after the training session. Thus, after training or competing, an optimal time for replenishing glycogen stores is within the first 30-45 minutes following exercise. The recommended intake is *1gm of carbohydrate per kilogram of bodyweight per hour.*

It is especially important to eat carbohydrates following hard training, such as strength and speed sessions, or following heavy contact and bruising after a game. Muscle damage delays muscle glycogen rebuilding particularly after the first 48 hours. Therefore it is important to maximize the time when there is an increase in glycogen building by providing a high post-exercise carbohydrate intake during the following 24 hours.

Historically, we classified carbohydrates as simple or complex carbohydrates. These days we classify them in terms of their glycemic index (GI). This refers to the relative rate of absorption of glucose from a particular food and the scale goes from 1 to 100 with 100 being the highest score meaning very rapid absorption of the carbohydrate into the bloodstream once eaten. For athletes, high GI foods are recommended immediately after training. The glucose from such foods is rapidly absorbed into the bloodstream and is available to be taken up by muscles and the liver to be available as energy for the next training session. However, if high GI foods are mixed with a food of low to moderate GI, the food with the low GI will slow the absorption rate of the high GI food. Thus, the smart masters athlete will take some bread, soft drink or sports drink to training and take it straight after training when the blood flow is still going to the trained muscles and the chemicals required to build the muscle and liver carbohydrate are very active. As discussed in the nutrition chapter shortly, some protein intake with the high GI foods is recommended after hard training such as weights, sprinting, contact sports, or hard endurance training.

*Table 15.6:* The glycemic index (GI) of a range of common foods.

| High GI | Moderate GI | Low GI |
| --- | --- | --- |
| White bread | Pasta/noodles | Apples |
| Wholemeal bread | Popcorn | Pears |
| Nutrigrain | Porridge | Peaches |
| Cornflakes | Special K | All-Bran |
| Weetbix | Boiled white rice | Baked beans |
| Potato | Sweet corn | Lentils |
| Rockmelon | Oranges | Ice cream |
| Watermelon | | Yoghurt |
| Raisins | | Mik |
| Honey | | Nuts |
| Soft drinks | | Brown rice |
| Sports drinks | | |
| Cordial | | |

Monitoring fluid loss can minimize the risks of dehydration. A bodyweight loss of 2% or more during exercise results in measurable physiological changes that can lead to a reduction in performance. Educating athletes to drink in order to keep pace with sweat rates is important and this can be monitored through urine checks (clear urine is ideal) and pre- and post-training weighing (1 kilogram of weight lost = 1 litre of fluid lost). For an event lasting less than 60 minutes, water should suffice for fluid replacement. However, for longer events isotonic sports drinks (*Gatorade, Exceed, Powerade, Staminade* etc.) help to stimulate the desire to drink and restore electrolyte balances as well as provide the replacement carbohydrate are recommended.

Antioxidants such as beta-carotene (pre-cursor of vitamin A), vitamin C, and vitamin E should also be taken to increase muscle antioxidant levels in order to reduce muscle damage in the next training session. Minerals and trace elements such as zinc and magnesium are important for muscle regeneration after training. However, extra intake of these by taking synthetic supplements may not be as effective as increased dietary sources, due to the reactivity of some elements and metals with other foodstuffs in the gut. Professional nutritional advice is recommended for those athletes who experience considerable muscle damage, or for those who are continually fatigued. Iron deficiencies or problems with absorption are not uncommon in athletes of both genders. If an athlete is consistently tired the following checklist (Table 15.7) may help to eliminate possible causes and direct the athlete to seek professional help if fatigue persists.

*Table 15.7:* Athlete and coach checklist of recovery strategies to use after training sessions and at the end of a day.

| *After each training session* |
| --- |
| Drink & eat |
| Walk / move (at least 5 minutes) |
| Stretch |
| Hot / cold shower |
| *Evening / end of day* |
| Hot / cold shower / spa / sauna |
| Stretch & self-massage (especially legs) |
| Practice relaxation 10 - 15 minutes before bed |
| Music, progressive muscle relaxation, reading, visualization, breathing exercises |

### Recovery Strategy 2: Active Recovery

Active recovery or cool down is greatly undervalued by athletes. The end of a quality training session is an ideal time to introduce active recovery activities. Active recoveries fulfill two main tasks. They help recover the physiological state of the athlete (e.g. light jogging, swimming, rowing, walking or cycling to remove lactic acid from the muscles) and they can focus on musculoskeletal recovery (e.g. stretching). Including both types of activities briefly at the end of a training session, especially after heavy speed or endurance training sessions, or a competition are simple ways to incorporate active recovery into training programs.

The cool down should consist of the following:
- *3-10 minutes of light aerobic work* similar to the activity just done. For example, a track running session should have a cool down consisting of jogging or walking.
- *Deep breathing* helps remove any accumulated lactic acid because lactic acid is

primarily buffered by bicarbonate ions in the blood that then turn into water and carbon dioxide. Deep breathing helps remove that carbon dioxide.
- *4-15 minutes of static stretching.* The harder or longer the training session, the longer the stretching session should be.

Active recovery needs to be very low intensity (e.g. 6-8 on the 6-20 RPE scale or less than 60% of maximum heart rate) and of short duration (10-30 minutes) and usually follows a hard training session or race. Examples of active recovery might be:
- Swimming 10-20 minutes continuously with flippers and / or pool buoy or doing a small set of say 10-20 x 50m swims on a long time cycle.
- Cycling for 30 minutes in the small chain ring on a flat course or spinning on rollers.
- Jogging for 10-20 minutes on a golf course or flat soft course such as a bush track or local park.

Cross training can often be used as a form of active recovery provided the work intensities are low (light aerobic) and the exercises undertaken are different to those normally performed in training. Pool work either walking or swimming, particularly backstroke and side stroke, are excellent modes of active recovery after a game or race and are now frequently used by many elite football teams and athletes. Cross training offers the masters athlete a number of advantages including reduced injury rate, variety, and the ability to train more intensely more often. For older athletes who need longer to recover than youngsters, this type of training makes sense.

Rest days are essential for competitive athletes of any age. At least one day per week should be a non- training day. This allows athletes time for physical recovery as well as time to develop interests outside their sport, so they can have a balanced lifestyle. The old truism that "*All work and no play make Jack a dull boy*" reflects the need for variety in order to prevent staleness and boredom. An athlete with one or two interests beside sport or work can provide for this stimulation more readily than the athlete who focuses on sport to the exclusion of everything else. Finding the balance between training, work, study and social and family commitments is one of the biggest challenges for most athletes. Rest days help masters athletes maintain a healthy balance in their lives. Let me know if and when you find the balance! We'll go into partnership, bottle it and make a fortune!

## Recovery Strategy 3: Hydrotherapies

Water therapies are much underused and undervalued in Australia. Contrasting hot and cold showers, or using a warm spa with a cold plunge pool provides an increase in peripheral (muscle/skin) circulation, and neural (nervous system) stimulation. The theory behind their success is that the alternate hot and cold induces a 'pump' action with alternating opening (heat) and closing (cold) of the blood vessels. Pressure from jets and shower nozzles enhance muscle relaxation by stimulating light contractions in muscles. Collectively these promote both physiological and nervous system recovery. Research has shown that the hot-cold contrasts should not be used immediately after injury but have been shown to be very useful after hard training for reducing stiffness and soreness.

Athletes need to be reminded to rehydrate before, during, and after this type of recovery strategy, as sweating tends to go unnoticed in wet environments. It is also important that treatment times are monitored carefully (Table 15.8). There is a tendency for athletes to linger in the warm environment and offset the benefits of the treatment through dehydration and nervous system fatigue. Athletes should feel relaxed but stimulated afterwards, not sleepy and lethargic.

*Table 15.8:* Protocols and notes for contrast hot and cold showers and spas.

| **Contrast Showers** Repeat three times Alternate cold and hot | |
|---|---|
| Cold ($10\text{-}15^\circ$ C / $50\text{-}60^\circ$ F) 10-30 seconds | Hot ($35\text{-}45^\circ$ C / $95\text{-}105^\circ$ F) 1-2 minutes |
| *Spa / Baths* Repeat three times Alternate cold and hot | |
| Cold ($10\text{-}15^\circ$ C / $50\text{-}60^\circ$ F) 3-4 minutes | Hot ($35\text{-}45^\circ$ C / $95\text{-}105^\circ$ F) 30-60 seconds |

**Notes:**
- Begin and end with the cold
- Rehydrate before, during, and after session
- Take a bottle of water or sports drink with you
- Clean skin with soap and shower off beforehand
- Spas and baths are best left till the end of the day
- Do not use a spa if you have a virus or cold or recent soft tissue injury.

Personally, I use the hot-cold contrast strategies only after hard or long training sessions and particularly after a race. If the triathlon or running race finishes near a cold pool, river or ocean, I'm in there straight away walking or lying and kicking my legs gently.

Another form of hydrotherapy is Deep Water Running (DWR). DWR is highly under rated. Most of us have seen other people running in pools with a flotation vest or running belt around their waist and wondered what they are doing. Using these devices (they cost about $70 AUS or can be hired at some pools) is a great recovery strategy after hard run training or competition, as an alternative to run training, or when injured or worried about a "niggle" that might become an injury.

DWR running equipment is available commercially but some people who are good floaters may find they can do without one. I have even heard of people using bike tubes partially inflated and wrapped around their waist.

Research has conclusively shown that aerobic capacity can be maintained for up to four weeks when using DWR when injured. Intervals can be replicated in the pool the same way they would be on the track so DWR makes a great alternative form of training, particularly if worried about injury. However, there is some evidence to suggest that heart rates may not reach the same levels. From my experience heart rates are generally about 10 beats lower than they would be on the running track. This is due to the pressure of the water helping return blood back to the heart.

DWR can be very boring because it takes minutes to move 25 meters or so. I can only handle 20-30 minutes of it in one straight hit but have found doing it with a training partner or mixing it up with intervals or swims a great way to break it up. I also find Saturday morning DWR wearing sunscreen, hat and sunglasses can while away the time.

## Recovery Strategy 4: Massage

Massage is the systematic manipulation of soft body tissues and assists in removing toxic energy metabolism by-products and residual fluid build-up resulting from damage to muscle. Theoretically, sports massage has six major physiological and psychological benefits, despite the limited research on sports massage suggesting any great benefits.

1. Increase blood flow that enhances the delivery of oxygen and nutrients to tired muscles as well as promoting the removal of metabolic by-products such as lactic acid. At rest, 4% of the small blood vessels (capillaries) of a muscle are open, during massage, 35% are open. By squeezing the muscle bellies in the direction of the heart helps empty the veins and enhance blood supply to muscles.
2. Removal of excess swelling often associated with muscle soreness after training is enhanced by the improved blood flow.
3. The warming and stretching of soft tissues via massage provides temporary flexibility gains.
4. The squeezing, stroking, compression and pushing of massage helps drain lymph fluid back to the heart and lymph glands, thus reducing the swelling that is believed to contribute to muscle soreness.
5. Massage helps stretch muscle adhesions, knots and micro trauma that can lead to scar tissue buildup. Such massage requires 5-10 sessions of deep tissue massage (can hurt this one!) lasting 5-10 minutes.
6. As tired and tight muscles relax there is a corresponding improvement in how we feel. Massage helps reduce tension, anger, and anxiety with athletes typically feeling less fatigued and more relaxed after a sports massage.

There are five basic terms describing massage techniques, vibration (shaking), tapotement (percussion or gentle blows along the length of the muscle surface with relaxed hands and commonly used pre-event as a muscle stimulant), petrisage (forceful rolling kneading from end of muscle to start of muscle and used commonly for recovery), effluerage (deep stroking along the long axis of the muscle back to the heart and used commonly for recovery), and friction (small range intensive stroking often used to decrease scarring after injury).

Sports massage uses different combinations of these techniques and it is regarded as one of the most effective means of recovery. Treatments are administered during three phases of

training:
1. *Within training session* massage can be given during training sessions to help cope with high quality training.
2. *Preparatory massage* as part of a warm-up can be given 15-20 minutes before competition and after a generalized warm-up such as a jog. Techniques can be varied so that the massage can either relax an over stimulated athlete or arouse an apathetic one. Sometimes the massage is localized to an injured area in an effort to prepare it for the hard work ahead.
3. *Recovery massage* is given after a training session or competition. Greater benefits are achieved if the massage is done after a hot shower, bath or sauna. The techniques used aim to reduce muscle tension and fatigue and lower stress levels. While young elite performers need at least two full body massages per week, time and cost would suggest once a week is suitable for the aging athlete with family and / or work commitments.

Sports massage has gained wide acceptance over the past ten years. There are now many well-qualified professionals available. If you are have private health insurance, attending a qualified masseuse may be claimable through your health fund. If the cost of these services is prohibitive, then self-massage techniques are easy to administer, particularly for the lower legs, chest, neck, shoulders and forearms. In particular, lower leg massages are an effective way to minimize compartment problems such as shin splints or repetitive strain problems. The techniques take a few minutes to perform and can be done in a relaxing atmosphere while watching television or in the shower or bath.

**Recovery Strategy 5: Rest and Sleep**

Sleep is the most important form of rest. A good night's sleep of seven to nine hours provides invaluable adaptation time for athletes to adjust to the physical and emotional stressors they experience during the day, and most importantly, aids in muscle repair. Growth and repair of tissues is greatest during rest or sleep. This is because the major hormone related to growth and tissue repair is growth hormone that is released at peak levels 30-60 minutes after falling asleep. Theoretically, particularly for aging athletes training hard on weekends when they may have time to sleep, it makes sense to schedule a midday snooze after a hard morning training session and a high GI meal with some protein to capitalize on the anabolic (muscle building) action of the growth hormone.

Research suggests that athletes sleep longer and deeper than non-athletes. One study examined the effects of training 4 times a week for 4 months in 43 men and women aged 60 years of age and compared them with a group that did no training. The exercise group increased their sleeping time from 5.96 hours per day to 6.8 hours per day while the control group did not change their sleeping habits at all.

Sleep deprivation can lead to decreased performance in athletes. A recent review of the effects of sleep on athletic performance stated that sleep deprivation can:

- Reduce cardiovascular endurance by 20% with 50 hours of deprived sleep
- Reduce cardiovascular endurance by 11% with 30-36 hours of deprived sleep
- Reduce reaction time by 20% with small amounts of sleep deprivation
- Reduce ability to process information
- Reduce emotional stability (poorer anger management, increased anxiety)

The same researcher developed a *Sleep Quiz* that aging athletes may find useful (see Table 15.9 below).

***Table 15.9:*** Sleep Quiz to assist athletes in deciding if they are getting enough or possibly too much sleep.

| |
|---|
| 1. Do you frequently fall asleep if given the opportunity (i.e. nod off for 10 minutes) |
| 2. Do you usually need an alarm clock to wake you? |
| 3. Do you tend to "catch up" on sleep on the weekends? |
| 4. Once awake, do you feel tired most mornings? |
| 5. Do you frequently take naps during the day? |
| 6. Do you consistently sleep more than 9.5 hours a night? |
| 7. Do you feel lethargic or "slow" throughout the day? |
| 8. Do you sleep longer during times of depression, anxiety and stress? |
| • If you answered yes two or more times to questions 1-5, chances are you need more sleep (go to bed earlier but at the same time ±30 minutes for 4-5 days in a row. |
| • If you answered yes two or more times to questions 6-8, you may need less sleep (reduce sleep by 30 minutes per week) |

Temperature extremes, psychological stress, overtraining and travel can disrupt sleep. Thus, controlling room temperature, reducing stress levels, avoiding overtraining, and maximizing sleep when traveling can help performance. Research has also shown that changing a person's sleep schedule for more than two days or sleeping more than one hour longer on weekends disrupts the sleep cycle. Maybe that explains "Mondayitis" after the Sunday sleep-in!

Getting to sleep can sometimes be difficult because of the excitement of the day's events so it is important that athletes develop habits to promote a good night's sleep. Four factors appear to typify a high quality sleeping environment:

1. *Quietness:* a fan, air conditioner, earplugs or music may mask any traffic noise.
2. *Darkness:* heavy curtains, blinds, eyeshades and towels at the bottom of doors.
3. *Coolness:* research has shown that 65°F is optimal for sleep. Bed covers/clothes and air conditioners/fans can help achieve this.
4. *Comfort:* each to their own regarding pillows, mattresses and sheets/blankets, but bigger beds have consistently shown to lead to improved sleep. People move 40-60 times a night so being able to move freely helps avoid sleep disruptions.

Table 15.10 below contains some tips to enhance good sleep habits.

*Table 15.10:* Actions that promote or prevent good sleep habits.

| Things to Do |
| --- |
| 1. Sleep in a cool, quiet and dark room and in a comfortable bed with comfortable clothing |
| 2. Sleepiness is bought on by lower body temperatures so a cool shower can help get to sleep, especially in warmer climates. In contrast, in cold weather, turn down the heating so the room can cool off. |
| 3. Practice relaxation techniques before going to bed. (relaxing music, muscle relaxation, breathing exercises, reading, visualization) |
| 4. Lie down to sleep **only** when you are sleepy |
| 5. Go to bed within 30 minutes of the same time every night. |
| 6. If you don't fall asleep within 30 minutes after turning out the light get up and do some relaxation work (see Point 1). |
| 7. If you wake up in the night and can't go back to sleep follow Point 3. |
| 8. Get up at the same time each day. |
| **Things to avoid (evening)** |
| 1. Caffeine (e.g. coffee, tea, coke, chocolate) – it acts as a stimulant |
| 2. Nicotine – it acts as a stimulant |
| 3. Alcohol – increases body temperature |
| 4. High protein meals – increases body temperature |
| 5. Reduce thinking and worrying in bed - learn to switch off. |

Although passive rest is an important component of recovery practices, the time spent during passive rest can be used to include meditation. Meditation trains the body to relax by controlling the parasympathetic (calming) nervous system through reducing 'noise' or stimulation to the brain. By controlling this system the athlete can lower blood pressure, heart rate, slow down breathing rates, relax muscles and calm the sympathetic (excitatory) nervous system. This technique is useful for controlling stresses from training or competition particularly if the athlete is over-aroused. Meditation skills take some time and plenty of practice to acquire.

Progressive muscle relaxation can be done at the end of training or before going to sleep. The technique involves tightening and relaxing specific muscle groups so that the athlete identifies the sensations of muscle tension and muscle relaxation in that body part. This reduces muscle tension and helps to improve body awareness so the athlete can recognize muscle tension and focus on reducing this. When this skill is used regularly in training it can significantly improve the quality of training and competitive abilities.

All athletes have an imagination that can be developed to contribute to their training potential. Imagery relaxation and visualization involve using the imagination to create a vivid scene. Four senses are used to generate the image: sight, smell, sound, and touch. Personally, I use this to relax but also see and feel myself in a race. I see the course I'm swimming, riding or running on. I imagine how I'm feeling, see myself feeling strong and in front. I also imagine things that could or might go wrong and try and picture myself calmly fixing that flat tyre or coping with missing an aid station on the bike. While on the one hand it takes effort and concentration to use imagery and visualization, I also find it very relaxing and a great way to go to sleep.

Breathing exercises are used frequently in the martial arts. Learning breathing techniques and focusing on relaxing tense muscles leads to a more relaxed state.

Although it is sometimes used in the weights gym to provide motivation for hard work, music is equally as effective in evoking a relaxation response if the appropriate music is selected. Many athletes have access to an *iPod*, MP3 player or bedside radio so they can create a bank of songs to generate a range of atmospheres, either stimulating or calming. These can be used in training, and because they are quite portable are excellent tools in competition or when an athlete is in an unfamiliar environment and is having difficulty relaxing. With practice an athlete can learn to manipulate mood states for optimal arousal or relaxation.

### The athlete and recovery training

All athletes regardless of age have two major responsibilities when it comes to recovery. Firstly, they need to learn to *listen to their bodies* to know when to rest and use recovery strategies; and secondly, they need to *look after themselves* physically and psychologically. Table 15.11 below may help masters athletes learn how to listen to their bodies as well as monitor the benefits of recovery training.

*Table 15.11:* Suggested monitoring and management strategies to assist masters athletes to optimise recovery and prevent fatigue or overtraining.

| Monitoring and Management Strategies |
|---|
| ***Daily*** |
| • Every morning monitor resting heart rate, body weight, and quality of sleep |
| • Each evening, rate fatigue/tiredness for the day |
| • Eat a balanced diet and plan meals and snacks to complement training |
| • Use shower/spa/bath for stretching, self massage, and hot and cold contrasts |
| • Before bed practice a relaxation (e.g. music, visualization, PMR, breathing exercises). |
| ***Weekly*** |
| • Have at least one rest day |
| • Plan active rest (e.g. stretching, cross training) |
| • Organise a massage (professional, partner) and use self massage at least three times. |
| • Weekly time management (plan in advance) |
| • Prioritize all weekly commitments (work, study, training, domestic, social events) |
| • Add a few varied recovery activities around these commitments (e.g. spa, sauna). |

### Recovery from training twice a day?

Competitive swimmers, rowers, triathletes and runners have been doing it for years. More recently, many high performance coaches of younger elite athletes have gotten into it and have even moved towards three or more short, sharp sessions in a day to maximize sports performance. While training twice a day or more is a luxury for most of us mere mortals with family, partners, work, or study in our lives, the following training and recovery strategies are equally important for the aging athlete who trains every day and in particular from an afternoon session to a morning session the next day.

Training twice a day (or more) means an aging athlete must optimize muscle energy stores, minimize dehydration, minimize fatigue and maximize recovery. Sport Science would suggest the following strategies be undertaken between training sessions.

1. *Stretch immediately after training.* One of the theories behind muscle soreness is that muscles stay slightly contracted and pull on the tendons and bones the tendons attach to. Stretching the muscle and tendon structures helps alleviate this problem. Immediately after training or competing, the muscles are still warm so stretches can be through a greater range of motion. It is widely recommended that stretching be done in a warm shower to enhance the stretch as a result of the increased temperature of the tissues being stretched. Stretching should continue at every opportunity (watching the news, current affairs, movie) and should focus on the major muscle groups and joints used in training.

2. *Get into a cool/cold pool or shower.* Another of the theories behind muscle soreness is pooling of blood and body fluids within the working muscles. Hitting cold water helps contract the blood vessels to "pump" the fluid out of the muscles and back into the circulation.

3. *Ensure high glycemic index (GI) foods are eaten within 30 minutes of finishing a training session.* It is common practice in high performance sport to ensure 50 grams of high GI foods (quickly absorbed) are eaten or drunk by athletes as soon as possible after training. Such items include: bread (3-4 slices), lollies (handful), raisins, soft drinks (4 cans), sports drinks (800 ml), weet-bix, watermelon, muesli bars (3). These foods and fluids are rapidly absorbed into the bloodstream by the gut and therefore available to be taken up by the muscles. Immediately after exercise is the best time to get those high GI carbohydrates in for other reasons as well. Firstly, immediately after exercise the blood flow is still getting to the muscles that were used in training to help them recover; and secondly, the glucose transporters that assist the passage of the blood glucose into the muscle are very active immediately after exercise.

4. *Ensure adequate daily carbohydrate intake.* Athletes training twice or more a day need to take in about 9-10 grams of carbohydrate per kilogram of body weight per day. For example, a 1990's study of rowers training twice-a-day showed that those athletes consuming this amount of carbohydrate were able to maintain higher muscle glycogen and, as a result, higher average power outputs on a rowing ergometer than athletes eating 5 g carbohydrate per kilogram of body weight per day. To help replace fluids as well as

the muscle glycogen used during training, provide about 50 grams of carbohydrate in the form of sports drink (about 600-900 ml), or a high-carbohydrate energy drink (*Lucozade, Gatorlode, Sustagen*) immediately after and at hourly intervals till the next training session. Examples of 50 gram serves of readily available carbohydrates include: 3.5 slices of bread, 1 cup of rice, 2 cups of oats, 3 oranges, 3 tablespoons of sugar, 2 pears, 4 cups of milk. Research has shown that eating about 1 gram of carbohydrate per kilogram of your body weight at two-hourly intervals for the next 4-6 hours also helps restore those muscle carbohydrate stores for the next session. Furthermore, to enhance muscle repair after high intensity training (sprints, weights, contact sports), about 10 grams of protein should be included with the carbohydrate. This enhances the muscle uptake of the carbohydrate by stimulating a greater insulin action and also gives the muscles amino acids to help repair damaged muscle fibers. Examples of snacks that have 50-75 grams of carbohydrate and 6-20 grams of protein are:

- 300 ml milkshake or fruit smoothie
- 300 ml *Sustagen* plus a few lollies or piece of fruit
- 2 x 200 grams tubs yoghurt or 1 tub with a muffin or bagel
- 1 bowl of breakfast cereal and low fat milk and a banana
- 250 grams tin of baked beans on two slices of toast
- Iced fruit bun
- 4 *Weetbix* with milk

5. *Ensure lost fluids are replaced to restore body weight.* Fluids should be drunk before, during and after training to maintain body weight and blood volume. Many athletes may not know it but it takes 2.7 grams of fluid to store 1 gram of carbohydrate in muscles and liver, highlighting just how important fluids are for recovery. Standard guidelines suggest 500 ml 30-60 minutes before exercise, 250 ml every 15 - 20 minutes during exercise, and drink 150% of lost body weight (1 kg lost = 1 L fluid) to replace fluids lost after exercise. The extra 50% is to allow for urinary and post-exercise sweat losses. Alcohol is NOT recommended. It makes us urinate so increases dehydration, it interferes with muscle carbohydrate recovery, and slows down muscle repair processes. Drink fluids until the urine is clear or light gold as this reflects a well hydrated state.

6. *Ensure electrolytes (NB. Sodium) are replaced.* This is particularly important during prolonged exercise in hot and/or humid weather. Sweat contains about 40 mEq/L of sodium. If an athlete loses 1-2 L/hr of sweat and trains for two hours without replacing sodium, between 80-160 mEq of sodium is lost through sweating. That's 2-4 gm of sodium that is 5-10 gm of salt - a lot. Try using sports drinks during and after training, and if you are a "big sweater", a sprinkle of salt over or in meals.

7. *Ensure availability of fluids.* Both water and sports drinks need to be readily accessible to the athlete. A coach can achieve this by ensuring that their athletes are educated to bring two drink bottles to training, preferably filled with sports drink. One is for drinking during training, the other for after training. Taps should also be available and if not, an

esky or water bottle filled with cold water.
8. *Use recovery therapies.* Recovery therapies include spas, hot and cold showers and massage. The guidelines for these are discussed above.
9. *Have complete rest.* This might include sleeping, reading, listening to music, watching a movie.

## Conclusion

For the aging athlete, time pressures with work and family may hinder producing better training results. Masters athletes often fall victim to illnesses associated with the excessive stress of training hard and trying to combine work and family pressures. Recovery training is the most forgotten training component and the most poorly understood of all the training principles. Yet recovery training is as important to a training program as are endurance, speed, strength, flexibility and mental skills training. The benefits from integrating recovery training effectively within programs are many and include:

- We learn how to monitor our training responses and manage ourselves so we can cope with workloads and stressors
- A spin-off from effective recovery is the reduction in injuries, illnesses and burnout often experienced by overstressed athletes
- Through recovery training, aging athletes and coaches acquire effective life skills in self awareness, self management, and self maintenance.

# CHAPTER 16

## NUTRITION FOR THE MASTERS ATHLETE

*Tell me what you eat and I will tell you what you are.*

Anthelme Brillat-Savarin

*I never met a carbohydrate I didn't like.*

David Lygre

*One should eat to live, not live to eat.*

Moliere

### Introduction

In early 2000, I was asked to write a book chapter for Australian Institute of Sport's Dietician, Professor Louise Burke's new *Clinical Sports Nutrition* book. The chapter focused on the nutrition for the aging athlete. In preparation for writing this chapter I did a huge literature search in University libraries, on the web and through vast computer databases. As I expected there were hundreds of studies examining the nutritional needs of young athletes and even more examining the needs of aging non-athletes. Little has changed with very few research papers having ever been written on this topic.

Recommendations for nutrition in masters athletes need to focus on both the nutritional requirements of the aging process and the nutrient needs for exercising. However, people age at greatly differing rates for genetic, environmental, lifestyle and cultural reasons. Furthermore, aging athletes participate in sports ranging from lawn bowls to Ironman triathlon. Moreover, these aging athletes participating in organised sport range from the physically dependent to the physically elite and participate for a wide variety of reasons including health, personal challenge, recreation, competition, social and public recognition. Masters athletes also exhibit an age-related decline in training intensity and volume compared to younger athletes, aging. Indeed, many do no physical training prior to competing in organised sport. Furthermore, 85% of the elderly population suffers from some type of chronic degenerative disease requiring medication(s) that may have potential drug-nutrient interactions that in turn may affect the intake, digestion, absorption, and utilisation of several nutrients. Indeed, a number of reports have suggested that between 14 and 25% of participants in masters sport have a pre-existing medical condition (primarily hypertension, asthma, coronary heart disease) with up to 34% taking medication (cardiovascular, respiratory, non-steroidal anti-inflammatory). Thus, the motivations, training practices, chronic illness and medication usage patterns, and variety of sports or activities participated in by masters athletes make general guidelines for nutrition in this group a challenge.

Recommended Daily Allowances (RDA) and Recommended Daily Intakes (RDI) are given to define "the level of intake of essential nutrients that, on the basis of scientific knowledge, are judged by the Food and Nutrition Board to be adequate to meet the known nutrient needs of practically all healthy persons". However, the data used to determine RDAs often does not include athletes or active individuals young or old. Furthermore, the oldest age group for which many recommendations have only recently been developed is 51 to 70 years and, for only several nutrients, greater than 70 years. These age ranges are very large and make little allowance for the metabolic and physiological changes that occur during these years or the activity levels or health status of aging individuals. Thus, the RDA may not be a valid means of evaluating the nutritional needs of the aging athlete in regular physical training.

The purposes of this chapter are to synthesise the few available studies examining nutritional practices of the older athlete, and to extrapolate data from studies completed on younger athletes or older sedentary populations. This will enable us to make recommendations on the dietary needs of masters athletes.

## Physiological changes in aging athletes

The aging process, at least in inactive people, is accompanied by many physiological changes that affect nutritional needs. These include loss of muscle mass, less efficient immune system, gut changes, decreased sensitivity to taste and smell, poor dental health, a loss of thirst sensitivity, decreased cardiovascular health, and decreased bone density. Whether these declines are the result of the aging process *per se* or the inactivity that accompanies the aging process remains to be conclusively evaluated. However, a number of studies appear to suggest that a number of these factors do decline with age, even in masters athletes. For example, several studies have shown that muscle mass declines with age in masters athletes, even in those with a lifetime of involvement in endurance, sprint and power events. Furthermore, bone mineral density in postmenopausal athletic women has been shown to be lower than in younger athletic women.

A number of physiological changes occur in the aging athlete that may affect not only training and competition performance, but also nutritional recommendations. Table 16.1 summarises the major changes that may affect the nutritional requirements of aging athletes.

*Table 16.1:* Major age-related changes that may influence nutrient requirements of masters athletes.

| Age-related change | Nutritional implication |
| --- | --- |
| Decreased muscle mass | Decreased energy requirements |
| Decreased aerobic capacity | Decreased energy requirements |
| Decreased muscle glycogen (CHO) stores | Decreased energy requirements |
| Decreased bone density | Increased need for calcium and vitamin D |
| Decreased immune function | Increased need for vitamins B6, E and zinc |
| Decreased gastric acid | Increased need for vitamin B12, folic acid, calcium, iron and zinc |
| Decreased skin capacity for vitamin D synthesis | Increased need for vitamin D |
| Decreased calcium bioavailability | Increased need for calcium and vitamin D |
| Decreased liver uptake of retinol | Decreased need for vitamin A |
| Decreased efficiency in metabolic use of pyridoxal (one form of vitamin B6) | Increased need for vitamin B6 |
| Increased oxidative stress status | Increased need for vitamins A, C and E |
| Increased levels of homocysteine (an amino acid related to heart disease) | Increased need for folate and vitamins B6 and B12 |
| Decreased thirst perception | Increased fluid needs |
| Decreased kidney function | Increased fluid needs |

However, when we talk about masters athletes who exhibit the changes outlined above, we must also consider the effects that exercise has on any individual young or old. Table 16.2 summarises the effects of both aging and exercise.

### Energy requirements of aging athletes

Meeting energy (Calories / kilojoules) needs is the first nutritional priority for all athletes. While a small energy deficit between energy intake and output can be tolerated for body fat loss, long term energy deficit or too rapid a weight loss, will lead to a loss of muscle mass and thus loss of strength and endurance, immune system problems, menstrual difficulties in females, and most importantly, lead to decreases in training and competitive performance. The most important factor that determines energy intake is energy expenditure, even in an aging population. Several research studies, including the famous Baltimore Longitudinal Study of Aging, have suggested that the daily energy requirements of an aging population decrease due to a decrease in both energy expenditure for physical activity and resting metabolism.

*Table 16.2:* The effects of aging and exercise on factors affected by nutrition.

| Factor | Aging Effect | Exercise Effect |
|---|:---:|:---:|
| Resting metabolic rate | ↓ | ↑ |
| Total energy expenditure | ↓ | ↑ |
| Thermic effect of food | ↓ | ↑ |
| Total body water | ↓ | ↑ |
| Total bone and muscle mass | ↓ | ↑ |
| Protein synthesis and turnover rate | ↓ | ↑ |
| Gut transit time of food | ↓ | ↑ |
| Appetite and energy intake | ↓ | ↑ |
| Glycogen storage capacity and uptake | ↓ | ↑ |
| Fat breakdown chemical activity | ↓ | ↑ |
| **Cholesterol** | | |
| Total | ↑ | ↓ |
| LDL Cholesterol | ↑ | ↓ |
| HDL Cholesterol | ↓ | ↑ |
| Growth hormone | ↓ | ↑ |

An age-related decrease in daily energy expenditure, at least in non-athletes, is primarily due to both age-related decreases in muscle mass and decreases in physical activity levels. Current RDAs for moderately-active men and women between 19 and 50 years of age have been established at 2,900 (12,200 kilojoules) and 2,200 (9,200 kilojoules) Calories per day, respectively. Current RDAs suggest that older individuals (≥ 51 years) have mean daily energy expenditures, and hence energy requirement, of 1.51 times the resting energy expenditure which is equal to 9.6 MJ/day (2300 kcal/day) for males and 7.9 MJ/day (1900 kcal/day) for females. However, research evidence from sedentary populations suggests that body composition (fat mass versus fat-free mass) changes dramatically with aging with an approximate doubling of body fat between 20 and 50-60 years of age and a fall in body fat after 70 years of age. Similar observations of decreased fat-free mass are also observed in older male and female endurance runners except that the body fat levels only increase marginally with age. This data suggests that the current RDAs need to be updated to account for these changes in body composition that influence the nutritional requirements of an aging population. In support of this suggestion, more recent accurate methods of energy expenditure, have suggested that the present RDAs for older persons are too low except in persons 75 years of age or greater.

Athletes of all ages require energy to maintain normal bodily functioning and provide fuel for working muscles when training or competing. Physical training (aerobic and / or resistance training) has been shown to effectively increase energy requirements and help maintain metabolically active muscle mass in healthy, previously sedentary aging individuals. A number of studies (see Table 16.3) examining the energy intakes of older athletes suggest that older athletes undertaking regular physical training have higher energy intakes than those of age-matched inactive but healthy people. Furthermore, a number of these studies have also found that the energy intakes of these older athletes are higher than those suggested for their respective age groups or gender in the RDAs. For example, energy intakes ranging between 10336 kJ/day and 11549 kJ/day have been observed for older (55-75 years) male endurance athletes with 8663 kJ/day intakes having been observed in 65-84 year old female endurance athletes undertaking physical training of at least one hour per day.

The limited available research has shown that energy intakes of older athletes are lower than those observed in similarly trained younger athletes. This may be due to an age-related decrease in active muscle mass, reduced training volumes (frequency, intensity, duration) of older athletes, or reduced leisure time activity levels commonly seen in older people.

For aging endurance athletes, it is suggested that between 45-55 Calories/kg body weight per day be consumed depending upon exercise intensity while for speed or strength trained athletes between 44-50 Calories/kg body weight per day be consumed.

The fuels burned during exercise depend on the intensity and duration of the exercise performed, the gender of the athlete, and the nutritional state of the athlete. All things being equal, an increase in exercise intensity will mean more carbohydrate being consumed. As the duration of the exercise increases, the source of the carbohydrate may shift from muscle glycogen (stored carbohydrate) to blood glucose. If blood glucose cannot be maintained, exercise performance decreases. This is the reason why sports drinks and sports gels and bars are consumed during long term exercise.

During both high intensity and low intensity exercise, fat is consumed at the same rate but proportionally decreases at high intensities of exercise because of the greater contribution of carbohydrate. Protein contributes less than 5% of total energy during rest and exercise. However, as exercise duration increases and glucose levels run low, protein can be used to make new glucose in the liver.

In general, the following percentages of daily energy intake (Calories or kilojoules) should be taken in by athletes both young and old:
- Carbohydrates 55-58%
- Fat 25-30%
- Protein 12-15%

Carbohydrate, fat and protein intakes are essential for meeting not only the energy requirements of masters athletes, but to ensure normal bodily functioning through the associated intake of fibre, vitamins and minerals. Age-related decreases in the intakes of these nutrients have been observed in a sedentary aging population. However, to my knowledge, no studies have examined the percentage contributions of these nutrients to those of younger, similarly-trained athletes.

*Table 16.3:* Summary of the limited research that has examined the dietary habits of masters athletes. RDA = Recommended Daily Allowance.

| Study | Age (yr) | Sample | Compared to | Results |
|---|---|---|---|---|
| Butterworth et al. (1993) | 72.5±1.8 | Female Endurance (n=12) | RDA | • Calcium (Ca) |
| | | | | • Energy intake |
| Butterworth et al. (1993) | 72.5±1.8 | Female Endurance (n=12) | Age-matched | • Energy intake |
| | | | Healthy controls | • Carbohydrate, Fat, Protein<br>• Fibre<br>• Vit B6, E, Folate<br>• Riboflavin, Thiamin, Niacin<br>• Ca, Ph, Mg, Fe, Zn, Na, K, Cu |
| Chatard et al. (1998) | 63±4.5 | Male Endurance (n=18) | RDA | • Mg, Vit D, Ca<br>• Energy intake<br>• Carbohydrate, Fat, Protein<br>• Fe, Vit A, B1, B12, C, E |
| Hallfrisch et al. (1994) | 66.6±1.3 | Male Endurance (n=16) | Age-matched | • Energy intake |
| | | | Healthy controls | • Carbohydrate, Protein |
| Reaburn & Le Bon (1995) | 50.6±4.2 | Male Runners (n=14) | RDA | • Protein (M & F), Fat (M & F) |
| | | Female Runners (n=15) | | • Riboflavin, Niacin, Thiamine (M & F)<br>• Vit A, C (M & F)<br>• Na, K (M & F)<br>• Ca (F), Fe (F), Zn (M & F), Mg (M&F |

## Carbohydrate Needs of Masters Athletes

Nutritionally, carbohydrates have numerous functions within the body, including energy provision, effects on feeling full after meals and gut emptying, effects on blood glucose and insulin metabolism, effects on protein breakdown, fatty acid production, and effects on bowel activity. Importantly for athletes, carbohydrate is the primary fuel source for working muscles and is stored in solid form within the liver and muscle as glycogen. During high intensity or prolonged endurance exercise, low muscle glycogen levels have been linked to exhaustion.

In older endurance athletes, glycogen storage per unit of muscle is lower than in similarly trained younger runners while glycogen utilisation per unit of energy expenditure is higher during sub-maximal exercise. However, following regular endurance training, older individuals are able to increase muscle glycogen storage and restore glycogen stores post-exercise at rates similar to younger athletes. Previous studies have also observed that healthy, previously inactive older individuals who undertake aerobic exercise training are able to improve glucose tolerance, the rate of insulin-mediated glucose removal from the blood, and increase muscle glucose transport activity from the blood to muscle.

The recommended carbohydrate intake for athletes is similar to that of the general population and therefore is similar for masters athletes since carbohydrate absorption and utilisation remains intact with aging. Thus, the older athlete should consume at least 55% of daily energy intake as carbohydrate obtained from a variety of food sources and the bulk of the carbohydrate-containing foods consumed should be those rich in complex carbohydrates and with a low glycemic index (see Table 16.14 in this chapter or http://www.glycemicindex.com/). A high percentage of this intake should be starchy carbohydrate (bread, cereals, rice, pasta, potato) that also provides protein, vitamin, mineral and fibre intake. However, too high a level of fibre (> 35 g/day) in these foods (e.g. wholegrain products, bran, wheat germ) may not be advantageous to older athletes due to the associated gastrointestinal discomfort or mineral imbalances that may arise as fibre can reduce the absorption of some minerals including calcium and iron. In an aging population, a diet high in cereals and fibre that meets the United States RDA of 30 g/day appears to:

- Assist with obesity prevention by increasing eating time, decreasing energy density, slow gut emptying rates, and affecting some gastrointestinal hormones that influence food intake
- Lower the risk of developing Type II diabetes by helping maintain lower blood glucose, insulin and blood fat levels through the relatively low glycemic index of cereals and other high fibre carbohydrates
- Reduce the risk of cardiovascular disease by lowering blood cholesterol, slowing carbohydrate, fat and protein absorption, and providing nutrients such as vitamin E and folic acid
- Play a role in cancer prevention
- Reduce the rates of constipation and diverticular disease
- Be protective against hypertension by reducing salt intake and increasing dietary fibre and magnesium
- Help prevent the age-related decline in immune function by increasing dietary Vitamin E and zinc, both of which have been shown to enhance immune function in older adults

Thus, apart from the physical benefits (enhanced performance and recovery) gained by a high carbohydrate diet of 5-10g/kg body weight/day, an older athlete can also derive great health benefits that may lower all-cause mortality and morbidity.

The *Australian Institute of Sport Sports Nutrition Department* (http://www.ausport.gov.au/ais/nutrition) lead by leading sports nutritionist and former elite triathlete, Professor

Louise Burke, suggests carbohydrate be consumed at different rates for different types of athlete and in different situations (normal diet, pre-event, during exercise, recovery). Table 16.4 summarises these suggestions.

*Table 16.4:* Recommended carbohydrate intakes before, during and after events or training.

| Situations | Recommended Carbohydrate Intake |
|---|---|
| *Single Event* | |
| Fuelling up for an event, recovering from an event | 7-10 gm/kg body weight/day |
| Rapid after-exercise recovery when less than 8 hrs between events | 1 gm/kg body weight immediately after exercise, repeated after 2 hours |
| Pre-event meal to increase carbohydrate availability prior to prolonged exercise | 1-4 gm/kg body weight eaten 1-4 hours before exercise |
| Carbohydrate intake during moderate intensity or intermittent (e.g. team sports) exercise | 0.5-1.0 gm/kg body weight/hour (30-60 gm/hour) |
| *Regular Training Day* | |
| Daily recovery/fuel needs for an athlete doing less than 1 hour per day of low intensity exercise | 5-7 gm/kg body weight/day |
| Daily recovery/fuel needs for an athlete doing 1-3 hours per day of moderate to high intensity exercise | 7-10 gm/kg body weight/day |
| Daily recovery/fuel needs for an athlete doing extreme hours hour per day (e.g. Tour de France) | 10-12 gm/kg body weight/day |

Table 16.5 shows the typical western, carbohydrate-rich foods consumed by athletes that contain 50 gram servings of carbohydrate. This table should help you check your carbohydrate intake relative to the table above which describes your carbohydrate needs.

Research has shown that typical young male athletes appear to achieve these carbohydrate intake goals but that young female athletes, particularly endurance athletes, are less likely to achieve these goals. This is most likely due to the chronic or periodic restriction of dietary intake done in order to maintain or achieve low levels of body fat. Thus, the following strategies might be suggested to increase carbohydrate and total energy intakes:

- Base meals and snacks around nutritious and carbohydrate-rich foods such as
  - Wholegrain breads and breakfast cereals
  - Rice, oatmeal, maize meal and other grain foods
  - Pasta and noodles
  - Fruits
  - Starchy vegetables (potatoes, corn, sweet potatoes)
  - Legumes (lentils, beans, soy products)
  - Sweetened dairy products (milk-shakes, flavoured-yoghurt)
  - Let these foods take up more than half of the space on your plate

*Table 16.5:* Variety of common foods and serving sizes that provide 50 grams of carbohydrate.

| Food | Serving | Food | Serving |
|---|---|---|---|
| **Cereals** | | **Fruit** | |
| Cornflakes/Wheaties | 60 gm (2 cups) | Canned fruit – light | 360 gm (1.5 cups) |
| Muesli | 65 gm (1-1.5 cups) | Canned fruit - heavy | 240 gm (1 cup) |
| Toasted Muesli | 90 gm (1 cup) | Fresh fruit salad | 500 gm (2.5 cups) |
| Porridge - milk | 350 gm (1.3 cups) | Bananas | 2 medium-large |
| Porridge - water | 410 gm (2 cups) | Mangoes, pears, grapefruit | 2-3 |
| Muesli bar | 2.5 | Oranges, apples | 3-5 |
| Rice cakes | 6 thick/10 thin | Nectarines, apricots | 12 |
| Rice boiled | 180 gm (1 cup) | Grapes | 470 gm (2 cups) |
| Pasta/noodles boiled | 200 gm (1.3 cups) | Melons | 900 gm (5 cups) |
| Canned spaghetti | 440 gm (large tin) | Strawberries | 760 (5 cups) |
| Crispbreads/dry biscuits | 6 large, 15 small | Sultanas, raisins | 70 gm (4 tbsp) |
| Plain sweet biscuits | 8-10 | Dried apricots | 115 gm (22 halves) |
| Bread | 110 gm (4 slices white, 3 thick grain) | **Vegetables/Legumes** | |
| Bread rolls | 110 gm (1 large) | Potatoes | 350 gm (1 large, 3 medium |
| Pita bread | 100 gm (2 pitas) | Sweet potatoes | 350 gm (2.5 cups) |
| Muffin | 120 gm (2) | Corn | 300 gm (1.2 cups creamed or 2 cobs) |
| Crumpet | 2.5 | Green beans | 750 gm (7 cups) |
| Pancake | 150 gm (2 medium) | Baked beans | 440 gm (1 large can) |
| Scone | 125 gm (3 medium) | Soy/kidney beans | 500 gm (3 cups) |
| Iced fruit bun | 105 gm (1.5) | Pumpkin or peas | 800 gm (4 cups) |
| **Dairy Products** | | **Sugars/Confectionery** | |
| Milk | 1 litre | Sugar | 50 gm |
| Flavoured milk | 560 ml | Jam | 3 tbsp |
| Custard | 300 gm (1.3 cups) | Syrups | 4 tbsp |
| Natural or diet yoghurt | 800 gm (4-5 tubs) | Honey | 3 tbsp |
| Fruit yoghurt – non-fat | 350 gm (2 tubs) | Chocolate | 80 gm |
| Ice cream | 250 gm (10 tbsp) | Jelly beans | 60 gm |
| **Drinks** | | **Sports Foods** | |
| Unsweetened fruit juice | 600 ml | Sports drink | 700 ml |
| Sweetened fruit juice | 500 ml | Meal supplement | 250 ml |
| Cordial | 800 ml | Sports bar | 1-1.5 bars |
| Soft drinks | 500 ml | Sports gels | 2 sachets |

Chapter 16 ~ Nutrition for the Masters Athlete

- Carbohydrate drinks (fruit juices, soft drinks, fruit smoothies), high- carbohydrate powders and liquid meal supplements provide high carbohydrate sources
- Increase the number of meals and snacks you eat rather than the size of each meal. Have some available at work.
- Choose low fibre sources when eating before exercise
- Eat a high GI (Glycemic Index) food (see Table 16.14) within 30 minutes of training or competing.
- Eat or drink carbohydrate during prolonged training sessions
- Have a carbohydrate "ready-reckoner" available to plan or assess your carbohydrate intake. These are available from health-food stores or sports nutrition texts in University or public libraries.

## Fat Needs of Masters Athletes

Dietary fat is essential as a source of essential fatty acids, fat-soluble vitamins (A, D, E, K), and as an energy source during low intensity or prolonged exercise at below 80% of maximum heart rate. The optimal daily intake of fat need only be between 25 and 30% of energy intake in both a young and older sedentary or masters athletes. It appears that older populations are meeting this recommendation with Australian National Nutrition Surveys showing that the mean percent energy intake for persons aged 25-65 years and over was approximately 32% for males and 33% for females with no difference between young and older groups. The consensus of scientific data suggests that saturated fats (the bad guys) be less than 10% of energy intake with no more than 10% as polyunsaturated fatty acids and 10-15% as monounsaturated fatty acids.

Older people retain the ability to digest, absorb and utilise fat. Masters athletes appear to consume fat in greater quantities than the recommended population targets or healthy but inactive age-matched controls. This might suggest that older athletes consume greater daily energy intakes, the RDA are not specific enough for older age groups, or more likely that an older population may not be as well educated as to the benefits of a low fat diet. Moreover, older athletes consuming greater than 30% of daily energy intake as fat may compromise cardiovascular health. As in younger athletes, older athletes on a low energy diet should consume between 20-25% of daily energy intake from fat sources in order for more energy to be derived from carbohydrate and protein. A daily energy intake containing less than 20% fat may compromise the absorption of fat-soluble vitamins (A, D, E, K) and limit the feeling of fullness between meals.

## Protein Needs and Aging

Inadequate protein intake has been shown to be related to the age-related decrease in muscle mass. The American College of Sports Medicine (ACSM) suggests that older non-athletes need approximately 0.9 grams or protein per kilogram of body weight per day (g/kg/d).

However, the current Recommended Dietary allowance (RDA) in the United States is 0.8 g/kg/d with this figure based on the needs of young people. The ACSM recommend a safe intake of 1.25 g/kg/d for older people, well below what many independent living older people take in (0.67-0.86 g/kg/d) according to surveys. Indeed, as discovered in one study, about 50% of independently-living men and women in the United States aged over 60 years consumed less than the RDA.

For older athletes, heavy weight training has muscle building effects. Weight training works to retain protein for both muscle repair and increasing muscle size. Moreover, athletes of any age have increased protein requirements due to the need for repair of the damage that training and competing have on muscle fibres, as well as the increased use of protein as an energy source, particularly in aging endurance athletes, and the need for increased protein to support increases in muscle mass that generally accompanies increased training intensities.

Protein is continually being broken down and made within the human body so that a dietary supply of the building blocks of protein, amino acids, is necessary to offset protein losses. Amino acids are used in the making of structural proteins (e.g. connective tissue such as ligaments and tendons, muscle tissue), functional proteins (e.g. chemicals for energy production, immune system antibodies, oxygen-carrying haemoglobin), and as an energy source in the absence of adequate carbohydrate (glucose) or fat (fatty acids).

The current United States RDA for adults of all ages is 0.8 g/kg/day and the Australian RDI 0.75 g/kg/day. However, one study examined the adequacy of the US RDA in men between 71 and 99 years of age and found that supplementation with 0.8 g of egg protein per kilogram of body mass per day was inadequate to maintain a positive energy balance. This suggests the RDA for older inactive populations need to be revisited.

An athlete's protein needs are even greater than a non-athlete because of increased use of protein during physical activity for making glucose, use of amino acids for energy production, and the tissue breakdown accompanying both training and competing. Furthermore, within an athletic population, the recommended dietary intakes for protein may vary depending upon exercise intensity, carbohydrate availability, exercise mode, energy balance, gender, training age, timing of food intake and age.

Insufficient overall dietary energy intake can lead to a protein loss given that there is a well-defined interaction between total energy intake and protein need. Moreover, increased protein requirements have been observed with high versus low intensity exercise and long versus short duration exercise. Thus, it has been suggested that younger endurance-trained athletes in regular training consume about 1.2-1.4 g/kg body mass/day (150% of current US RDA) and young strength-trained athletes 1.6-1.7 g/kg body mass/day (200% of current US RDA).

Older endurance or power athletes may require a lower protein requirement than suggested above for a number of reasons. First, the aging process is accompanied by a decline in muscle mass in both healthy active individuals and masters athletes secondary to an age-related decrease in both whole-body protein turnover and protein synthesis. Secondly, older athletes appear not to train with the same intensity and/or volume as younger athletes. Thirdly, although not conclusively investigated, there may be an age-related reduction in the absorptive capacity of the gut for amino acids. Fourthly, due to a number of underlying problems (dietary recall problems or inadequate energy intakes given by researchers in protein studies), the protein requirements suggested in the RDAs may have been overestimated. Taken together, the above factors suggest that older athletes may require a lower daily protein intake than those suggested above for younger athletes.

Thus, although the protein needs of different aged athletic populations is not considered, it has recently been suggested that aging exercisers may require 0.8-1.0 g/kg body weight/day with one leading researcher suggesting older exercisers may require 1.0-1.25 g/kg body weight/day in order to promote a positive protein balance. Adjustments may have to be made for illness, chronic disease, or suboptimal total energy intakes. This figure of 1.0-1.25 g/kg body weight/day approximates the observed protein intakes of 1.25-1.45 g/kg body weight/day observed in older athletes and regular exercisers from a variety of training backgrounds. However, older athletes in heavy training, particularly those involved with strength and power sports, may require increased protein intakes (e.g. 1.5-1.7 g/kg body weight/day) since resistance exercise increases muscle protein synthesis in both elderly and young individuals. Table 16.6 shows common foods and their protein content.

*Table 16.6:* Quantity of protein found in a variety of common foods and the associated serving sizes.

| Food | Typical Serve | Protein Content (grams) |
|---|---|---|
| Beef, lamb, pork | 100 gm cooked | 31 |
| Ham, salami, corned beef | 1 slice (30 gm) | 7 |
| Sausage | 1 cooked (90 gm) | 13 |
| Chicken, turkey | 100 gm cooked | 28 |
| Seafood | 100 gm cooked | 23 |
| Milk (incl. Soy) | 250 ml glass | 9 |
| Hard cheese | 20 gm slice | 5 |
| Cottage cheese | Tablespoon (20 gm) | 3 |
| Flavoured yoghurt | 200 gm carton | 10 |
| Ice-cream | 1 scoop (50 gm) | 2 |
| Rice | 1 cup cooked | 5 |
| Pasta | 1 cup cooked | 7.5 |
| Bread, fruit loaf, crumpet | 1 slice (30 gm) | 3 |
| Breakfast cereal | 1 cup (30-45 gm) | 3-5 |
| Eggs | 1 cooked | 7 |
| Tofu | 100 gm | 8.5 |
| Baked beans | 1 cup (220 gm) | 10 |
| Nuts | 50 gm | 10 |

Recent research suggests that taking amino acid supplements may stimulate protein synthesis in an elderly male population. However, other studies have observed either no anabolic effect of high protein diets or no relationship between protein intake (adjusted for body mass and physical activity) and muscle mass. Taken together, these data suggest that protein intake above the RDA is not linked to preservation of muscle mass in older people.

There appear to be a number of possible negative side effects of an increased protein intake that have recently been suggested to have been overestimated in the past. These include impaired kidney function, increased calcium loss and effects on plaque build up in arteries. While it is acknowledged that older people with impaired kidney function should not consume high protein diets, there appears no convincing evidence that a normally functioning kidney cannot handle the additional nitrogen excretion that accompanies a high protein diet. High protein diets may also increase calcium loss and therefore be hazardous for older female athletes with an increased risk of osteoporosis. However, it appears that the observed calcium loss may be associated with protein supplementation as opposed to normal protein foods, the phosphate content of which negates this adverse effect. Finally, it has also been recently suggested that diets containing protein in the ranges 1.2-1.7 g/kg body mass/day will not adversely affect cardiovascular health.

While not guaranteed as indicators of the need for more protein in the diet, the following have been suggested as indicators of possible protein inadequacy:

- Frequent colds and sore throats
- Slow recovery between training sessions
- Slow fingernail growth
- Easily broken nails
- Sugar cravings

## Vitamin and Mineral Intakes

Vitamins and minerals are essential for efficient energy production and numerous other bodily functions affecting sports performance such as the making of haemoglobin to carry oxygen in the blood, maintenance of bone health, immune system function, and the antioxidants protection of tissue damage. They are also required to build and repair muscle tissue after exercise.

Athletes both young and old may have an increased need for vitamin and mineral intakes for a number of reasons:

- Increased need for them due to high energy turnovers
- Increased loss due to sweating, urination or muscle damage
- Increased need for tissue maintenance and repair

Research has shown that a direct relationship exists between overall energy intake and vitamin and mineral intake. High-energy intakes are required by both younger and older athletes in order to meet the energy demands of physical training and competition. It would thus be expected that the micronutrient intake in these groups should be in excess of the

RDAs, assuming that a well-balanced diet is eaten. Thus, vitamin and mineral deficiency may be aggravated in athletes who restrict energy intakes to reduce body weight or have chronic medical conditions that may disturb micronutrient absorption or utilisation.

Numerous studies examining the dietary practices of younger athletes have shown that dietary intakes of the minerals zinc, iron, magnesium, copper and calcium, together with the vitamins $B_6$, $B_{12}$, and D are below the RDA. The few studies that have examined nutritional intakes of older endurance athletes suggest low intakes of the minerals calcium, iron, zinc, and magnesium and vitamin D, despite consuming energy intakes above the RDAs (See Table 16.3).

Masters athletes may be at a greater risk of micronutrient deficiencies for a number of reasons. Deficiencies may be due to age-related changes in the ability to absorb and metabolise these compounds, different baseline requirements, increased medication use, and the presence of chronic disease states. Those older athletes at greater risk of vitamin and mineral deficiencies may also be those on low-fat diets, those on weight loss diets and those with limited intakes of fruit and vegetables.

The following section will examine the available evidence on dietary intakes of micronutrients in masters athletes, to extrapolate information from studies of aging non-athletes, and to make recommendations as to the micronutrient needs of the aging athlete.

## Vitamins

### Vitamin A

Vitamin A (retinol) is essential for vision, growth, maintenance of tissues, and the integrity of the immune system. Together with ß-carotene, vitamin A's precursor, this vitamin has been suggested as an antioxidant in athletes and thus beneficial in preventing tissue damage and facilitating tissue repair. In a healthy aging population, the clearance of vitamin A is decreased by about 50% compared to younger adults, thus suggesting the current RDA for retinol of 1000 and 800 µg/day for older males and females, respectively, may be too high. In support of this finding is that a number of international nutritional surveys have observed both adequate dietary intakes and high serum retinol values in elderly populations.

Supplementation of vitamin A may lead to vitamin A toxicity (skin peeling, headaches, vomiting) or a decreased immune response if consumed in large amounts. Thus, aging athletes should focus on consuming vitamin A precursors, the carotenoids, in order to take advantage of the antioxidant and immune system benefits of vitamin A. These foods include the orange-coloured fruit and vegetables apricots, carrots, mangoes, pumpkin, and sweet potatoes.

### Vitamin $B_6$

Vitamin $B_6$ is involved in amino acid and glycogen (carbohydrate) metabolism and aids in the formation of haemoglobin (blood oxygen carrier) and myoglobin (muscle oxygen carrier) and thus plays a crucial role in any athlete's diet. The requirement for vitamin $B_6$ increases as the intake of protein increases because of its role in amino acid metabolism. Since vitamin $B_6$ and protein tend to occur together in the diet (meat, fish, poultry, cereals, vegetables, whole grains), dietary adequacy of this vitamin is common in younger individuals eating the normal western diet.

The current US RDA for vitamin $B_6$ is 1.7 and 1.5 mg/day for elderly (≥51 years) males and females, respectively and does not differ from those recommended for younger adults. Most dietary intake surveys have confirmed that the intake of vitamin $B_6$ in elderly persons is inadequate to meet the RDAs. In an aging population, the blood concentrations of vitamin $B_6$ appear to decrease and there appears to be a greater amount of the vitamin needed to ensure immune system functioning in elderly people. Furthermore, vitamin $B_6$ plays a crucial role in reducing the risk factor in cardiovascular disease. Thus, for both health and performance reasons, it might be suggested that the RDA for vitamin $B_6$ be increased in aging athletes to 2.0 mg/day.

### *Vitamin $B_{12}$*

Vitamin $B_{12}$ is required for the making of blood cells and acts as a co-factor in energy metabolism and thus plays an important role in an athlete's diet. The major dietary intakes of vitamin $B_{12}$ come from red and organ meats such as liver and kidney. As such, an aging population tends to have decreased intakes of these sources because of the high cholesterol and fat content contained in these meats. Moreover, strict vegetarians may have trouble meeting the RDA for vitamin $B_{12}$ of 2.4 µg/day. Furthermore, an Australian study observed a decreased vitamin $B_{12}$ intake over a five-year period in Australians with 3-10% of adult men and 10-17% of women consuming less than the RDI.

A decrease in the overall energy intake of masters athletes relative to younger athletes might suggest a decrease in the need for the B group of vitamins. However, an age-related decrease in gut size seen in approximately 30% of people over 60 years of age and the subsequent decrease in stomach acid secretion may be a cause of the observed deficiency in vitamin $B_{12}$ in sedentary aging individuals through malabsorption of vitamin $B_{12}$.

Despite the suggestion that older athletes may have an increased need for vitamin $B_{12}$, the only published study to date that examined vitamin $B_{12}$ intake in older endurance athletes on a mixed diet showed intake of this vitamin was above the French RDA. However, it has been suggested that the dietary needs of vitamin $B_{12}$ and folate necessary to prevent anaemia in older persons may be less than that required to maintain low homocysteine levels necessary for cardiovascular health. Thus, it has been suggested that the RDA for vitamin $B_{12}$ be increased to 150% of the current US RDA (2.4 µg/day) in order to prevent deficiency symptoms. Researchers have thus suggested that an RDA of 2.8 µg/day may be needed for older persons undertaking regular exercise, particularly for those who are vegetarians or have reduced secretion of stomach acids.

### *Vitamin C*

Vitamin C has the ability to work as an antioxidant and is thus suggested to benefit athletes through preventing connective tissue damage, enhancing tissue repair, and thus enhancing recovery from physical training and competition. Moreover, vitamin C enhances iron absorption, and facilitates iron availability. Importantly for an older population more at risk of chronic disease, vitamin C has also been linked to reduced risk of cancer, cardiovascular disease and cataracts. Major sources of vitamin C include citrus fruits, tomatoes, green peppers and salad greens.

At present, there is no research evidence to suggest that vitamin C absorption or utilisation is impaired with age or that dietary intake in an aging sedentary population or aging athletes are lower than the current RDAs of 30-60 mg/day. While vitamin C has also been shown to be sensitive to factors such as temperature and pollution and may thus be recommended for older endurance athletes from sub-tropical or tropical cities, their appears no suggestion to encourage supplementation of vitamin C in older athletes. Importantly for an older population with increased rates of chronic disease, megadoses of vitamin C (> 1000 mg/day) have been shown to cause side effects such as kidney stone formation, precipitate gout in those predisposed to this disease, impair copper absorption, destroy vitamin $B_{12}$ and have been associated with "runners diarrhoea".

## *Vitamin D*

Vitamin D is widely regarded as promoting growth and mineralisation of bones, as well as enhancing the absorption of calcium. Importantly for athletes undertaking heavy training loads, vitamin D is also important to the body's immune response. Research over the past few decades has uncovered several new potential roles of vitamin D. Many types of cells in the body can use vitamin D to help regulate critical cellular functions. Vitamin D deficiency could thus lead to several potential health problems including an increased risk of colon and other cancers, heart disease, diabetes and multiple sclerosis, and perhaps to some infectious diseases such as tuberculosis. Apart from dietary intake of vitamin D (meats, fortified cereals and margarines, dairy products, eggs), human skin also has the capacity to synthesise vitamin D in the presence of sunlight.

Adequate intakes of vitamin D appear crucial for older individuals given its importance in maintenance of bone integrity. However, there appears to be up to a 50% age-related decrease in the capacity of aging skin to synthesise vitamin D relative to younger persons. Vitamin D production within the skin may also be compromised by factors such as seasonal variations, latitude, use of protective clothing, and sunscreens. Moreover, there appears to be an age-related reduction in the kidney production of vitamin D and a decreased intake and absorption of vitamin D in healthy but sedentary aging populations. Taken together, these findings strongly suggest that older individuals and health practitioners need to encourage older people to ensure an adequate intake of vitamin D and sun exposure in moderate doses.

The USA's National Research Council observed that about 75% of elderly Americans ($\geq$ 51 years) only met two-thirds of the vitamin D RDA of 5 µg/day. Moreover the Australian National Nutrition Survey also confirmed that the dietary intake of vitamin D was inadequate in aging Australians. In light of the importance of vitamin D in calcium absorption and bone mineralisation and thus osteoporosis prevention, these findings suggest an increase in the RDAs to 10 µg/day in persons over 51 years of age and 15 µg/day in those over 70 years of age. Thus, vitamin D supplementation may be recommended in aging athletes, particularly those with poor dietary intakes or with little exposure to sunlight.

### Vitamin E

Vitamin E is the major antioxidant protecting against cell membrane breakdown that can result from exercise that is prolonged or eccentric (muscles contracting while lengthening) such as during running or weight training. Elderly populations have been shown to benefit from vitamin E supplementation through improved immune function, reduced incidence of cataracts, cancers and cardiovascular disease.

No evidence of vitamin E deficiency has been observed in older athletes with one study of 18 older male endurance athletes suggesting a more than adequate intake of vitamin E. However, it is a nutrient that is notoriously deficient in low-fat diets. The current US RDA for vitamin E is 10 and 8 mg of tocopherol equivalents (TE) per day for males and females, respectively.

Vitamin E is found within vegetable oils, nuts and seeds, green leafy vegetables and wheat germ. No negative side effects have been observed with supplementation of up to over 700 mg TE/day. Thus, a review of nutrition for elderly exercisers has suggested that older individuals undertaking endurance training and concerned with cardiovascular problems, may consider a supplement of 100-200 mg TE/day. Aging athletes with high blood pressure, or anticoagulant medicines that prevent blood clots, check with your sports medicine doctor before taking vitamin E supplements as vitamin E may raise the risk of stroke and interfere with the action of the drugs.

### Riboflavin

Riboflavin or vitamin $B_2$ is a major constituent of two co-factors involved with energy metabolism and as such is of importance to athletes, particularly those embarking on a new or increased physical training program. The current US RDA for riboflavin is 1.4 and 1.2 mg/day for elderly males and females, respectively. A number of studies have suggested the dietary intakes of riboflavin to be lower than the RDA for the respective country. In Australia, depending upon the age group concerned, between 14-26% of men and 4-11% of women exhibit intakes of riboflavin below the RDI. It has been suggested that low riboflavin intakes are commonly observed in countries with low dietary intakes of dairy products.

Older athletes may have a greater need for riboflavin than the present RDA. A 1990's study identified that older women (50-67 years) undertaking an exercise program and having a riboflavin intake equal to the US RDA, displayed decreased urine riboflavin excretion rates which is indicative of riboflavin depletion. This has lead to the suggestion that older athletes should strive to consume at least 1.5 mg/day through whole grain or fortified breads and cereals. Moreover, some researchers have suggested the RDA for older persons be the same as for younger persons (1.7 mg/day for males and 1.3 mg/day for females).

### Folate

Folate is important for protein metabolism and red blood cell formation. In young athletes consuming high-energy intakes from yeast, legumes, green leafy vegetables, fortified cereals and fruits, folate deficiency is rare. Results from an Australian National Nutrition Survey also suggest that older persons consuming a western diet are not at risk of folate deficiency. This is most probably due to the increased trend of folate fortification of foods or an adequate intake of folate-rich foods (nuts, seeds, dark green leafy vegetables, legumes, meats, milk products). However, in older athletes with gut problems so common in elderly persons, the associated decrease in stomach acid production may lead to decreased folate absorption. A folate deficiency has been shown to elevate plasma homocysteine levels (an amino acid) and even a moderate elevation in homocysteine levels has been shown to be an independent risk factor in cardiovascular disease. Thus, it has recently been suggested that aging athletes take in at least 200 µg/day of folate, as long as vitamin $B_{12}$ intake is adequate since high levels of folate can mask vitamin $B_{12}$ deficiency.

## Minerals

Research has shown that the minerals low in the diets of all athletes, especially females, are calcium, iron and zinc. Low intakes of these minerals are usually attributed to dieting, or avoidance of animal products such as meat, fish, poultry, and dairy products.

### *Calcium*

Calcium is essential for nerve-muscle transmission, blood coagulation, muscular contraction, and bone health. Calcium becomes even more important with age given that there is an age-related loss of bone minerals in both males and females as a result of bone resorption predominating over bone formation, particularly after menopause. In older athletes, particularly those undertaking repetitive weight-bearing activities such as running, adequate calcium intake is crucial given that stress fractures are most likely to occur in athletes with low bone density and low calcium intake. Moreover, such repetitive activities particularly in a hot and / or humid environment, may lead to significant calcium loss via sweating. Thus, calcium is important for long-term bone health in older athletes, particularly menopausal/post-menopausal women.

An Australian study showed that between 18-32% of men and 32-58% of women had calcium intakes below the RDI. As well as a poor dietary intake, there appears to be an age-related decrease in calcium absorption, particularly in post-menopausal women, and an impaired ability to increase calcium absorption when eating a low calcium diet such as that observed in older athletes (see Table 16.3). The availability of calcium in the body is also affected by gut problems common in older persons as a result of decreased stomach acid decreasing the dissociation of calcium from food. Another factor significantly affecting calcium absorption is that calcium and vitamin D are interactive in their role on bone health. The active form of vitamin D is produced in the kidneys that show an age-related decrease in function. This deterioration in kidney function has been attributed to the age-related decrease in circulating active vitamin D and thus calcium absorption. Other factors that have shown to lead to vitamin D deficiencies and thus threaten calcium absorption are sunlight deprivation, dairy product avoidance, lactose intolerance and malabsorption of fat-soluble vitamins A, D E and K, factors that are often observed in older populations. In aging endurance athletes, it might also be suggested that consumption of sports drinks containing high levels of sodium chloride to enhance fluid absorption and taste may reduce calcium availability since sodium chloride has been shown to increase urinary calcium loss.

The RDI for calcium in Australia is 800 mg/day for males over 64 years and 1000 mg/day for females over 54 years. In older (> 65 years) healthy females, mean calcium intakes from an Australian National Nutrition Survey were only 68% of the RDI, a major concern given the causes of osteoporosis, risks of fall fractures, and the role of calcium in bone mineralisation. In the United States of America, the current RDA for calcium is 1200 mg/day for all people over 51 years of age. However, calcium balance studies have suggested intakes of 1000 mg/day for oestrogen-treated post-menopausal females and 1500 mg/day for untreated females. On the other hand, the National Institute of Health Consensus Development Panel on Optimal Calcium Intake recommended 1000 mg/day for males and oestrogen-sufficient females less than 65 years of age and 1500 mg/day for males and females older than 65 years of age.

Given the fact that athletes, particularly those undertaking strenuous endurance exercise in hot and/or humid environments, lose significant quantities of calcium in sweat, it would thus appear prudent to suggest calcium intakes at the higher end of these recommended ranges for older athletes. Table 16.7 contains examples of calcium contents of typical foods.

*Table 16.7:* Amount of calcium found in a variety of common calcium-rich foods and the associated serving sizes.

| Food | Amount | Calcium Content (mg) |
|---|---|---|
| Plain yoghurt, non-fat | 1 cup | 450 |
| Plain yoghurt, low-fat | 1 cup | 350-415 |
| Fruit yoghurt, low-fat | 1 cup | 250-350 |
| Skim milk | 1 cup | 300-320 |
| Milk, 2% fat | 1 cup | 315 |
| Dried figs | 10 | 270 |
| Orange | 1 medium | 60 |
| Spinach | 1 cup cooked | 140-250 |
| Broccoli | 1 cup cooked | 175 |
| Salmon, canned with bones | 1 cup | 240 |
| Sardines, canned with bones | 1 cup | 235 |

In masters athletes, both exercise and calcium-enriched diets have been shown to have independent effects on bone mineral density in postmenopausal women. The majority of available research evidence on aging athletes suggests older persons in regular physical training are not getting enough calcium in the diet (see Table 16.3). Thus, consideration should be given to calcium supplementation in a dose that brings the dietary intakes up to the RDA for age and gender.

Calcium supplements come in many forms but the amount of elemental calcium is what to look for. Taking these supplements with food in doses of less than 500 mg appears to improve absorption. If taking two calcium supplements, it appears that taking them at separate meals will enhance the uptake. It appears that calcium citrate malate is better absorbed than calcium carbonate in post-menopausal women with low dietary intakes of calcium and is more effective in reducing bone demineralisation and lowering bone fracture rate. Indeed, it has recently been suggested that calcium supplementation (~ 1,000 mg/day) can reduce bone loss in both pre-menopausal and late post-menopausal women consuming 700 to 1,000 mg calcium/day in their diet. Many calcium supplements contain vitamin D to improve calcium absorption during digestion.

Finally, older female athletes who have been involved in sports such as swimming, track and field, and gymnastics since childhood may face a higher than normal risk of osteoporosis or stress fractures as a result of delayed menarche or secondary amenorrhoea. These masters athletes should be carefully monitored for calcium intakes and / supplementation. A number of researchers have recently suggested that the following strategies are major components in preventing osteoporosis in aging men and women:

1. Ensure optimal bone mass through childhood, adolescence and early adulthood
2. Ensure adequate dietary calcium and vitamin K intake throughout life
3. High load exercise
4. Avoidance of tobacco and excessive alcohol
5. Avoid steroids and anticonvulsants
6. Avoid excess phosphorous consumption
7. Avoid excess dietary protein, sodium and caffeine
8. Ensure adequate calcium and vitamin D throughout the lifetime
9. Hormone replacement therapy.

## *Iron*

In athletes of any age, particularly those involved with endurance exercise, iron is an integral component of the oxygen carrying capacity of both haemoglobin in the blood and myoglobin within muscle. Moreover, iron is also crucial for the production of aerobic energy within muscle cells.

Iron deficiency has been shown to reduce both performance capacity and maximal aerobic power in younger athletes and is commonly observed in both younger endurance athletes, particularly those who are females and vegetarians. It also appears that weight-bearing endurance athletes such as runners are more prone to iron deficiency since iron losses occur with excessive sweating, gastrointestinal bleeding and red blood cell breakdown as a result of pounding the roads. While the iron losses of older athletes have not been examined, my unpublished observations are that the dietary intakes of older male and female endurance athletes are below the RDI for Australians of 5-7 mg/day. This observation is despite an

Australian National Nutrition Survey finding that the average iron intake for Australians was 14-15 and 11-12 mg/day in 65-80-plus year old males and females, respectively. Thus, as a result of the increased iron losses in endurance athletes and the suggestion of reduced iron intakes in this group, the dietary intakes of male endurance runners and post-menopausal women has been suggested to be as high as 18 mg/day.

Absorption of dietary iron depends on the form of iron ingested. One form, *heme iron* is more highly absorbed (23% efficiency) and is found in meat, fish and poultry whereas the *non-heme iron* form is absorbed less efficiently (3-8%) and is found in legumes and vegetables. Thus, older vegetarian athletes appear to be at a greater risk of depleting their iron stores than athletes consuming *heme iron* sources. The iron content of some common foods is found in Table 16.8.

*Table 16.8:* Amount of iron found in a variety of common iron-rich foods and the associated serving sizes.

| Food | Serving | Iron (mg) |
|---|---|---|
| Heme-iron sources | | |
| Liver | 100 gm | 11 |
| Steak | 100 gm | 4 |
| Fish | 100 gm | 0.6-1.4 |
| Chicken breast, skinless | 100 gm | 1.2 |
| Oysters | 100 gm (10) | 3.9 |
| Salmon | 100 gm | 1.5 |
| Non-heme sources | | |
| Eggs | 2 | 1 |
| Wholegrain bread | 2 slices | 1.4 |
| Dried apricots | 50 gm | 2 |
| Tofu | 100 gm | 1.9 |
| Cooked spinach | 1 cup | 4.4 |
| Almonds | 50 gm | 2.1 |
| Kidney beans/Lentils cooked | 2/3 cup | 2.5 |

The requirements for iron decrease with age due to an age-related increase in iron stores in males and post-menopausal females. In an aging male inactive population, nutritional iron deficiency is rarely exhibited and any observed anaemia is most commonly associated with chronic illness that may decrease iron absorption. However, an Australian survey has suggested that up to 30-45% of adult females had estimated dietary intakes of iron below the RDI. The US RDA for both elderly males and females is 10 mg/day and should be adequate for aging athletes. However, older athletes who are female and / or vegetarians involved with intense endurance running in hot environments might be suggested to consume a diet that provides up to 15 mg/day of iron.

## Zinc

Dietary zinc is an important mineral in older individuals due to its role in both tissue growth and repair and, most importantly for older athletes undertaking physical training, the functioning of the immune system. Zinc is also an essential component of a large number of chemicals that make and breakdown carbohydrates, fats, and proteins. Zinc is primarily lost through urine, faeces and sweating and thus dietary intakes of this mineral become more important in older endurance athletes, particularly those training and competing in hot environments.

There is no evidence to suggest that the zinc balance is different between young and older populations on the same diet. While there is evidence of decreased zinc absorption in elderly persons, there is evidence that zinc excretion is also diminished, thus zinc balance is maintained.

An Australian National Nutrition Survey revealed that the average zinc intake for older males (> 65 years) was borderline but was below the recommended dietary intake of 12 mg/day for similarly-aged women. A further Australian study has observed poor dietary zinc intakes with the finding that between 30 and 69% of Australian adults had intakes less than the RDI. Deficiencies in dietary intakes of zinc are also commonly observed in both younger and older athletes. This may be related to the athletes' relatively high fibre diets that contain phytates that reduce the bioavailability of zinc from foods such as cereals and grains. Moreover, the bioavailability of zinc can be further compromised in athletes taking calcium or iron supplements with food. Thus, older athletes who are vegetarians, who consume small amounts of meat or seafood, or take calcium or iron supplements, may have trouble meeting the RDA for zinc and may warrant zinc supplementation. Food sources of zinc include meat, dairy products, cereals, legumes, nuts, soy products and eggs.

There is also a suggestion that zinc may be implicated in anaerobic exercise. Some research suggests that zinc may be required during muscular work that predominantly depends on a high production of lactic acid such as sprint or middle-distance swimmers and runners. This would suggest the need for older power athletes, team players, or endurance athletes undertaking high intensity interval training, may have increased needs for dietary zinc or zinc supplementation.

Given that the available evidence suggests zinc deficiency may be a problem in an aging population or older endurance athletes with high sweat rates and high starchy carbohydrate diets, it might be suggested that dietary intake of zinc be increased to the 15 mg/day for both males and female aging athletes who train hard.

Table 16.9 below summarises the food sources, bodily functions, deficiency symptoms and symptoms of excessive consumption of the minerals calcium, iron and zinc.

*Table 16.9:* Food sources, bodily functions, deficiency symptoms and symptoms of excessive consumption of the minerals calcium, iron and zinc.

| Mineral | Food Sources | Functions | Deficiency Symptoms | Symptoms of Excessive Consumption |
|---|---|---|---|---|
| Calcium | Dairy products (milk, cheese, yoghurt, ice cream) egg yolk, dried peas and beans, dark green vegetables) | Bone formation, nerve impulses, muscle contraction | Osteoporosis, impaired muscle contraction, cramps | Constipation, kidney stones, calcification of soft tissues |
| Iron | Organ meats (liver, kidney), shellfish (NB oysters), dried peas and beans, wholegrains, green leafy vegetables, dried apricots, dates, figs and raisins, iron cookware | Hemoglobin and myoglobin, aerobic energy production | Fatigue, anemia, decreased resistance to infection | Liver damage, hemochromotosis (excessive absorption of iron leading to bronzed pigmentation and eventual heart failure) |
| Zinc | Organ meats, meat, fish, poultry, oysters, dairy products, nuts, wholegrains, asparagus, spinach | Co-factor in energy metabolism, protein synthesis, immune function | Depressed immunity, impaired wound healing | Increased cholesterol, impaired immune function |

## Water

Fluids are lost from the body via breathing, faeces, urine and sweating. Table 16.10 shows the normal daily fluid loss and fluid intake in a non-exercising adult male and female.

*Table 16.10:* Normal daily fluid loss and fluid intake in a non-exercising adult male and female.

| | Water Loss | | | Water Intake | | |
|---|---|---|---|---|---|---|
| | *Male* | *Female* | | *Male* | *Female* |
| Urine | 1500 ml | 1100 ml | Fluids | 1300 ml | 1000 ml |
| Faeces | 200 ml | 100 ml | Water in food | 1000 ml | 700 ml |
| Lungs | 400 ml | 200 ml | Water from metabolism of fat and carbohydrate | 300 ml | 300 ml |
| Skin | 500 ml | 600 ml | | | |
| TOTAL | 2600 ml | 2000 ml | TOTAL | 2600 ml | 2000 ml |

In athletes, particularly those involved in endurance sports, sweat losses of up to 2L/hr have been reported during long duration, high intensity exercise in hot and humid conditions. Moreover, up to 100 ml/hr has been reported lost from the lungs during heavy breathing such as is seen during prolonged endurance exercise. Factors affecting sweat rates in athletes include the body surface area, the number of sweat glands per unit of surface area, gender, exercise intensity, the environment (temperature, humidity), hydration level, aerobic fitness level, acclimatisation, and age.

The aging process is associated with a number of age-related changes that may make masters athletes more susceptible to hydration problems than younger athletes. First, the commonly-observed decrease in total body protein (including muscle mass) leads to an age-related decrease in total body water. Secondly, it appears that kidney hormone receptors that detect dehydration lose their efficiency leading to increased water excretion by the kidney. Thirdly, an age-related reduction in thirst sensation is caused by a decrease in receptors that are sensitive to blood concentrations of fluid regulating hormones and electrolytes. One research study took older "average fit" (~ 60 years) and younger (~ 20 years) males and systematically dehydrated them for three hours. The older men rated themselves less thirsty, despite reducing blood volume and increasing blood thickness to a greater extent than the younger men. Together, these age-related changes suggest that older individuals may have problems with maintaining fluid volume. Fourthly, during exercise in the heat, aged skin exhibits decreased blood flow (25-40%) due to a reduced ability to open the blood vessels of the skin. Finally, there appears an age-related decrease in sweat production together with a delay in the onset of the sweat response. However, a number of research studies have reported that lifelong aerobic exercise may retard the suggested decrease in sweat production reported in earlier studies.

Taken together, these age-related changes strongly suggest that aging athletes may have problems with heat exchange and fluid balance. Thus, masters athletes should be cautious about fluid intake during exercise, particularly during prolonged endurance exercise in hot environments. This topic was discussed in detail in Chapter 11 of this book that examines heat and cold regulation in masters athletes. However, the following fluid intake guidelines have been suggested for both young and older athletes:

- *Before exercise*: drink 400 - 600 ml (13-20 oz)
- *During exercise*: drink 600-1200 ml (20-40 oz) per hour with 150-350 ml (6-12 oz) every 15-20 minutes. Plain water is suggested for events shorter than one hour but drinks containing 4-8% carbohydrate (4-8 grams/100 ml) are suggested for longer events. Sodium in the drink at 0.5-0.7 grams/litre is suggested for events longer than one hour as it enhances the taste and drive to drink, as well as prevents a lowering of the blood sodium levels that can cause a decrease in performance.
- *After exercise*: based on body weight lost (1 kilogram lost = 1 litre lost), drink 150% of fluid lost to account for urine and sweat losses after exercise. Drinks with sodium in will help stop urination and water storage.

**Nutrients, Health and Chronic Disease**

A wide variety of nutrients have been associated with a variety of diseases or health states, often with varying degrees of association. Table 16.11 summarises the available information.

*Table 16.11:* Nutrients that have been associated with positive or negative effects on health and disease.

| Disease State | Protective Effect | Increased Incidence |
|---|---|---|
| Cancer | Carotenes<br>Vitamins C, D & E<br>n-3 fatty acids<br>High intakes of fruits/vegetables | Low vitamin A and folate intakes<br>High total fat intake<br>Low fibre intake |
| Cardiovascular Disease | Vitamins C, D & E<br>High dietary fibre intakes<br>Low intakes of saturated fats<br>Higher intakes of mono- and poly-unsaturated fats | Low folate intakes<br>High sodium intakes<br>High magnesium intakes<br>High iron intakes |
| Immunocompetence | Glutamine<br>n-3 fatty acids | Malnutrition<br>Zinc, copper, iron and selenium deficiencies<br>Vitamin A, $B_6$, C & E deficiencies |
| Osteoporosis | High calcium intakes<br>Magnesium, flouride, and vitamin C and D intakes | Low calcium intakes<br>High sodium and protein intakes |
| Anaemia | | Folate and vitamin $B_{12}$ deficiency<br>Copper deficiency |
| Cataract/Macular Degeneration | Antioxidants | |
| Diabetes | Chromium<br>Fibre, complex carbohydrate<br>Resistant starch<br>Monounsaturated fats | Low vitamin E |
| Bowel Health | n-3 fatty acids<br>Oligosaccharides | High intakes of fat & total protein |

## Medications - Nutrient Interactions

There are many nutrient-nutrient interactions such as the relationship between calcium intake, protein intake, vitamin D and sodium intake in the prevention or cause of osteoporosis. With up to 85% of older persons having at least one chronic medical condition, the aged population use more medications compared to younger persons. There also appears a high rate of chronic illness in aging athletes (primarily hypertension, asthma, coronary heart disease) and thus it is not surprising that up to 34% of masters athletes take medication (primarily cardiovascular, respiratory, non-steroidal anti-inflammatory). The purpose of the following section is to overview some of the important medication-nutrient interactions that may affect the health or performance of masters athletes.

The number of medications used is an important predictor of the adverse nutrient interactions occurring since the number of reactions increases exponentially with the number of drugs used. These interactions are further complicated by an age-related decrease in hormone function, prescribed dietary restrictions and the degenerative physiological changes that occur with aging. While prescribing drugs with a meal is an effective means of reminding older persons to take their medication, the interaction of food and drug may not maximise absorption of either. For example, cholesterol-controlling drugs may change gastrointestinal tract motility or antacids may alter the pH within the same tract.

Certain drugs can affect nutritional status and may lead to over- or under-nutrition. Table 16.12 summarises the major medication-nutrient interactions that may affect older athletes. In summary, nutritional status can be affected by a decrease or increase in appetite, malabsorption of nutrients, stimulation of basal metabolic rate, and changes in the glycemic level of food. Given the complexity of the drug-nutrient interaction, it is important that the masters athlete work closely with a health professional to maximise both nutrient and drug effectiveness.

*Table 16.12:* The major medication-nutrient interactions that may affect older athletes and their nutrient status.

| Drug | Effect | Nutrients affected |
|---|---|---|
| Diuretics (e.g. *Aldactone, Chlotoride, Lasix*) | Alterations in renal tubular function | Loss of sodium, potassium and magnesium |
| Antipsycarbohydratetic / psycarbohydrateactives | Disinterest in food | Protein and calories intake reduced |
| Cardiac glycosides (e.g. *Digoxin*) | Anorexia, nausea, vomiting, disinterest in food | Protein and calories intake reduced |
| Anticonvulsants (e.g. *Phenytoin, Dilantin, Phenobarbitone*) | Induction of liver enzymes<br><br>Reduced absorption of folic acid | Altered vitamin D metabolism<br>Folic acid |
| Salicyclate (e.g. *Aspirin, Voltaren, Nurofen, Orudis*) | Gastrointestinal blood loss | Iron deficiency |
| Corticosteroids (e.g. *Prednisone, Prednisolone, Cortisone*) | Inhibition of calcium absorption, alterations in glucose metabolism and electrolyte imablance<br><br>Increased excretion of vitamin C | Calcium imbalance (osteoporosis), hyperglycemia, sodium retention and potassium deficiency<br>Vitamin C |
| Antacids | Decreased absorption of phosphate | Phosphate |
| Tetracycline | Increased excretion of vitamin C | Vitamin C |
| Bile acid sequesters | Malabsorption of fat-soluble vitamins | Vitamins A, D, E and K |
| Mineral oil laxatives (e.g. *Agarol*) | Inhibition of fat-soluble vitamins absorption<br>Depletion of Potassium | Vitamins A, D, E and K malabsorption<br>Potassium |

## Supplementation

It is well recognised that physically active people eating well-balanced diets and following the recommended dietary guidelines (e.g. Table 16.13) may not need to take vitamin supplements. Moreover, most experts agree there is little harm in taking multivitamin / multimineral capsule(s) containing the recommended quantity of each vitamin or mineral, particularly in those with marginal intakes. However, it is important to recognise that a number of negative side effects, including adverse effects on the immune system, can present not only by deficiencies but also excessive intakes of certain nutrients.

Athletes in physical training tend to increase food and energy intake and thus meet carbohydrate, fat, protein and vitamin and mineral recommendations. Moreover, vitamin and mineral supplementation appears to have no effect on performance when standard dietary guidelines are met. However, supplementation may be recommended in masters athletes with low energy intakes, high energy outputs or excessive sweat losses, specific diseases affecting micronutrient requirements, a diagnosed micronutrient deficiency, or with poor dietary practices.

Research suggests that up to 60 % of older persons have been reported to use supplements on a daily basis. It also appears that the majority of elderly supplement users are more health conscious and physically active than non-users, and that the more active individuals aged 68-90 years were vitamin supplement users. These findings are similar to those observed in studies examining supplement use in younger athletes. It might be suggested that a daily multivitamin/mineral supplement that provides no more than 100% of the RDA may be recommended for aging exercisers involved in regular physical training. Furthermore, it is suggested that single-nutrient supplements should be limited to calcium, iron and zinc and vitamins $B_6$, $B_{12}$, D and E depending on an individual's risk for certain diseases and food consumption patterns.

Only recently have a couple of studies examined supplement use in older athletes. A German study examined supplement use in 598 male and female masters athletes competing in the World Masters Indoor Athletic Championships in 2004. They observed that 60.5% of all participants used supplements with the predominant substances being vitamins (35.4%) and minerals (29.9%). In contrast to younger elite athletes who use such supplements for performance enhancement, the masters athletes in this study used these substances predominantly for health reasons that were linked to health professional's advice. Other findings of interest from this study were that:

- only 0.4% used illicit drugs or doping substances
- supplement users tended to train with a higher frequency than non-users
- supplement users compared to non-users showed no differences for age, gender, family status, education, disciplines, training years, or use of alcohol

The most frequent reasons for using supplements included injuries (25.5%), health reasons (19.9%), success in sports (18.3%), increased endurance and performance (17.3%), and increased strength (10.3%).

## Summary

Nutritional recommendations for older athletes must consider the following important factors:

1. Age-related changes in physiology
2. Dietary changes that occur with exercise
3. Type of exercise (power, endurance)
4. Training volumes (frequency, intensity, duration)
5. Presence of chronic illness or disease
6. Nutrient-medication interactions
7. Goals of the older athlete (competitive, health and fitness or recreational).

In summary, it appears the small amount of available research examining the nutritional practices of older athletes or exercising older adults suggest the need for older athletes to monitor and possibly supplement vitamins $B_6$, $B_{12}$, D and E and the minerals calcium, iron and zinc. Apart from the need to possibly focus on dietary intakes or supplementation of these nutrients, there are a number of risk factors that may make the aging athlete at risk of dietary inadequacy. These include:

- Poverty
- Social isolation
- Depression
- Use of multiple drugs
- Surgical procedures
- Acute or chronic illness
- Disability
- Bereavement
- Dementia
- Alcoholism
- Oral health problems
- Institutionalisation

Moreover, aging athletes should become aware of guidelines such as the *Dietary Guidelines for Older Australians* (Table 16.13) that emphasise the need for maintaining energy balance through selection of a wide variety of foods high in vegetables (including legumes) and fruit, cereals, breads and pastas and low in saturated fat.

Now that we have examined the dietary needs and concerns of aging athletes, let us turn our attention to the general and specific guidelines related to issues pertaining to sports nutrition in athletes of any age.

*Table 16.13:* The Dietary Guidelines for Older Australians typical of those throughout the world and designed to assist older adults maintain and promote healthy eating habits.

| |
|---|
| 1. Enjoy a wide variety of nutritious foods |
| 2. Keep active to maintain muscle strength and a healthy body weight |
| 3. Eat plenty of vegetables (including legumes) and fruit |
| 4. Eat plenty of cereals, breads and pastas |
| 5. Eat a diet low in saturated fat |
| 6. Drink adequate amounts of water and/or other fluids |
| 7. If you drink alcohol, limit your intake |
| 8. Eat carbohydrate foods low in salt and use salt sparingly |
| 9. Include foods high in calcium |
| 10. Use added sugars in moderation |
| 11. Eat at least three meals every day |
| 12. Care for your food: prepare and store it correctly |

The fundamental difference between an athlete's diet and that of the general population are that athletes require additional fluid to cover sweat losses and additional energy to fuel training and competing. In summary, the *Joint Position Statement on Nutrition and Athletic Performance* developed by the American College of Sports Medicine, American Dietetic Association and Dieticians of Canada in 2009 (http://www.ms-se.com/pt/pt-core/template-journal/msse/media/0309nutrition.pdf) suggest that athletes should:

- Athletes need to consume adequate energy during periods of high-intensity and/or long-duration training to maintain body weight and health and maximize training effects.
- Carbohydrate recommendations for athletes range from 6 to 10 g/kg body weight/day (2.7–4.5 g/lb body weight/day)
- Protein recommendations for endurance and strength-trained athletes range from 1.2 to 1.7 g/kg body weight/day (0.5–0.8 g/lb body weight/day). These recommended protein intakes can generally be met through diet alone, without the use of protein or amino acid supplements. Energy intake sufficient to maintain body weight is necessary for optimal protein use and performance.
- Fat intake should range from 20% to 35% of total energy intake. Consuming ≤20% of energy from fat does not benefit performance. Fat, which is a source of energy, fat-soluble vitamins, and essential fatty acids, is important in the diets of athletes. High-fat diets are not recommended for athletes.
- Athletes who restrict energy intake or use severe weight-loss practices, eliminate one or more food groups from their diet, or consume high- or low carbohydrate diets of low micronutrient density are at greatest risk of micronutrient deficiencies. Athletes should consume diets that provide at least the recommended dietary allowance (RDA)

- for all micronutrients.
- Before exercise, a meal or snack should provide sufficient fluid to maintain hydration, be relatively low in fat and fibre to facilitate gastric emptying and minimize gastrointestinal distress, be relatively high in carbohydrate to maximize maintenance of blood glucose, be moderate in protein, be composed of familiar foods, and be well tolerated by the athlete.
- During exercise, primary goals for nutrient consumption are to replace fluid losses and provide carbohydrates (approximately 30–60 g/hr) for maintenance of blood glucose levels. These nutrition guidelines are especially important for endurance events lasting longer than an hour when the athlete has not consumed adequate food or fluid before exercise or when the athlete is exercising in an extreme environment (heat, cold, or high altitude).
- After exercise, dietary goals are to provide adequate fluids, electrolytes, energy, and carbohydrates to replace muscle glycogen and ensure rapid recovery. A carbohydrate intake of approximately 1.0–1.5 g/kg body weight (0.5–0.7 g/lb) during the first 30 min and again every 2 h for 4–6 h will be adequate to replace glycogen stores. Protein consumed after exercise will provide amino acids for building and repair of muscle tissue.
- In general, no vitamin and mineral supplements are required if an athlete is consuming adequate energy from a variety of foods to maintain body weight. Supplementation recommendations unrelated to exercise, such as folic acid for women of childbearing potential, should be followed. A multivitamin/mineral supplement may be appropriate if an athlete is dieting, habitually eliminating foods or food groups, is ill or recovering from injury, or has a specific micronutrient deficiency. Single-nutrient supplements may be appropriate for a specific medical or nutritional reason (e.g. iron supplements to correct iron deficiency anaemia).
- Vegetarian athletes may be at risk for low intakes of energy, protein, fat, and key micronutrients such as iron, calcium, vitamin D, riboflavin, zinc, and vitamin B12. Consultation with a sports dietician is recommended to avoid these nutrition problems.

## Is Your Diet Fit For Sports Performance?

The following dietary quiz may help you focus more on the dietary needs as an athlete.

| Eating Patterns | |
|---|---|
| I eat at least three meals a day with no longer than 5 hours in between | Yes/No |
| **Carbohydrate Checker** | |
| I eat at least 4 slices of bread each day (1 roll = 2 slices of bread) | Yes/No |
| I eat at least 1 cup of breakfast cereal each day or an extra slice of bread | Yes/No |
| I usually eat 2 or more pieces of fruit each day | Yes/No |
| I eat at least 3 different vegetables or have a salad most days | Yes/No |
| I include carbohydrates like pasta, rice, and potato in my diet each day | Yes/No |
| **Protein Checker** | |
| I eat at least 1 and usually 2 serves of meat or meat alternatives (poultry, seafood, eggs, dried peas/beans or nuts) each day | Yes/No |
| **Fat Checker** | |
| I spread butter or margarine thinly on bread or use none at all | Yes/No |
| I eat fried food no more than once per week | Yes/No |
| I use polyunsaturated or mono-unsaturated oil (canola or olive) for cooking *(say yes if you never fry in oil or fat)* | Yes/No |
| I avoid oil-based dressings in salads | Yes/No |
| I use reduced fat or low fat dairy products | Yes/No |
| I cut the fat off meat and take skin off chicken | Yes/No |
| I eat fatty snacks such as chocolate, chips, biscuits or rich deserts/cakes etc. no more than twice per week | Yes/No |
| I eat fast or take-away food no more than once per week | Yes/No |
| **Iron Checker** | |
| I eat lean red meat at least 3 times per week or 2 servings of white meat daily or for vegetarians, include at least 1-2 cups of dried peas and beans (e.g. lentils, soy beans, chick peas) daily | Yes/No |
| I include a vitamin C source with meals based on bread, cereals, fruit and vegetables to assist the iron absorption in these 'plant' sources of iron | Yes/No |
| **Calcium Checker** | |
| I eat at least 3 serves of dairy food or soy milk alternative each day (1 serves = 200 ml milk or fortified soy milk; 1 slice (30 gm) hard cheese; 200 gm yoghurt) | Yes/No |
| **Fluids** | |
| I drink fluids regularly before, during and after exercise | Yes/No |
| **Alcohol** | |
| When I drink alcohol, I would mostly drink no more than is recommended for the safe drink driving limit *(say yes if you don't drink alcohol)* | Yes/No |

Score a point for every "yes" answer. The scoring scale is:

- 18-20   Excellent
- 15-17   Room for improvement
- 12-14   Just made it
- 0-12    Poor

Very active people will need to eat more breads, cereals and fruit than on this quiz, but to stay healthy no one should be eating less.

## The Glycemic Index and Masters Athletes

Most aging athletes are aware that eating a diet high in carbohydrates is important for good health, training and race performance, and recovery between training sessions or after events. What many may not know is that there is now more to the humble carbohydrate than meets the eye. Historically we looked at carbohydrates in terms of complex and simple carbohydrates. Sport and exercise science now looks at them in terms of their *glycemic index*.

## The Glycemic Index

The *glycemic index* (GI) is a number system of measuring how fast 50 gm of a carbohydrate food triggers a rise in circulating blood sugar relative to 50gm of glucose. The higher the number (up to 100), the greater the blood glucose response to the food. Thus, a low GI food will cause a small rise in blood glucose, while a high GI food will trigger a sharp rise (see Figure 16.1). You can also apply the GI to mixed meals or snacks by taking a weighted average based on the energy content (Calories/kilojoules) of each food that makes up the meal.

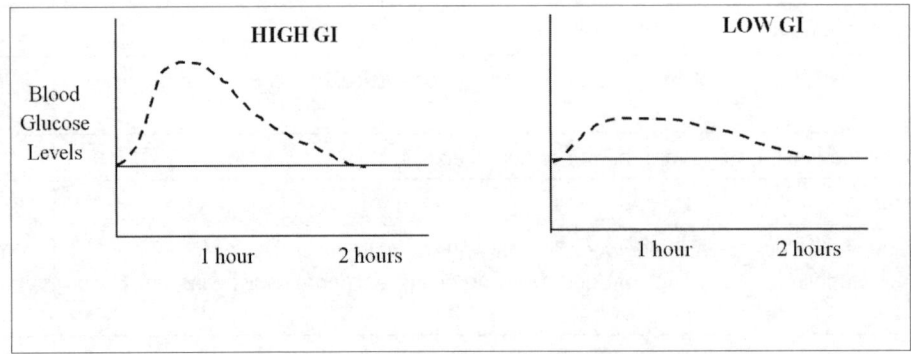

*Figure 16.1:* Blood glucose response to consuming 50gm of glucose showing the effects of both a high and low glycemic index food on blood glucose levels.

For pre-event meals, it makes sense that low to moderate GI foods are suggested to allow a slow release of glucose during the race. In contrast, in the 30 minutes or so after training or racing, a high GI food is suggested as it triggers a sharp rise in blood glucose that in turn triggers a sharp rise in insulin that then, with the advantage of glucose-carrying blood still flowing to the muscles that did the work, will push glucose into those tired muscles to replace the glycogen (storage form of carbohydrate) used in training or racing.

*Table 16.14:* High, moderate and low glycemic index foods and their actual GI score.

| | Food | GI (Glucose = 100) |
|---|---|---|
| **High GI (>70)** | Sports Drink | 95 |
| | Rice (low amylose) | 88 |
| | Baked potato | 85 |
| | Cornflakes | 84 |
| | Instant mashed potato | 83 |
| | Jelly beans | 80 |
| | Cocopops | 77 |
| | Honey | 73 |
| | Watermelon | 72 |
| | Weetbix | 70 |
| | White bread | 70 |
| | Wholemeal bread | 69 |
| **Moderate GI** | Muesli | 68 |
| | Soft drink | 68 |
| | One-minute oats | 67 |
| | Arrowroot biscuit | 66 |
| | Sugar | 65 |
| | Muffins | 62 |
| | Porridge | 61 |
| | Ice cream | 61 |
| | Ripe banana | 61 |
| **Low GI (<55)** | Mangoes | 55 |
| | Baked beans | 48 |
| | Mixed grain bread | 45 |
| | Orange | 43 |
| | All Bran | 42 |
| | Pasta | 41 |
| | Apple | 36 |
| | Flavoured yoghurt | 33 |
| | Milk | 2 |

## Pre-Event Nutrition Strategies

There is no doubt that a pre-event meal 1-4 hours prior to an event should be high in carbohydrate food and drink, particularly if the athlete has low carbohydrate stores due to prior events or training or if the event is long and/or hard. In general, low to moderate GI foods are suggested for pre-event meals. Why? If the foods were high GI, the rise in insulin would be high. This elevated insulin level suppresses the breakdown and use of fat as a fuel that in turn increases glucose demand and usage at a time when we are wanting to save the carbohydrate for the event.

Despite the popular belief that carbohydrate in the hour before exercise should be avoided, the majority of research suggests there is no negative effect of such a practice in most athletes. However, as always, athletes should try their own pre-event strategy in training. In any case, ensure that the carbohydrate-rich food used is low GI. The following guidelines must be considered when planning your pre-event meal:

- Be taken 1-4 hours before depending on personal preferences, experience and event intensity, length and starting time. The closer the meal to the event, the smaller the meal.
- 200-300 grams of carbohydrate for meals 3-4 hours before exercise have been shown to enhance performance
- Include fluids (400-600 ml)
- Low in fat and fibre to help stomach and intestine emptying and minimise gut upsets
- Be familiar foods
- High in carbohydrate to maintain blood glucose and maximise muscle and liver glycogen stores
- Be moderate in protein
- Know what works and doesn't work for you and practice the planned strategy before the major goal.

Examples of pre-event meals might include:
- Cereal with low-fat milk and fruit
- Bread, toast, muffins or crumpets with jam, honey or banana
- Pancakes with honey, jam or syrup
- Pasta or rice with low-fat topping
- Rice cakes or bread rolls with banana
- Sports bars
- Commercial liquid meal supplement
- Creamed rice
- Fruit salad and yoghurt

In the 1-3 days leading up to a major endurance event or series of matches at a tournament, the following pre-event tips are suggested in order to maximise the levels of carbohydrates within muscle and liver:

- Increase carbohydrate intake three days out
- Spread the intake of carbohydrate foods and drinks over smaller and more frequent meals or snacks
- Reduce fat and protein intake to leave more room for the carbohydrates

- Increase fluid intake as carbohydrate need water to be stored
- Avoid alcohol in the 24-48 hours leading up to the event

For the long distance endurance athlete (e.g. marathoner, Olympic distance or longer triathletes, ultra distance athlete), the principle of *carbohydrate loading* might be considered. Any of the recommended methods below have been shown to significantly increase the body's normal stores of muscle carbohydrate above normal levels. I personally have used the depletion method referred to in Table 16.15 below for years with none of the negative side-effects (irritability, fatigue) often mentioned with this method. Sports scientists from the University of Western Australia developed the recent method below. It requires high intensity endurance and sprint work close to the day of competition and would only be recommended for endurance athletes used to training at very high intensity.

*Table 16.15:* Variety of carbohydrate loading methods used before major endurance events or for team players playing in lengthy carnivals or championships.

| Day | Method 1 (Classic Depletion) | Method 2 (More Common) | Method 3 (Recent) |
|---|---|---|---|
| 1 | Depletion exercise (long and/or hard) | Optional depletion exercise | Normal diet<br>Normal training |
| 2 | High fat/protein diet<br>Low carbohydrate<br>Tapering exercise | Mixed diet<br>Moderate carbohydrate<br>Tapering exercise | Normal diet<br>Normal training |
| 3 | High fat/protein diet<br>Low carbohydrate<br>Tapering exercise | Mixed diet<br>Moderate carbohydrate<br>Tapering exercise | Normal diet<br>Normal training |
| 4 | High fat/protein diet<br>Low carbohydrate<br>Tapering exercise | Mixed diet<br>Moderate carbohydrate<br>Tapering exercise | Normal diet<br>Normal training |
| 5 | High carbohydrate<br>Tapering exercise | High carbohydrate<br>Tapering exercise | Normal diet<br>Normal training |
| 6 | High carbohydrate<br>Tapering exercise | High carbohydrate<br>Tapering exercise or rest | Normal diet<br>Normal training |
| 7 | High carbohydrate<br>Tapering exercise | High carbohydrate<br>Tapering exercise or rest | Depleting exercise (3 minutes hard)<br>High GI and high carbohydrate (90%) diet |
| 8 | Competition | Competition | Competition |

### During Event Nutrition Strategies

A number of research studies have conclusively shown that eating or drinking carbohydrate during exercise longer than 60 minutes in duration will improve performance. In athletes that train in the morning after not eating overnight and depleting their liver carbohydrate stores (this provides the energy needed by your body overnight), such a practice is strongly recommended. The longer the event, the more important eating or drinking carbohydrate becomes to maintain the blood glucose levels and improve performance. For athletes who have not carbohydrate loaded, consumed a pre-exercise meal or are dieting to lose fat weight, taking in carbohydrates during exercise is even more important.

Research has also shown that the maximum rate at which carbohydrate can be used as a fuel is 60 grams of carbohydrate per hour of exercise (approximately 0.7 gm carbohydrate/kg body weight/hour). This is the reason why sports drinks that contain 6 grams of carbohydrate per 100 ml (what we call 6%) are suggested consumed at 250 ml every 15 minutes or one litre per hour – this delivers 60 grams of carbohydrate. Taking any more carbohydrate in has been shown to lead to gut upsets and slow fluid uptake in the gut, not a good thing when fluids might be crucial.

If carbohydrate is the priority during an event, then a high GI food or drink with high GI food makes sense. If not, then sports bars, gels or fluids that deliver the optimal amount of carbohydrate (30-60grams/hourr) are suggested. The higher the exercise intensity, the greater the carbohydrate intake need. The form of carbohydrate does not appear to be important so sucrose, glucose, maltodextrins, are suggested but research suggests avoid fructose (and thus fruits) during exercise as this sugar has been linked to gut upsets and slower glucose release.

Thus, in summary, the following guidelines are suggested for nutrition during exercise:
- Start shortly after starting exercise (15-20 minutes)
- Focus on glucose with a mixture of other sugars
- Sports drink or gels with water (to get 4-8 grams with 100 ml water) are optimal
- The higher the intensity, the greater the amount of carbohydrate needed
- Maintain fluids at 150-350 ml/hour depending on fluid losses.

## After Exercise Nutritional Recovery Strategies

It takes 90 -180 minutes of continuous exercise at a slow to fast pace to deplete the body's carbohydrate stores. However, muscle carbohydrate can also be depleted after only 15-30 minutes of very high intensity training such as interval work or speed work. It can take up to 24 hours to replace these stores. Thus, for athletes training hard twice a day or for athletes doing a number of consecutive hard days, there is a need to replenish the carbohydrate stores prior to the next training session or event.

Research has shown that muscle carbohydrate is remade at about 5 units per kilogram of muscle per hour. On the assumption that a muscle topped-up with carbohydrate contains about 100 units per kilogram of muscle, it takes about 20 hours to completely recover the hungry muscle's stores. This has strong implications for athletes that train twice daily or trains in the afternoon and then goes again the next morning. This research strongly suggests the need to have an easy session following or before the hard one where fats become the primary fuel and muscles have a chance to recharge their carbohydrate tanks.

After training or racing, athletes need to consume carbohydrate that can be very quickly converted to blood glucose and then transported in the blood to the muscles. To help us get the carbohydrate quickly into the blood and to the muscles, carbohydrates with a high GI are recommended (see Table 16.14). The high GI foods should also be combined with fluid intake since it takes about 3 grams of water to store 1 gram of carbohydrate in a muscle.

Three dietary factors dictate the rate of carbohydrate rebuilding in muscle after training or racing.

1. *Rate of carbohydrate intake.* Sport scientists recommend an intake of about 1.2-1.5 gram per kilogram of body weight per hour every thirty minutes for up to 4-5 hours to recover carbohydrate stores.

2. *Type of carbohydrate.* High to moderate GI foods appear equally effective for carbohydrate recovery over the longer term with high GI preferred immediately after training or racing. Research also suggests that carbohydrate in liquid or solid moderate-to-high GI form is equally effective as solids. However, if fluids are needed after a session of high sweat rates, then the fluid forms are the recommended alternative. Sports drinks, soft drinks, and cordials fit this bill. Taking the carbohydrate with up to 6 grams of protein also appears to enhance recovery and muscle repair.

3. *Timing of the carbohydrate intake.* During the first two hours after a workout, the rate of muscle carbohydrate rebuilding is 7-8% per hour with some suggestion that this rate is even higher in the 30 minutes following exercise. This indicates the need to eat or drink moderate-to-high GI foods or fluids straight away after training or competing. If you're like me and can't eat straight away after training, then drink a sports drink, cordial or soft drink. As above, these high-moderate GI foods should be taken at the rate of 1.2-1.5 gram per kilogram of body weight per hour for up to 4-5 hours until the next large meal where low to moderate GI foods are the go for health reasons because such a meal will (hopefully!) contain vitamins and minerals.

Finally, apart from all the obvious sports performance benefits of the GI, research has recently shown that low to moderate GI foods are closely linked to lower rates of cardiovascular disease and lowered risk to certain forms of cancer. Thus, for aging athletes, such foods will not only benefit sport performance but health as well.

### Table 16.6: Recommended Websites for Sports Nutrition

- http://www.americanheart.org/presenter.jhtml?identifier=3004604 is a page within the American Heart Association's webpage and has numerous health-related information regarding healthy lifestyle and nutrition-related issues.

- http://www.americanheart.org/presenter.jhtml?identifier=851 contains the most recent American Heart Association Dietary Guidelines.

- http://www.health.gov/dietaryguidelines/ contains the most recent dietary guidelines for Americans developed by the Department of Health and Human Services (HHS )and the Department of Agriculture (USDA).

- http://www.acsm-msse.org contains the Joint Position Statement on Nutrition and Athletic Performance jointly developed by the American College of Sports Medicine, American Dietetic Association and Dieticians of Canada in 2008. It can also be found at: http://www.eatright.org/ which is the home of the American Dietetic Association

- http://www.ausport.gov.au/ais/nutrition that is the home of the Australian Institute of Sport Sports Nutrition Group. An excellent page with numerous resources and links.

- http://www.sportsdietitians.com/ is the home page of Sports Dieticians Australia. It has some excellent fact sheets available online and a search engine to find a sports dietician near you if you live in Australia.

- http://www.glycemicindex.com/ is the homepage of the leading research group in Australia examining the role of the GI in both sports performance and health. It has large database in which to check the GI value of all foods.

- http://www.gssiweb.com is the homepage of the Gatorade Sports Science Institute. It has an excellent range of articles relating to sports performance and good health and an easy-to-use search engine.

# CHAPTER 17

## WEIGHT CONTROL AND THE MASTERS ATHLETE

*Perhaps no one realizes how important a good diet has been for me. I can't describe how important it is. You go along for years weighing too much. Then you change your diet, you start feeling good and you don't even mind looking in the mirror. Gradually, you rise to a different physical and mental level. It reflects on all your life, not just on your ability as an athlete.*

**Jack Nicklaus**


*Nature is a wonderful teacher.
When we put on weight, she pushes us further away from the table.*

**Anonymous**


*He must have had a magnificent build
before his own stomach went in for a career of its own.*

**Margaret Halsey**


### Introduction

As an aging athlete, one of the hardest things I find is to control my waistline. I'm not alone in this regard. Recent research suggests that 38% of men in their early 20s are overweight with this number jumping to 76% of men aged 45-64 years being overweight but dropping after 65 years, most likely due to the overweight men having died of heart disease and other obesity-related diseases. Sadly, the same research suggests that by the year 2015, 80% of all males may be overweight. Obviously, for an aging athlete, maintaining weight by controlling body fat levels, is crucial for not only sports performance reasons but also general health and well-being.

For body weight to be maintained, energy intake (Calories or kilojoules consumed) must equal the energy expended. If an athlete is trying to increase body weight, energy intake must exceed energy expenditure. Conversely, if an athlete wants to reduce body weight, energy output must exceed energy intake. Although a number of popular diets (high-protein/high fat, low carbohydrate diets) claim to induce body weight loss by altering the diet's composition, body weight will not be lost unless the energy value (kilojoules or Calories) of the food and fluids taken in is less than that expended, regardless of what diet we use.

While alterations in energy intake or energy expenditure are the primary determinants of body weight, changes in the types and amounts of fat, protein, carbohydrate and alcohol and the usage of these energy sources must be managed for long-term weight maintenance. Interestingly, under normal physiological conditions, protein, carbohydrate and alcohol are not easily converted to fat. What happens is that by increasing their intake, we increase their use as an energy source within the body and in doing so, burn them up. However, when it comes to fat intake, an increase in dietary fat does not mean an immediate increase in its use as a fuel. Thus, excess fat intake will mean increased storage as body fat. Thus, the type of food we eat can influence the amount of energy intake and expenditure each day.

Let's look at the basic biochemistry and physiology of each of the major nutrients we eat or drink:

1. *Carbohydrate.* The balance of carbohydrate (CHO) in the body is regulated so that the amount of carbohydrate taken in matches the amount used in a day. Importantly for athletes, taking in CHO stimulates glycogen (solid CHO) storage in muscles and liver and the use of glucose as a fuel. It also inhibits the use of fat as a fuel. The conversion of excess CHO to fat tissue is very limited in normal-weight people. However, if large amounts of CHO (>85% of daily energy intake) are consumed over several consecutive days and total energy intake exceeds energy expenditure, the excess CHO will be stored as fat.

2. *Protein.* As with CHO, the body adjusts to excess protein intake by burning it off as an energy source if any excess protein intake is not used for body growth, repair and body maintenance. The adequacy of total energy intake and CHO intake in particular, seem to affect this process. Too little energy intake overall, or too little CHO intake, result in a negative protein balance with protein being used as an energy source rather than for its major role as a body builder and repairer. Conversely, if energy and CHO intake are too high, protein as an energy source is reduced. Once the body has used the protein it needs for growth, repair and maintenance, any excess is then converted to fat. Sport scientists and sport dieticians recommend between 20-25% (1.5-2.0 gm/kg body weight) of daily energy intake be protein. Apart from its requirement for growth and repair, protein has been shown to increase the energy used in digestion and makes us feel full. However, too much of it can lead to a higher fat intake (the two are often together in foods such as meat), increased calcium loss and stress on the kidney as the kidney tries to excrete end products of protein breakdown.

3. *Fat.* Fat balance isn't as precisely regulated as CHO and protein. As the intake of fat increases, there is not a proportionate increase in its use as an energy fuel. Thus, excess intake of fat leads to increased storage and thus excess body fat. Importantly, fat is also an energy dense fuel with 9 Calories of energy for every gram consumed whereas CHO and protein have 4-5 Calories per gram. This means fat is a great store of energy but no good on the energy intake side of the body weight equation.

4. *Alcohol.* Drinking a few (or many!) quiet (or loud!) ones will cause a rapid rise in the

use of alcohol as an energy source until it is cleared from the body via the liver. It is used preferentially as an energy source over either fat, CHO or protein. Excess alcohol cannot be converted to fat or glycogen but in heavy drinkers may contribute to fat storage by preventing the burning up of fat as an energy source. It can also contribute greatly to overall energy intake because it contains 7 Calories of energy per gram.

## Body Composition and Normal Aging

The typical patterns of body composition changes seen in your normal aging person are summarised in Table 17.1.

*Table 17.1:* Body composition changes with aging and implications for exercise recommendations.

| Body Compartment | Age-Related Change | Exercise Recommended |
| --- | --- | --- |
| Body fat | • Fat mass ↑<br>• Internal fat deposits ↑<br>• Body trunk fat deposits ↑ | Aerobic or weight training |
| Skeletal muscle | • Muscle mass ↓<br>• Fast twitch fibre number ↓<br>• Fast twitch fibre size ↓<br>• Intramuscular fat/connective tissue ↑ | Weight training, speed training, weight/speed training, aerobic or weight training |
| Bone | • Bone density ↓<br>• Bone strength ↓ | Weight-bearing aerobic training, weight training and high impact, high velocity loading of affected sites |

The extent to which these changes occur are dependent upon genetics, lifestyle (nutritional and exercise habits), and disease-related factors that are all inter-related. However, these changes appear most greatly affected by how active a person remains with more active people being less fat and more able to maintain muscle and bone mass. For example, a classic 1999 United States study (called the Fels Longitudinal Study) has followed 102 men and 108 women with an average age of 53 years over a 20-year period and observed the following:

- Decreased muscle mass and height in aging men and women
- A direct relationship between physical activity levels, body weight and body fat in men
- A direct relationship between physical activity levels, body fat and increased muscle mass in women
- Postmenopausal women had higher body fat than pre or peri-menopausal women
- The longer the time since menopause, the greater the increases in body weight and body fat

## Body Composition of Masters Athletes

A classic 1997 study by Dr Michael Pollock and his colleagues from Florida in the United States followed 21 older (70±9 years) endurance athletes over a 20-year period. They divided the group of athletes into three groups according to how hard they continued to train – high, moderate and low. The major findings were:

- Height decreased in all groups by about 2.5 cm.
- Total body weight remained constant for the high and moderate intensity groups but increased in the low intensity group.
- Body fat in each group increased 3-5%.
- Waist circumference increased by about 5 cm in the group as a whole but was most obvious in the low intensity group.

The percent body fat of these older endurance athletes (10-15%) has been shown to be greater than elite younger endurance runners (5-7%) but significantly lower than that observed in age-matched non-athletes (20-24%). Importantly, 16 of the 21 athletes were weight training to help maintain strength and muscle mass. The results of this study showed that these athletes better maintained their muscle mass compared to the 5 athletes who did no weight training.

## Weight Control and Exercise

Fat loss can be achieved by restricting how much energy we take in and increasing how much energy we use up. Research has shown that decreases in total body fat and abdominal fat deposits, together with increased bone density, are achieved by both aerobic exercise and weight training while significant changes in total body fat are best achieved by these activities combined with an energy-restricted diet. What this means is that we can lose about 5% of our total body fat but about a 25% decrease in tummy fat. This is great news for getting rid of that tummy. Not only for appearances sake but also disease prevention given that abdominal fat has been linked to most chronic diseases including diabetes, cardiovascular disease, and high blood pressure.

For masters athletes wanting to lose or control body fat and improve that PB or win a gold, it is also important to hold on to or develop muscle mass. This is only achieved by weight training. Weight training also has the added benefits of helping to prevent diabetes, increase the resting metabolic rate that helps burn energy without doing any exercise, reducing the risk of falls and fractures in the very old athlete, and keeping us functionally independent into old age. All good news for those of us like me who dread ending up in a nursing home!

## The Energy Balance

Weight gain is caused by an imbalance between energy intake (food and drink) and energy expenditure (activity) (Figure 17.1). Although many factors contribute to individual differences in metabolism, it has been estimated that, at the population level, weight gain is caused by a modest positive energy balance. At the individual level, the amounts of physical activity needed to prevent weight gain, and to lose weight, vary considerably.

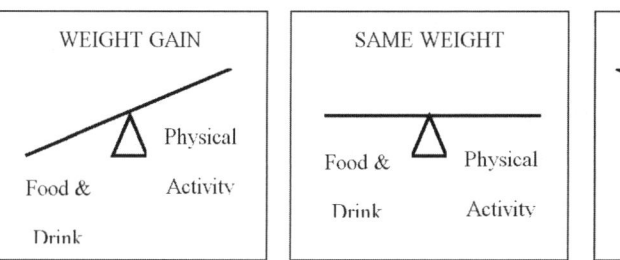

*Figure 17.1:* The effect of exercise and food and drink on body weight.

## Daily Energy Intake

In the United States, regular National Health and Nutrition Examination Surveys (NHANES) are carried out to examine physical activity, dietary habits and other health activity patterns of normal North Americans. These surveys have conclusively shown that there is a substantial decline in food intake with advancing age. For example, the third NHANES showed that between the ages of 25 and 70 years, energy intake decreases by as much as 1000 to 1200 Calories/day for men and 600 to 800 Calories/day for women. By age 80, 1 in 10 men consumed less than 890 Calories/day and 1 in 10 women less than 750 Calories/day. These low energy intakes can lead to inadequate intakes of protein, vitamins and minerals. Indeed, the NHANES III data showed that protein, zinc, calcium, and thiamine, riboflavin, vitamins $B_6$, $B_{12}$, and E intakes were below the recommended daily allowances in older people.

Athletes of all ages require energy to maintain normal metabolism and provide energy for working muscles when training or competing. Physical training (aerobic/speed/weight training) has been shown to increase energy requirements and maintain muscle energy utilising muscle mass in previously sedentary older people.

The same observations have been made in aging athletes. A number of studies have shown that aging athletes have higher energy intakes than age-matched non-athletes. For example, while the *National Research Council* suggests an energy intake of 2,300 Calories/day (9.6 MJ/day) for males and 1,900 Calories/day (7.9 MJ/day) for females over the age of 51 years, energy intakes of between 10,336 and 11,549 kJ/day (2,500-2,750 Calories/day) have been reported for older male endurance athletes 55-75 years of age and 8,663 kJ/day (2,060 Calories/day) for 65-84 year old female endurance athletes training at least one hour per day.

The reported energy intakes of aging athletes are lower than those observed in similarly-trained younger athletes. This may be due to an age-related decrease in active muscle mass, reduced training volumes and intensities commonly observed in aging athletes, or reduced leisure time activity levels commonly observed in older people.

## Daily Energy Expenditure

Daily energy expenditure declines progressively throughout adult life. For example, a research study measured total daily energy expenditure measured over a 10-day period in 35 youngsters (22.7±0.6 years) and compared it with that of 35 older non-athletes (68.0±1.5 years). The researchers found that the daily energy expenditure of the youngsters was 14.5 MJ/day while that of the elder statesmen was 11.3±5.4 MJ/day, a 22% difference. The researchers observed, as discussed below, significant age-related declines in the energy consumed in daily physical activity, resting metabolic rate, and the energy required for digestion. As in Figure 17.2 below, these three factors affect the total amount of energy (Calories or kilojoules) we expend in a day.

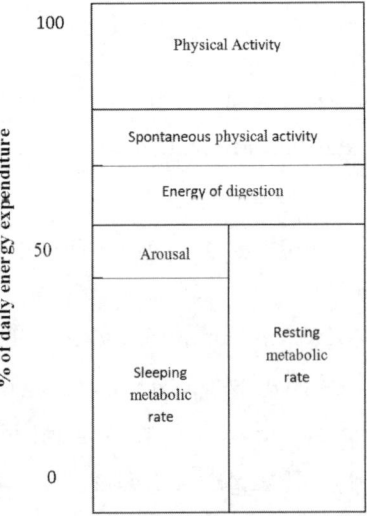

*Figure 17.2:* The major factors affecting total daily expenditure in healthy adults.

1. *Resting metabolic rate* is the energy required to maintain the body's systems and regulate the body temperature at rest. It is the main determinant of daily energy expenditure and accounts for between 60-80% of daily energy expenditure. In an active athlete, this percentage will vary greatly since many endurance athletes consume 4,100-8,300 kJ/day (1000-2000 Calories/day). Thus, in athletes young or old who train long and/or hard on a daily basis, resting metabolic rate (RMR) might only account for between 40-50% of daily energy expenditure. Indeed, RMR has been reported to be as low as 20% of daily energy expenditure on days of heavy competition such as long distance triathlons or ultra marathons. A number of factors have been shown to influence RMR and include:
   a. *Gender.* Men have a larger muscle mass which increases RMR
   b. *Body size.* The larger the body size, the higher the RMR
   c. *Muscle mass.* The larger the muscle mass, the greater the RMR. Hence, hypertrophy (muscle enlargement) weight training is great for people wanting to lose fat weight.
   d. *Genetics*
   e. *Menstrual cycle phase.* RMR is highest at end of the menstrual cycle
   f. *Training.* Can increase muscle mass and thus RMR. Strenuous exercise can cause

muscle damage that requires rebuilding and repair and thus consumes energy. Moreover, following training, the body keeps using oxygen and thus energy to return the body back to normal resting state. The longer and/or harder the training session, the greater the energy needed to return the body back to normal and thus the greater the energy consumed.

g. *Age*. RMR decreases by 10 to 20% with age due directly to an age-related decrease in lean body mass (muscle, bone, organs) that has been shown to decrease with age by about 15% between 30 and 80 years of age. This decreased RMR combined with a lower physical activity level is the major reason why older people increase their fat mass. Weight training that works to increase or maintain muscle mass will help preserve the muscle mass and thus influence the RMR. Importantly, the RMR of older athletes is higher than non-athletes, even though they too lose muscle mass and should undertake weight training to hold on to muscle mass for both weight control and performance reasons. This finding of increased resting metabolic rate is particularly noticeable in older weight-trained and/or endurance athletes who train hard.

A number of equations have been developed over the years to estimate RMR (Calories)

**Males: 66.47 + (13.75 x weight in kg) + (5 x height in cm) − (6.76 x age in yrs)**
**Females: 655.1 + (9.56 x weight in kg) + (1.85 x height in cm) − (4.68 x age in yrs)**

These equations were developed in 1919 and based on 239 people with an average age of 27±9 yr (men) and 33±14 yr (women), not an aging population. This equation has more recently been suggested to overestimate RMR by as much as 15%. In 1985, the World Health Organization (WHO) developed a series of equations to estimate RMR (Calories/day) for various age-groups. These are shown in Table 17.2 below.

*Table 17.2: World Health Organization* (WHO) equations to estimate Resting Metabolic Rate (Calories/day) for various age-groups.

| Age-Group (yr) | Males | Females |
|---|---|---|
| 10-18 | (17.5 x weight in kg) + 651 | (12.2 x weight in kg) + 746 |
| 18-30 | (15.3 x weight in kg) + 679 | (14.7 x weight in kg) + 496 |
| 30-60 | (11.6 x weight in kg) + 879 | (8.7 x weight in kg) + 829 |
| 60 + | (13.5 x weight in kg) + 487 | (10.5 x weight in kg) + 596 |

Recently, another equation has been developed for estimating RMR in young male athletes: RMR (Calories/day) = − 857 + (9 x weight t in kg) + 11.7 (height in cm). While it was developed in Italy on water polo players and martial artists, as long as it is used consistently like any of the equations mentioned above, it can give you a rough estimate of your RMR.

2. **Energy Cost of Physical activity**. The second major contributor to daily energy expenditure is physical activity. This is the most variable part of the daily energy

expenditure and includes the energy consumed doing the activities of daily living (e.g. dressing, cooking) and the energy cost of physical activity including training. It also includes the cost of spontaneous physical activity such as fidgeting. The energy of physical activity accounts for 10-15% of daily energy expenditure in non-exercisers, but can reach 50% in heavy trainers.

Research has conclusively shown that as we age, we undertake less physical activity. Even in older athletes this appears to be the case, since research has shown that older athletes train less often, for shorter durations, and with less intensity than they did as younger athletes. Moreover, masters athletes are more likely to be less active both in the workplace as they move into less physically demanding roles and at home where automation and other family members share the physical workload. In a recent review of the role of exercise in weight control of 60 plus year olds, Dutch researchers found, in contrast to what we know about younger people (20-50 years), no relationship between higher levels of physical activity and body weight, total energy expenditure or fat mass. That is, body fat levels appear the same in both older (> 60 years) exercisers and non-exercisers. However, when exercise levels are increased, body fat decreases and muscle mass increases as they do in younger people. Importantly, weight training appears to be more beneficial in that it increases energy burning muscle mass that increases resting metabolic rate.

3. *Energy cost of metabolising food.* The third major contributor to daily energy expenditure is the increase in energy expenditure that results from consuming food throughout a day. It includes the energy involved in food digestion, absorption, transport, metabolism and storage. It generally represents about 8-10% of daily energy expenditure and is generally slightly lower in women (6-7%).

Research on aging people suggests that they tend to eat less, which suggests that this component of the daily energy expenditure also decreases with age. A number of factors have been shown to influence the energy cost of metabolising food and include:

a. *Energy content of the meal.* The higher energy content (Calories or kilojoules) required to metabolise food, the more energy is consumed in metabolism.

b. *Type of food.* Glucose increases the energy expenditure by 5-10%, fat by 3-5% and protein by 20-30%.

c. *Fluid versus solids.* Solids take more energy to be broken down.

d. *Other factors.* Factors such as cold, fear, stress and medications or drugs (e.g. smoking, alcohol, caffeine) are also known to increase daily energy expenditure.

This is one of the reasons regular small snacks are recommended when trying to lose fat mass.

To *estimate* your daily energy expenditure, the *National Research Council* in the United States came up with the following table (Table 17.3) that is easy to use but well and truly just an *estimate*.

*Table 17.3: The National Research Council* methods of estimating daily energy expenditure as a function of Resting Metabolic Rate.

| Level of Activity | Factor | Range |
|---|---|---|
| **Resting** (sleep, reclining) | RMR x 1.0 | |
| **Very Light** (sleeping then doing normal, non-strenuous household activities etc) | RMR x 1.5 | 1.5-2.5 |
| **Light** (sleeping then gardening, easy walking, shopping etc) | RMR x 2.5 | 2.0-4.0 |
| **Moderate** (sleeping then moderate walk, mowing, tennis, slow swimming, stretching, dancing) | RMR x 4.0 | 3.0-5.0 |
| **Strenuous** (sleeping then jogging, competition tennis, moderate swimming, aerobics, weights, squash, soccer) | RMR x 7.0 | 5.0-9.0 |
| **Very strenuous** (sleeping then racing or doing fast pace training in endurance sports) | RMR x 10.0 | 7.0-13.0 |

In summary, it appears that the most important factor that determines energy intake is energy expenditure, even in an aging population. Moreover, it appears that the daily energy requirements of an aging population decrease due to a decrease in both energy expenditure for physical activity and a decrease in resting metabolic rate secondary to a reduced muscle mass that accompanies aging.

## Weight Loss Strategies Are Important for Older Athletes

Since hitting 35 years of age, I've had a never-ending "battle of the bulge". I just seem to have a problem losing that fat weight, particularly round the tummy. My wife, Claire, tells me it's the "bum and thighs" for the ladies. While we may not be able to prevent what mum and dad look like or gave us genetically, a low body fat in athletes of any age is important for five reasons:

1. *Aesthetics* (e.g. dancers/gymnasts/bodybuilders/divers/skaters, looks and ego). Most of us want to look good but in some sports it is factored into performance.
2. *Improved speed/power* through not having to carry as much weight (runners, cyclists, jumpers). Excess body fat hinders performance in sports where the body needs to jump or be moved against gravity or water. For example, some Australian scientists have estimated that increasing fat mass by 2 kg increases 4,000 m pursuit cycling time 1.5 sec or 20 m in distance and a 40 km time trial slows by 15 sec or about 180 m. In runners, United States researchers showed that oxygen usage increased by 0.2 litres of oxygen per kilometre for each extra kilogram of weight carried, leading to a significant decrease in performance. In swimmers there has been conjecture that increased fat mass may improve buoyancy but this has yet to be proved.
3. *Achieving a weight category* (e.g. lightweight rowing, wrestling, judo, karate)
4. *Helping dissipate heat.* Excess body fat insulates the body and holds in heat. For endurance athletes, this may hinder performance, especially in hot and humid conditions.

5. *Health*. Australian research has shown that even a small increase in BMI (Body Mass Index which is your weight in kilograms [1 kg = 2.2 lb] divided by your height in metres squared) can significantly increase your risk of chronic diseases such as diabetes and coronary heart disease. For example, the same study showed that increasing BMI from between 25-26.9 to 27-29.9 doubled the risk of chronic disease in both adult men and women.

## Goal Weight

A goal body weight for a competitive masters athlete should be discussed in consultation with a sports dietician. They will be aware that numerous factors influence what the optimal body weight and composition might be for an athlete, regardless of age. These include:

- *Genetics*. Scary thing getting older. You start to see just how powerful a thing mum and dad's genes are. I for one have seen three of my younger brothers, all extremely active in football (real football that is – Rugby!), surf lifesaving and surfing in their youth, all blow out at various times – and look just like my dad does – carrying excess body fat and with exactly the same body shape. A world-renowned sport geneticist, Claude Bouchard from Canada, studies identical and non-identical twins and suggests about 25-40% of fat gain is due to genetics. These same researchers suggested that genetics can also explain food preferences and dietary intakes.

- *Energy intake and Source of Food*. Historically, it was thought that a kilojoule or Calories from fat, protein, CHO or alcohol was the same when it came to maintaining weight. We thought that eating excess of any of these would lead to fat being deposited. As discussed at the start of this chapter, we now know that each of these food types is used differently by the body and it really is, in a normal well-balanced diet, only the excess fat that leads directly to fat deposits on the hips, thighs or tummy. Excessive intake of CHO and protein stimulate the uptake of each for storage (CHO as glycogen in liver or muscle) or energy provision. Endurance athletes are at an advantage when it comes to burning up fat as a fuel since long distance training encourages the use of fat as a fuel. Power athletes and even athletes who train for long hours but not continuously (gymnasts, skaters, divers) may not get this benefit of fat burning.

- *Training and Appetite*. There is some research to suggest that hard and/or long training will suppress the appetite in the short-term but in most people it appears that increased energy output (training/competing) leads to an increased drive to eat.

- *Physical Activity and Energy Expenditure*. Over 50% of adult Aussies and Americans are overweight with the rise in obesity paralleling a decrease in daily physical activity. Apart from the energy consumed during training, any form of physical activity (mowing, gardening, walking the dogs, dish-washing etc) will consume energy. Thus, masters athletes who get injured or sick, sit and read a lot, sit at a desk at work (heh, that's me!), or love to watch the sport on TV or read the newspaper sport on weekends (heh, that's me!) aren't getting the benefit that they could when trying to lose fat weight.

- *Access to Food.* Eating behaviours are a strong influence on maintaining goal weight. Access to buffet or smorgasbord type meals has been shown to lead to over-consumption of food. Food is also social, so being around other athletes in a team environment or on trips can influence intake quantities. Sadly these days, it's also easier to access the convenience and fast food stores and see high fat foods more readily available than the healthier choices. We also can drive through a KFC or Macca's much easier than a fruit and vegetable shop.
- *Competition Influences.* Leading up to an event, we generally taper our training so we are training less often and for shorter periods. Do we lower our food intake to compensate? Travelling also presents a problem before a major competition, because we sit a lot, thus reducing our energy expenditure compared to normal and eating convenience foods in transit. Thus, tapering time and travel are times to watch the food intake.
- *Bodyweight History.* Most of us know through experience what our body weight or amount of body fat was that gave us the best performance. This should be factored in to decisions on goal weights.
- *Sport and/or Position.* Different sports have different demands on the amount of body fat or muscle mass we need. For example, masters open water swimmers may need extra body fat for buoyancy or insulation for a long distance swim, an older runner may need to lose body fat to run faster over a 10k run, or a Hawaii Ironman triathlete may want to lose fat weight to help cope with the heat better.
- *Current Body Composition.* A sports dietician will have the ability to estimate your body fat and even muscle mass using measures of skinfolds, body girths, height and weight or breadths of some bones. Importantly for health, the American College of Sports Medicine recommends that male athletes should be no lower than 5% and female athletes no lower than 10-12% body fat
- *Dietary Habits, Likes and Dislikes.* Obviously, recommending activities or a diet that doesn't suit your food likes and dislikes will not work. A professional dietician will factor your food preferences and eating habits into their recommendations.

## Common Athlete Approaches to Weight and Fat Loss

Leading Australian sports dieticians, Professor Louise Burke and Vicki Deakin, recently completed an excellent review of the common ways used, correctly or incorrectly, by young athletes to lose body weight and fat weight. Below is a summary of these methods.

1. **Low-Fat versus Low-Energy Diets.** Research has shown neither type of diet is any better than the other. This is because a low-fat diet is generally related to a low-energy (total

kilojoules, Calories) diet. Conversely, high-energy diets contain relatively high levels of fat. Research has consistently shown that weight and fat loss are related to low-fat diets that by their nature are a low-energy diet. For all athletes, CHO is essential for energy provision so it makes sense when losing weight or fat mass via a low-energy diet, to increase CHO intake at the expense of fat in the diet.

2. **Low-CHO Diets.** These include the *Doctor Atkins, Scarsdale, Sugarbusters, Zone* (more on this one later) diets that have come and gone in and out of fashion over the last 20-30 years. The marketers of these and other such diets tell us that CHO is the key factor in getting fat and getting diabetes and heart disease. Like many of the marketing claims that are "too good to be true", research does NOT support these assertions. As discussed earlier, body fat in a normal person comes from eating too much fat, NOT CHO that tends to be stored in muscles and the liver as energy producing glycogen or used immediately as an energy source. Moreover, a little known fact is that 1 gm of glycogen (stored CHO) takes about 3 gm of water to be stored with it. So, if we eat low CHO-diets we don't give our body's enough dietary CHO for physical activity or our brain and nervous system to operate (they only use CHO as their energy source), the body has to break down the glycogen as an energy source. With the breakdown of 1 gm of glycogen comes a loss of 3 gm of the stored water. Thus, these low-CHO diets lead to a very quick loss of weight, most of it water. So when we weigh ourselves on a set of scales, the low-CHO diet appears to be working. In fact, it's a bloody miracle! Medium-term though, particularly in athletes who need CHO as a major energy source to train effectively, low CHO diets lead to protein (muscle) breakdown, bad breath from protein breakdown end-products in our breath, tiredness, headaches and nausea. Longer term, low CHO diets don't give an athlete enough energy to train with any intensity. If muscles are being broken down to provide energy, we also lose muscle mass that means that eventually the biggest consumer of energy (kilojoules, Calories) at rest, muscle mass, is reduced even more than the aging process itself does. As discussed earlier, aging athletes need to hold onto muscle mass for performance reasons. Losing more muscle mass just doesn't make sense. Like most of these fad diets, once we go off them and back onto some CHO, water is stored and on goes the weight we thought we'd lost!

3. **High-Protein Diets.** These diets are a variation of the low CHO diets that are marketed as being low-fat, and therefore healthier, or promoted as good for holding onto muscle mass. These facts are true BUT AGAIN; weight loss is primarily via the loss of stored CHO and thus water and weight loss and fat loss due to the low energy intake, rather than the restricted food types.

4. **The Zone (Dr Barry Sears) Diet.** This diet targets athletes by suggesting that it promotes endurance, fat loss and muscle mass maintenance. Sears suggests limiting CHO intake to 40% of daily energy intake (sport scientists and dieticians recommend athletes have 60%), fat 30%, and protein intake 30% and having three meals and two snacks a day according to prescribed blocks. The low CHO intake lowers insulin and another blood

sugar-promoting hormone levels that in turn promotes the breakdown of fat as an energy source. Another action of these hormones is to promote other chemical messengers that open up blood vessels that he promotes will increase blood flow, oxygen delivery and thus endurance (thus you enter the "zone").

While some of Dr Sear's suggestions are based on fact, research has shown that insulin levels are only reduced with diets that consist of less than 25% CHO, not the 40% he advocates. Some of his foods prescribed as high blood-glucose producing such as pasta are also incorrect. Like many of these fad diets, they are difficult and impractical to implement in a busy schedule of work, family and training, particularly if you are sensitive new-age guy like me and do some cooking at home for the family. Sports dieticians have also noted that some of his actual suggested recipes contradict his own plan and that the recommended snacks are difficult to prepare (the *PR Bar* known to triathletes meets the Sear's guidelines).

Again, like many of these relatively low CHO diets, this diet is impractical for masters athletes. It is low energy (4,200-8,400 kJ/day, 1,000-2,000 Cal/day) when most aging athletes need more than this. It does not contain enough CHO for athletes in training. Combining low energy intake, normal energy output via training and RMR, and we'd expect weight loss, even if the majority is via water loss. However, as athletes, we do NOT want the accompanying tiredness and decreased training and racing performance that comes with not getting enough CHO.

5. **Food-Combining Diets.** The *Fit for Life* diet was around about 10 years ago and promoted such eating practices as combining certain foods, eating fruit before midday and avoiding any food after 8pm. Its major premise was avoiding combining protein and CHO suggesting that this combination was hard to digest and resulted in the build up of "toxins" that negatively impacted on health and increased body weight. Sure protein *takes longer* to break down in the digestive system but like all foods, the gut does it easily. All food is broken down to its basic constituents so I'd ask what these "toxins" might be? Like most of these fad diets, testimonials from people including high profile athletes are used in marketing. However, scientific rigour in their formulation is often missing. Like most of the fad diets above, this diet is low energy and low fat, thus leading to weight loss. It also restricts the amount of CHO that an athlete badly needs for training and competition performance. As we saw in the recovery chapter of this book, restricting the combination of some protein and CHO during recovery from hard training may also compromise the recovery process.

6. **High-Fat Diets.** Endurance athletes need to efficiently use fat as an energy source. By using their huge reserve of fat as a fuel they preserve their limited supply of CHO that is only found in muscles, the liver and the blood. The theory is that by eating a high-fat diet we promote the use of fats. This is correct but what athletes may not know is that fat will be used primarily during low intensity exercise and it will only be used, for biochemical reasons, if some glucose (CHO) is available. When we start to exercise at

higher intensities, we use more and more CHO the higher the intensity of exercise. Most of us race at high intensity!! Obviously, another negative of high fat diets is the increased risk of cardiovascular disease that accompanies high fat diets in masters athletes.

7. *Liquid Diets*. Use of fluid diets such as *Modifast* or *Optifast* provide about 400-600 Calories/day (1680-2,500 kJ/day) of energy and will obviously lead to rapid weight loss (1.5-2 kg/week) due to the low energy intake. However, long term, there are too many negatives. While the majority of these supplements contain enough protein to maintain muscle mass, they don't contain enough CHO (about 100 g/day) for training athletes, are expensive, and require vitamin and mineral supplementation which is another expense. Again, the weight loss with this diet is primarily water from the increased use of stored CHO in the form of glycogen being used as an energy source for exercise and the nervous system. Apart from fatigue, other potential negative side effects for athletes include bad breath, nausea, hunger, headaches, and precipitation of gout in those susceptible.

8. *Weight Loss Centres or Groups*. All of us are aware of *Jenny Craig* or *Weight Watchers*. The majority of these centres cater for the general public, not athletes, and certainly not aging athletes. While relatively expensive, if you feel the need to use them, insist on going to those that have accredited dieticians and/or medical practitioners in house.

9. *Dietary Supplements*. Both the gym and health food industry are riddled with myths about supplements. Some supplements are marketed that they "burn fat". Two that have been shown to be effective are chromium (400µg/day) and pyruvate, but ONLY in obese people, not young or masters athletes. Research suggests that NO magic pill or powder can accelerate body fat loss. Many supplement companies falsely push products (e.g. carnitine) as "fat burners" and get away with it because the products are not drugs and are therefore free from government legislation and no standards are in place to control them.

10. *Drugs*. A number of legal and illegal (banned by the IOC) are commonly used for weight loss. These include:
    a. *Diuretics*. The IOC has banned these drugs in that they 'mask' other drugs such as anabolic steroids. They lead to rapid weight loss by causing rapid fluid loss for up to a period of 24 hours after which drinking will replace the fluid lost. Commonly used in weight category sports such as wrestling, boxing or rowing, the negative side effects include loss of calcium and sodium leading to weakness, low blood pressure and dehydration.
    b. *Appetite Suppressors*. This range of drugs is commonly used in obese people. One type of appetite suppressor "bulks up" the gut causing a feeling of fullness. Methylcellulose is one such agent. Drugs such as *phentermine, benzphetamine, phendimetrazine, mazindol,* and *diethypropion* have been shown to be effective appetite suppressors when combined with diet and exercise. Because these drugs stimulate the nervous and cardiovascular systems, the IOC has banned their use by athletes.
    c. *Acarbose* prevents the breakdown of sugar in the gut so reduces overall energy intake and thus weight loss.

d. ***Orlistat*** has recently come onto the market. Its aim is to prevent the breakdown of fat in the gut. 120 mg is taken at every meal and causes some 30% of fat not to be absorbed and therefore passed through to the bowel. Its use must be incorporated with a low-fat diet or diarrhoea and anal loss of fat and oil may result. Apart from this problem (that would do me!), negative side effects include abdominal pain and the loss of vitamins (A, D, E, K) that are commonly found in fat. It is not an IOC-banned drug.
   e. ***Ephedrine***. While it is a banned drug for athletes, taken at a dose of 150 mg/day it has been shown to lower body weight and fat in obese people by increasing heart rate and energy metabolism as well as suppressing the appetite. It has been shown to work best in combination with caffeine (20 mg ephedrine, 200 mg caffeine). Side effects include increased heart rate, nervousness, and increased blood pressure and muscle tremors and are not recommended for athletes requiring a steady hand or who have heart or blood pressure problems.
   f. ***Caffeine***. Good old caffeine has not been shown to be effective in weight loss when used alone.
   g. ***Nicotine***. Smokers have been shown to increase RMR both overnight and after a cigarette. This explains the weight gain after smoking cessation in smokers. Suggesting the use of nicotine in any form would be ridiculous for an aggressive anti-smoker like myself – I've seen what it's done to my mum!

## Exercise Prescription for Weight and Fat Loss

Research has conclusively shown that a moderate dietary restriction of energy intake and a low-fat diet combined with exercise is the best method for weight and fat loss. Simply put, we decrease energy intake by eating less and increase energy expenditure by exercising more. Sure we can do the little extra things that over a day or a week add up to a lot of energy expenditure. These might include:

- Parking the car away from work or shopping and walk briskly to and from the car
- Gardening, mowing, other yard work
- Vacuuming, dusting, sweeping, ironing – get to it fellas!
- Using stairs instead of lifts or escalators or the airport moving walkways
- Walk during morning or afternoon tea or lunch breaks
- Playing with the kids or grandkids

So the question beckons. If I decide to exercise more, should I go short and hard or long and easy? For overweight non-athletes, the research says go longer (about 60 minutes) and slower (about 60% of maximum heart rate). Truth be known, this strategy is all that older overweight people with low motivation, at risk of injury including heart attacks, and with poor fitness, can handle. For older athletes, things are different.

A classic study in 1994 followed 17 young adults over 20 weeks to see if high-intensity or low-intensity endurance programs lead to the greatest weight and fat loss. While the total overall energy used during exercise was much lower in the high-intensity group, the high intensity group reduced their skinfold thickness nine times greater than the lower intensity group. Research has shown that high intensity exercise uses fat as a fuel during recovery and that recovery takes much longer than low intensity training. Furthermore, high intensity training helps maintain or increase muscle mass, particularly athletes not used to such training. This increased muscle mass will lead to increase in RMR and thus greater energy burning at rest.

So which type of exercise should I do to lose weight or fat? While little research has been done on this, it appears both scientifically and anecdotally, that running is preferable to cycling and swimming. While research has shown that swimming and running at the same intensity use the same energy *during* exercise, running appears to increase energy expenditure *after* exercise. This appears due to the higher body temperatures generated during running. In older athletes, if injury is a risk with running, then fast walking or cycling might be suggested, as both will lead to increased body temperatures compared to swimming.

Is weight training better than aerobic training? The American College of Sports Medicine suggest aerobic work is the best of these alternatives in the short term in that it leads to greater energy expenditure for a one-hour workout. Table 17.4 below suggests why. However, longer term weight training that builds muscle mass may be more beneficial because this will increase muscle mass, the largest contributor to resting metabolic rate which is the largest contributor to total daily energy expenditure.

*Table 17.4:* Table comparing the energy expenditure during either an hour of running or weight training.

| Weight training | Running |
|---|---|
| Vigorous weight training | Vigorous running (11.5 min/mile) |
| 7.2 Calories/min | 10.8 Calories/min |
| 60 minute workout | 60 minute workout |
| 432 Calories | 648 Calories |

## Problems with Rapid or Too Much Weight Loss

Apart from a lack of energy, fatigue during training, possible headaches and bad breath, low energy or low CHO diets can also lead to more serious problems. These include:

- *Menstrual and Hormonal Disturbances.* In the 1980s I left PE teaching and worked in a gym frequented by a number of lean high-performance female endurance athletes. Many were concerned about long-term problems as a result of having irregular periods or complete loss of the menstrual cycle. Put on body fat was my answer as in those days we believed that a body fat of 17% was needed to initiate a period. These days we know that each woman is different and that it's not just body fat levels that determine loss of the menstrual cycle. Factors such as energy restriction, the rapidity of fat loss or level of protein intake may be related to the loss. Indeed, factors such as low-fat diets, high-fibre diets, vegetarianism, and strenuous training programs have been linked to low levels of the hormone oestrogen and menstrual irregularities.

Given that such problems lead to decreased bone density, stress fractures may become a problem in masters female athletes, particularly as bone mineral density has been shown to decrease from young adulthood. This loss of bone mineral appears not to be completely reversible so older female athletes approaching menopause need to take care in this regard. Rapid weight loss in males can also cause disturbances in the hormone testosterone, an anabolic hormone that is crucial for developing muscle mass, recovery from training, and performance.

- *Reduced Muscle Mass and RMR.* As discussed earlier, lean body mass is the major determinant of RMR. Muscle mass also decreases with age, even in aging athletes who maintain high-intensity training. In people who lose weight or body fat quickly by using the fad diet methods above, not only can muscle mass reductions lead to decreased RMR, but the thyroid hormones that are essential for carbohydrate metabolism are affected. Taken together, these factors can lower RMR by as much as 15% following very low energy diets. This creates a viscious cycle in that a low RMR makes further weight loss very difficult long-term.
- *Performance Decrements.* Decreases in both strength and endurance have been observed in athletes who maintain low-energy diets for long periods.
- *Illness and Decreased Immunity.* In athletes, a reduced energy intake decreased CHO levels, reduced protein intake or lack of vitamin/mineral intake make athletes more susceptible to illness. Low CHO diets used incorrectly for weight loss in athletes lead to increased levels of a stress hormone called cortisol that suppresses the immune system.

## Recommended Safe Weight Loss Strategies

An energy deficit of 3500 Calories (14,700 kilojoules) leads to the loss of one pound (0.45kg) of body fat, which can be safely achieved in one week by a daily deficit of 500 Calories (2,100 kilojoules). The acronym GOWADA, highlights the major factors to consider for healthy weight loss in athletes of any age:

- Gradual. Rapid weight loss is more likely to cause loss of muscle and bone tissue as well as carbohydrate fuel, and promote undesirable changes in hormones, metabolic rate, vigour and mood. Sports Dieticians recommend a weight loss of 0.5-1.0 kg/week which equates to 2,100-4,200 kJ/day or 500-1,000 Calories/day.
- *Off-season.* If possible, significant weight loss should occur during the off-season to avoid an energy drain that can compromise training and skill development during the competitive season.

- *Weight-training.* For both young and masters athletes, research has shown that older people who undertake weight training can increase their metabolic rate as well as burn energy while weight training. It also has the advantage of reducing body fat and increasing muscle mass to benefit performance, particularly in speed and power events. In masters athletes with type II diabetics, it also helps improve insulin action.
- **A**ctivity. Some athletes may be able to increase their calorie burning by adding aerobic conditioning. While low intensity aerobic work appears "best", higher intensity exercise that can be sustained for 30-60 minutes may be more beneficial although it may place an overweight aging athlete more at risk of injury or cardiac problems.
- **D**iet. For many athletes, diet will be the focus of weight loss efforts. Research shows that adequate carbohydrate (6-8 g/kg), protein (1.5-2 g/kg), vitamins and minerals (at least 100% of RDA), and a low fat (15-25% of energy) diet of about 500 kcal (2100 kJ) less per day than required for maintaining body weight is best for weight loss. This will lead to a weight loss of approximately 0.5-1.0 kg/week. Foods high in fibre and/or having a low glycemic index may help reduce the desire to eat.
- **A**void. Although tempting for rapid results, dehydration in spas/saunas, fad diets, supplements, and drugs should never be used by masters athletes for weight loss as well as health and performance reasons. We should also avoid fatty foods and limit fatty add-ons such as sour cream, high-fat salad dressings, butter and margarine.

### What are some of the dangers of rapid weight loss?

Some athletes, particularly in sports requiring weight classes, try and lose weight by saunas, exercising in "sweats" or using diuretic tablets. These methods lead to rapid weight losses but the weight lost is all fluids lost through sweating or urinating. Some of the problems for athletes using these methods include:

- decreased performance
- kidney problems
- higher heart rates
- decreased ability to lose heat
- muscle cramping
- fatigue

Apart from reducing performance and increasing the risk of heat injury, dehydration has contributed to the death of athletes in both weight class and endurance sports. Importantly, with the majority of weight loss being sweat and thus fluids, athletes will get thirsty, drink, and put the weight straight back on.

Some athletes may also drastically reduce carbohydrate intake to lose weight. However, this type of diet increases urine output due to the fact that one gram of stored carbohydrate takes 2.6 grams of water to be stored. The increased urine output leads to dehydration and electrolyte losses. These diets are also low in key nutrients for energy production and thus training performance. A restricted diet can also lead to irritability, difficulty concentrating or low blood sugar because of lack of carbohydrate in the diet. This is particularly true around 3-4pm when many athletes want to train but have not eaten since lunch or not eaten at all.

## What About Weight Gain?

Some masters athletes may wish to increase their muscle mass to enhance performance, particularly in speed and power events or sports. In fact, it is strongly suggested that the older the athlete, the more important it is to maintain or gain muscle mass.

Muscle makes up about 40-50% of our body weight and about 50% of the body's total protein. This muscle protein is being continually turned over, with new proteins being made and old ones degraded. In resting adults, body protein turns over at about 3-4 grams of protein per kilogram of body weight per day. Thus, to gain muscle mass, we need to increase the amount of proteins being made or decrease the breakdown of older ones, or both. Hormones such as insulin, insulin-like growth factor-I (IGF-I), growth hormone, and testosterone are anabolic (protein building) hormones while the stress hormone cortisol is a catabolic (protein breakdown) hormone. Immediately after weight training, the concentrations of all these hormones are increased in both men and women with the concentrations being higher after a higher volume of training. Apart from the hormonal influence on muscle mass, a number of other factors can increase or decrease muscle mass and are summarised in Figure 17.3 below.

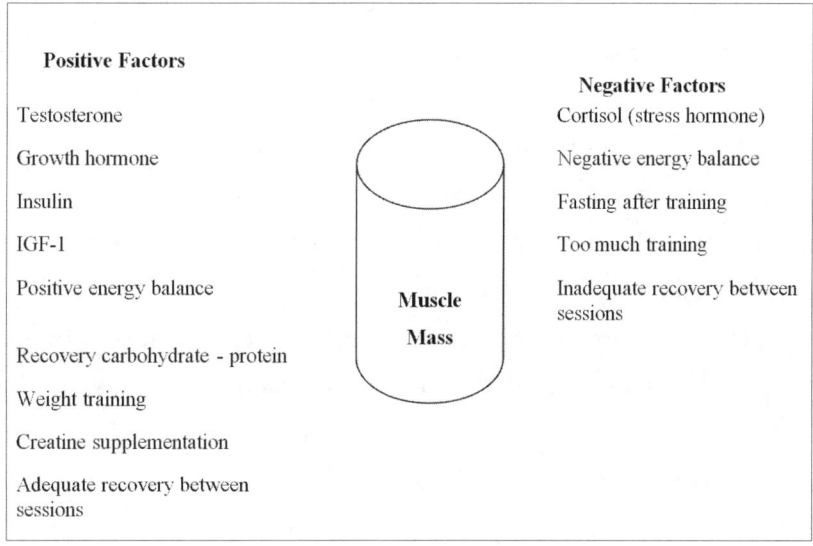

*Figure 17.3:* Factors that can increase or decrease muscle mass in athletes.

The following strategies are suggested for increasing muscle mass in masters athletes:
1. *Weight training* to stress the major muscle groups with repeated sets of 8-12 RM (repetition maximum) loads with relatively short recovery between sets and exercises. See Chapter 7 for more detail on this type of *hypertrophy* (muscle building) weight training.
2. *Adequate recovery* between training sessions of 2-3 days.

3. *A positive energy balance* promotes protein building, even in the absence of weight training. Thus, eat more Calories/kilojoules than is needed to maintain daily energy balance when trying to put on muscle mass.
4. *Frequent meals/snacks* are preferable to a few meals. Why? One of the factors promoting muscle building is increased uptake of amino acids from the blood. More frequent snacks help maintain blood amino acid levels.
5. *Extra protein intake* may promote muscle protein building. A well-balanced diet, slightly energy-positive, provides enough protein to meet an athletes needs. An athlete commencing weight training to put on muscle mass may need up to twice the amount of protein (1.6-2.0 gm/kg) than that recommended for a non-athlete of the same age (0.8-1.0 gm/kg). However, most athletes who eat well will get enough protein without the need for expensive protein powders.
6. *After training eating* is important. A combination of protein and carbohydrate intake straight after weight training increases the anabolic (muscle building) effect of the weight training alone in stimulating protein building. It also increases the level of the hormones needed to help build muscle. There is no scientific evidence to suggest that amino acid or protein supplementation enhances muscle mass gain. However, recent research suggests that creatine loading at 20-25 gm/day for 5-7 days followed by a maintenance dose of 1-2 gm/day can lead to significant increases in muscle mass when combined with weight training.

Research suggests that the rate and amount of muscle gain in younger athletes is dependent upon the training load, the training nutrition, the athlete's body type, and genetic factors. There is no reason to suggest the same factors would not apply to masters athletes wanting to gain weight since studies have shown similar percentage gains in muscle mass in 90+ year-olds as in youngsters doing heavy weight training.

In younger body-builders, it appears that the amount of muscle mass able to be put on with weight training depends on the initial body type of the athlete. Research has shown that an athlete with a solid build can expect to gain more muscle mass than an athlete with a slender build. There is also no doubt that muscle mass development only occurs if the muscles are overloaded. For aging athletes, this type of hypertrophy (muscle enlargement) weight training is essential given the loss of muscle mass that occurs with aging in both non-athletes and athletes, particularly after age 70 years. This type of training and the details of how to go about it are discussed in Chapter 7 of this book.

Apart from the weight training, a well-balanced diet that provides enough protein and carbohydrate is required, particularly following recovery from the weight training. It has been estimated that an extra 2,500 Calories or 10,500 kilojoules of energy are required to develop 1 pound (0.45 kg) of muscle. Assuming this amount of muscle can be developed slowly over a week, this would suggest an extra 350 Calories/day (1,470 kJ). Research suggests that the best way to get the required energy in the day while gaining weight is to eat/snack at least 5 times per day.

There is a common belief that protein powders are needed to provide the protein needed to build the extra muscle mass desired. However, NO research paper has found the need for this. While the protein needs are greater in an athlete wanting to gain muscle mass through weight training (1.5-2.0 gm/kg body weight versus 0.8-1.0 gm/kg body weight in non-athletes), a normal healthy diet with the increased energy of 350 Calories/day will provide this amount of protein. Save the money and eat natural foods.

Finally, research has shown that an important aspect of muscle gain is sleep and rest. For masters athletes with family, work and training commitments, this becomes a factor to consider if trying to maximise the hypertrophy weight training. My solution to this problem is to do the hypertrophy work over the triathlon off-season so that I reduce my endurance training volume, frequency and intensity but replace it with the weight training. Once back into triathlon endurance training, I get to the gym 1-2 / week rather than 3-4 / week like I was in the off-season.

## Conclusion

Using the GOWADA principles outlined above, losing 0.5-1.0 kg of fat weight per week is suggested in masters athletes through lowering the fat-dense foods and replacing them with the low calorie foods such as fruits and vegetables. While not always available to many athletes, a visit to a sports dietician for a consultation is strongly recommended. Their professional input may help you win the "battle of the bulge", improve your health, and boost performance as well.

CHAPTER 18

# PERFORMANCE-ENHANCING SUPPLEMENTS AND THE MASTERS ATHLETE

*Don't be fooled if something sounds too good to be true – it probably is.*

H. Jackson Brown Jr

*I don't understand what goes through all those athletes' minds. It doesn't make any sense. I mean – why do they do it? Why do they use steroids? Are they afraid of hard work?*

Greg Louganis

*All the athletes I know use drugs, even those who are considered role models. I don't know anyone who is absolutely clean.*

Ben Johnson

## Introduction

Health food shops, bike shops, chemists, sporting and fitness magazines and the internet promote supplements that will *enhance performance, increase recovery, improve stamina, improve strength, lose body fat etc*. It all sounds too good to be true and in general, it is. Government agencies do not review such supplements for safety, effectiveness, purity or potency before they are marketed. It's only after they appear on the market that these agencies can take action if it can be proved these claims are false or misleading. Thus, the marketers have a free rein to promote a product with bright, catchy claims that in general are unsubstantiated by science but are supported by testimonials from high-profile people and athletes. For example, a 1993 research study evaluated 624 commercially available products targeted at body-builders and found over 800 performance claims for these products, most of which were not supported by published research. In 2000-01, the International Olympic Committee (IOC) commissioned a study of nutritional supplements from 215 suppliers in various countries. The study included supplements purchased in shops, on the internet and by telephone order. Of the 634 products analysed, 94 (14.8 per cent) contained prohibited substances, but the prohibited substances were not declared on the label.

Regardless, athletes young and old will take supplements for a number of reasons including:

- Compensating for poor diet or lifestyles
- Meet the demands of long-duration or intense training
- Benefit performance

In 1996, United States consumers spent $6.5 billion on supplements. Some high profile supplements, despite in some cases lack of scientific evidence to support their use, have enormous sales. For example, *creatine* first came to the public eye after the 1992 Olympics success of Lynford Christie. Worldwide sales of creatine are now estimated at 2.7 million kilograms. While this supplement does enhance performance in intermittent sports such as touch or soccer, it is often marketed to improve endurance with no evidence to support this claim. Another example of marketing power is the *HMB (hydroxy-methyl butyrate)*, a supplement promoted in the mid-90s to improve muscle mass and strength despite no scientific evidence, but now reaching sales of $30-50 million in the USA alone.

## Harmful Supplements

A number of popular supplements to enhance weight loss by increasing resting energy burning levels (e.g. *Ma Huang, Mormon Tea*) contain *ephedrine* that increases heart rate and blood pressure thus placing masters athletes with cardiac risk factors at greater risk. Combining these products with *caffeine (coffee, guarana)* will further increase the risk. The IOC has banned the use of *ephedrine*.

*Androstenedione* is a "prohormone" steroid that can be converted to testosterone in the body and thus potentially increase muscle mass, aid recovery, and build strength. However, research has shown it fails to meet any of these claims. However, it also has negative side effects such as lowering the concentration of good (HDL) cholesterol in the body – a worry for an aging athlete focused on good health. The IOC has also banned it.

## Safe and Effective Supplements that can cause problems in high doses

Some supplements can benefit an athlete of any age if taken according to the manufacturer's recommendations. For example, *Vitamins and Mineral Supplements* can benefit an athlete on a poor or weight-reducing diet who may not be getting enough vitamins and/or minerals through the diet. However, large doses of them can be toxic. For example, iron deficiency is relatively common in endurance athletes, particularly menstruating females, and directly affects performance by reducing the oxygen carrying capacity of the blood. However, megadoses of iron can create imbalances in other minerals such as copper because high iron intakes inhibit copper absorption in the gut. High levels of iron can also increase the risk of cardiovascular disease.

*Creatine* has been shown to benefit repeated sprint-performance in sports such as team sports where sprints are interspersed with rest or recovery periods of low intensity such as soccer, basketball or touch. Athletes are recommended to load with 20-25 grams/day over 5 days then maintain with 1-2 grams/day to maximise the benefits. While not often taken in larger doses, in those people susceptible to kidney problems, the loading phase and regular use may be not recommended.

Kidney function may also be reduced in athletes taking in more than 2.8 grams/kg body weight/day of *protein*. Athletes are recommended protein dosages of between 0.8-1.6 grams/kg body weight/day with possible larger doses of 2.0 grams/kg body weight/day for masters athletes wanting to put on muscle mass via weight training.

*Caffeine* has been shown to legally enhance endurance performance with minimal side effects when used in dosages of 3-6 mg/kg body weight (one *No-Doze* tablet contains 100 mg caffeine). Higher dosages often result in nausea, dizziness, gut upsets and insomnia. Taking amounts greater than 6 mg/kg body weight also causes excretion of caffeine to levels seen by the IOC as doping.

## Evaluating Ergogenic Supplements

As a sport scientist I am often asked to give my opinions on such products. However, few masters athletes have access to sport scientists or information to make informed decisions on whether the vast range of products do in fact legally benefit performance in athletes. The following guidelines may help decide whether a product has legal performance-enhancing properties or is just marketing hype.

1. Are the claims based on sound physiological or biochemical principles? Speak to a reputable coach, Health and/or Physical Educator, Dietician, Doctor or Exercise Scientist. If you are taking medications for a medical condition a visit to your doctor is a must to ensure no interactions of the supplement with your medication(s).

2. Are the claims based on scientific fact or testimonials of high-profile athletes or individuals? If it's testimonials alone, be sceptical. Check out the scientific claims by a web search. See the websites recommended in Table 18.1 following. In particular, check out whether the claims have been scientifically validated and written up in scientific journals (check out: http://www.ncbi.nlm.nih.gov/entrez/query.fcgi/ that is the National Library of Medicine (USA) website and free to access. If papers in this database support the claims, have faith of the claim's validity.

3. Is the supplement safe, ethical and legal? Check out the Australian Sports Anti-Doping Authority (ASADA) website (www.asada.gov.au/) for information on most drugs and supplements.

4. Who operates the website or produced the marketing? If it is a non-profit organization such as the government, a University, reputable organization rather than a for-profit business, it's more likely unbiased.

5. Did someone with a qualification (e.g. PhD or degree in medicine or dietetics) produce the marketing blurb? If so, it's more likely the information is correct.

6. Are the claims *too good to be true*? If so, it probably is!

7. Check out the labels on the products and if there is not enough information there,

contact the manufacturer on the telephone or by mail and then evaluate the information as above.

An excellent paper on evaluating supplements is available at the United States Food and Drug Administration for Food Safety and Applied Nutrition website at: http://www.cfsan.fda.gov/~dms/ds-savvy.html

### Table 18.1: Recommended Websites for Evaluating Supplements

- http://www.consumerlab.com  This site provides independent test results and information to help the reader and health professionals evaluate and select dietary supplements.
- http://www.ausport.gov.au/ais/nutrition/supplements/classifications is a website maintained by the nutritionists at the Australian Institute of Sport. One of the most readable sites on the topic of supplements in sport.
- http://www.supplementwatch.com Supplement Watch is dedicated to educating consumers about the potential benefits and risks of dietary supplements and provides an independent and science-based evaluation of supplements.
- http://www.quackwatch.org/index.html is the homepage of Quackwatch, Inc., a member of Consumer Federation of America. It is a non-profit corporation whose purpose is to combat health-related frauds, myths, fads, and fallacies.
- http://www.cfsan.fda.gov/~dms/ds-savvy.html The United States Food and Drug Administration for Food safety and Applied Nutrition website that gives excellent advice to coaches, athletes and health professionals when it comes to supplements.
- http://ods.od.nih.gov/databases/databases.html is the homepage of American National Institutes of Health Office of Dietary Supplements. Reliable information on just about any supplement can be found.
- http://www.gssiweb.com is the homepage of the Gatorade Sports Science Institute. It has an excellent range of articles relating to sports performance and good health and an easy-to-use search engine.

### Marketed supplements with proven performance benefits

A number of products have shown benefits in specific sports or events following well-controlled scientific trials. It is essential that the smart athlete be aware that these products have been shown to work in most people, not necessarily themselves, and in certain situations with certain dosages and methods of administration. The smart athlete will check the required dosages and methods of taking the supplement and check out some of the websites in Table 18.1 to see exactly what sport, event, gender, age-group, level of athlete benefited from the supplement. It is widely known that not all people will respond positively to the supplement, indeed some individuals may respond negatively to them. Thus, it is essential to try the supplement prior to using them in competition as well as ensuring they are used to the scientifically-proven methods (e.g. dosage, timing) suggested.

1. *Creatine*

    Creatine is a muscle fuel derived from amino acids and stored primarily in muscle. Most of it is stored as creatine phosphate, a substance used as a fuel for explosive efforts lasting 5-10 seconds such as a 100m sprint on the track, the start of a swim sprint, or sprints in a team game such as hockey or soccer. The body turns over about 1-2 grams of creatine a day with this amount replaced naturally by eating animal products such as meat and eggs, making vegetarians more prone to benefit from supplementation. Additional creatine needs are made in the liver from amino acids and then transported to the muscles for uptake and use. Research suggests the amount of creatine in the body declines with aging, at least in non-athletes.

Research has shown that 70% of people who load their bodies with creatine monohydrate can increase their muscle stores of creatine phosphate, thus increasing their capacity for speed and power. The correct loading method involves 4-5 doses a day for five days with 5 grams/dose, thus giving a total of 20-25 grams/day leading into a major competition or when trying to put on muscle mass. Once the supplementation stops, it appears the muscle levels of creatine return to normal after 4-5 weeks. Thus, once loaded, a maintenance dose of 1-2 grams/day appears enough to maintain muscle creatine levels. An alternative loading method is to use 3 grams/day for 28 days. Of interest may be the following table (Table 18.2) that shows the creatine content of relatively common foods before cooking that leads to small decreases in the creatine content.

*Table 18.2:* Creatine content of foods relatively high in creatine.

| Food | Creatine Content (grams/kg) |
|---|---|
| Herring | 6.5-10 |
| Pork | 5.0 |
| Beef | 4.5 |
| Salmon | 4.5 |
| Tuna | 4.0 |
| Cod | 3.0 |

Recent research has shown that taking creatine with 75-100 grams of carbohydrate (2 bananas, 4 slices of bread, litre of sports drink) enhances creatine uptake. Creatine appears to benefit repeated 6-30 second efforts with 20 second to 5 minute recoveries in between. The benefit appears to be gained by enhancing the resynthesis of the fuel used in these efforts – creatine phosphate. Thus, players of team or racquet sports, weight trainers, or sprinters doing interval training appear to gain the greatest performance benefits of creatine monohydrate loading. It does NOT appear to benefit one-off sprint efforts or endurance performance, despite what the magazines or websites might say. In some sports that are weight-sensitive such as rowing, rock-climbing, or cycling, creatine's use is only recommended if the weight gains (around 1 kg during loading) are not at the expense of power.

Other benefits commonly seen with creatine supplementation are increases in muscle mass and strength. Given that aging leads to decreases in muscle mass, muscle strength and sports performance, there has been a lot of research on the possible benefits of creatine monohydrate supplementation on older people, including aging athletes. In summary, the studies on older non-athletes (70 years of age) suggest that older people cannot increase their creatine stores as much as younger people after creatine supplementation. However, creatine supplementation at 0.3 gram/kg body weight/day for a week appears to lead to increased muscle mass, strength, and the ability to repeatedly do maximum efforts. However, the improvements are less than those observed in younger people.

To date, few studies have examined the effects of creatine monohydrate supplementation on performance in older athletes. French sport scientists compared the maximum cycling power and repeated cycling capacity of 14 older cyclists (66±1.2 years) with those of 14 inactive men (70.1±1.2 years) and 14 young (26±1.2 years) non-athletes. Before and after 5 days of creatine loading (3 x 5 grams/day), each person did a 5 x 10-second all out sprints with 60-seconds between efforts. While the young and older non-athlete groups improved their performances, the older athletes showed no improvement in performance. While this might suggest older athletes may not benefit from creatine supplementation, it remains to be seen whether an increased dose similar to that used by younger athletes (20-25 grams/day) would increase older athletes repeated sprint performance.

There has been much speculation over negative side effects of creatine loading. Anecdotally, nausea, gut upsets, headaches, muscle cramps, and muscle strains have been linked to its use. However, research has shown no liver, muscle or kidney dysfunction when healthy people consume creatine to the above recommended doses. Masters athletes with kidney problems may be advised to seek medical advice on loading with creatine or use the 28 day, 3 grams/day loading method that will not overload the kidneys as much as the 20-25 gram/day method. Because creatine uptake by muscles requires water, dehydration may be a problem such that increased fluid uptake is recommended during loading.

2. *Caffeine*

*Caffeine* is a naturally occurring stimulant found in coffee, tea, chocolate and cola drinks that provide between 30-100 mg/serve (see Table 18.3 overleaf). Some non-prescription medications such as *No-Doz* can provide between 100-200 mg of caffeine /tablet.

Caffeine has been well-documented by research to have the following benefits:
- Central nervous stimulant – increases perception and reduces feeling of effort
- Improved strength – by stimulating the release and uptake of calcium by muscles that enhances the force of muscle contraction
- Increased endurance as measured by time to exhaustion – by increasing the use of fats as a fuel and thus sparing the stored carbohydrate (glycogen), particularly during the first 15-20 minutes

Caffeine doses of between 3-6 mg/kg of body weight taken 45-60 minutes prior to performance appear to not only enhance performance but also keep the IOC-legal urine level of less than 12 micrograms/ml in check. Research has shown that doses as high as 9-mg/kg body weight take the urinary level to the IOC-limit and not have any further benefit on performance.

*Table 18.3:* Caffeine content of common foods, drinks and other sources.

| Food | Caffeine Content Range (mg) |
|---|---|
| **Coffee (/cup)** | |
| Drip brewed | 110-150 |
| Percolated | 65-125 |
| Instant | 40-110 |
| Decaffeinated | 2-5 |
| **Tea (/cup)** | |
| Brewed 1 minute | 9-33 |
| Brewed 2 minutes | 20-46 |
| Instant | 12-28 |
| **Soft Drinks (/can)** | |
| Coke and Diet Coke | 46 |
| Pepsi/Diet Pepsi | 36-38 |
| Mountain Dew | 54 |
| Mello Yellow | 52 |
| **Other Sources** | |
| *No Doz* tablet | 100 |
| Chocolate bar (250 gm) | 12-15 |

3. *Sodium Bicarbonate*

   *Sodium Bicarbonate* (yep, good old baking soda!) has been shown to benefit performance in events requiring maximum effort lasting 1-7 minutes. This includes rowing, kayaking, 100-400m swim events, 400-1500m track events and track cycling events up to the 4000m pursuit. During such events, large amounts of lactic acid are produced in the working muscles. The increased acidity of the muscles leads to reduced energy metabolism and an inhibition in the ability of the muscles to contract effectively, thus leading to fatigue. Once produced in the muscles, the acid is pumped to the blood to be removed. The largest remover of acidity in the blood is bicarbonate found naturally in large quantities in the blood. Thus, ingesting more bicarbonate means a greater capacity to "buffer" the acid produced in the muscle and thus will assist in delaying fatigue and enhancing performance.

   Sodium bicarbonate is taken at a dose of 0.3 grams/kg of body weight, mixed with 1-1.5 litres of water or diet cordial (to remove the terrible taste!) and drunk slowly 1-2 hours before the event. Another source is *Ural* available from chemists.

There appear no negative health effects of bicarbonate loading except the risk of gut upsets such as stomach cramps or diarrhoea. The IOC has not banned its use because of the wide range of normal values that exist in people. However, given the possibility of losing control over the bowels on the start line (not a pretty sight!), as with caffeine and creatine and any other supplement, try it in event simulations in training or lead-up events to see how you respond.

## Marketed supplements with mixed performance benefits

A number of widely available supplements have been shown to benefit performance in some studies and not in others. This is most likely due to the different methods employed by the researchers. These different methods may have included different subjects (aged vs. young; recreational athletes vs. elite), different dosages, or different performance measures (speed-power vs. endurance).

1. *Antioxidants*

   *Antioxidants* are any substance that helps reduce the severity of oxygen stress and are designed to remove what are called "free oxygen radical species" that are produced during periods of high muscle oxygen consumption. These free radicals have been linked to muscle cell damage and as a cause of aging as discussed in Chapter 1. In both young and aging athletes, a sudden increase in training volume or intensity that causes muscle damage or inflammation, or training in a stressful environment such as heat, cigarette smoking, psychological stress, pollution or altitude, have been shown to increase the production of these free oxygen radicals. Indeed, the rate of production of these free oxygen radicals increases directly in proportion to the rate of oxygen use, that is, the harder we exercise aerobically. However, increases in free radical production have also been observed following weight training. The free radicals can damage cells of the immune system making us more susceptible to illness, damage muscle cells leading to muscle damage, or damage cholesterol leading to heart attacks.

   While the body produces its own antioxidants that are able to "mop up" these free radicals, use of dietary antioxidant supplements during periods of hard aerobic training may also provide protection against the damage caused by these free radicals. Beta-carotene – a precursor needed for production of vitamin A, and vitamins C and E are the most important dietary antioxidants. While the body increases its own antioxidant defences with training, it is still uncertain as to whether dietary antioxidants work, which dietary antioxidant(s) provide the greatest protection, and what the optimal doses to take are.

   Research in aging non-athletes has shown that the body's own antioxidant defence system declines with age and that the levels of free radicals are also elevated in older non-athletes. We can therefore assume that masters athletes, especially those undertaking high intensity endurance training, might need to consider taking in extra dietary antioxidants or making an effort to eat foods high in the pre-cursor of vitamin A in the body, beta-carotene and vitamins C and E (see Table 18.4). Vitamin C appears to be involved in preventing free radical damage of cells involved with the immune system, the reason why vitamin C is touted as the one to prevent "colds". Research has also suggested that a mix of these three vitamins boosts the activity of each. Maybe this is why mum says to mix the colours of your vegetables on a plate! Some minerals such as copper, iron, manganese, selenium and zinc are involved in the body's production of its own antioxidants. This research suggests the need for multi-vitamin / multi-mineral supplementation in masters athletes.

*Table 18.4:* Food sources high in antioxidants vitamins A, C and E.

| Antioxidant | Food Source |
| --- | --- |
| *Vitamin A (beta-carotene)* | Spinach |
| | Liver |
| | Sweet potato |
| | Carrots |
| | Pumpkin |
| | Apricots |
| | Dairy products |
| *Vitamin C* | Oranges |
| | Blackcurrants |
| | Strawberries |
| | Capsicum |
| | Brussels sprouts |
| *Vitamin E* | Wheat germ oil |
| | Sunflower seeds |
| | Sweet potatoes |
| | Green leafy vegetables |
| | Margarine |
| | Nuts |

There is also some concern that some antioxidants (e.g. vitamin C) may promote free radical damage to cells when taken in very large doses. While further research is needed to confirm the need for antioxidants and the exact amounts needed in athletes of any age, most sport scientists support that antioxidant supplements protect against oxidative stress due to exercise and perhaps enhances recovery and minimises muscle soreness. However, most also agree that athletes on a normal, well-balanced diet rich in fruits and vegetables obtain enough antioxidants and do not need supplementation and if they do, they will get it from simple vitamin/mineral supplementation rather than another pill taken separately as an antioxidant. At risk groups may be masters endurance athletes who are on low-fat diets since vitamin E is fat soluble and found in fatty foods such as meats. Other at risk groups may the aging 'weekend warrior" who is unfit, as research has shown that regular training increases the body's own antioxidant ability.

Finally, if your diet or training habits suggest the need for antioxidant supplements, the following dosages are recommended:
- Vitamin E – 400-800 international units (mg)
- Vitamin C – 500-1000 mg
- Beta-carotene – 400-800 international units (mg)

While these are well above the recommended daily allowances, they are below the levels suggested as toxic.

2. *Protein and Amino Acid Supplementation*

Research has conclusively shown that supplementing the diet with extra protein supplements is expensive and unnecessary except during periods of heavy training, when trying to increase muscle mass, or when used as a recovery meal to enhance muscle repair and carbohydrate replacement simultaneously. Many sports drinks, liquid meals, powders, and sports bars have been developed over the years promoting these benefits. However, the research suggests that, if money or convenience aren't an issue, a normal well-balanced, well-timed diet will do the trick in providing these needs.

a. *Branched-chain amino acids* (leucine, isoleucine, and valine) have been pushed by marketers because they make up about a third of muscle protein; have a role in protein metabolism for energy production, and a suggested role in nervous system fatigue. Theoretically, their use might be suggested. However, few studies have found supplementation of these amino acids to benefit actual sports performance. They have also been promoted as enhancing recovery but with no scientific proof of this. Everyday foods or liquid meals that have a mix of carbohydrate and protein have similar benefits. I personally use a *Musashi* product called *Loaded Protein* after hard or long triathlon training and have anecdotally found it works. It contains these branched-chain amino acids, other protein, and carbohydrate. It is thus suggested that you might like to try some of the commercially-available products that contain these amino acids and find out for yourself if they benefit your performance or rate of recovery.

b. *Arginine, ornithine and lysine* have been shown to increase the release of growth hormone, an anabolic hormone that increases muscle mass and thus strength as well as decreasing body fat. Arginine and ornithine have also been suggested to stimulate the release of insulin so that, when taken in with carbohydrate, will stimulate the uptake of the carbohydrate from the blood to muscle where the carbohydrate is stored as glycogen. However, the available research has been contradictory and in general shown that the suggested amounts of these amino acids (2-3 grams/day) are just as easily obtained from eating dairy products (milk, yoghurt) and eggs.

High intakes of these and other amino acids have been linked to muscle cramping and diarrhoea, yet another reason to save the money and eat a normal, well-balanced diet.

c. *Glutamine* is the most commonly found amino acid in the body. It is essential for many immune system functions and is an energy source for many of the cells that fight infection. Levels of glutamine have been shown to decrease after long and/ or hard training and to remain depressed during recovery from this type of training. Furthermore, a number of researchers who have examined overtraining in athletes have shown long term suppression of glutamine levels. This has lead to the belief that glutamine supplementation may help athletes prevent getting sick during periods of heavy training. While the data from research is conflicting in this regard, the aging athlete might be recommended to use glutamine during periods of heavy training, particularly since the aging process itself has been shown to suppress the immune system.

d. *Glycerol* is a substance naturally produced in the body during the breakdown of fat for energy production. When taken orally with a large volume of fluid, it is rapidly absorbed and acts to retain water in the body and reduce urination. It might thus have a benefit when competing in events of long duration and/or high intensity in hot and humid conditions where dehydration might affect performance.

The protocol for its use is 1-1.5 grams/kg of body weight taken with 25-35 ml/kg of body weight of fluid (water, sports drink or diet cordial) during the 1-2.5 hours leading up to the event. It is available from chemists as glycerine and on the net. Side effects in some people include nausea, bloating, gut upsets, or headaches.

While its use has been shown to be beneficial in some events and not others, it appears that it may confer some protection from dehydration in endurance events held in hot and humid environments. I personally have used it in long distance triathlons at Yeppoon (hot and humid) and Goondiwindi (hot and dry). While the bloating was a factor, it disappeared while racing. I felt it helped my performance but urge you to try it in training at race pace.

e. *HMB (hydroxy-methyl butyrate)* is the latest product marketed to increase muscle mass and strength when combined with weight training, lower body fat levels, and enhance recovery. The marketers tell us it will minimise protein breakdown and elevate protein building. While some early uncontrolled studies on untrained people showed improved strength and muscle mass, more recent and better controlled studies showed no performance benefit or increases in muscle mass or strength in trained men taking 0, 3, or 6 grams/day of HMB for 28 days. However, a number of more recent studies over longer periods of 8-10 weeks have shown that taking 38 mg/kg body weight/day of HMB over this length of time while weight training (80% of maximum lift) three-days per week does lead to increased muscle mass and reduced muscle damage. Thus, it appears that HMB may have role in developing muscle mass in aging athletes, as long as they combine the HMB intake with moderate to heavy weight training.

## Marketed supplements with no performance benefits

A number of widely-used supplements have been marketed so well to athletes via the popular press for so long that they appear entrenched in the sporting culture. However, little scientific support exists for their use by athletes.

1. *Ginseng* extracts have been suggested to reduce fatigue, improve endurance, strength, mental functioning and recovery. To date, there is a lack of scientific data to support any of these claims.

2. *Carnitine* is naturally-produced in the liver and kidney from amino acids found in the diet and is found naturally in most animal foods, some of which is lost during cooking. Its main function is to assist in the transport of fatty acids into the muscle cell where oxygen combines with the fatty acid to create aerobic energy. Thus, carnitine supplementation has been suggested to lower body fat levels, explaining why body-builders suggest its use at 1-6 grams/day is great for 'getting ripped' or 'cutting up'.

   However, research has failed to show that fatty acid transport is enhanced by carnitine supplementation and that the body's own levels of carnitine are enough to cope with demand. Research has also shown that the body produces enough of its own carnitine, can get enough in the diet, and that supplementing with carnitine does not lead to increased muscle carnitine levels.

   If you decide to use carnitine, be sure to get the L-carnitine form and that the commercial product is >99% L-carnitine as the other form, D-carnitine, has been shown to lead to decreased L-carnitine levels.

3. *Coenzyme Q10* or ubiquinone is commonly found in animal foods and in low amounts in plant foods. It is a vital link in the processes involved with the creation of aerobic energy in muscle and has been suggested to be an antioxidant. It has thus been marketed to "promote vigour", "enhance aerobic capacity", and reduce the oxidative damage of exercise.

   However, recent research from the world-renowned Karolinska Institute in Sweden has suggested that instead of acting as an antioxidant, it actually increases oxidative damage in athletes undertaking high intensity training. The claims of enhanced aerobic capacity are also yet to be conclusively proven.

4. *Chromium picolinate* is an essential element required by the body to enhance the action of insulin in taking up glucose from the blood. It is found naturally in yeast, nut and legumes (beans, seeds), some fruit and vegetables, chocolate, wine and beer. Thus, like many nutrients, it is the athletes on restricted energy diets that are at risk of reduced chromium intakes. While there is some research to suggest that training increases its loss through the urine, some studies have shown that training may enhance the absorption and retention of chromium.

   The marketers suggest that chromium will enhance the metabolism of glucose, fat and protein and thus increase muscle mass and strength while lowering body fat – all very attractive to an athlete of any age. However, well-controlled studies have shown no benefit in any of these areas other than what training alone can provide. However, if an athlete is not getting the dietary intake of chromium via the foods mentioned above, then low levels of supplementation might be needed as high levels have been shown to be linked to iron deficiency.

5. *Medium chain triglycerides (MCT's)* are fatty acids found in butter, palm, coconut and kernel oil. They can also be found on the web or in some health food shops as *MCT Fuel, MCT Oil, MCT Gold, Prozone Drink, MCT Powder,* or *UltraGel.* Because they are smaller than most fats (called long-chain triglycerides) found in the normal diet, they empty from the stomach more easily, are more easily absorbed by the small intestine, and enter the energy making part of muscle cells (mitochondria) more easily than the long-chain triglycerides. Thus, the bodybuilding community has pushed them as less likely to lead to fat deposits and more likely to be used as an energy source. In endurance exercise, if they are consumed during exercise, they theoretically might spare carbohydrate and thus improve endurance in long events. One often quoted 1996 study by Van Zyl and others showed a 2.5% improvement in 40-km cycling time trial performance following MCT ingestion. However, no study since then has shown improved performance. Indeed, taken collectively, these later studies have shown that MCT use does not improve performance, does not spare muscle carbohydrate and in large doses causes gut upsets such as nausea and diarrhoea. This is most likely due to the low rate at which MCT's are metabolised by the body and the small amounts (approximately 30 grams) that can be taken in without causing gut upsets. Further support for not using MCT's is the fact they lead to elevated blood cholesterol and trigyceride levels, thus increasing the risk of heart disease in aging athletes.

6. *Prohormones (DHEA, Androstenedione)* are so named because they are precursors in the steroid pathway leading to the anabolic (muscle building) hormone, testosterone. Some commercially available products such as *Tribulus* and *Saw Palmetto* are marketed as having similar anabolic activity as the prohormones. Since they are all marketed as dietary supplements rather than drugs, the government regulations are loose in regards to quality control and the marketers' claims.

Despite being banned by the IOC, prohormones are marketed to athletes as a way to promote fat loss, gain muscle mass and strength, increase sex drive, reverse the effects of aging, and improve the immune system. However, in one of the few studies that has examined these claims following training, a study examined the effect of 300 mg/day of androstenedione during 8 weeks of weight training in healthy young but untrained males, half of whom took the hormone and half who didn't. Testosterone levels did not change, the good cholesterol (HDL) decreased, and the female hormone levels increased in the group that took androstenedione! As expected with weight training, muscle mass and strength increased and fat levels decreased in both groups, all of whom had normal levels of testosterone before and after the study. However, the group that took the prohormone *and* the group that took none both changed the same amount, suggesting that the positive changes were due to the weight training and not the prohormone. However, the researchers suggested that androstenedione might be useful in older males and females or endurance athletes, all of whom are characterized by lower than normal testosterone levels.

DHEA decreases with aging and has been investigated as a performance-enhancing agent. A similar study to the one above found that DHEA (like androstenedione taken at 100 mg/day) did not lead to any increases in testosterone or significant increase in muscle mass or strength compared to that effect expected after 8 weeks of weight training. A similar study of the effect of *Tribulus* by the same group, also showed no effect on performance.

In summary, the studies examining the effects of prohormones on muscle mass and strength to date have found no benefit on testosterone levels, no increases in strength and muscle mass, and some negative side-effects that place an older person more at risk of heart disease. A little bit of trivia (!?) regarding anabolic steroid use in athletes. We have for many years known about the negative side effects of anabolic steroid use. These include increased risk of heart disease, sudden death, increased cholesterol levels, and heart size abnormalities. However, some long-term studies have recently been completed on the death rates of anabolic steroid users who were monitored over a 12-year period from the early 1980s. The rate of death amongst the users was 12.9% compared to 3.1% in a normal age-group, a rate 4.6 times higher than normal.

7. *Colostrum* is a protein-rich substance found in breast milk of mothers during the first few days after birth. It has been suggested to improve the immune system. It has recently been commercially produced from cow's milk and appears on the shelf as *Bioenervie* or *Intact*. Taken at the dosage of 60 grams/day, athletes in a number of Australian studies found improved rowing performance and run performance in their subjects. However, the studies were funded by the manufacturers of *Intact*, had small subject numbers, and were verbally presented at a conference and thus not published and subject to review by other researchers. Thus, the weight of evidence to support its use to benefit performance or enhance the immune system is lacking. At a cost of $80/week for the recommended four weeks it takes to see benefits, it is also very expensive!

## Conclusion

The marketing of sports supplements can blur a masters athletes vision! While there are a number of legal supplements (caffeine, sodium bicarbonate, and creatine) that have been shown to enhance performance in certain sports and events, there are many, many supplements that science has shown to have no benefit to a masters athlete's training or performance. However, research has also shown that the aging process in masters athletes may lead to possible dietary deficiencies in a number of vitamins and minerals. This would suggest the need for multi-vitamin multi-mineral supplementation in masters athletes, especially those involved with endurance training or regular high performance training.

# CHAPTER 19

## The Female Masters Athlete

*The female of our species has been hindered by the propagation of myths regarding her abilities to withstand stress, to perform heavy work, to run, to jump, or just plain play.*

**Christine Wells**

*I hated the easy assumption that girls had to be slower than boys.*

**Dawn Fraser**

*They train and compete just as intensely as their male counterparts and produce performances that are equally outstanding.*

**Judy Daly and Wendy Ey**

### Introduction

There are increasing numbers of older woman coming back into sport or starting a sporting career for the first time. Performances in every age group of female sports continue to improve at a rapid rate due to increases in participation rates, increases in competitive opportunities, better training techniques and better coaching.

Many women are combining careers, family and sport as times thankfully change and more opportunities are opening up for women. However, there also many changes that occur as a woman ages. These include the physical changes to the body as well as lifestyle changes such as career, home-life and family changes, all of which impact on whether or not to participate in masters sport and to what level.

### Aging Female Athletes and Barriers to Participation

As discussed at length in chapter 5 *(Coaching the Aging Athlete)*, there are numerous barriers to older women becoming more actively involved in sport. In summary, these factors include:
- Lack of confidence
- Fear of failure
- Body image
- Lack of time
- Lack of support

- Urinary incontinence
- Lack of money
- Medical considerations
- Lack of awareness

In order to increase the number of mature women in sport, a number of strategies have been suggested by one of the leaders of sport for mature-aged women; Wendy Ey OBE (now deceased). These include:

1. *Come 'n Try sessions* for women of all ages who have little or no background in sport in a non-threatening environment.
2. *Awareness campaign* of opportunities for older women. Such a campaign should de-emphasise former champions and include the numerous human interest stories found in mature-aged sport.
3. *Skill coaching sessions.* Accredited coaches with an awareness of the needs of female masters athlete need to be developed by sports. An older person will want to be coached by an older person who better understands their motivations and goals. While the number of female accredited coaches is small relative to that of men, older female coaches should be encouraged to be involved.
4. *Female role models* in the media that are more mature would attract older women to sport.
5. *Female-only opportunities.* Women's only events that highlight participation and enjoyment rather than competition will help encourage older women who feel uncomfortable in a mixed group.
6. *Child care, transport and cost subsidy.* With the trend towards having children later in life, and many women maintaining their career along side family involvement, these support systems are needed to attract and maintain women's involvement in sport.
7. *Health and body image campaign.* A campaign is needed that emphasises role models from mature-aged sport (not former champions), focuses on health benefits (reduced osteoporosis, reduced obesity, reduced heart disease, reduced diabetes and blood pressure control), points to the exercise benefits of weight loss and improved body shape, and highlights the psychological benefits of exercise (lower stress levels, improved socialisation).

## Effects of Menstrual Cycle on Performance

The menstrual cycle is the result of the interplay between different parts of the brain (hypothalamus), the anterior pituitary gland that produces hormones (follicle stimulating hormone (FSH) and luteinizing hormone (LH)) and the ovaries that produce the hormones oestrogen and progesterone that regulate changes in the uterus to prepare for a fertilised egg. If fertilisation does not occur, the lining of the uterus becomes menstrual flow (the 'period').

The menstrual cycle has three phases:

1. *Menstrual phase* of 1-5 days when the hormones FSH, LH, oestrogen and progesterone

are low and the lining of the uterus fall away.
2. *Proliferative phase* of 6-14 days when FSH and oestrogen levels rise as the uterus lining starts to build and ovulation occurs at about day 14 as a result of a sudden release of the hormone LH.
3. *Secretory phase* of 15-28 days when progesterone levels rise and bring about a rise in blood supply to the uterus. If fertilisation doesn't occur, progesterone and oestrogen levels fall and the menstrual cycle starts over again.

Thus, a very precise, rhythmic variation in hormones is required to maintain a normal menstrual cycle. Anything that upsets the precise balance will lead to menstrual irregularities such as the conditions oligomenorrhoea (irregular periods) and amenorrhoea (loss of three or more sequential cycles) that will soon be discussed.

Studies examining the effect of different phases of the menstrual cycle on endurance and speed events suggest that the menstrual cycle itself does not compromise performance but the presence of premenstrual and menstrual symptoms such as cramping, headaches, water retention, tender breasts, mood swings, irritability and fatigability might negatively affect sports performance in some individual athletes. Research has consistently shown that different women respond in different ways to different events (speed, endurance, strength) during different phases of the menstrual cycle. Indeed, world records have been set in any phase of the cycle. Each woman should experiment to find out what works for them. However, from a theoretical perspective, Table 19.1 may enable the female athlete to plan training more effectively.

## Menstrual Irregularities

While the benefits of regular physical activity are well documented (reduced risk of heart disease, reduced risk of developing high blood pressure, colon cancer and diabetes, reduce blood pressure in people with hypertension, maintain healthy bones, muscles, joints, control body weight, develop muscle and reduce body fat, and reduce the symptoms of anxiety and depression), recent research has suggested a link between vigorous physical activity such as that undertaken by aging female athletes and menstrual cycle disorders in pre-menopausal women.

Irregular periods and amenorrhoea are part of a continuum of severity and are very common in pre-menopausal athletic women, especially female endurance athletes. Indeed, research has shown that the incidence of amenorrhoea or loss of three menstrual cycles in a row occurs at the following rates:

    a.  General female population – 5%
    b.  Female athletes overall – 10-20%
    c.  Female endurance athletes – 50%

*Table 19.1:* Summary of menstrual cycle changes and training effects.

| Days | Cycle Phase | Hormone Levels | Changes | Effect on Training |
|---|---|---|---|---|
| 1, 2, 3, 4, 5 | Early Follicular | Low levels of: oestrogen progesterone testosterone | Immune system low Mood changes and stress Poor reaction times Increased perception of effort | Eliminate skill and precision training. Reduce training volume. Last few days include strength and power work |
| 6, 7, 8 | Mid Follicular | Oestrogen rising Progesterone low | | Include high intensity speed and power work |
| 9, 10, 11, 12, 13 | Late Follicular | Oestrogen peak | Increased glycogen storage (carbohydrate) Increased water storage | Include low intensity and high volume aerobic work. |
| 14 | Ovulation | Testosterone peak | | Strength training |
| 15, 16, 17, 18, 19, 20 | Early Luteal | Progesterone rising | Increased glycogen storage (carbohydrate) Increased water storage Low blood sugar levels | Include high intensity, low volume work. Speed and power work. |
| 21, 22, 23, 24 | Mid Luteal | Oestrogen peak Progesterone peak | Increased protein breakdown Low muscle endurance Increased water storage | Include low intensity and high volume aerobic work. |
| 25, 26, 27, 28 | Late Luteal | Oestrogen, progesterone and testosterone low | Immune system low Mood changes and stress Poor reaction times Increased perception of effort | Recovery week. Eliminate skill and precision training. |

It is characterised by a decrease in the production frequency of LH and lower levels of oestrogen and progesterone, the balance of which is crucial for normal menstrual cycle functioning. In athletes, the following causes have been suggested to lead to athletic amenorrhoea:

- Rapid weight loss
- Imbalance between energy intake (Calories/kilojoules) and energy expended
- Low body weight and percent body fat
- Sudden onset of strenuous exercise
- Psychological stress (home, work, study, training)
- Pregnancy
- Anorexia nervosa

- Polycystic ovaries
- Thyroid disorders
- Drug use
- Medications
- Endocrine disorders
- Pituitary tumour

Treatments for athletic amenorrhoea include medical intervention for any of the non-sport related causes, reducing exercise duration or frequency or both by 10-20%, increasing body weight by 2-3%, improving energy intake to 2600-3300 Calories per day, and reducing stress levels. If the menstrual cycle does not return, hormone replacement therapy might be warranted if amenorrhoea last more than six months. Oestrogen (0.625 mg/day), in combination with progesterone, may be prescribed, but frequently low-dose oral contraceptives are the most convenient form.

Any condition that affects menstrual function appears to affect the *luteal phase* (the time between ovulation and the onset of the period – about 14 days) first. This is the phase where the hormones oestrogen and progesterone are normally high. In athletic women, this phase is often shortened to less than 10 days and lower progesterone levels are observed. The main effects are infertility, reduced fertility, and reduced bone density. Thus, for the aging female wanting to become pregnant this presents a concern. Ovulation can be assessed by observing a rise in body temperature of 0.2-0.6 degrees Celsius (I vividly remember graphing this on an old MacIntosh computer with my wife, Claire, who was swimming training often and hard at the time!), the presence of premenstrual tension signs, and mid-cycle pain. If pregnancy is desired, decreasing training duration and intensity and increasing body fat levels through higher energy intake via food and drinks are suggested.

In female athletes with amenorrhoea, there is a higher prevalence of lower limb stress fractures due to the associated reduced bone density that accompanies menstrual irregularity. The younger the athlete, the more of a concern this loss of bone density and higher incidence of stress fractures are as both these factors have been linked to a higher incidence of osteoporosis in older age.

## The Female Athlete Triad

While not common in female masters athletes, the *female athlete triad* refers to the interrelationships between disordered eating, amenorrhoea, and osteoporosis. A relationship exists between disordered eating and intense sporting activity, in particular in sports where physical appearance (gymnastics, figure skating) or low body weights (endurance running, triathlons) are important or weight categories (martial arts, rowing, judo, boxing) exist. In October, 2007, the American College of Sports Medicine released a position stand (www.acsm.org) on the female athlete triad. They defined the three components of the female athlete triad as:

1. *Disordered eating* refers to a wide spectrum of harmful and often ineffective eating behaviours used in attempts to lose weight or achieve a lean appearance. The spectrum of behaviours ranges in severity from restricting food intake, to binging and purging, to the disorders of anorexia nervosa and bulimia nervosa (both mental disorders). Table 19.2 below shows the characteristics of these two disorders as defined by the *Diagnostic and Statistical Manual of Mental Disorders*.

*Table 19.2:* Characteristics of the most common eating disorders.

| Anorexia Nervosa | Bulimia Nervosa |
|---|---|
| Refuses to maintain body weight at or near normal (for age/height) | Recurrent binge eating in a single period |
| Intense fear of gaining weight/becoming fat, even when underweight | Recurrent compensation (self-induced vomiting, use of laxatives, enemas, diuretics, fasting, excessive exercise) to prevent weight gain |
| Disturbed way of evaluating own body weight or shape with denial of seriousness | Binge and compensation ($\geq$ 2/week for 3 months) |
| Amenorrhoea | Self-evaluation distorted |

2. *Amenorrhoea.* While primary amenorrhoea (delayed menarche or start of periods) is defined as the absence of menstruation by age 16 in a girl with other sex characteristics, for our purposes, secondary amenorrhoea is the absence of three or more consecutive menstrual cycles.

3. *Osteoporosis* is a disease characterised by low bone mass and microarchitectural deterioration of bone tissue leading to enhanced skeletal fragility and increased risk of fracture.

Prevention of the female athlete triad involves:
- knowing the athlete's early athletic history (e.g. delayed menarche or onset of periods, stress fractures, volume and intensity of training, menstrual history, dietary history)
- dietary analysis to ensure energy output is matched by energy intake and nutrient densities of carbohydrates, fats and proteins
- examination of current training practices
- educate athlete and coach as to signs, symptoms, causes and consequences (fatigue, decreased immunity, depression)
- educate on nutrition (energy balance, food choices, eating habits)
- early multidisciplinary (coach, trainer, doctor, psychologist, nutritionist) intervention

Treatment of the female athlete triad involves:
- Medical management to:
  - Elevate oestrogen levels to minimise bone loss through hormone therapy (e.g. oral contraceptive pill) or oestrogen replacement therapy which may be contraindicated in some medical conditions such as:
    - Hypertension

- Abnormal liver function tests
- Cancer of the breast or endometrium
- History of deep vein thrombosis
    - Laboratory tests to determine hormone levels of FSH, LH, prolactin, and thyroid-stimulating hormone (for carbohydrate metabolism)
    - Rule out pregnancy
- Nutrition and exercise counselling
    - Energy intake equals energy output
    - Adequate carbohydrate, fat and protein intake
    - Calcium intake (up to 1500 mg/day for athletes with amenorrhea)
    - Reduce training load
- Psychotherapy
    - Discuss training stressors
    - Address other stressors

### Exercise around Menopause

The average age at which menopause occurs is about 50 years, with an age range of between 35 and 59 years. The cause of menopause is the failure of the ovaries to produce the hormones progesterone and oestrogen. As a result of the lowered levels of oestrogen (small amounts are still produced by the breasts and fat tissue), a woman stops ovulating and menstruation gradually disappears. The process can take five years.

The most common symptom of lowered oestrogen levels is hot flushes. In addition, the bladder, uterus and vagina lose tissue and become thinner, making them drier, less elastic and more prone to infections. The lining of the urethra that takes the urine from the bladder to the exterior becomes thinner and bladder control becomes poorer leading to possible incontinence. Furthermore, the amount of collagen (tissue that builds the body's tissues) produced falls after menopause and a woman's skin loses its tone. Bone also loses calcium, causing a loss of bone density and increasing the risk of osteoporosis and fractures. Thus, hormone replacement therapy is often recommended for masters female athletes. For each individual woman, the experience will be different and depend upon their lifestyle, influences around her, and her physical and psychological response to this lifecycle change. For example, psychological changes such as depression may be exacerbated by children leaving home, loss of a partner or close friends, or financial problems.

The symptoms of menopause can be divided into physical and psychological and are summarised in Table 19.3 below.

*Table 19.3:* Physical and psychological changes symptoms of menopause.

| Physical Changes | Psychological Changes |
|---|---|
| **Vasomotor instability**<br>• Hot flushes<br>• Night sweats<br>• Heart palpitations<br>• Headaches | • Depression<br>• Mood swings<br>• Tiredness<br>• Insomnia<br>• Memory difficulties<br>• Loss of libido |
| **Genital tract changes**<br>• Vaginal dryness<br>• Infection<br>• Vaginal discharge | |
| **Urinary tract changes**<br>• Cystourethritis (inflammation of the bladder and urethra)<br>• Dysuria (burning or stinging sensation when urinating)<br>• Incontinence | |

In addition to these symptoms of menopause, there are major diseases that are associated with menopause. The most common cause of death in post-menopausal women is heart disease. It is believed that the hormones oestrogen and progesterone confer some protection against coronary heart disease. Given that the production of these hormones declines at menopause, hormone replacement therapy again should be considered for the menopausal female athlete. Osteoporosis or decreased bone density is also common in both older men and women and is related to over 50% of bone fractures in adults. However, the older female is 2-4 times more likely to have an osteoporotic fracture than a man of the same age, most likely due to the larger muscle mass of the men offering some protection against falls. In the 3-6 years after menopause there is an accelerated loss of bone. Again oestrogen deficiency is a major contributing factor to osteoporosis, but other factors such as low energy (kilojoules/ Calories) intakes, low body weight, poor dietary intake of calcium and vitamin D, lack of weight bearing activity, family history and smoking are contributing factors as well.

A self-assessment oestrogen level score chart (Table 19.4 overleaf) has been developed and may help the aging female athlete diagnose oestrogen deficiency.

A score of 15 or more indicates the possibility of oestrogen deficiency. A score of 30 or more indicates a very low oestrogen level. A visit to your sports physician or gynaecologist is suggested in either case to discuss options that may enable you to better perform in training and competition.

*Table 19.4:* Oestrogen Level Self-Assessment Chart.

| Oestrogen Deficiency Symptom | Score *(see below table)* |
|---|---|
| Fatigue | |
| Muscle pains | |
| Joint pains/increase in arthritis | |
| Backache | |
| Hot flushes and / or night sweats | |
| Sleeplessness / altered sleep patterns | |
| Light headedness / dizziness | |
| Headaches | |
| Crawling / itching / burning of the skin | |
| Dry skin / sudden wrinkling | |
| New facial hair | |
| Dry vagina or itching | |
| Discomfort during sexual intercourse | |
| Reduced sexual desire | |
| More frequent urination and / or discomfort | |
| Mood changes | |
| Anxiety | |
| Depression | |
| Irritability | |
| Unloved feelings / unappreciated | |
| Poor memory and / or concentration | |
| TOTAL SCORE | |

*0: absent   1: mild   2: moderate   3: severe*

## Training the Menopausal Woman

All of the age-related declines in aerobic capacity, strength, speed, power and flexibility that occur in aging men also occur in aging women. The ability to improve endurance fitness and lose body fat does not appear to be dependent on menopausal status. For example, a 1992 study of aerobic capacity in female aging runners (35-70 ye5ars) showed that reductions in VO$_2$max from pre- to post-menopause was attributed to age-related changes in functional capacity and decreases in training load rather than changes in menopausal status.

As is typical of endurance training programs of men and women of all ages, the degree of improvement in aerobic capacity is strongly related to the initial fitness level (the lower the fitness, the greater the improvement). At all initial levels of fitness, the improvement in endurance capacity is also related to a higher intensity and frequency of training. Training studies on menopausal women have shown that improvements in aerobic capacity are possible provided the principles of overload (working progressively harder) are adhered to. As with younger athletes, the training program should commence at moderate intensity and progress gradually in intensity, frequency and duration. The risk of injury is of primary concern. Therefore, appropriate activities for menopausal women beginning to exercise include low impact aerobics, walking, cycling, swimming, aquarobics, and circuit weight training under supervision.

Age-related losses in muscle mass and strength also strongly contribute to decreases in endurance, speed and power in the female masters athlete. Research has shown that post-menopausal oestrogen deficiency accelerates the age-related decline in one of the hormones that contributes to muscle mass development – growth hormone. This helps explain the accelerated loss of muscle mass and strength that occurs as women age and again argues strongly for hormone replacement therapy in the aging female athlete. Weight training in older women has been shown to significantly increase muscle strength, power and endurance and help maintain muscle mass. Weight training also helps control obesity by burning energy and maintaining muscle mass that is the largest burner of energy in daily living.

Most aging people increase their body fat levels as they age. This increase is most likely due to the decreased leisure- and occupational-activity levels that accompany aging, at least in aging non-athletes. Another reason may be the age-related decrease in muscle mass, the biggest energy consumer in the body. As we age, if we do not curtail our energy (food and fluid) intake, and we maintain or decrease our energy expenditure, then body fat levels will rise. However, there is no scientific evidence to suggest that this accumulation of body fat is related to menopause, oestrogen deficiency or other hormone deficiency.

Where the body fat is deposited is important. It has been demonstrated by research that abdominal fat is a risk factor in both heart disease and diabetes. While aerobic exercise helps lose abdominal fat more than other sites, the relative resistance of thigh fat deposits to exercise, may discourage many women with heavy thighs.

A number of research papers and consensus statements have been produced over the last decade that point to the following recommendations for a successful exercise training program for the menopausal woman. They are guidelines only for recreational older athletic women or for women just beginning a training program. The more competitive older female athlete needs to consult a strength and conditioning specialist for advice.

- Strength Training
    - Use large and small muscle groups
    - Perform 2-3 sets of 8-15 repetitions at 40-80% of 1 RM (maximum lift)
    - Take 3-5 minutes between sets
    - Start low in weight and go slow!
    - Perform each exercise through the full range of motion
    - Increase weights gradually every 2-3 weeks
    - Train 2-3 days / week for novices, 3-4 days / week for intermediate level athletes

and 4-5 days / week for experienced athletes
- *Endurance Training*
    - 4-5 days / week
    - 20-60 minutes
    - 60-75% of heart rate reserve ([220-age]-resting heart rate)
- *Flexibility Training*
    - Hold stretch for 30-60 seconds
    - Move each joint through the full range of motion
    - Don't stretch to the level of pain but to point of mild discomfort
- *Functional Training*
    - Choose multi-joint exercises that involve large muscle groups
    - Mimic the tasks of daily living or sport (e.g. stair climbing for cyclists)
    - Work at intensity greater than that used in daily activities.

The following table suggests some strength training exercises for improving function.

*Table 19.5:* Suggested weight training exercise for menopausal women to improve physical functioning.

| Exercise | Joints Involved | Functional Benefits |
| --- | --- | --- |
| Squat or Leg Press | Hip, knee, ankle | Picking up objects off the floor, lifting grandchildren, controlling downwards motions, stability, getting up and own to floor, climbing stairs |
| Lunge (caution with knee problems or lack of hip flexibility) | Hip, knee, ankle | Recover from tripping |
| Push-Up (against wall or on knees) or bicep curls | Wrist, elbow, shoulder | Push own body weight, opening heavy doors, carrying groceries |
| Dips (between chairs or benches) | Wrist, elbow, shoulder | Lower into bath or chair |
| Stair Climbing | Hip, knee, ankle | Climb stairs |

## Hormone Replacement Therapy (HRT)

Hormone Replacement Therapy is used to treat the symptoms of menopause and to help prevent Alzheimer's disease, heart disease, arthritis and osteoporosis. Competitive female masters athletes wanting to maintain performances during and after menopause may use HRT. The type of HRT used should be designed individually in consultation with the woman's own doctor or specialist. It will usually include oestrogen with progestogen or oestrogen alone for women who have had a hysterectomy. HRT may include testosterone for surgical menopause and conditions not responding to oestrogen alone.

The forms of HRT are under the skin implants, skin patches, tablets and gels. While tablets remain the most popular form, the implant has proved to be the most effective in delivering the hormones and maintaining stable levels of these. Aging female athletes might look to HRT to increase energy levels, overcome fatigue and to help maintain training levels and performance. These athletes should be aware that some HRT contains testosterone, a banned substance given that high level masters competitions have drug testing.

## Is HRT the Answer for the Menopausal and Post-Menopausal Athlete?

From the above discussion, it might be suggested that HRT is the answer to preventing the symptoms of menopause and possibly holding onto athletic abilities during and after menopause. However, research has led many women to question whether to use or continue using hormone therapy (HRT) as a result of the halting of the United States Women's Health Initiative (WHI) study on combined oestrogen and progestin use in healthy postmenopausal women. The study found that in 10,000 United States women using HRT for more than five years that in a given year:

- 8 more (than those without HRT) will develop breast cancer
- 7 more will have a heart attack
- 8 more will have a stroke
- 18 more will develop blood clots on the lungs
- 6 fewer (than those without HRT) had colorectal cancer
- 5 fewer had hip fracturs

Experts from the *American College of Obstetricians and Gynecologists* (ACOG) have carefully reviewed the published study results. The following is a summary of this research extracted from their website (http://www.acog.org):

> *The Women's Health Initiative is a long-term study sponsored by the National Institutes of Health (NIH) that is looking at ways to prevent heart disease, breast and colon cancer, and osteoporosis. One part of that study followed 16,608 healthy women with a uterus, who were ages 50 to 79 when they entered the study, and who took either oestrogen and progestin therapy (combined hormone therapy, or HRT) or a placebo. The goal of this 8-year trial was to study the relationship between HRT and its possible benefits for heart disease and hip fracture, as well as its possible risks for breast cancer, endometrial cancer, and blood clots. The trial was not intended to study the effect of HRT on menopausal symptoms or on other conditions such as Alzheimer's disease.*
>
> *On July 9, 2002, the NIH halted this trial after 5.2 years, concluding that the risks for the study group on combined HRT outweighed the benefits. (The published report is in the July 17, 2002 issue of the Journal of the American Medical Association. Additional information on the WHI can be found at the website www.whi.org.) Risks included small but significant increased risks of breast cancer, coronary heart disease, stroke, and blood clots for the group of women on HRT. Benefits of HRT use included lower risks for hip fractures and colon cancer. There was no difference between the two groups in death rates. A separate WHI trial*

*on the use of oestrogen alone (ERT) in women who have had a hysterectomy is continuing, because study officials have apparently not seen comparable risks in those women. The data and safety monitoring board of the WHI will continue to review data from this trial every six months.*

*The NIH is continuing to review a number of the statistics that were part of the WHI study, conducting what are known as subset analyses of the WHI data. So far, the NIH has issued its published JAMA report but has not released the underlying WHI data to outside organizations including ACOG. As the WHI data become available and as NIH announces the results of subset analyses, there may be further clarification of HRT issues and further revisions to ACOG recommendations.*

Since it is not a substitute for medical advice, ACOG urges each reader to consult her personal physician when deciding about HRT. Thus, it is suggested that the aging female athlete considering HRT should consult with her family doctor, sports physician or endocrinologist.

## The Pregnant Female Aging Athlete

The appropriateness of various forms of exercise during pregnancy remains controversial as indicated recently in Australia by a *Netball Australia* stand on pregnant players playing first class netball being challenged by the players. Numerous physiological and anatomical changes during pregnancy affect a woman's ability to exercise and her body's response to exercise. For example, placental blood flow, the potential for hyperthermia (overheating) and trauma, changes in coordination and balance, body position during exercise, increased nutritional requirements, and the potential for back and pelvic pain must all be considered in light of each woman's particular exercise program, her prior fitness and prior history during pregnancy.

Pregnant women come from diverse exercise backgrounds. Some are recreational athletes, some fitness enthusiasts, while others are competitive athletes. To appropriately counsel each athlete, it is important to understand how exercise affects the physiologic adaptations that occur during pregnancy. However, there is no doubt that participation in sport usually must be modified during pregnancy and continued participation in competitive sports is of special concern.

## Anatomical and Physiological Changes During Pregnancy

The anatomical changes of pregnancy alter balance, flexibility, and coordination. Physiological changes occur in the cardiovascular, respiratory, musculoskeletal, and gastrointestinal system and all affect the pregnant woman's response to exercise.

1. *Cardiovascular.* The heart adapts to the increased demands placed on it by the enlarging uterus and growing foetus. The major change is a 30-50% increase in the amount of blood pumped by the heart over the pre-pregnancy level. However, when a pregnant woman is lying down, the amount of blood pumped per the minute decreases beyond the

pre-pregnant baseline, especially after 28 to 32 weeks. The resting heart rate increases by up to 7 beats per minute in the first trimester and by 15 beats per minute in the second and third trimesters.

Another significant circulatory adaptation is an increase in blood volume of 35% to 45% over the pre-pregnancy level. This increased volume is partially offset by an increase in the carrying capacity of the veins, so that blood pressure is not increased and may actually decrease in the second trimester. The increase in the blood carrying capacity of the veins contributes to the blood vessels of the skin opening up, which increases heat loss. This adaptation helps to prevent hyperthermia during exercise. Anaemia during pregnancy is not uncommon and results from a relatively greater increase in the fluid volume of the blood with a smaller increase in red blood cell number. This increases the oxygen carrying capacity of the blood. Performance in endurance athletic activities may improve during the first 12 to 15 weeks of pregnancy, before the increase in body weight precludes involvement in competitive sport. This increase in performance probably results from the increased blood volume and red blood cell mass.

2. *Respiratory.* The respiratory system is affected anatomically by the enlarging uterus and physiologically by hormonal changes. Uterine enlargement can elevate the diaphragm by as much as 4 cm, which increases the chest diameter but reduces lung capacity. A resting hyperventilation occurs in response to increased blood levels of the hormone progesterone. Resting oxygen consumption is also increased by up to 20%.

3. *Gastrointestinal.* The gastrointestinal system is affected anatomically by the enlarging uterus and physiologically by increased blood levels of the hormone progesterone, a smooth muscle (the type of muscle found in the stomach and intestines) relaxant. The combined effects of these changes contribute to constipation and a slowing of the gut actions. The increase in progesterone also promotes relaxation of the junction between the stomach and the throat, which leads to increased gastric reflux and heartburn.

4. *Musculoskeletal.* Multiple adaptations of the musculoskeletal system can affect the ability to exercise. The forward positioning of the enlarging uterus changes the woman's centre of gravity and exaggerates normal curve of the back. The increase in hormone levels, especially progesterone, promotes ligament and joint looseness, which is needed to bring about the pelvic relaxation and pelvis widening that permit an easier vaginal delivery. The enlarging breasts also affect the woman's centre of gravity, and their increased weight can contribute to upper back and shoulder pain.

## Anatomical and Physiological Changes When Exercising During Pregnancy

A number of changes occur during exercise that affects both the foetus and the mother's response to exercise. These include:

1. *Placental blood flow.* Changes in uterus and placental blood flow probably occur with exercise; however, this phenomenon is relatively difficult to study. Some studies of

pregnant women exercising have demonstrated increased foetus heart rates, though this response is variable. Some have suggested that exercise-induced increased heart rate in the developing foetus is a sign of foetal distress and decreased uterus-placenta blood flow during exercise. However, other researchers feel that the flow of blood through the placenta remains unchanged, but that the flow of blood to the pregnant uterus is reduced, as it is for any organ during exercise. Still other researchers believe the increased heart rate in the foetus is primarily a response to circulating maternal adrenaline or the increased blood temperature during exercise. As a result of this controversy, increases in foetus heart rate during exercise are not considered a marker of foetal distress in exercising pregnant women.

2. *Hyperthermia*. During exercise, significant elevations in the mother's body temperature should be avoided. Some researchers have suggested that hyperthermia during pregnancy causes nervous system defects, because of observations that women who experience an illness that raises body temperature in the first trimester give birth to a greater number of infants with congenital defects than women who have not had such an illness. It is also widely accepted that dehydration and hyperthermia resulting from strenuous exercise lower the mother's blood volume and reduce the flow of blood through the uterus and to the foetus.

3. *Coordination*. The balance and coordination skills required for most sports are affected by the enlarging uterus and the resulting changes in the centre of gravity. Activities that require significant balance skills will need to be modified for women in their second and third trimesters of pregnancy. Participation in sports where there is the potential for falls may need to be eliminated. Joint looseness and an increase in the fluid volume in the weight-bearing joints, lead to decreased body awareness and diminished coordination. All of these changes probably increase the risk of ligament strains and bone injuries, such as ankle or wrist fractures during a fall.

4. *Injury*. Participation in competitive sports that pose a risk of injury, such as basketball, touch or netball, should only be undertaken with the pregnant patient's full understanding that abdominal trauma to a pregnant uterus carries the risk of placental damage, premature labour, and possibly, pre-term delivery. These concerns are most relevant to a woman who is at more than 20 weeks pregnant, when the uterus has become large. Before 12 to 15 weeks, the uterus is relatively protected by the bony structures of the pelvis. The period of 15 to 20 weeks is considered a *grey zone* for participation in competitive sports, and the possible risks should be fully discussed with the athlete, her doctor and her coach.

5. *Body position*. The position required to perform various types of exercise is also of concern during pregnancy. Lying down exercise, such as some aerobic exercises, sit-ups, and weight lifting on a bench press machine, should be avoided, as in this position the pregnant uterus compresses a major vein returning blood from the lower body, thus compromising blood return to the heart. In the exercising pregnant woman, this can

decrease blood flow to other areas of the body, such as the brain and muscles, possibly leading to fainting. This compressive effect is greatest after the uterus has become large, usually after 20 weeks of pregnancy.

6. *Nutrition.* Pregnancy increases energy intake requirements by approximately 150 Calories (630 kilojoules) per day in the first two trimesters, and by 300 kcal (1260 kilojoules) per day in the third trimester. Exercise during pregnancy further increases calorie requirements, and nutrition supplementation should take into account these increased needs. Vitamin and iron supplements are generally recommended for pregnant women, though few research studies of routine vitamin or iron supplementation for pregnant women have been conducted. An exception to this is folic acid, which at a dose of at least 1 mg per day prior to pregnancy and during the first trimester has reduced the incidence of neural tube defects.

7. *Back and pelvic pain.* Exercise during pregnancy may exacerbate back and pelvic pain. It is estimated that at least 50% of pregnant women experience some degree of back pain that may be exacerbated by strenuous exercise. Separation of the bony joint in the front of the pelvis and inflammation of this joint may result from weight-bearing exercise.

## What Do Exercise and Pregnancy Guidelines Say?

Over the past decade, controversy has arisen regarding recommendations for exercise during pregnancy. In the 1980s, The American College of Obstetricians and Gynaecologists (ACOG) published guidelines based on the consensus opinion of a panel of obstetricians. They recommended exercise of no longer than 15 minutes, a maternal heart rate not to exceed 140 beats per minute, and a core temperature not to exceed 38°C (100.4°F). These guidelines were designed to ensure the safety of the majority of pregnant women, but were later thought to be too restrictive for most trained female athletes.

In 1994, ACOG published another document on exercise during pregnancy and the period after delivery of the baby. The previous guidelines on heart rate and duration of exercise were eliminated, and the recommendation was modified to read that most women *"can exercise moderately to maintain cardiorespiratory and muscular fitness throughout pregnancy and the postpartum period."* There are no data in humans to indicate that pregnant women should limit exercise intensity and lower target heart rates because of potential adverse effects. For women who do not have any additional risk factors apart from being pregnant, the following recommendations may be made:

1. During pregnancy, women can continue to exercise and derive health benefits even from mild to moderate exercise routines.
2. Regular exercise (at least three times per week) is preferable to intermittent activity.
3. Women should avoid exercise in the supine position (lying on the back) after the first trimester.
4. Prolonged periods of motionless standing should be avoided.

5. Women should be aware of the decreased oxygen available for aerobic exercise during pregnancy. They should be encouraged to modify the intensity of their exercise according to maternal symptoms. Pregnant women should stop exercising when fatigued and not exercise to exhaustion.
6. Weight-bearing exercises may under some circumstances be continued at intensities similar to those prior to pregnancy throughout pregnancy.
7. Non-weight bearing exercises such as cycling or swimming will minimize the risk of injury and facilitate the continuation of exercise during pregnancy.
8. Loss of balance could be detrimental to maternal or foetal well being, especially in the third trimester. Further, any type of exercise involving the potential for even mild abdominal trauma should be avoided.
9. Pregnancy requires an additional 300kcal/d in order to maintain metabolic homeostasis. Thus women who exercise during pregnancy should be particularly careful to ensure an adequate diet.
10. Pregnant women who exercise in the first trimester should augment heat dissipation by ensuring adequate hydration, appropriate clothing and optimal environmental surroundings during exercise.

Many of the physiologic and morphologic changes of pregnancy persist 4-6 weeks after delivery. Thus pre-pregnancy exercise routines should be resumed gradually based on a woman's physical capability. After a normal vaginal delivery, gentle exercise like walking can be commenced immediately and gradually increased. Excessive stretching and lifting should be avoided. After a Caesarean section, strenuous activity should be avoided for six weeks and weight lifting for 12 weeks.

**Contraindications to Exercise during Pregnancy**

The above recommendations are intended for women who do not have any additional risk factors for adverse mother or baby outcome. A number of medical and obstetric conditions may lead the obstetrician to recommend modifications of these principles. The following conditions should be considered contraindications to exercise during pregnancy:

- Pregnancy induced hypertension
- Severe hypertensive disease
- Pre-term rupture of membranes
- Pre-term labour during the prior or current pregnancy or both
- Incompetent cervix/cerclage
- Persistent second or third trimester bleeding
- Intrauterine growth retardation
- Multiple foetuses
- Congestive heart failure
- Valvular heart disease

- Incompetent cervix

In addition women with certain other medical or obstetric condition including:
- Hypertension
- Cardiac, vascular or pulmonary disease
- Anaemia
- Thyroid disease
- Medication-controlled diabetes
- Breech presentation in the third trimester
- Excessive weight gain or loss

have a relative contraindication to exercise and should be evaluated carefully by an obstetrician or gynaecologist or sports physician in order to determine whether an exercise program is appropriate.

## Safety Tips for Exercising Pregnant Women

Apart from the exercise guidelines given above, the following safety tips are suggested for the pregnant female athlete when training:

1. Fluid intake during and after exercise should be adequate to prevent dehydration and loss of blood volume. Taking regular breaks to drink is suggested.
2. Clothing worn during exercise should allow for adequate ventilation and prevention of hyperthermia. Loose fitting, light coloured, cotton clothing is suggested.
3. Exercise during any illness that elevated body temperature at rest is contraindicated.
4. Exercise on a sprung wooden floor or tightly carpeted surface to avoid slipping and falling and to absorb shock.
5. Exercises that require repetitive bouncing and jerky movements should be avoided, especially in the third trimester.
6. Hard stretching of joints should be avoided due to the hormonal influence on joint looseness.
7. Bouncing stretches should be avoided for the same reason.
8. Recommended exercise regimens should emphasise low-impact activities, such as stationary bicycling, swimming, walking, and low-impact aerobics.
9. Activities that involve potential low-oxygen states, such as scuba diving and mountain climbing, are contraindicated.
10. The exercising pregnant woman should be encouraged to follow a diet that emphasises complex carbohydrates to replace muscle glycogen (carbohydrate) lost during exercise.
11. Participation in competitive team sports is acceptable in the first 15 weeks of pregnancy if the woman understands that there are potential but unproved risks for foetal loss from pelvic trauma, abdominal trauma, or both.
12. Exercises requiring significant use of Valsalva's manoeuvre (breath holding), such as weight lifting, should be avoided, especially in the third trimester.

## Nutritional Concerns for the Aging Female Athlete

Chapter 16 of this book examines in detail the nutritional needs of aging male and female athletes. However, in this section the importance of calcium and iron will be highlighted as these two minerals are of prime concern for the female masters athlete's diet.

Calcium is a mineral that plays an essential role in growth, muscle contraction, nerve impulse transmission, and in particular the development of strong bones. Table 19.6 below shows the recommended amounts of calcium required during different stages of a woman's life.

*Table 19.6:* Dietary requirements for calcium in females of various ages.

| Group | Dietary Requirement (mg/day) |
|---|---|
| Girls 12-15 years | 1000 |
| Girls 16-18 years | 800 |
| Menstruating women | 800 |
| Athletic women with irregular or absent menstruation | 1000-1500 |
| Post-menopausal women | 1000 |
| Pregnant/lactating women | 1100-1200 |

Despite widespread knowledge of these values and campaigns to highlight awareness of them, research has shown that a significant number of women are not getting enough dietary calcium. For example, one Australian research study observed that over 40% of women between 25 and 85 years of age had calcium intakes below 60% of those recommended in Table 19.6. In younger adult female athletes, calcium intakes in the range of 700-900 mg per day are common, well below the values suggested. Adequate calcium intake is essential in the younger adult athlete as the higher the peak bone mass at adulthood (20-30 years of age), the less the likelihood of osteoporosis post-menopause. Given the aging female athlete, particularly post-menopause, has an increased risk of osteoporosis and fractures, calcium intake should be a strong focus for the aging female athlete. The following list of foods contains approximately 300 mg of calcium:

- 200 ml of low fat/skim fortified milk
- 200 gm (1 tub) of yoghurt
- 40 gm hard cheese
- 80 gm sardines/salmon
- 2.5 cups baked beans
- 250 gm tofu

If the normal dietary requirements cannot be met, then calcium supplementation is suggested. Calcium carbonate or calcium phosphate supplements should be taken *after* a meal when the intestine acids have been stimulated. A more acidic environment in the intestines stimulates calcium absorption. For lactose intolerant women, soy drink (calcium enriched) is the easiest way to obtain calcium as 250 ml of this drink contains 365 mg calcium. To enhance calcium absorption by the intestine, some foods should be avoided as they inhibit the calcium absorption process. These include excessive caffeine, unprocessed bran, oxalate (found in spinach and rhubarb), and alcohol. In contrast, the sugar lactose improves absorption. Diets high in salt or protein reduce the body's ability to retain calcium.

Iron is an essential component of haemoglobin that carries oxygen on the red blood cells from the lungs to the muscles. It also plays a role in aerobic energy production within muscles. Thus, for the aging female endurance athlete, particularly if menstruating and losing blood, dietary iron is a priority. Table 19.7 below shows the recommended amounts of iron required during different stages of a woman's life.

*Table 19.7:* Dietary requirements for iron in females of various ages.

| Group | Dietary Requirement (mg/day) |
|---|---|
| Children | 6-8 |
| Adolescents | 10-13 |
| Adult women | 12-16 |
| Athletic women | Minimum 16 |
| Pregnant women | 22-36 |

The following list of foods contains approximately 2 mg of iron:
- 50 gm lean beef
- 250 gm chicken
- 20 gm liver
- 0.5 cup spinach

Iron is found in the diet in two main forms:
1. *Haem iron* is found in foods such as red meat, poultry and seafood. Liver and kidney are the best sources. It is well absorbed by the body.
2. *Non-haem iron* is found in plant foods such a breakfast cereals, dried fruit, rice, pasta, vegetables (NB green leafy), legumes and tofu. This type of iron is not as well absorbed by the body as haem-iron but taking vitamin C (I have two oranges immediately after every dinner) and haem-iron food with non-haem sources enhances the uptake. Conversely, tea, caffeine (coffee, colas, chocolate) and excess fibre reduce the absorption of non-haem iron.

If insufficient iron is obtained from food, iron-deficiency anaemia is likely to occur. Female endurance athletes (iron is lost in sweat, urine, faeces and menstrual flow) who are vegetarians and / or dieting, particularly runners (red blood cells are destroyed by impact), are at risk. A blood test that measures blood iron levels (haemoglobin) and body iron stores (ferritin) is needed to diagnose this condition. Decreased performance, fatigue and shortness of breath are symptoms. Treatment is via iron supplements taken under supervision by a doctor or dietician) and an iron-rich diet are used to treat anaemia.

## Gynaecological Issues

A number of conditions may affect the training and competitive performance of the female masters athlete. Below is a brief discussion of each of these.

1. *Menstrual Cramps* or dysmenorrhoea is abdominal pain associated with uterine contractions or loss of blood flow to the uterus during menstruation. They are caused by release of a chemical from the lining of the uterus called prostaglandin. There is no reason to suggest avoiding exercise. If the symptoms are mild, analgesics such as *Panadol* may be appropriate. If the symptoms are severe, antiprostaglandin medication such as *Naproxen Sodium* or *Ibobrufen* if taken 24-48 hours before the onset of the period in order to slow the release of prostaglandins. The oral contraceptive pill may also reduce the severity of menstrual cramps.

2. *Pre-Menstrual Tension* (PMT) relates to a group of symptoms beginning at ovulation and improving with the onset of menstruation. Symptoms include emotional symptoms (mood swings, anxiety, depression, insomnia, irritability, and change in libido) and physical symptoms (headaches, fluid retention, breast soreness and enlargement and fatigue). Regular exercise may decrease or eliminate PMT. However, treatment is aimed at preventing ovulation and the development of the lining of the uterus. The oral contraceptive pill can be effective in this regard. Taking vitamin B6 (pyridoxine) at 200-600 mg per day for up to two weeks may reduce fluid retention and breast tenderness. Diuretics reduce fluid retention but increase the risk of dehydration and are banned by the IOC and high level masters competition organisers.

3. *Contraception*. The choice of contraception depends upon the frequency of sexual intercourse, pregnancy plans and medical history. Female athletes with menstrual irregularities or loss of menstrual flow should still use contraception as ovulation can still take place and the condition may resolve itself spontaneously. Mechanical barrier methods are popular choices. The diaphragm should be left in for at least six hours after intercourse and may thus be in place during training or competition. If uncomfortable, a smaller size barrier or alternative method might be suggested. Intra-uterine devices (IUD's) impose a risk of pelvic infection and may alter future fertility. It may thus be a good choice for older female athletes who have regular sexual intercourse and completed child rearing. However, IUD's are commonly associated with more cramping and heavier bleeding, either of which may affect performance.

4. *Oral Contraception*. Most "pills" contain a combination of the hormones oestrogen and progesterone. For female athletes, there are benefits and disadvantages in the use of the "pill" (see Table 19.8 opposite).

*Table 19.8:* Advantages and disadvantages of oral contraceptive use in female athletes.

| Advantages | Disadvantages |
|---|---|
| Reduced menstrual cramping | Water retention |
| Source of hormone oestrogen for non-menstruating athletes | Alter glucose metabolism by progestin component |
| May reduce iron deficiency anaemia by reducing blood loss during menstruation | Possible decrease in aerobic capacity ($VO_2max$) |
| Enable athlete to manipulate menstrual cycle | |

Research suggests few major effects on athletic performance in those female athletes using the "pill". However, some female athletes are contraindicated for the use of the "pill". These include pregnancy, smokers over 35 years of age, those with undiagnosed abnormal uterine bleeding, previous thromboses (blood clot inside a blood vessel), breast cancer, oestrogen-dependent cancers, active liver disease, intestine malabsorption disease, uncontrolled hypertension, diabetes with blood vessel complications and artery disease.

5. *Manipulation of the Menstrual Cycle.* Research has shown that the sports performance of individual women is affected during different phases of the menstrual cycle. The use of the oral contraceptive pill has been used to take advantage of this. The "pill" can be stopped 7-10 days before a major event to induce a withdrawal bleed early to avoid menstruating during the event. Alternatively, the athlete might skip the seven day sugar tablet interval and continue into the next packet thus preventing the withdrawal bleed. For those female athletes not on the "pill", a bleed can be induced 10 days prior to the event by taking progesterone for 10 days, finishing 10 days prior to the event.

| Table 19.9: Recommended Websites for Female Masters Athletes |
|---|
| • http://www.coach.ca/eng/women/index.cfm is run by the Coaching Association of Canada and is for "Women in Coaching". There is free access to the journal Canadian Journal for Women in Coaching plus numerous other resources. |
| • http://www.acog.org/ is the homepage of one of the lead world agencies in the area, The American College of Obstetricians and Gynecologists. It has a search engine and authoritative information on most issues pertaining to women's health. |
| • http://www.physsportsmed.com/index.php?page=home is the home page of one of the best free on-line journals for any matter pertaining to Sport - The Physician and Sports Medicine Journal. It has a great search engine. |
| • http://www.acsm.org is the website run by the American College of Sports Medicine, the premier sport and exercise science organization in the world, and has a wide range of sport and exercise-related topics to peruse. It has a great search engine. |